Alexis vs Summer Vacation

D0943180

For the Secret Masters of MJC—gamers extraordinaire!
—Sarah

For my family, friends, and partner.
Without you, this book wouldn't be possible.
—Veronica

Center for Responsive Schools, Inc., is a not-for-profit educational organization.

© 2019 by Center for Responsive Schools, Inc.

First edition, June 2019
10 9 8 7 6 5 4 3 2 1

Written by Sarah Jamila Stevenson
Illustrated by Veronica Agarwal
Edited by Heather Kamins and Sera Rivers
Book design by Liz Brandenburg and Hannah Collins
Printed in the United States of America

ISBN: 978-1-892989-96-3
Library of Congress Control Number: 2019932503

Avenue A Books
An imprint of
Center for Responsive Schools, Inc.
85 Avenue A, P.O. Box 718
Turners Falls, MA 01376-0718
800-360-6332
avenueabooks.org
crslearn.org

Alexis vs Summer Vacation

Sarah Jamila Stevenson • Veronica Agarwal

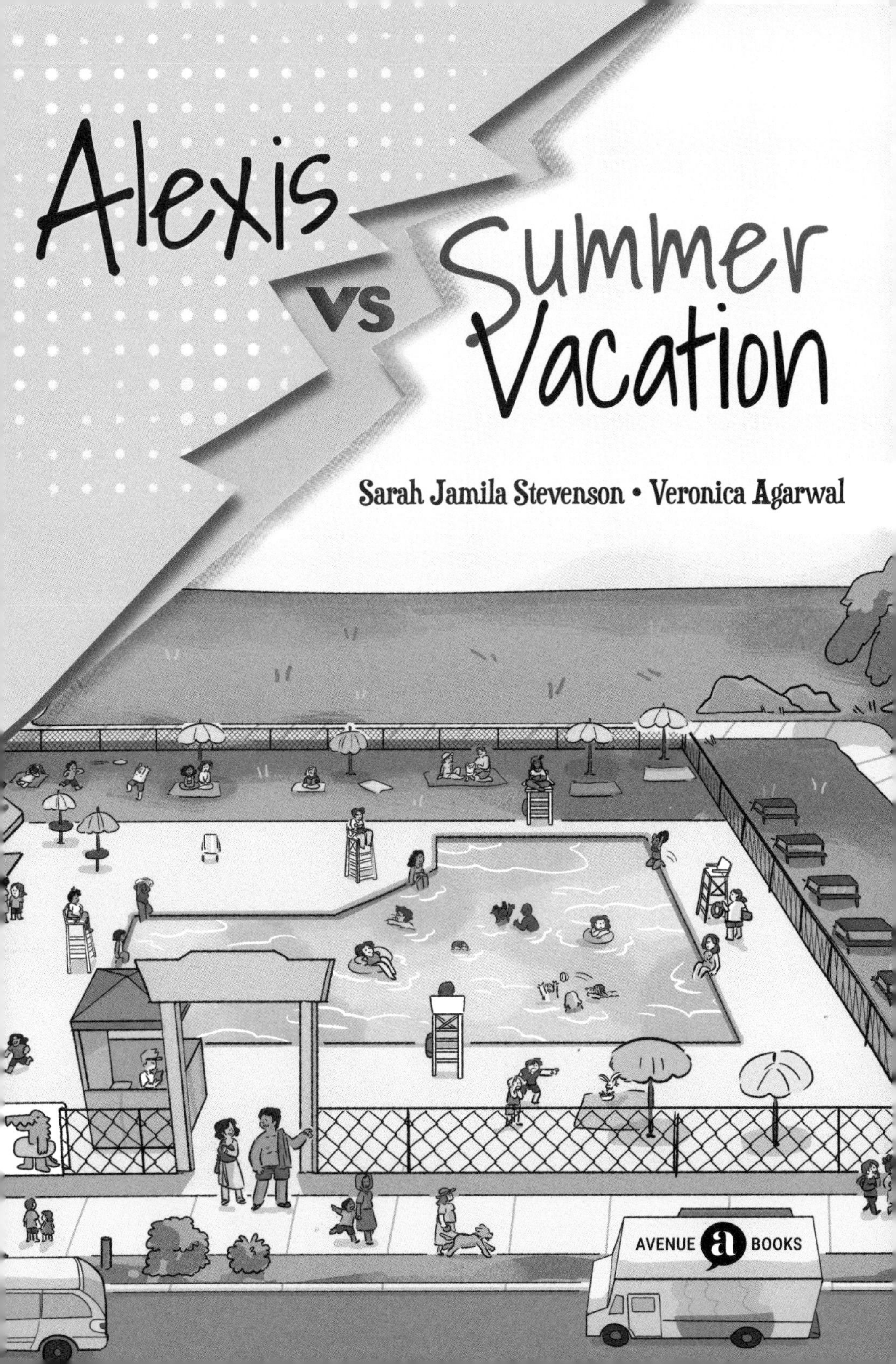
AVENUE a BOOKS

Table of Contents

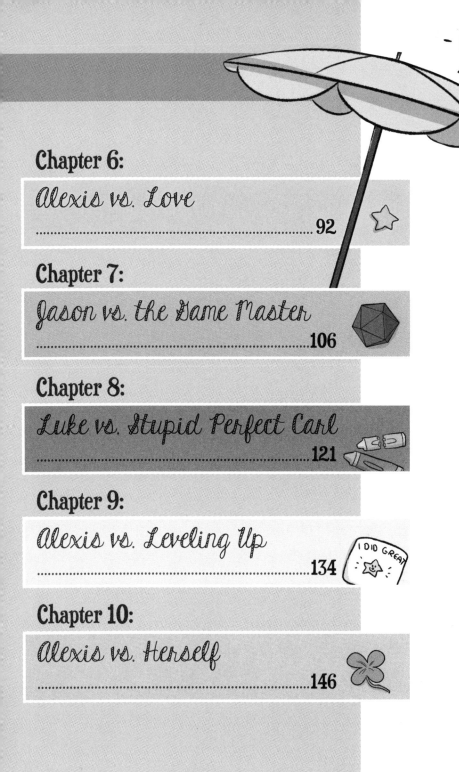

Chapter 1

Alexis vs. Summer Vacation

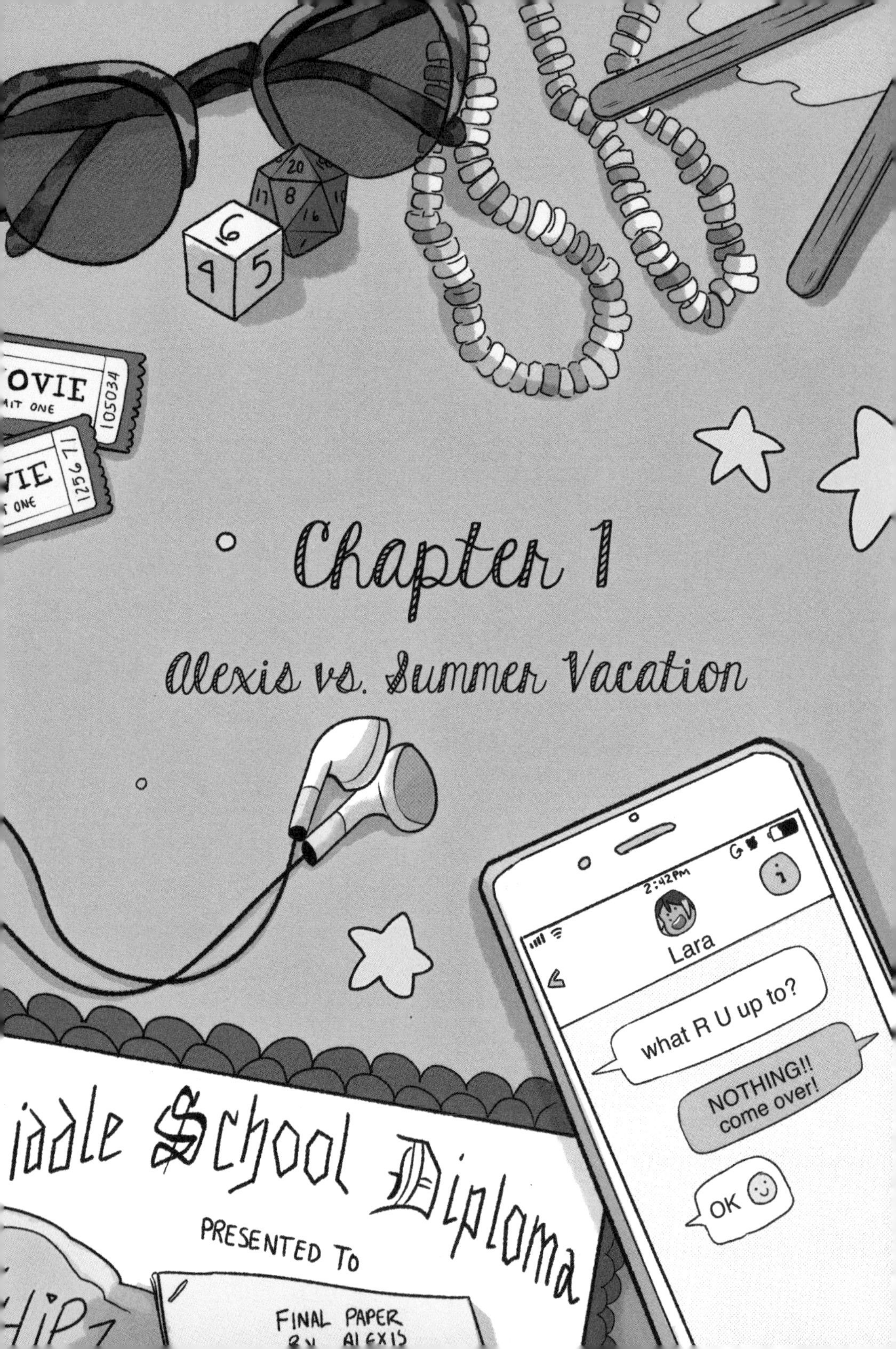

OVIE
105034
VIE
125671
2:42PM
Lara
what R U up to?
NOTHING!! come over!
OK
iddle School Diploma
PRESENTED TO
FINAL PAPER

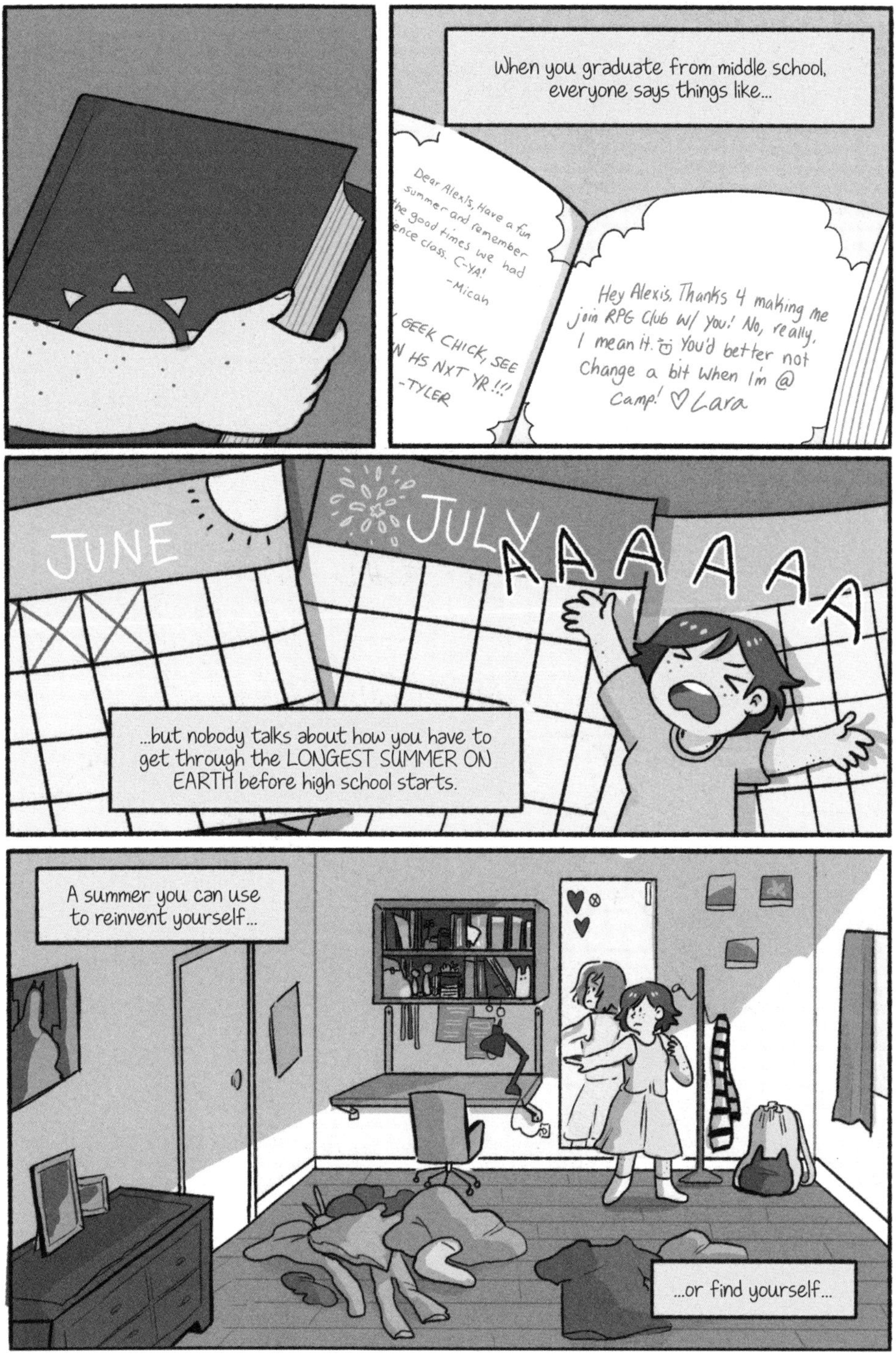
When you graduate from middle school, everyone says things like...
Dear Alexis, Have a fun summer and remember the good times we had ence class. C-YA! -Micah
GEEK CHICK, SEE N HS NXT YR!!! -TYLER
Hey Alexis, Thanks 4 making me join RPG Club w/ you! No, really, I mean it. You'd better not change a bit when I'm @ Camp! ♡ Lara
JUNE
JULY
AAAAAA
...but nobody talks about how you have to get through the LONGEST SUMMER ON EARTH before high school starts.
A summer you can use to reinvent yourself...
...or find yourself...

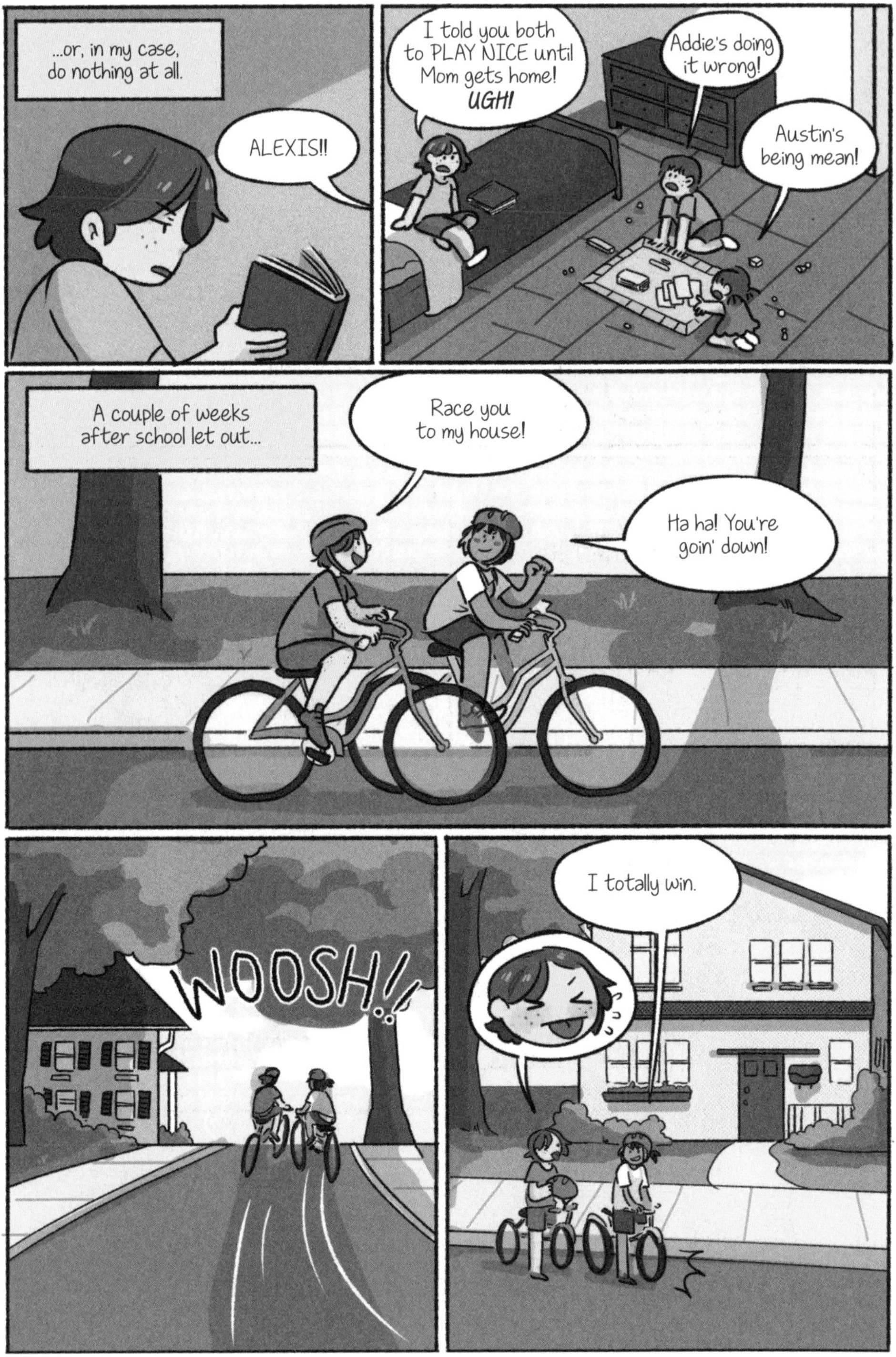
...or, in my case, do nothing at all.
ALEXIS!!
I told you both to PLAY NICE until Mom gets home! UGH!
Addie's doing it wrong!
Austin's being mean!
A couple of weeks after school let out...
Race you to my house!
Ha ha! You're goin' down!
WOOSH!!
I totally win.

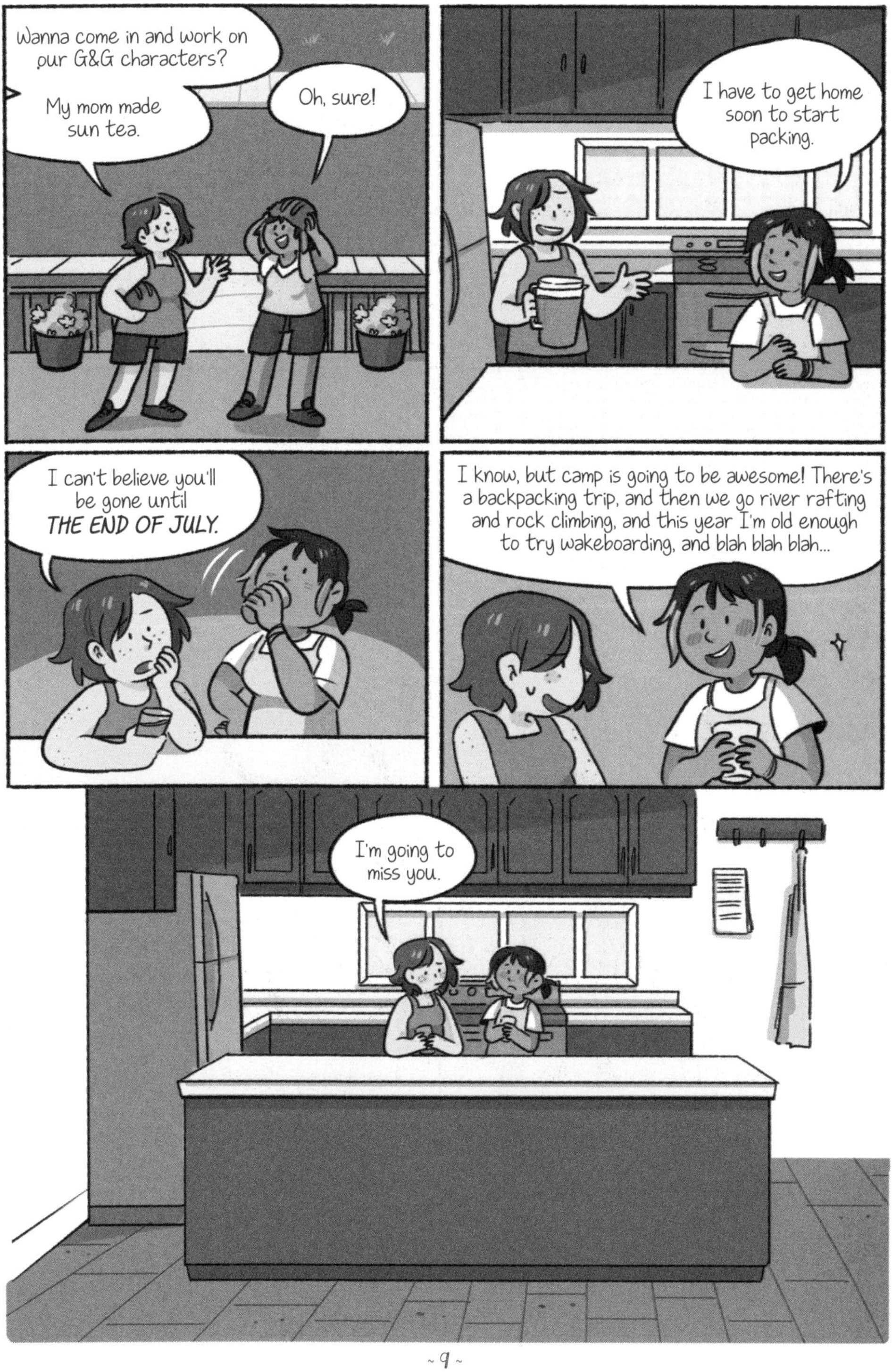
Wanna come in and work on our G&G characters?
My mom made sun tea.
Oh, sure!
I have to get home soon to start packing.
I can't believe you'll be gone until THE END OF JULY.
I know, but camp is going to be awesome! There's a backpacking trip, and then we go river rafting and rock climbing, and this year I'm old enough to try wakeboarding, and blah blah blah...
I'm going to miss you.

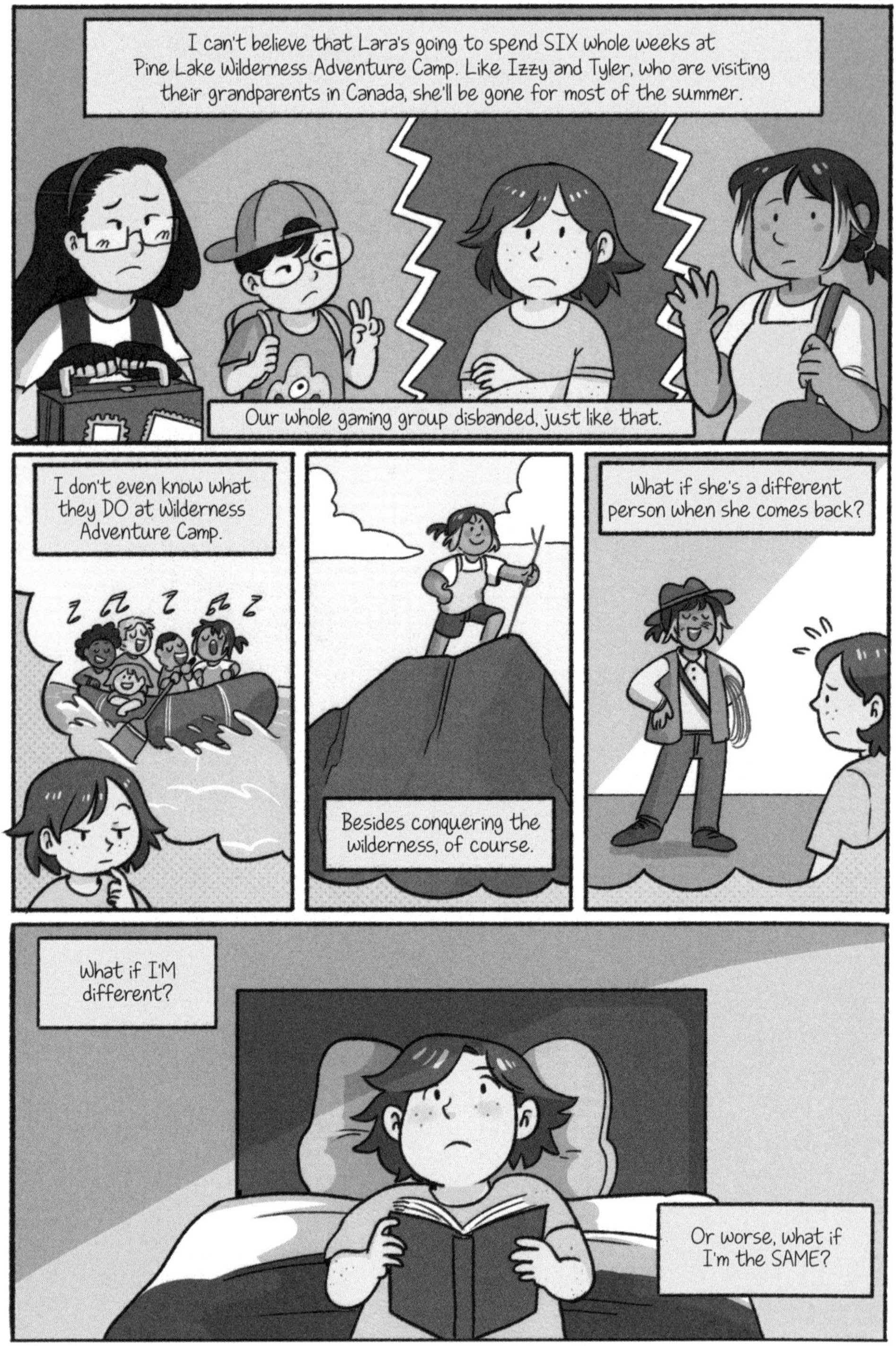
I can't believe that Lara's going to spend SIX whole weeks at Pine Lake Wilderness Adventure Camp. Like Izzy and Tyler, who are visiting their grandparents in Canada, she'll be gone for most of the summer.
Our whole gaming group disbanded, just like that.
I don't even know what they DO at Wilderness Adventure Camp.
Besides conquering the wilderness, of course.
What if she's a different person when she comes back?
What if I'M different?
Or worse, what if I'm the SAME?

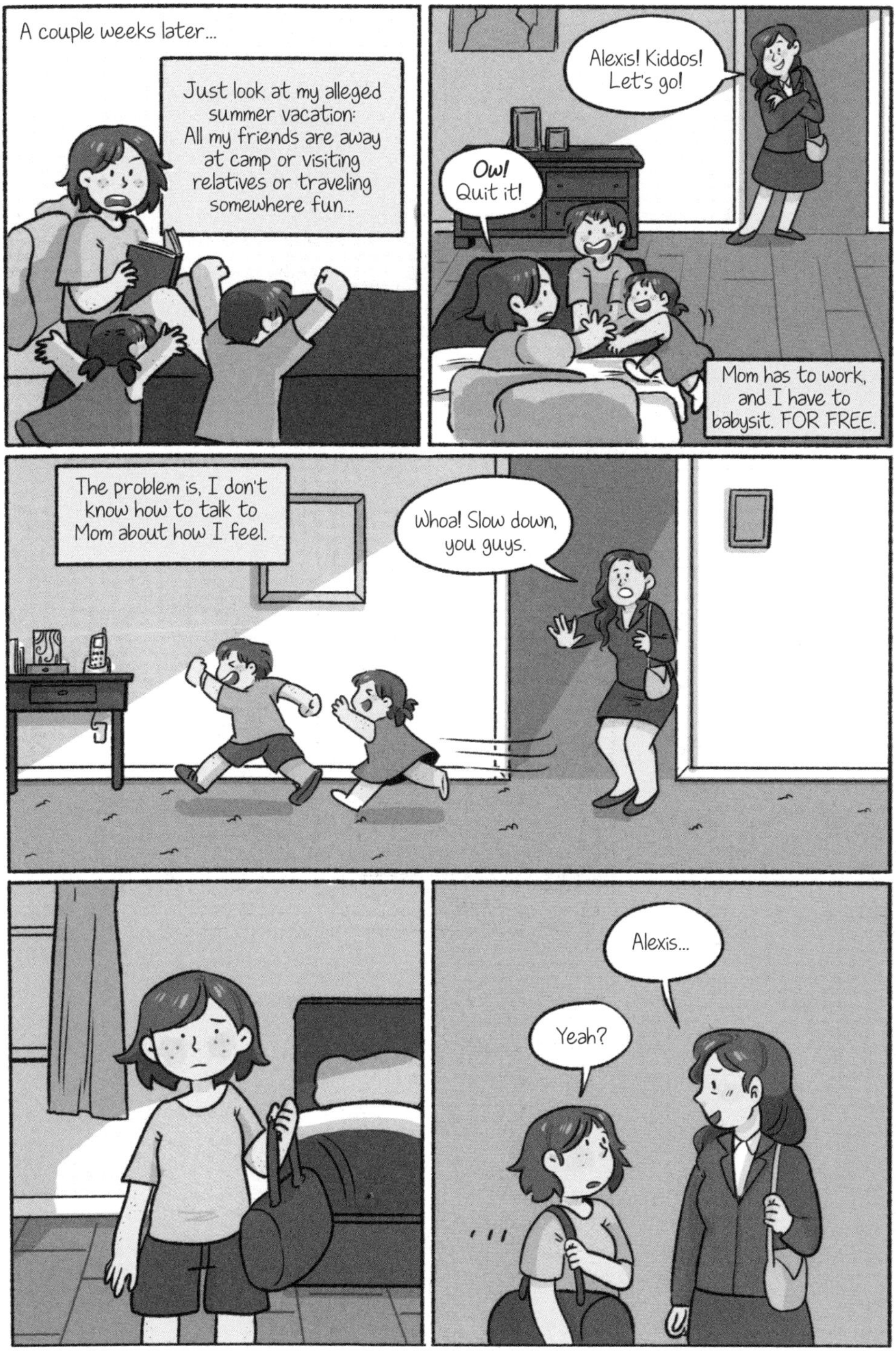
A couple weeks later...
Just look at my alleged summer vacation: All my friends are away at camp or visiting relatives or traveling somewhere fun...
Alexis! Kiddos! Let's go!
Ow! Quit it!
Mom has to work, and I have to babysit. FOR FREE.
The problem is, I don't know how to talk to Mom about how I feel.
Whoa! Slow down, you guys.
Alexis...
Yeah?

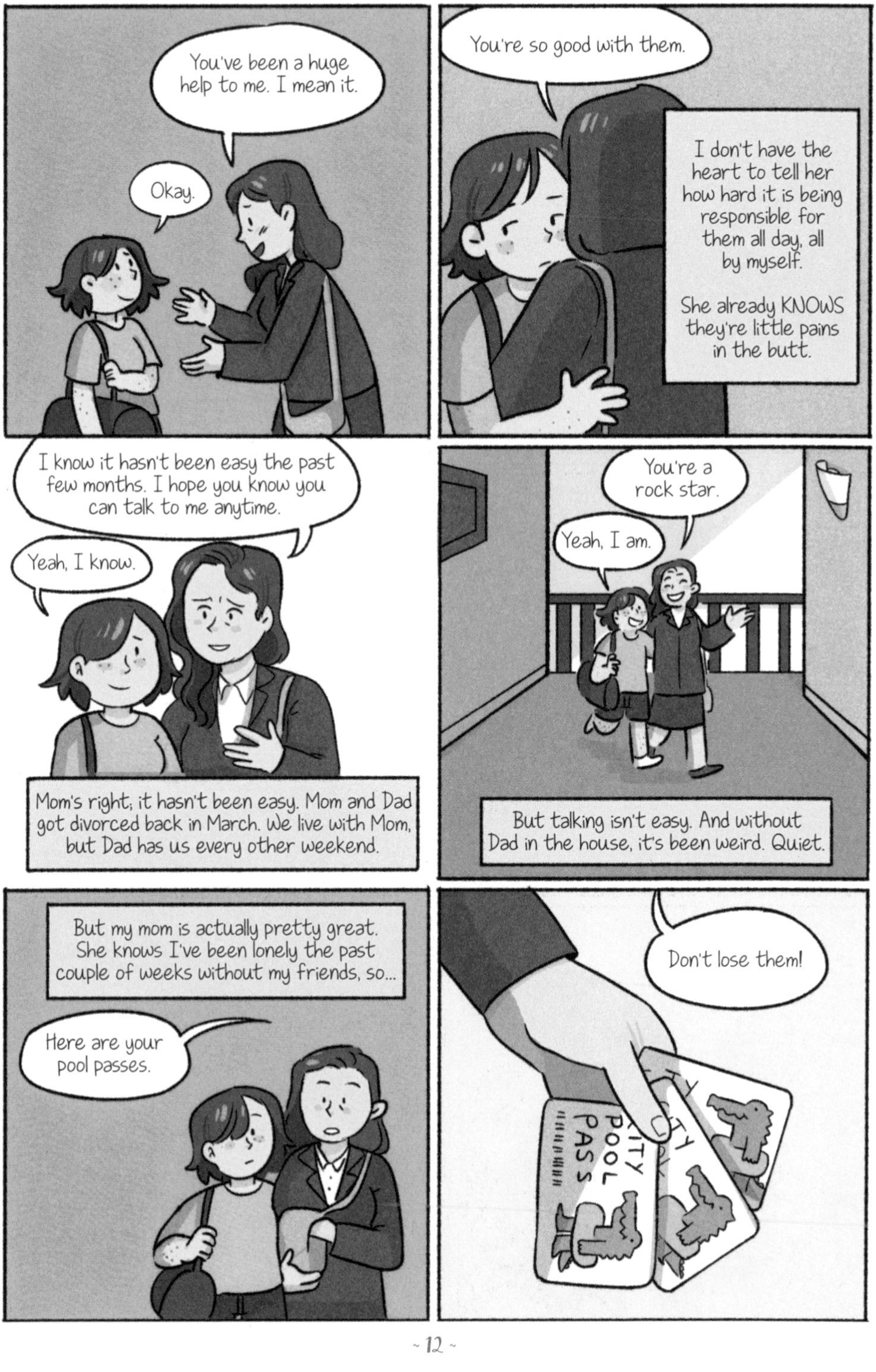
You've been a huge help to me. I mean it.
Okay.
You're so good with them.
I don't have the heart to tell her how hard it is being responsible for them all day, all by myself.
She already KNOWS they're little pains in the butt.
I know it hasn't been easy the past few months. I hope you know you can talk to me anytime.
Yeah, I know.
Mom's right; it hasn't been easy. Mom and Dad got divorced back in March. We live with Mom, but Dad has us every other weekend.
You're a rock star.
Yeah, I am.
But talking isn't easy. And without Dad in the house, it's been weird. Quiet.
But my mom is actually pretty great. She knows I've been lonely the past couple of weeks without my friends, so...
Here are your pool passes.
Don't lose them!
CITY POOL PASS

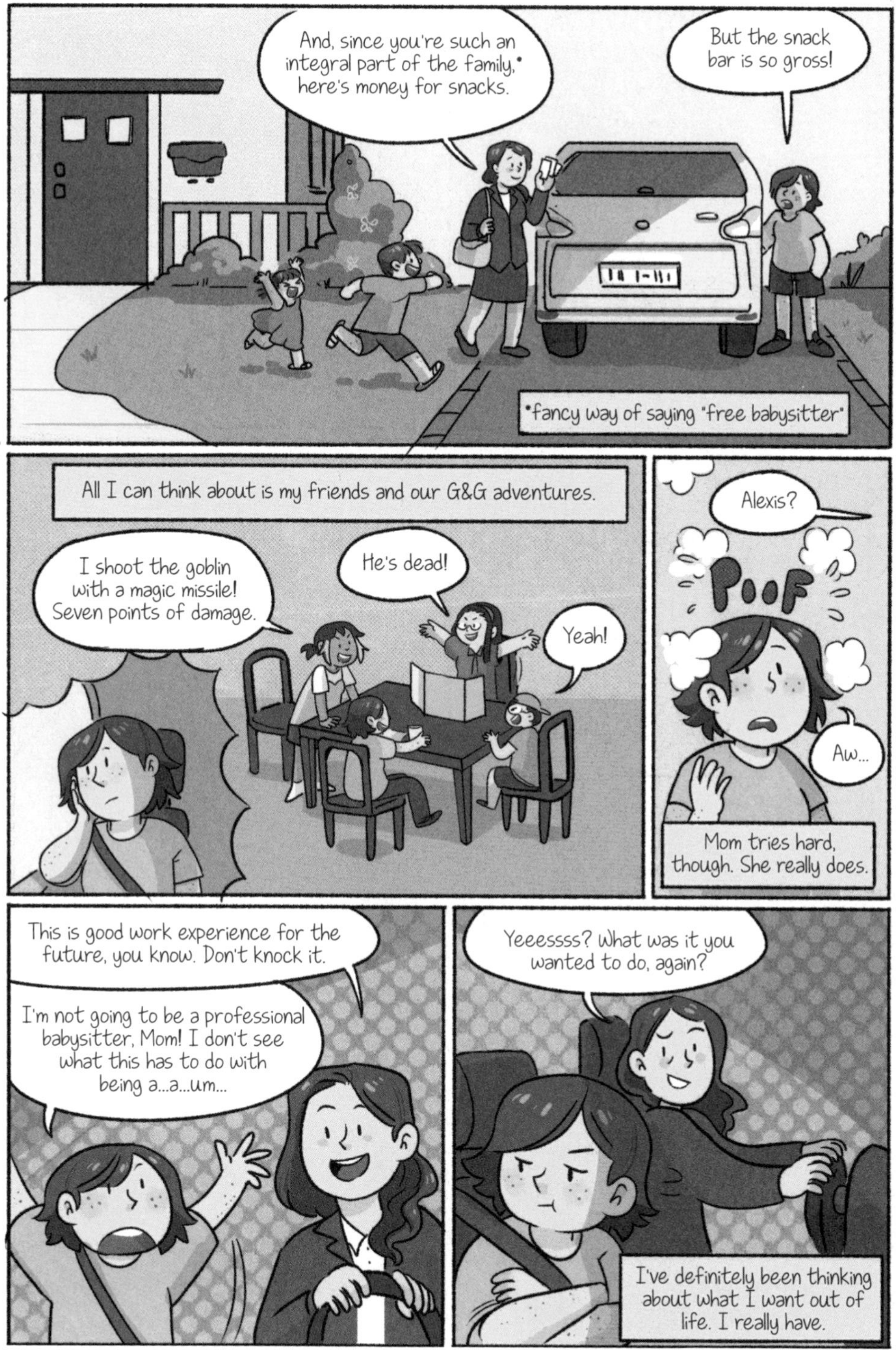
And, since you're such an integral part of the family,* here's money for snacks.
But the snack bar is so gross!
*fancy way of saying "free babysitter"
All I can think about is my friends and our G&G adventures.
I shoot the goblin with a magic missile! Seven points of damage.
He's dead!
Yeah!
Alexis?
POOF
Aw...
Mom tries hard, though. She really does.
This is good work experience for the future, you know. Don't knock it.
I'm not going to be a professional babysitter, Mom! I don't see what this has to do with being a...a...um...
Yeeessss? What was it you wanted to do, again?
I've definitely been thinking about what I want out of life. I really have.

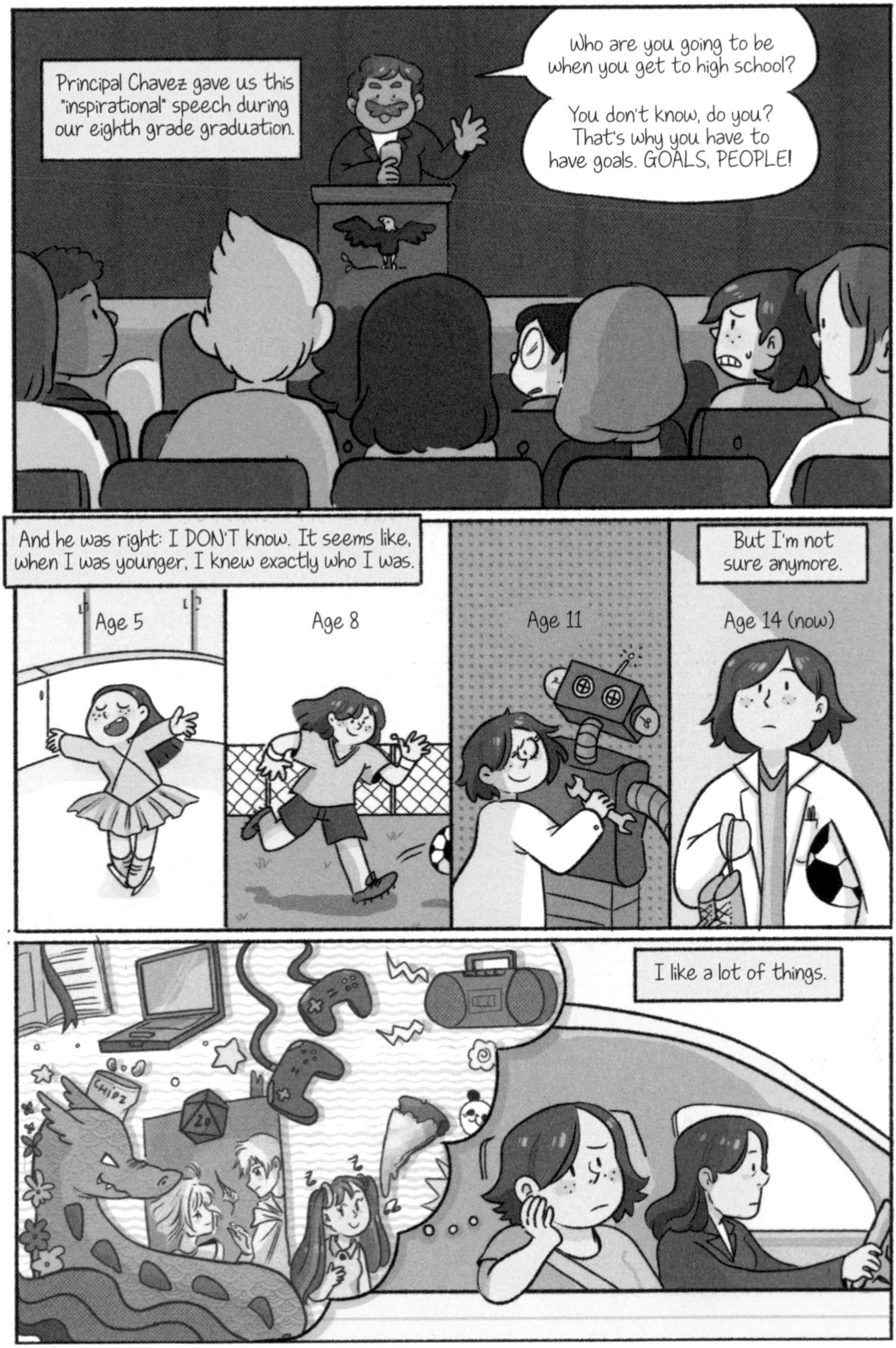
Principal Chavez gave us this "inspirational" speech during our eighth grade graduation.
Who are you going to be when you get to high school?
You don't know, do you? That's why you have to have goals. GOALS, PEOPLE!
And he was right: I DON'T know. It seems like, when I was younger, I knew exactly who I was.
Age 5
Age 8
Age 11
But I'm not sure anymore.
Age 14 (now)
I like a lot of things.
CHIPZ
20

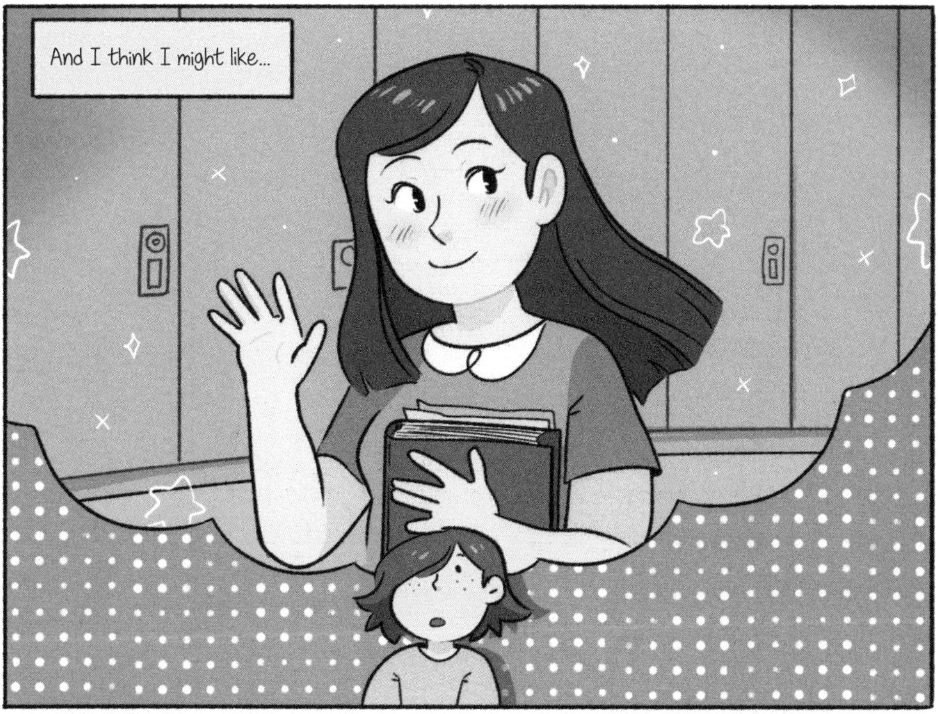
And I think I might like...

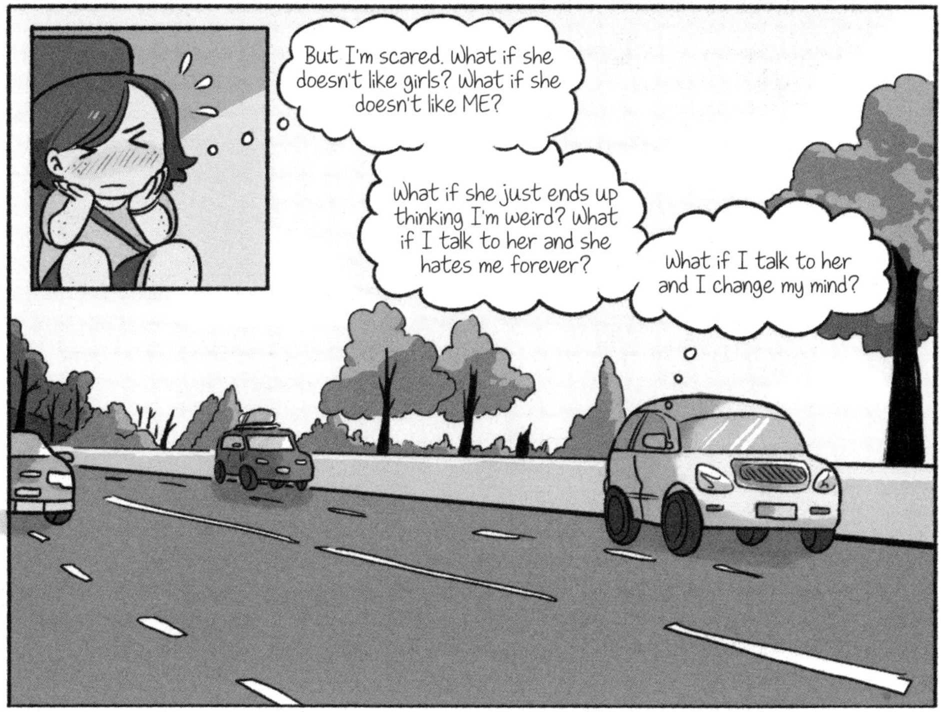
But I'm scared. What if she doesn't like girls? What if she doesn't like ME?
What if she just ends up thinking I'm weird? What if I talk to her and she hates me forever?
What if I talk to her and I change my mind?

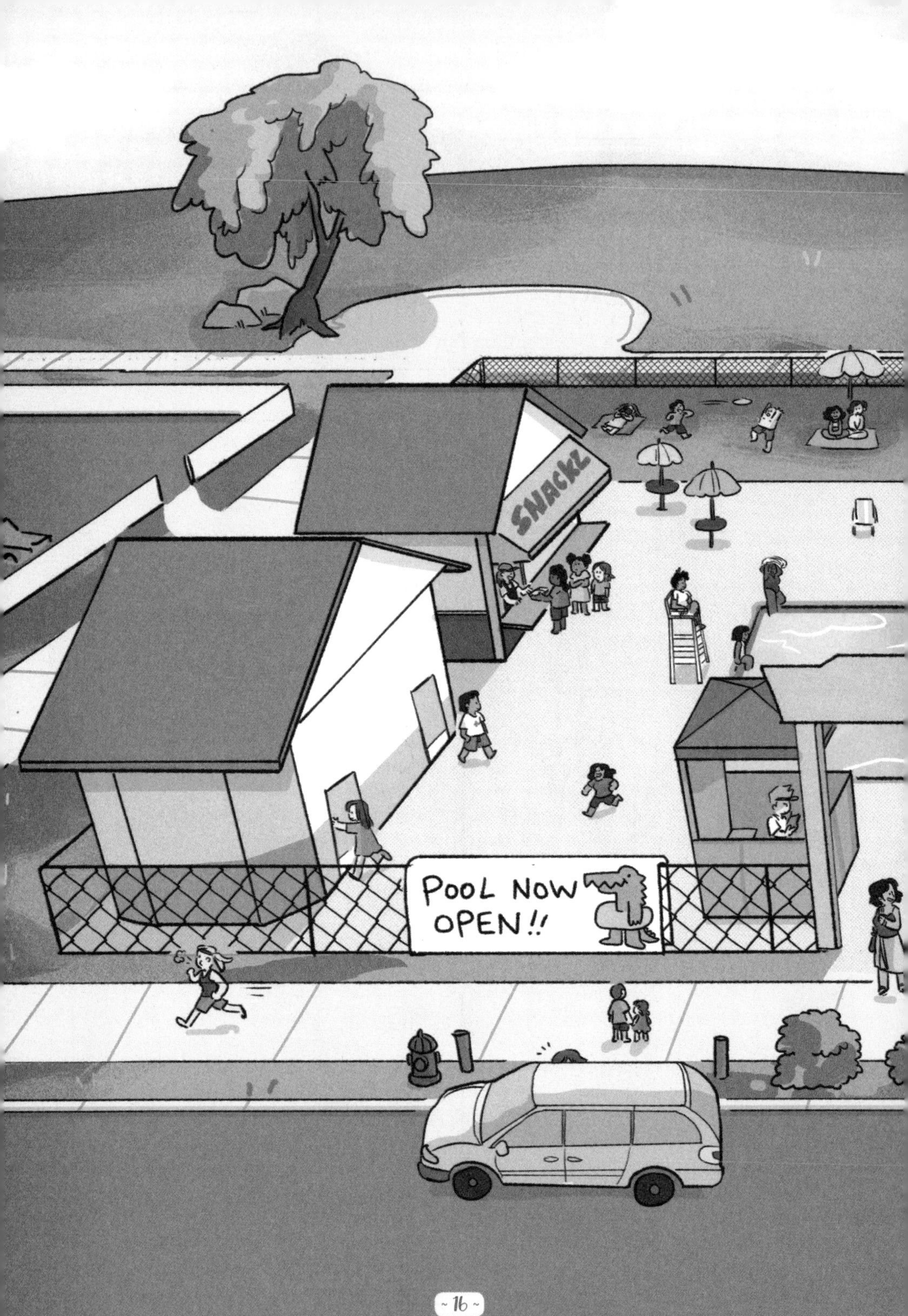
SNACKS
POOL NOW OPEN!!

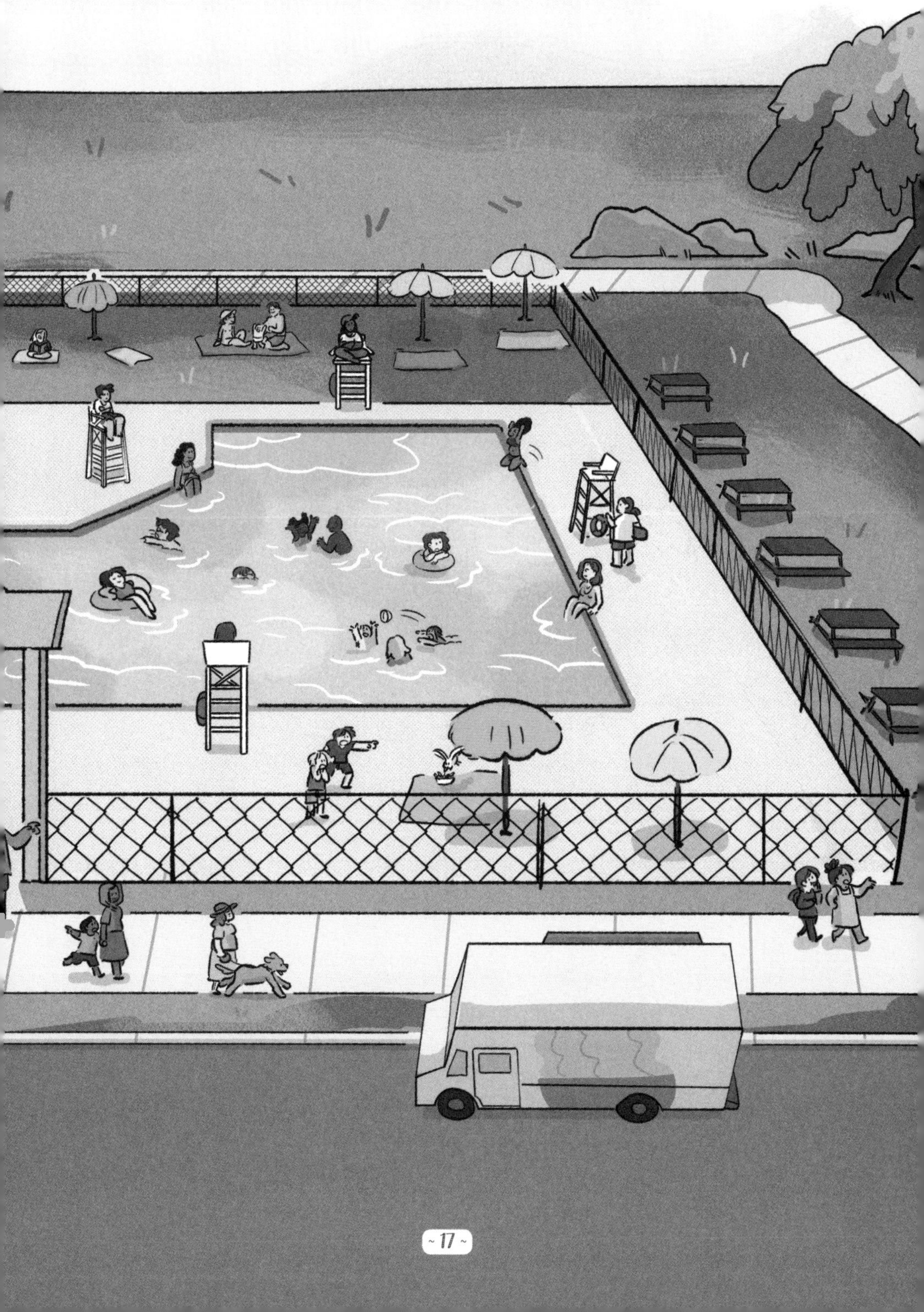

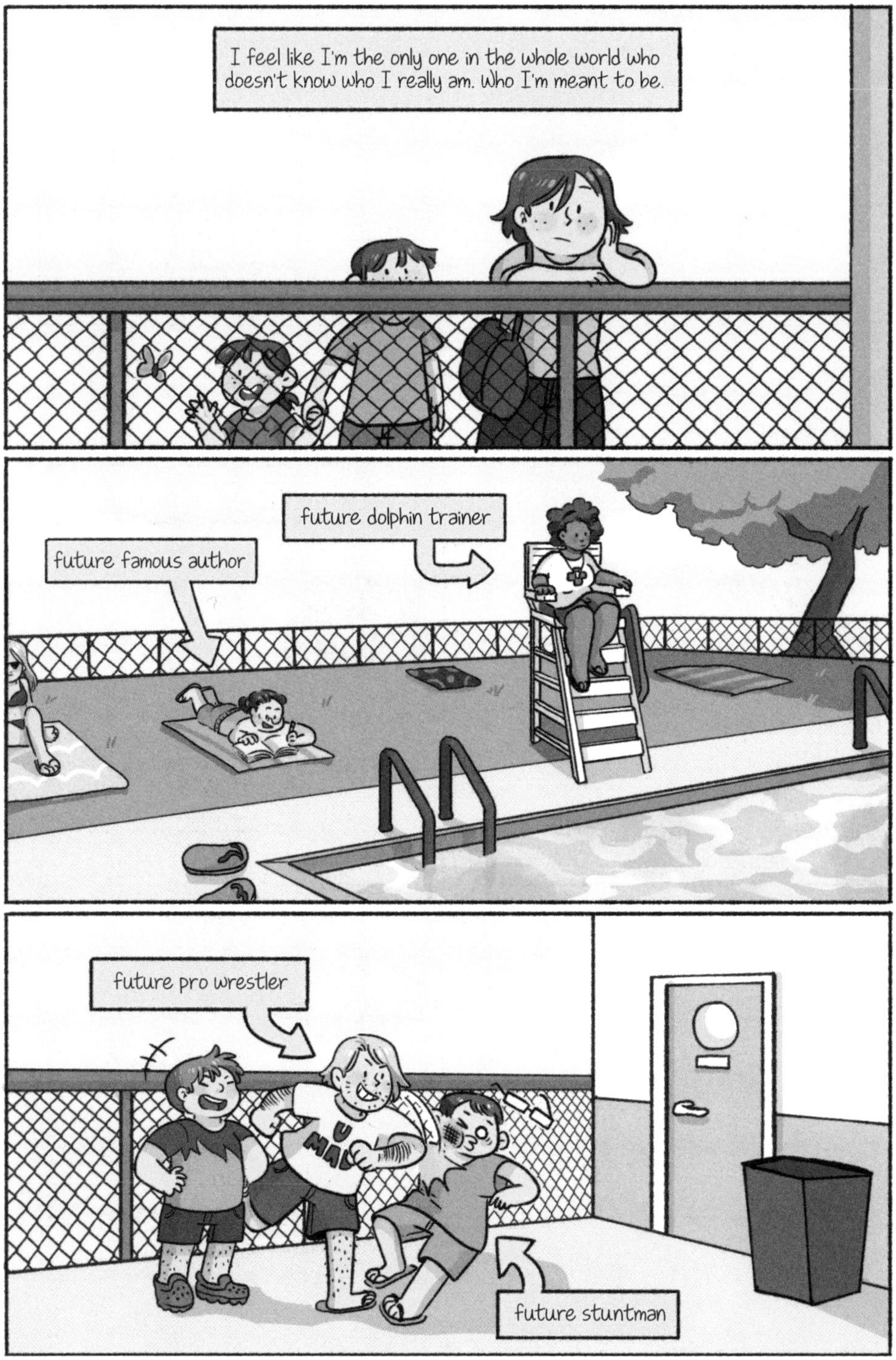
I feel like I'm the only one in the whole world who doesn't know who I really am. Who I'm meant to be.
future famous author
future dolphin trainer
future pro wrestler
future stuntman

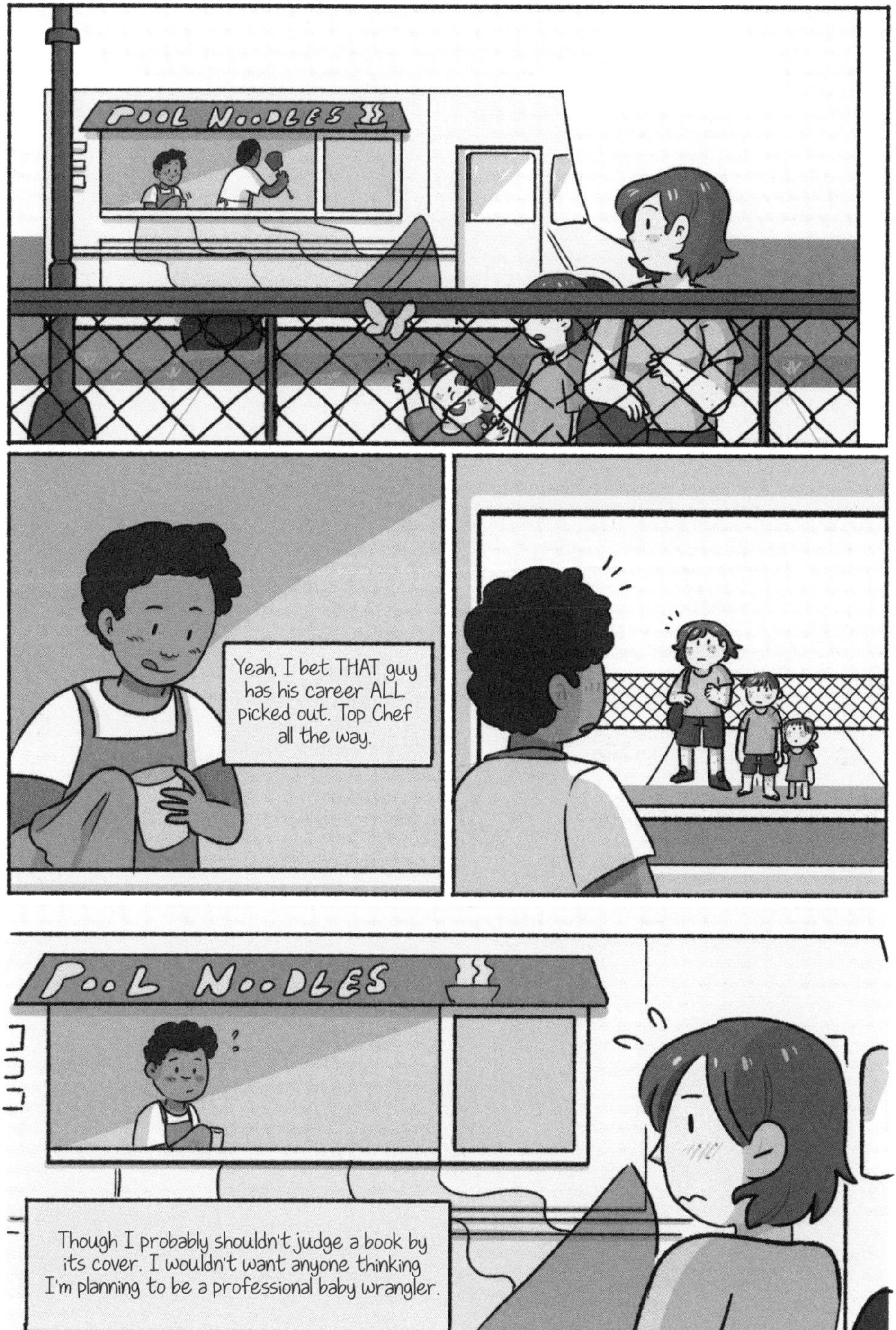

POOL NOODLES
Yeah, I bet THAT guy has his career ALL picked out. Top Chef all the way.
POOL NOODLES
Though I probably shouldn't judge a book by its cover. I wouldn't want anyone thinking I'm planning to be a professional baby wrangler.

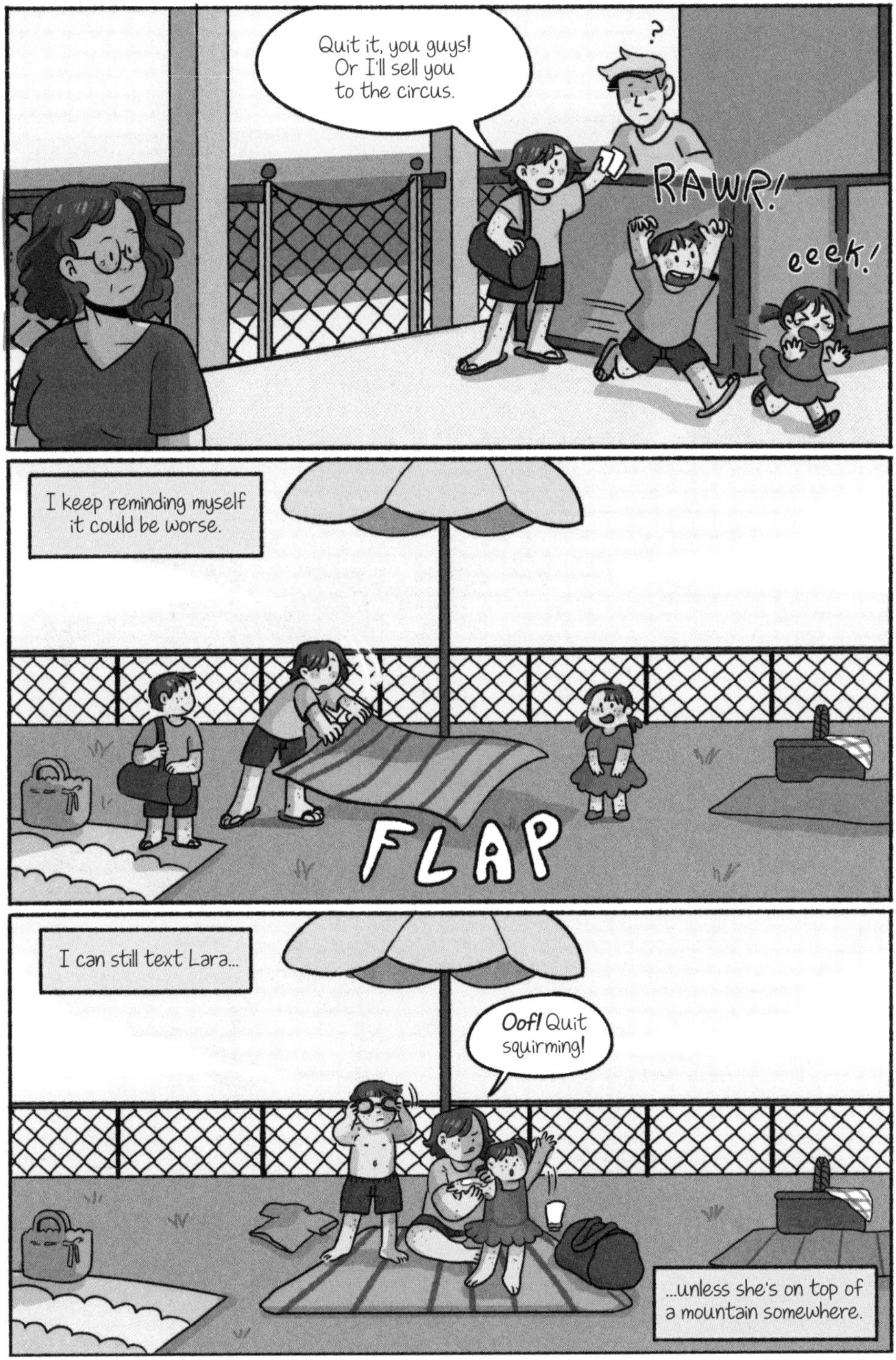
Quit it, you guys! Or I'll sell you to the circus.
?
RAWR!
eeek!
I keep reminding myself it could be worse.
FLAP
I can still text Lara...
Oof! Quit squirming!
...unless she's on top of a mountain somewhere.

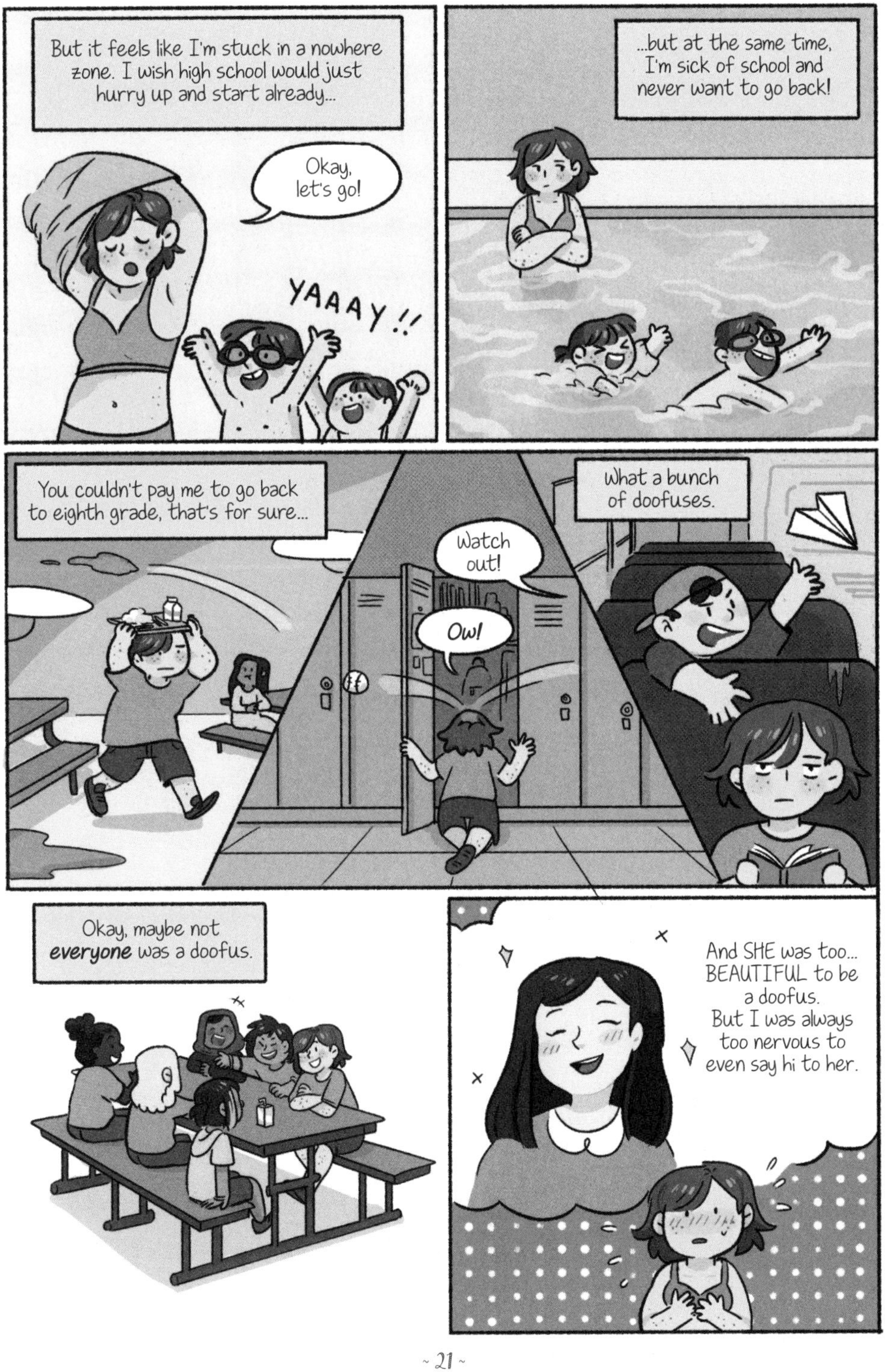
But it feels like I'm stuck in a nowhere zone. I wish high school would just hurry up and start already...
Okay, let's go!
YAAAY!!
...but at the same time, I'm sick of school and never want to go back!
You couldn't pay me to go back to eighth grade, that's for sure...
Watch out!
Ow!
What a bunch of doofuses.
Okay, maybe not **everyone** was a doofus.
And SHE was too... BEAUTIFUL to be a doofus. But I was always too nervous to even say hi to her.

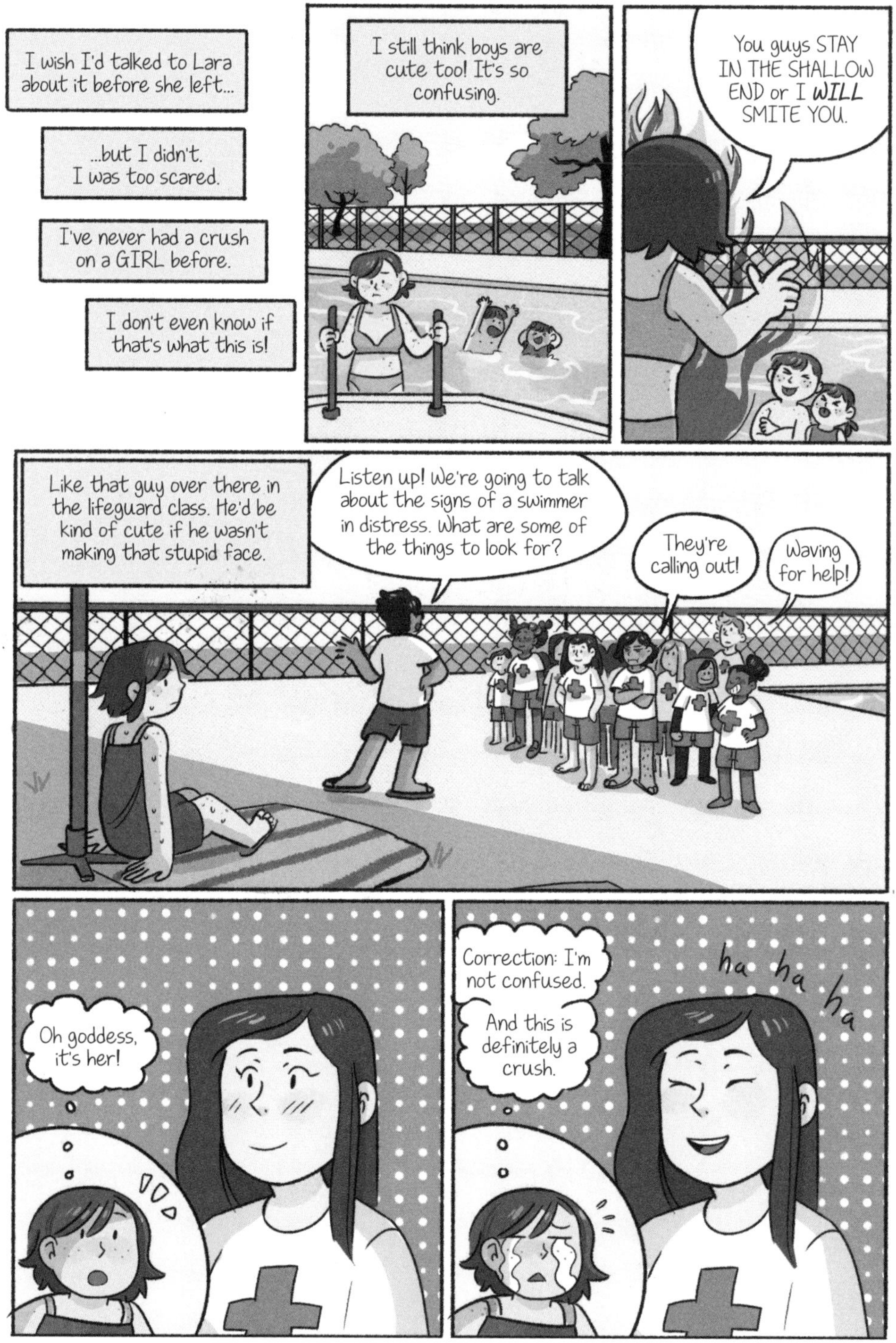
I wish I'd talked to Lara about it before she left...
...but I didn't. I was too scared.
I've never had a crush on a GIRL before.
I don't even know if that's what this is!
I still think boys are cute too! It's so confusing.
You guys STAY IN THE SHALLOW END or I **WILL** SMITE YOU.
Like that guy over there in the lifeguard class. He'd be kind of cute if he wasn't making that stupid face.
Listen up! We're going to talk about the signs of a swimmer in distress. What are some of the things to look for?
They're calling out!
Waving for help!
Oh goddess, it's her!
Correction: I'm not confused.
And this is definitely a crush.
ha ha ha

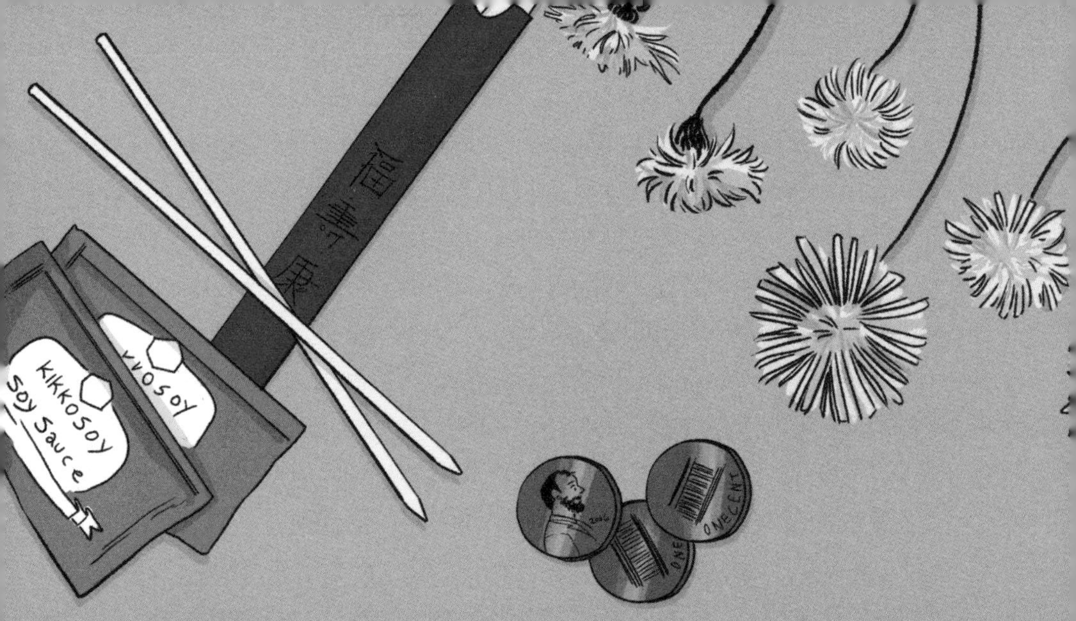
福壽康
Kikkosoy
Soy Sauce
ONE CENT

Chapter 2

Jason vs. the Meathead

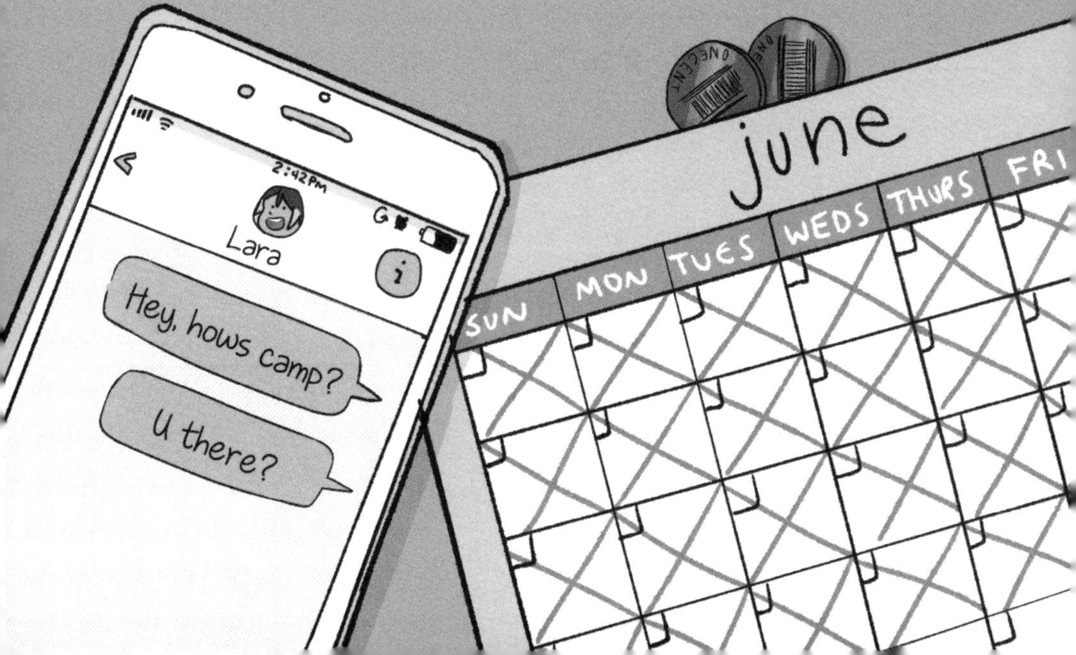
2:42PM
Lara
Hey, hows camp?
U there?
june
SUN
MON
TUES
WEDS
THURS
FRI

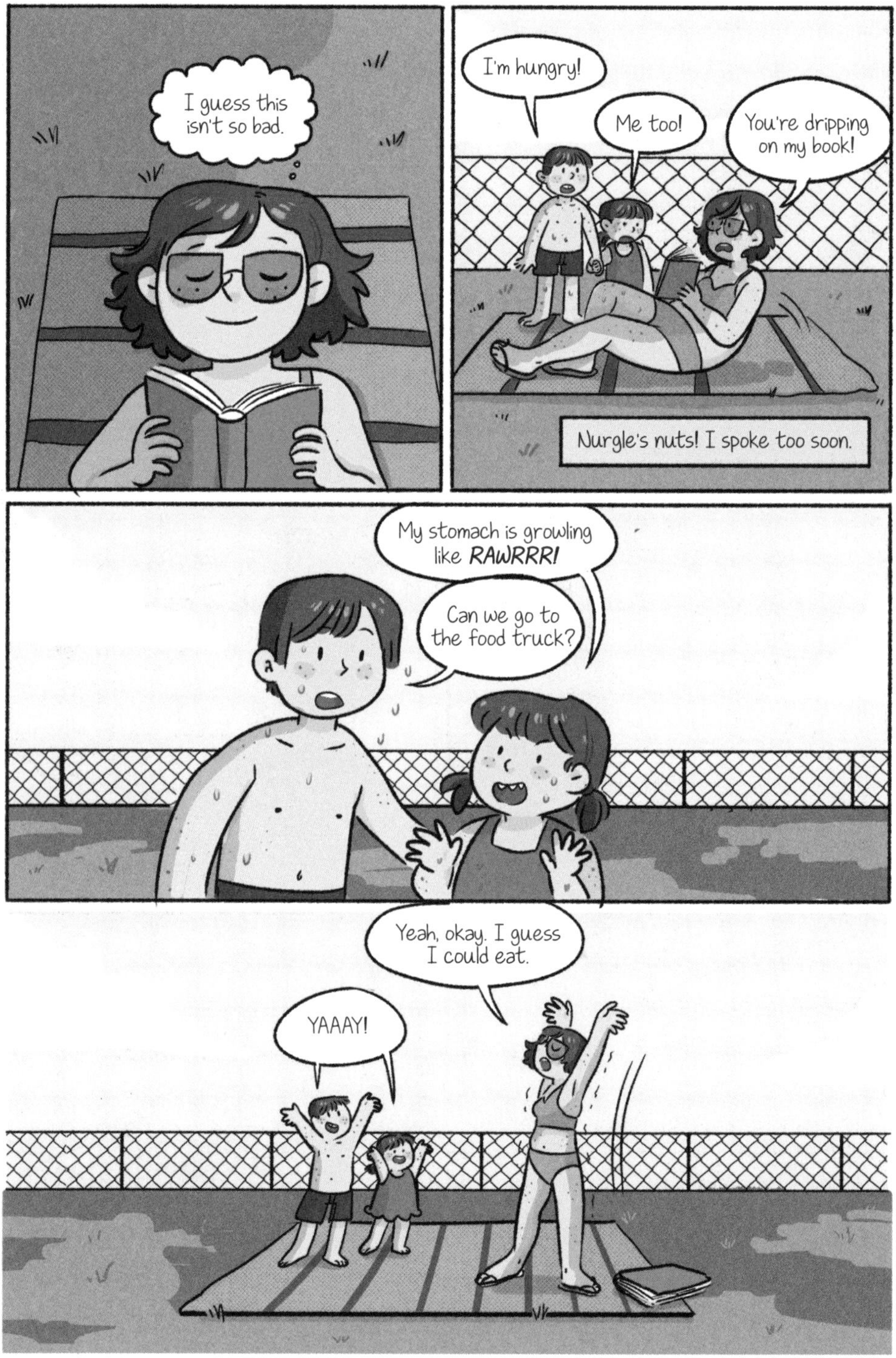
I guess this isn't so bad.
I'm hungry!
Me too!
You're dripping on my book!
Nurgle's nuts! I spoke too soon.
My stomach is growling like **RAWRRR!**
Can we go to the food truck?
Yeah, okay. I guess I could eat.
YAAAY!

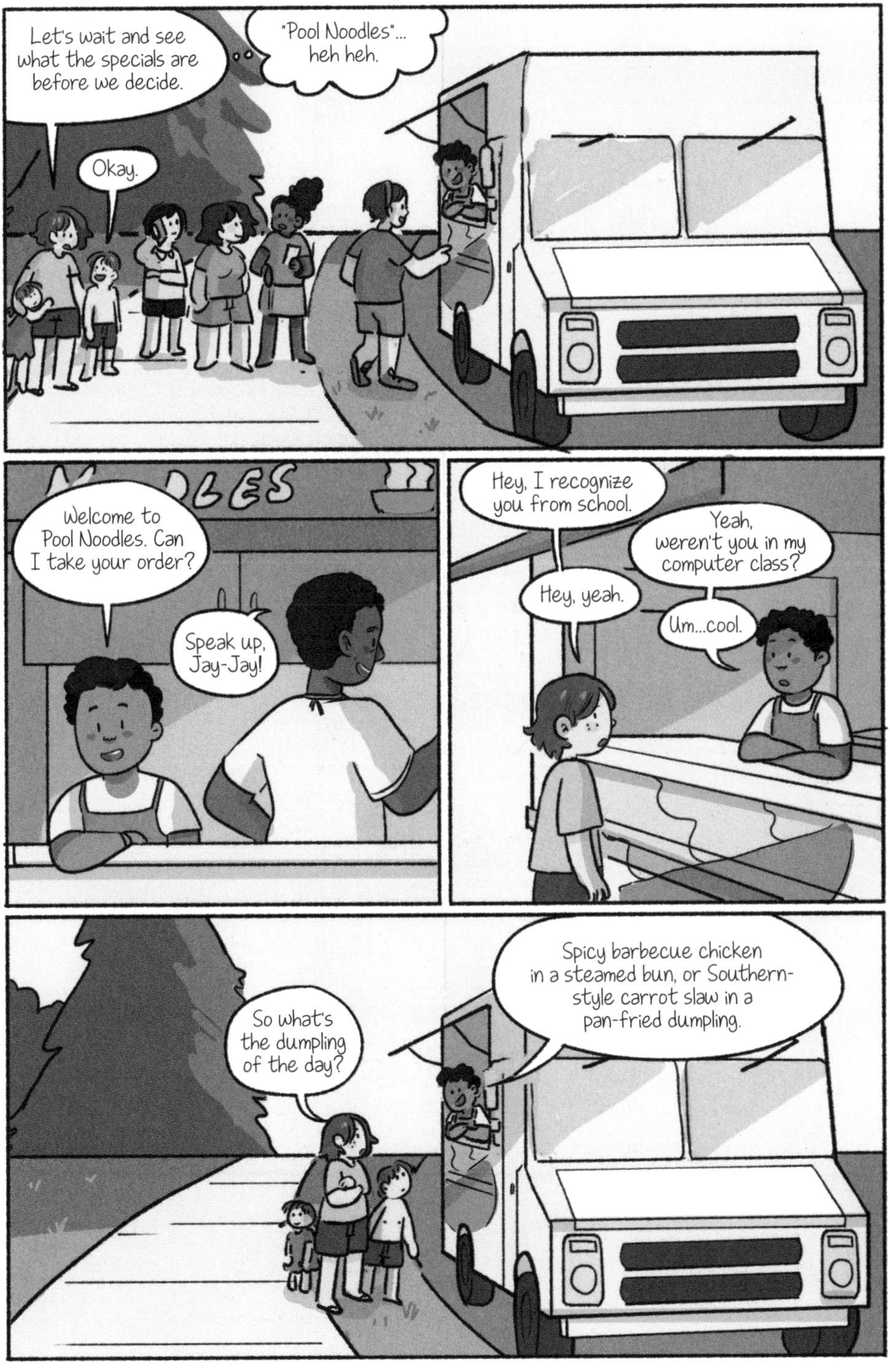
Let's wait and see what the specials are before we decide.
"Pool Noodles"... heh heh.
Okay.
NOODLES
Welcome to Pool Noodles. Can I take your order?
Speak up, Jay-Jay!
Hey, I recognize you from school.
Yeah, weren't you in my computer class?
Hey, yeah.
Um...cool.
So what's the dumpling of the day?
Spicy barbecue chicken in a steamed bun, or Southern-style carrot slaw in a pan-fried dumpling.

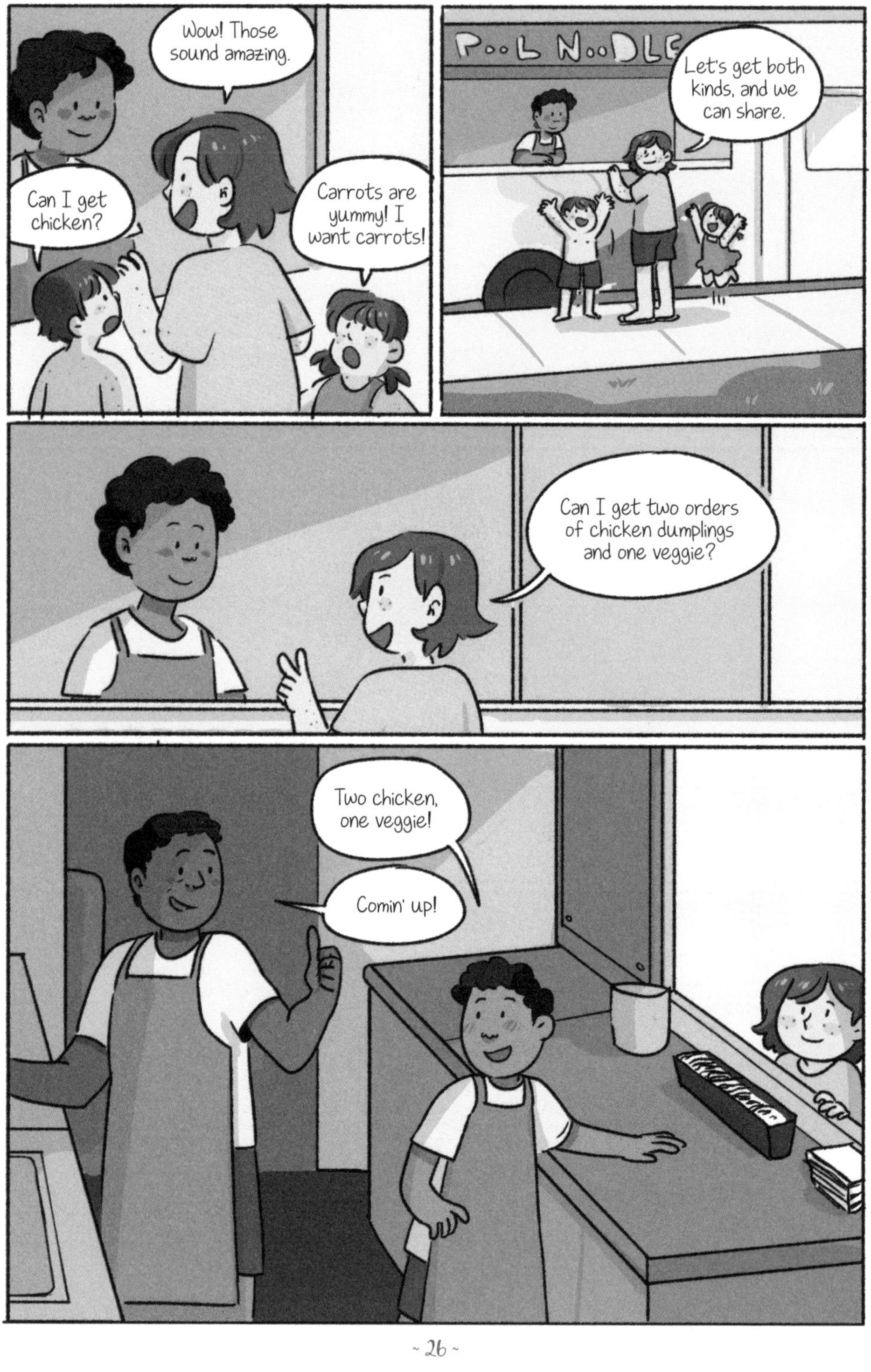
Wow! Those sound amazing.
Can I get chicken?
Carrots are yummy! I want carrots!
POOL NOODLE
Let's get both kinds, and we can share.
Can I get two orders of chicken dumplings and one veggie?
Two chicken, one veggie!
Comin' up!

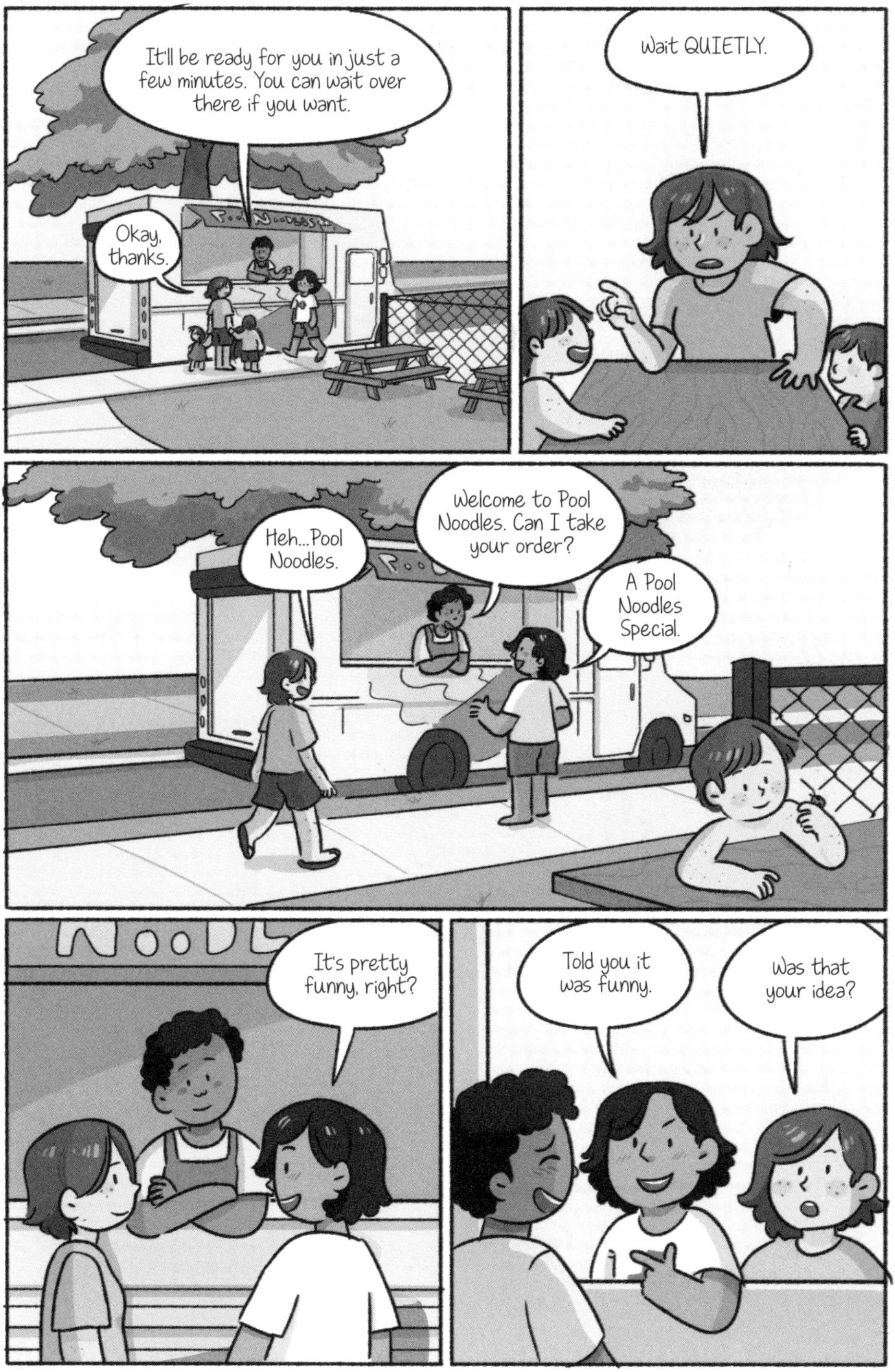
It'll be ready for you in just a few minutes. You can wait over there if you want.
Okay, thanks.
Wait QUIETLY.
Heh...Pool Noodles.
Welcome to Pool Noodles. Can I take your order?
A Pool Noodles Special.
It's pretty funny, right?
Told you it was funny.
Was that your idea?

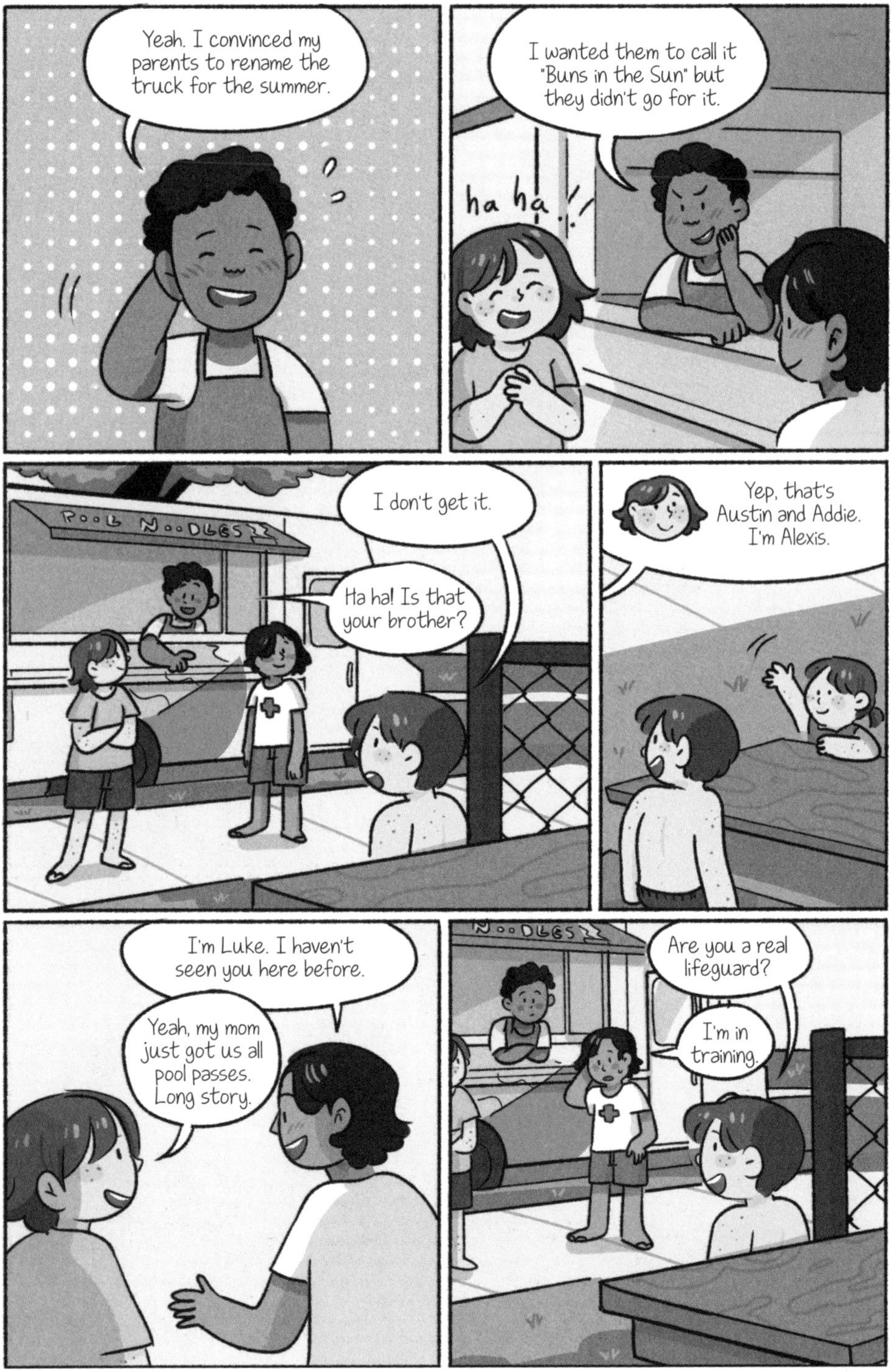
Yeah. I convinced my parents to rename the truck for the summer.
I wanted them to call it "Buns in the Sun" but they didn't go for it.
ha ha
POOL NOODLES
I don't get it.
Ha ha! Is that your brother?
Yep, that's Austin and Addie. I'm Alexis.
I'm Luke. I haven't seen you here before.
Yeah, my mom just got us all pool passes. Long story.
NOODLES
Are you a real lifeguard?
I'm in training.

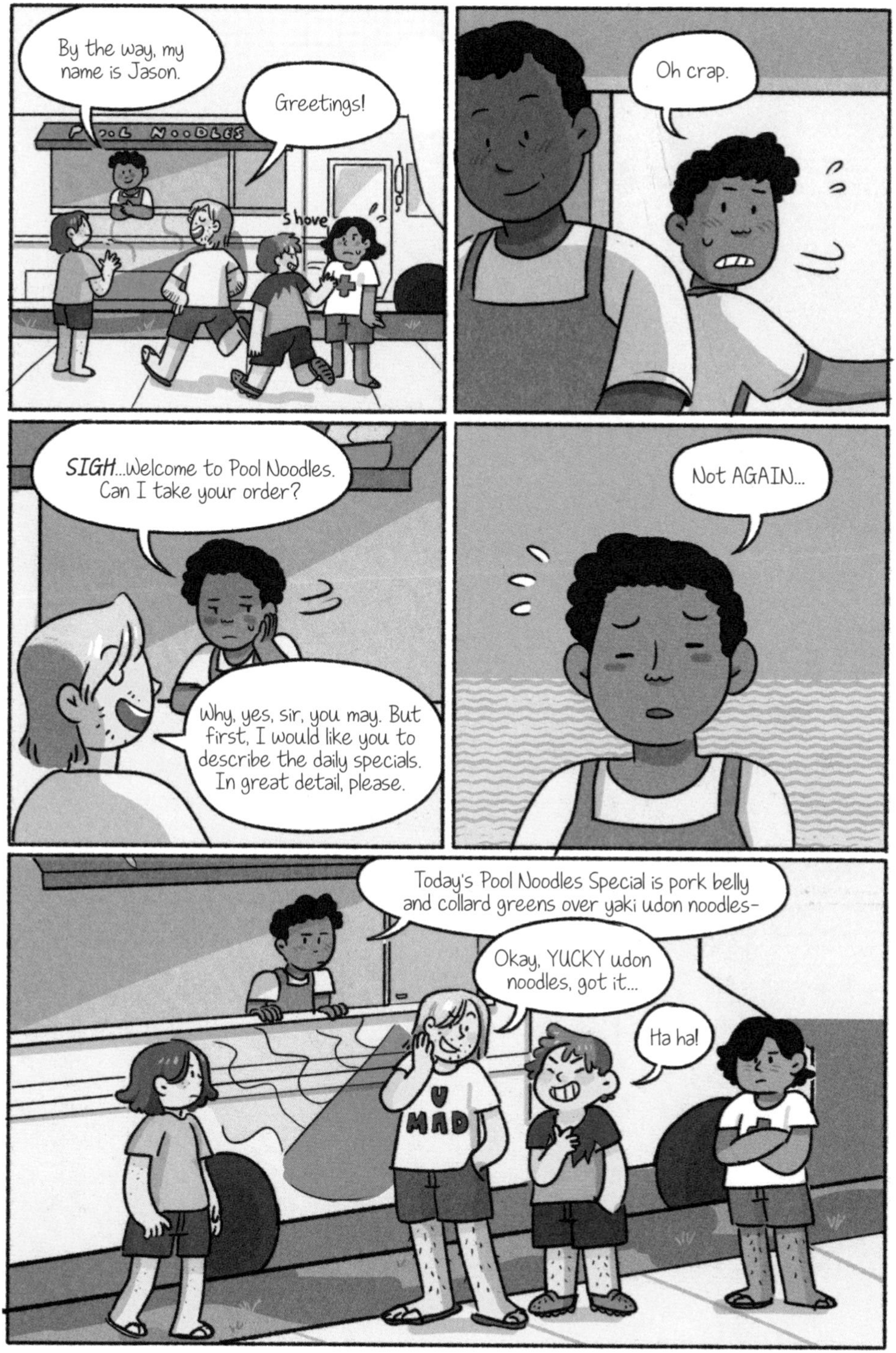
By the way, my name is Jason.
Greetings!
POOL NOODLES
Shove
Oh crap.
SIGH...Welcome to Pool Noodles. Can I take your order?
Why, yes, sir, you may. But first, I would like you to describe the daily specials. In great detail, please.
Not AGAIN...
Today's Pool Noodles Special is pork belly and collard greens over yaki udon noodles-
Okay, YUCKY udon noodles, got it...
Ha ha!
U MAD

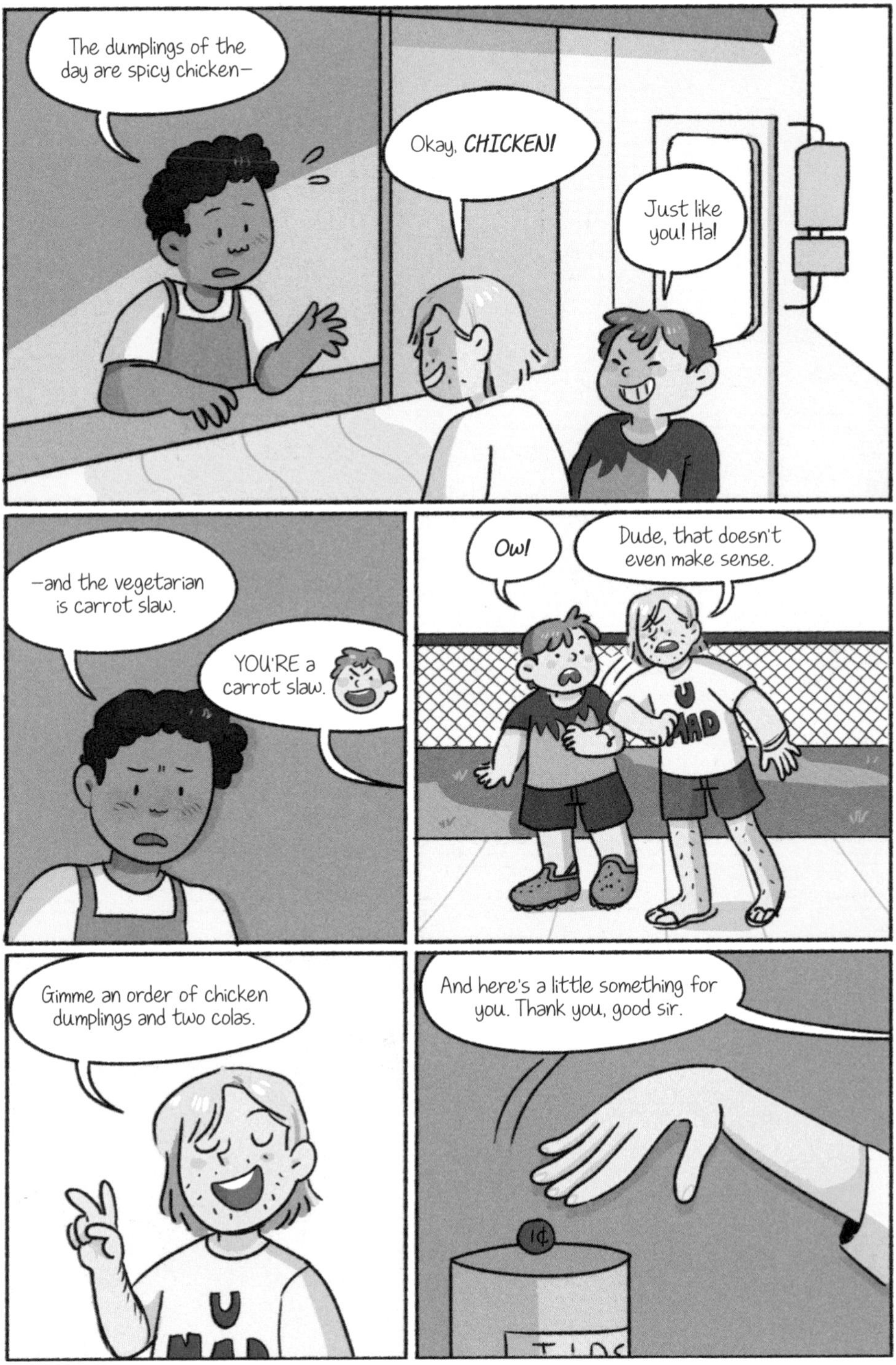

The dumplings of the day are spicy chicken—
Okay, CHICKEN!
Just like you! Ha!
—and the vegetarian is carrot slaw.
YOU'RE a carrot slaw.
Ow!
Dude, that doesn't even make sense.
Gimme an order of chicken dumplings and two colas.
And here's a little something for you. Thank you, good sir.
1¢

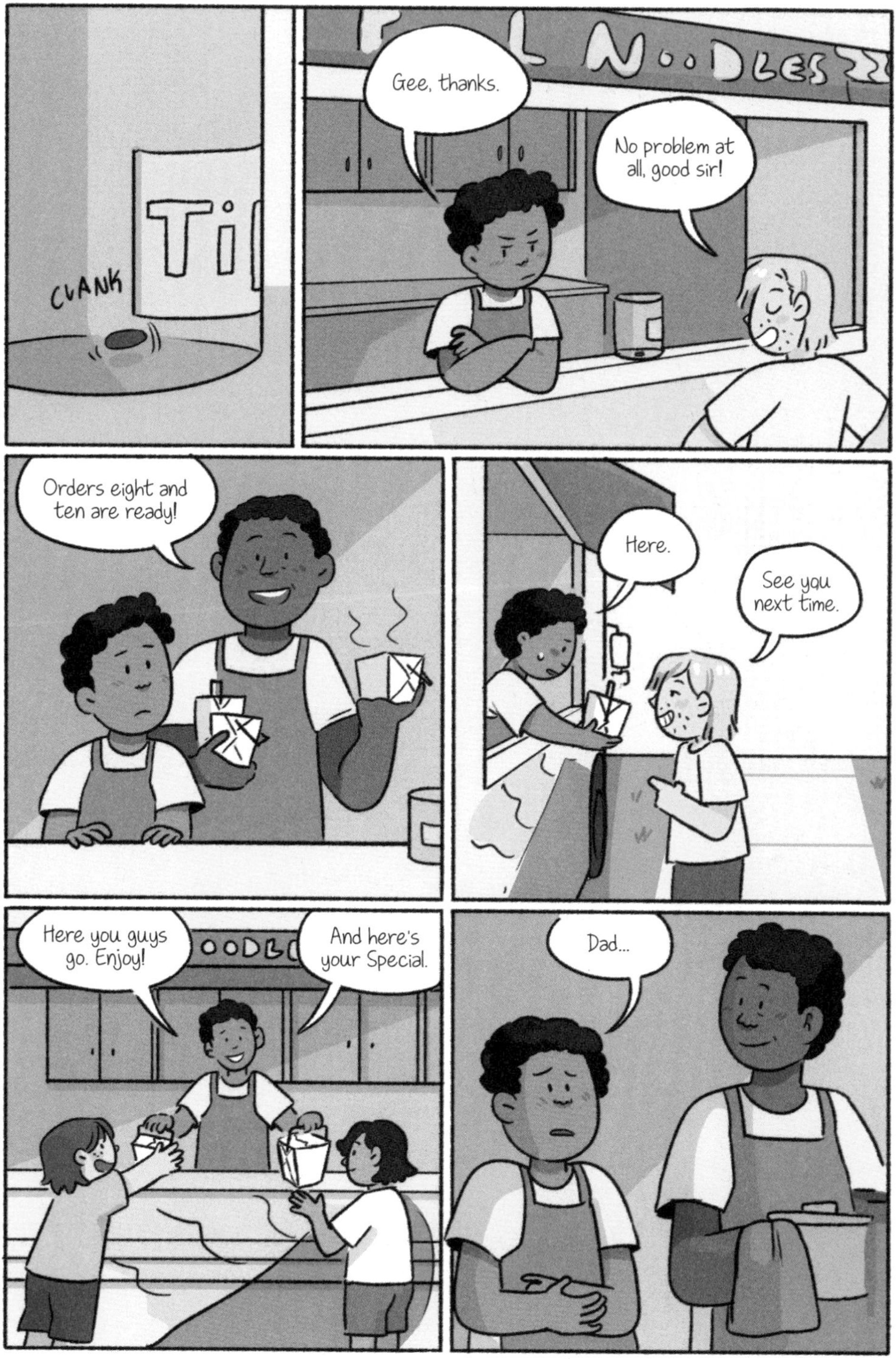
CLANK
Ti
L NOODLES
Gee, thanks.
No problem at all, good sir!
Orders eight and ten are ready!
Here.
See you next time.
Here you guys go. Enjoy!
OODL
And here's your Special.
Dad...

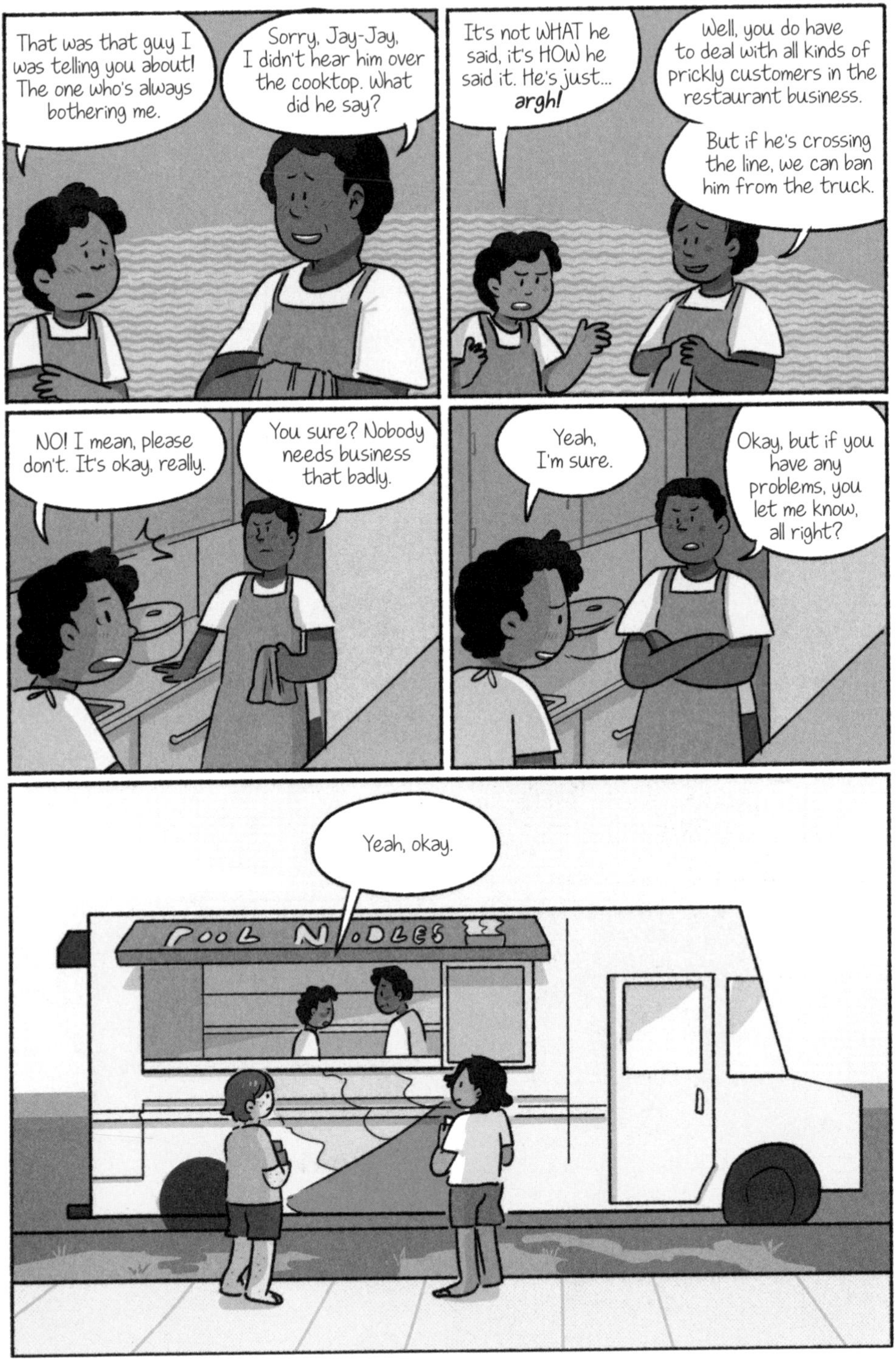

That was that guy I was telling you about! The one who's always bothering me.
Sorry, Jay-Jay, I didn't hear him over the cooktop. What did he say?
It's not WHAT he said, it's HOW he said it. He's just... argh!
Well, you do have to deal with all kinds of prickly customers in the restaurant business.
But if he's crossing the line, we can ban him from the truck.
NO! I mean, please don't. It's okay, really.
You sure? Nobody needs business that badly.
Yeah, I'm sure.
Okay, but if you have any problems, you let me know, all right?
Yeah, okay.

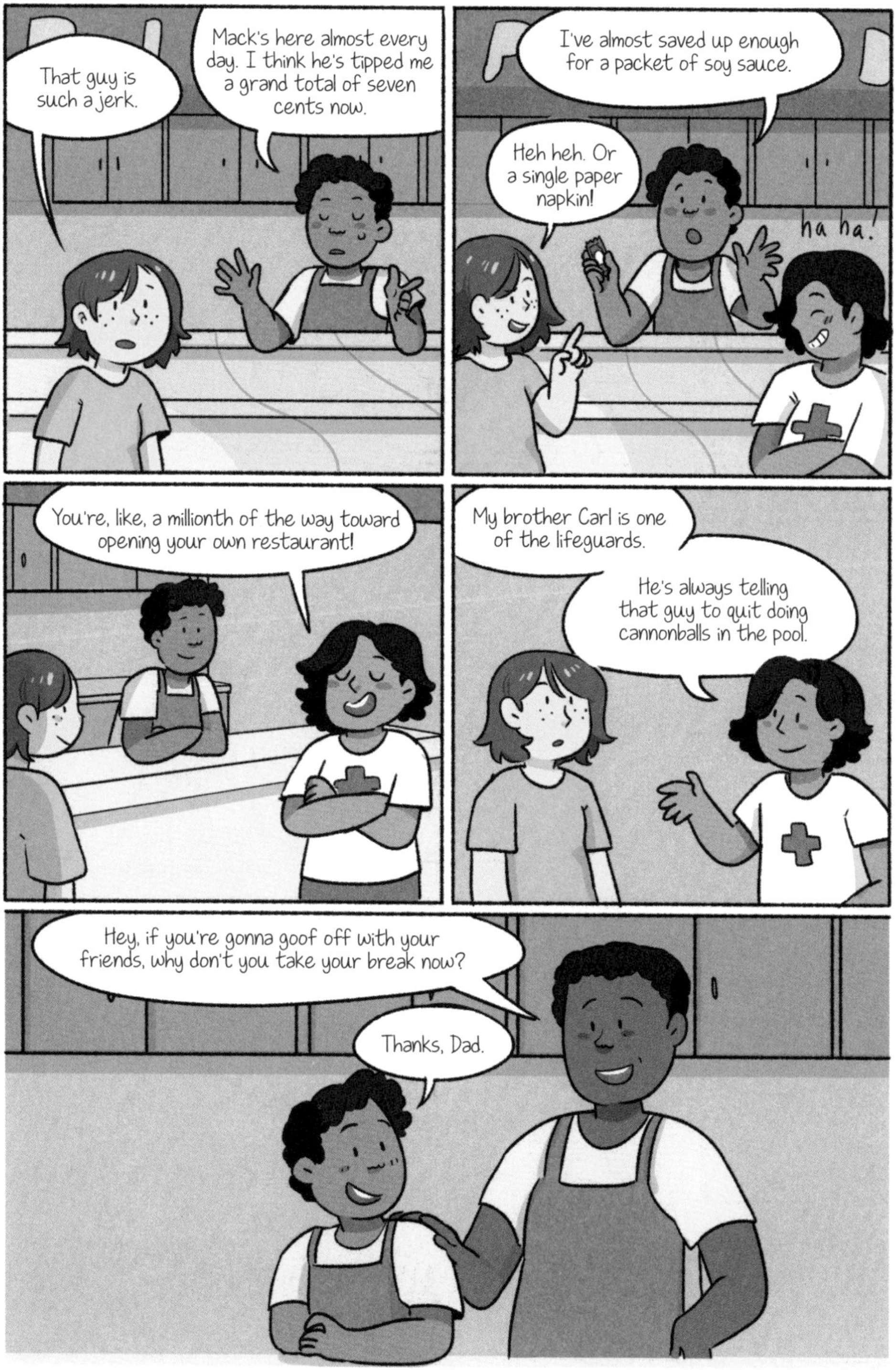
That guy is such a jerk.
Mack's here almost every day. I think he's tipped me a grand total of seven cents now.
I've almost saved up enough for a packet of soy sauce.
Heh heh. Or a single paper napkin!
ha ha!
You're, like, a millionth of the way toward opening your own restaurant!
My brother Carl is one of the lifeguards.
He's always telling that guy to quit doing cannonballs in the pool.
Hey, if you're gonna goof off with your friends, why don't you take your break now?
Thanks, Dad.

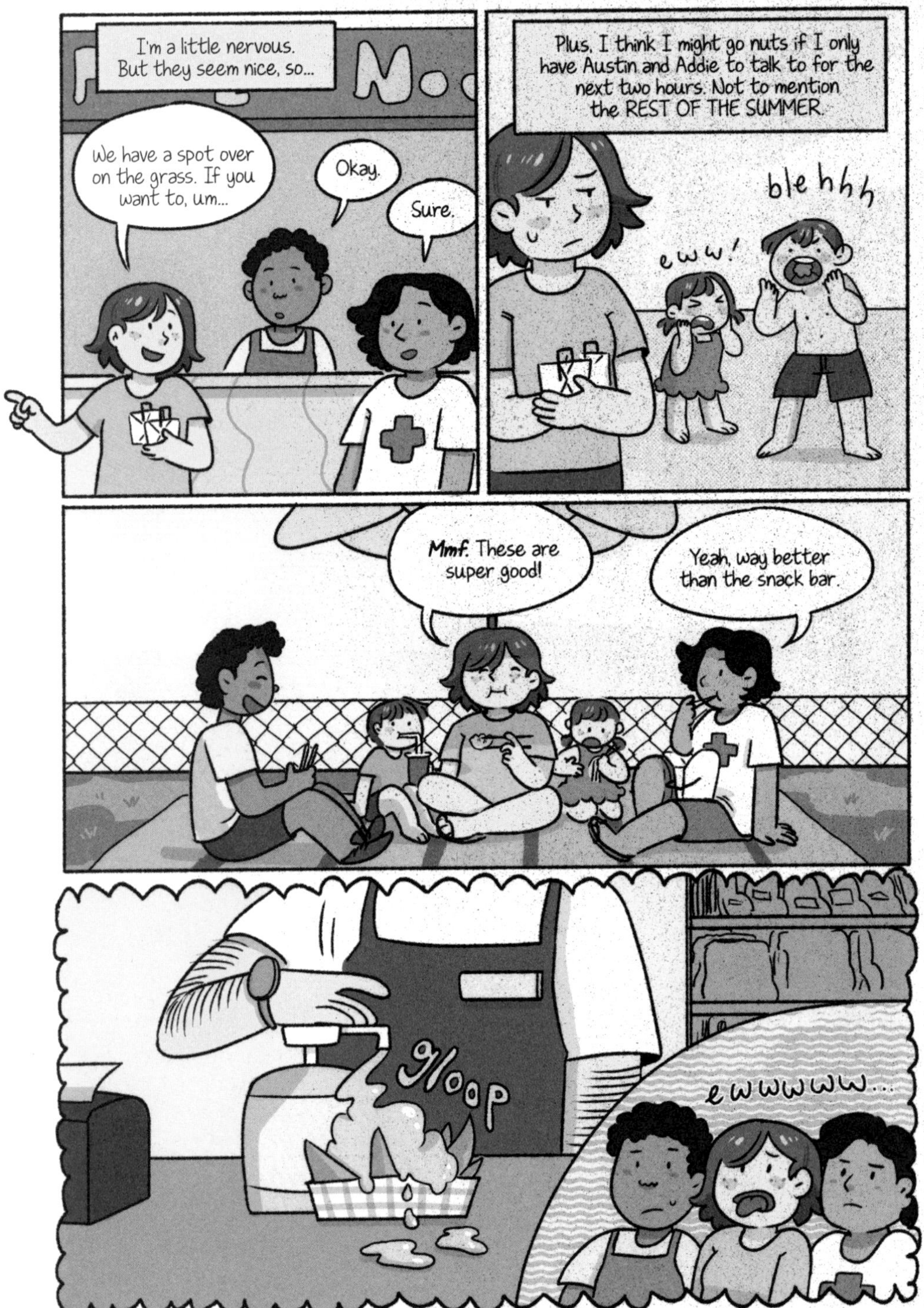

I'm a little nervous. But they seem nice, so...
We have a spot over on the grass. If you want to, um...
Okay.
Sure.
Plus, I think I might go nuts if I only have Austin and Addie to talk to for the next two hours. Not to mention the REST OF THE SUMMER.
blehhh
eww!
Mmf. These are super good!
Yeah, way better than the snack bar.
gloop
ewwwww...

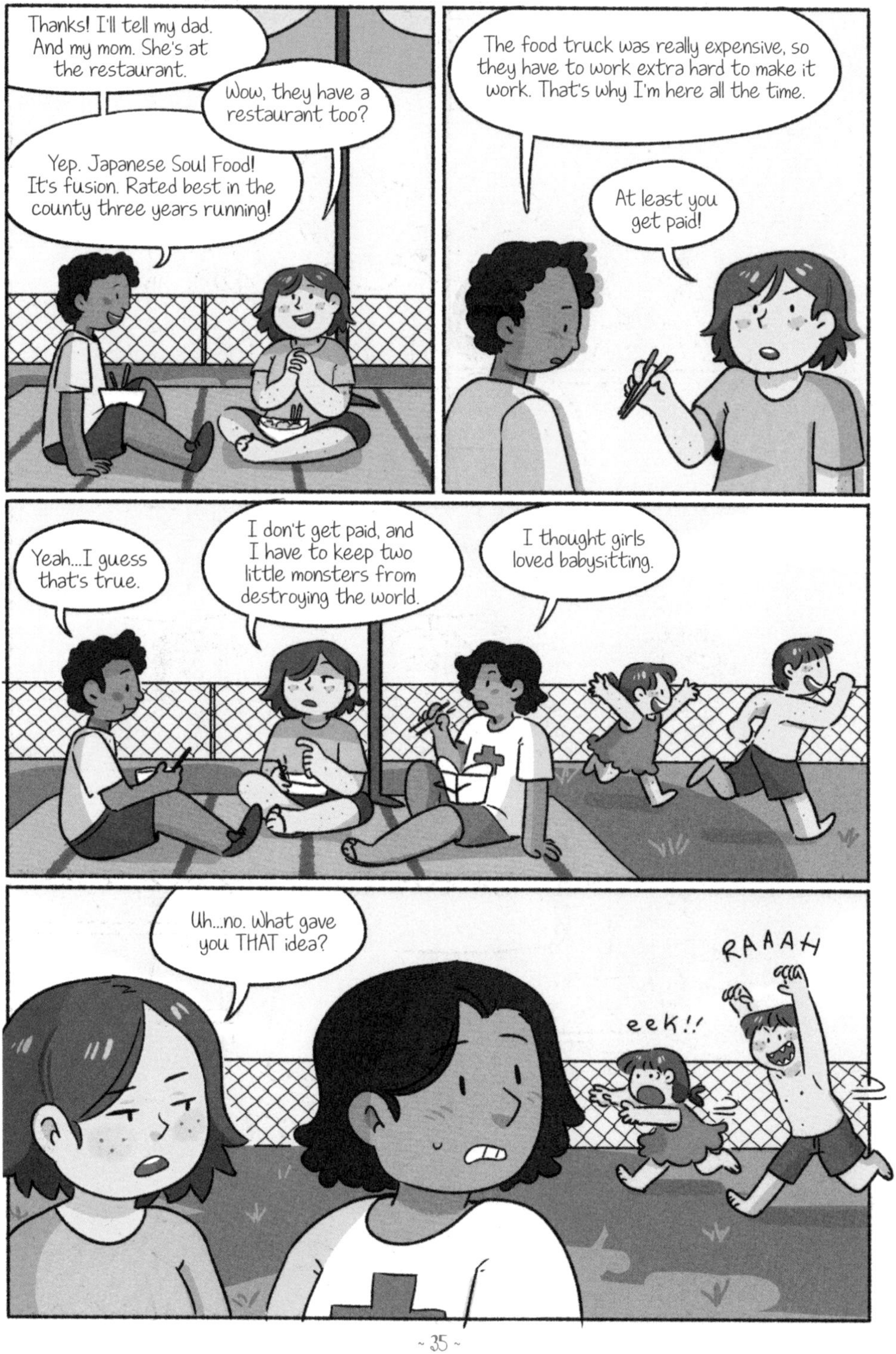
Thanks! I'll tell my dad. And my mom. She's at the restaurant.
Wow, they have a restaurant too?
Yep. Japanese Soul Food! It's fusion. Rated best in the county three years running!
The food truck was really expensive, so they have to work extra hard to make it work. That's why I'm here all the time.
At least you get paid!
Yeah...I guess that's true.
I don't get paid, and I have to keep two little monsters from destroying the world.
I thought girls loved babysitting.
Uh...no. What gave you THAT idea?
RAAAH
eek!!

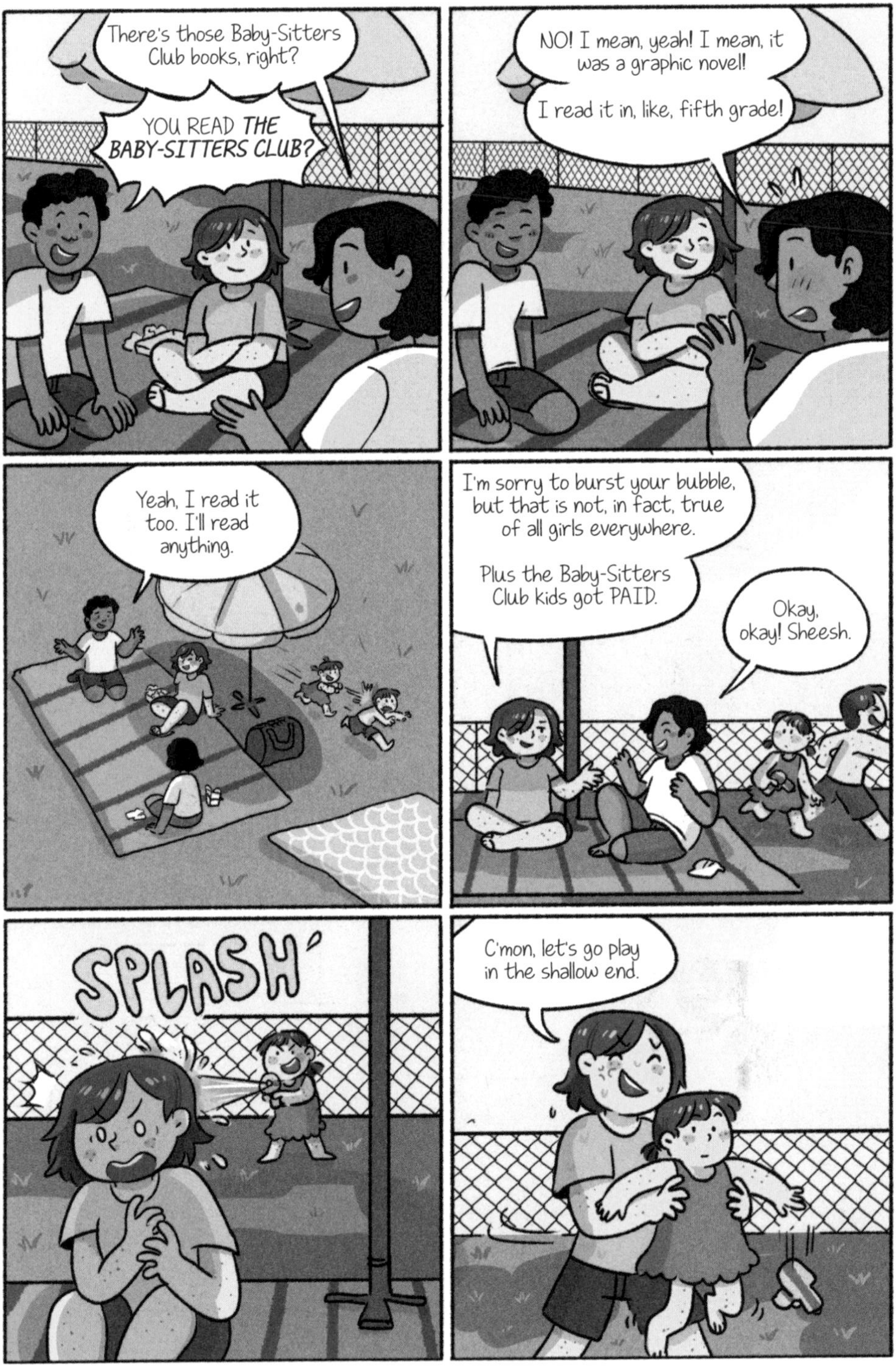
There's those Baby-Sitters Club books, right?
YOU READ THE BABY-SITTERS CLUB?
NO! I mean, yeah! I mean, it was a graphic novel!
I read it in, like, fifth grade!
Yeah, I read it too. I'll read anything.
I'm sorry to burst your bubble, but that is not, in fact, true of all girls everywhere.
Plus the Baby-Sitters Club kids got PAID.
Okay, okay! Sheesh.
SPLASH
C'mon, let's go play in the shallow end.

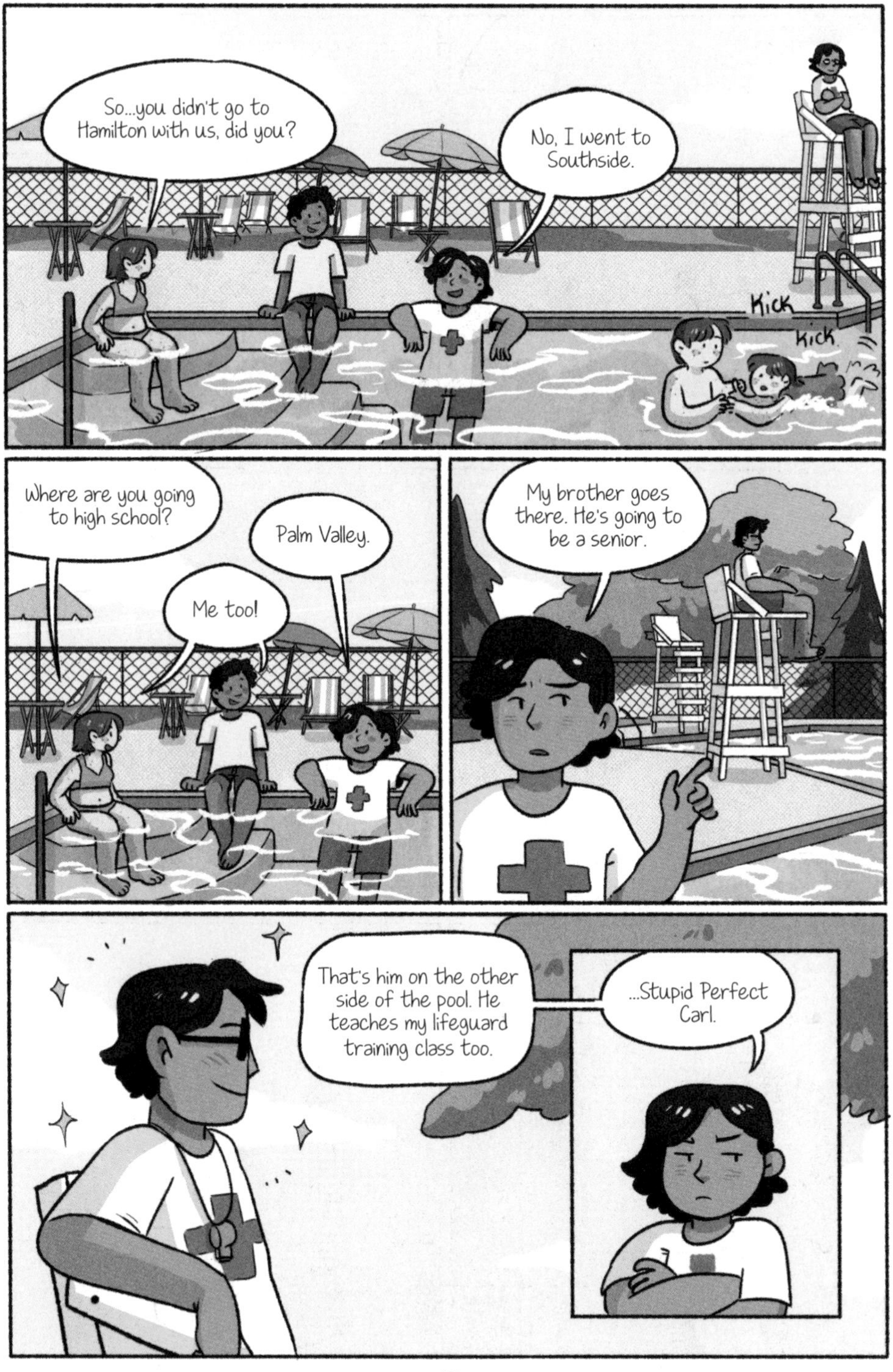
So...you didn't go to Hamilton with us, did you?
No, I went to Southside.
KICK
KICK
Where are you going to high school?
Palm Valley.
Me too!
My brother goes there. He's going to be a senior.
That's him on the other side of the pool. He teaches my lifeguard training class too.
...Stupid Perfect Carl.

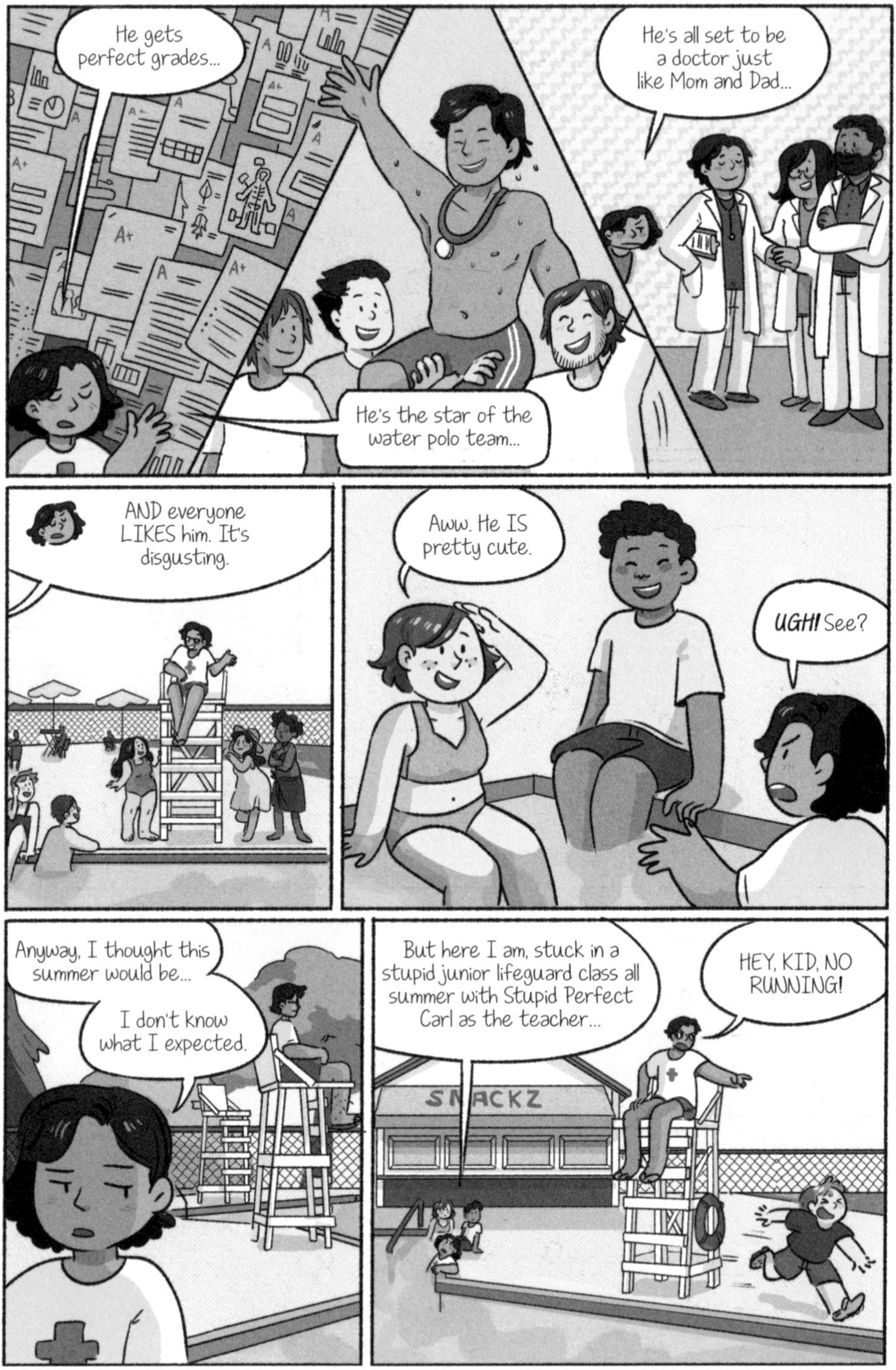
He gets perfect grades...
He's the star of the water polo team...
He's all set to be a doctor just like Mom and Dad...
AND everyone LIKES him. It's disgusting.
Aww. He IS pretty cute.
UGH! See?
Anyway, I thought this summer would be...
I don't know what I expected.
But here I am, stuck in a stupid junior lifeguard class all summer with Stupid Perfect Carl as the teacher...
HEY, KID, NO RUNNING!
SNACKZ

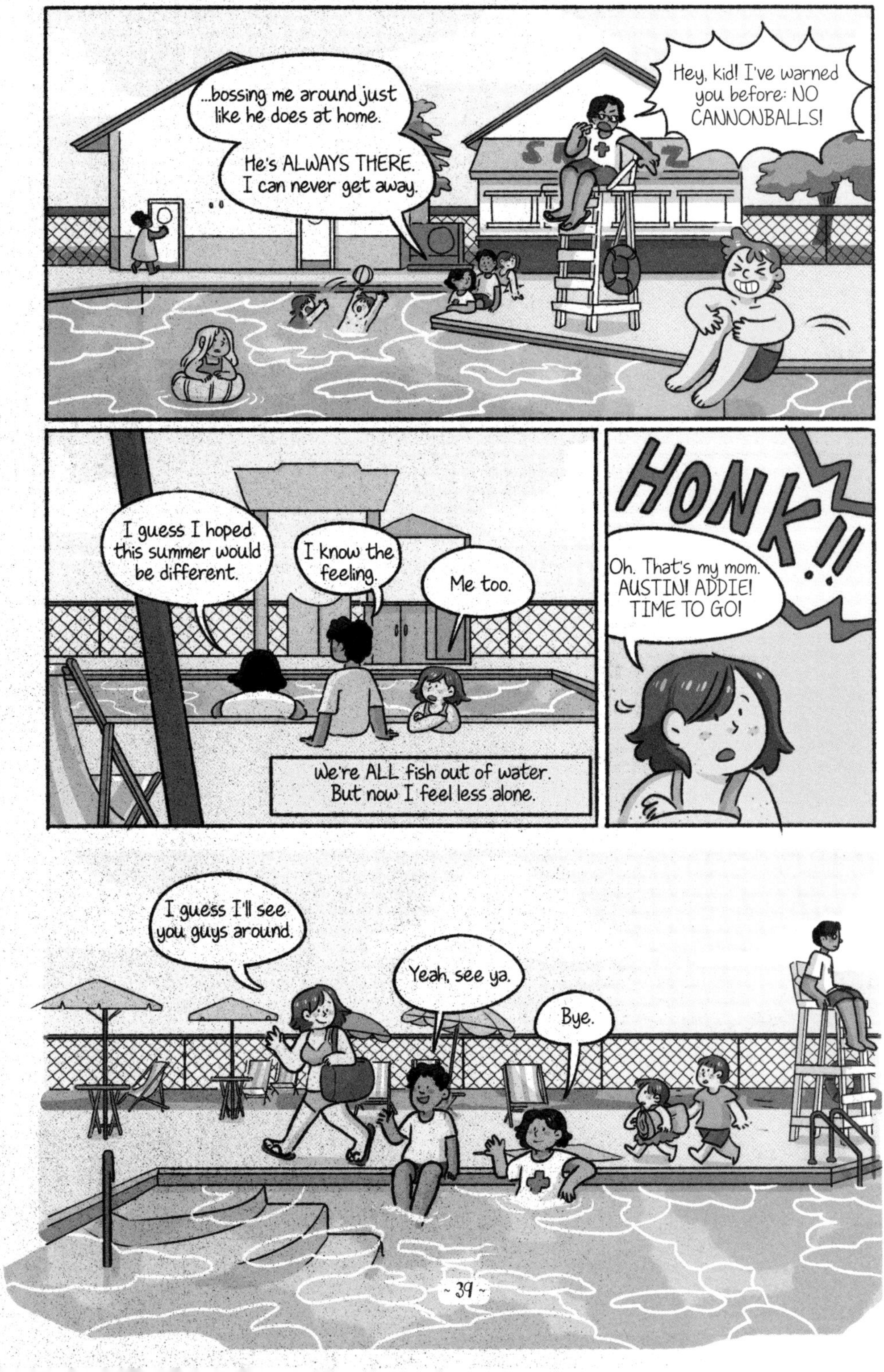
...bossing me around just like he does at home.
He's ALWAYS THERE. I can never get away.
Hey, kid! I've warned you before: NO CANNONBALLS!
I guess I hoped this summer would be different.
I know the feeling.
Me too.
We're ALL fish out of water. But now I feel less alone.
HONK!!
Oh. That's my mom. AUSTIN! ADDIE! TIME TO GO!
I guess I'll see you guys around.
Yeah, see ya.
Bye.

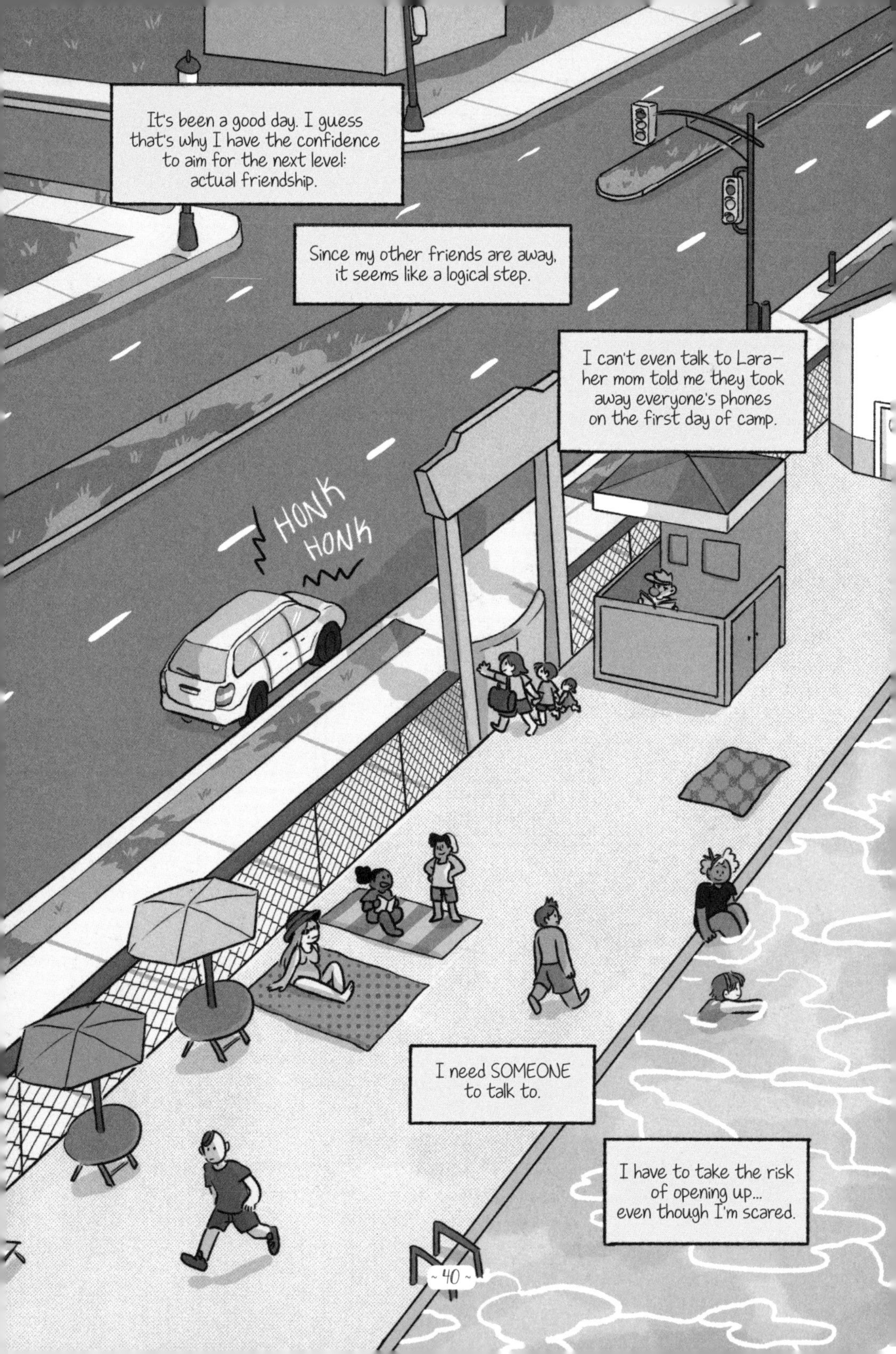
It's been a good day. I guess that's why I have the confidence to aim for the next level: actual friendship.
Since my other friends are away, it seems like a logical step.
I can't even talk to Lara— her mom told me they took away everyone's phones on the first day of camp.
HONK HONK
I need SOMEONE to talk to.
I have to take the risk of opening up... even though I'm scared.

Chapter 3

Luke vs. Initiative

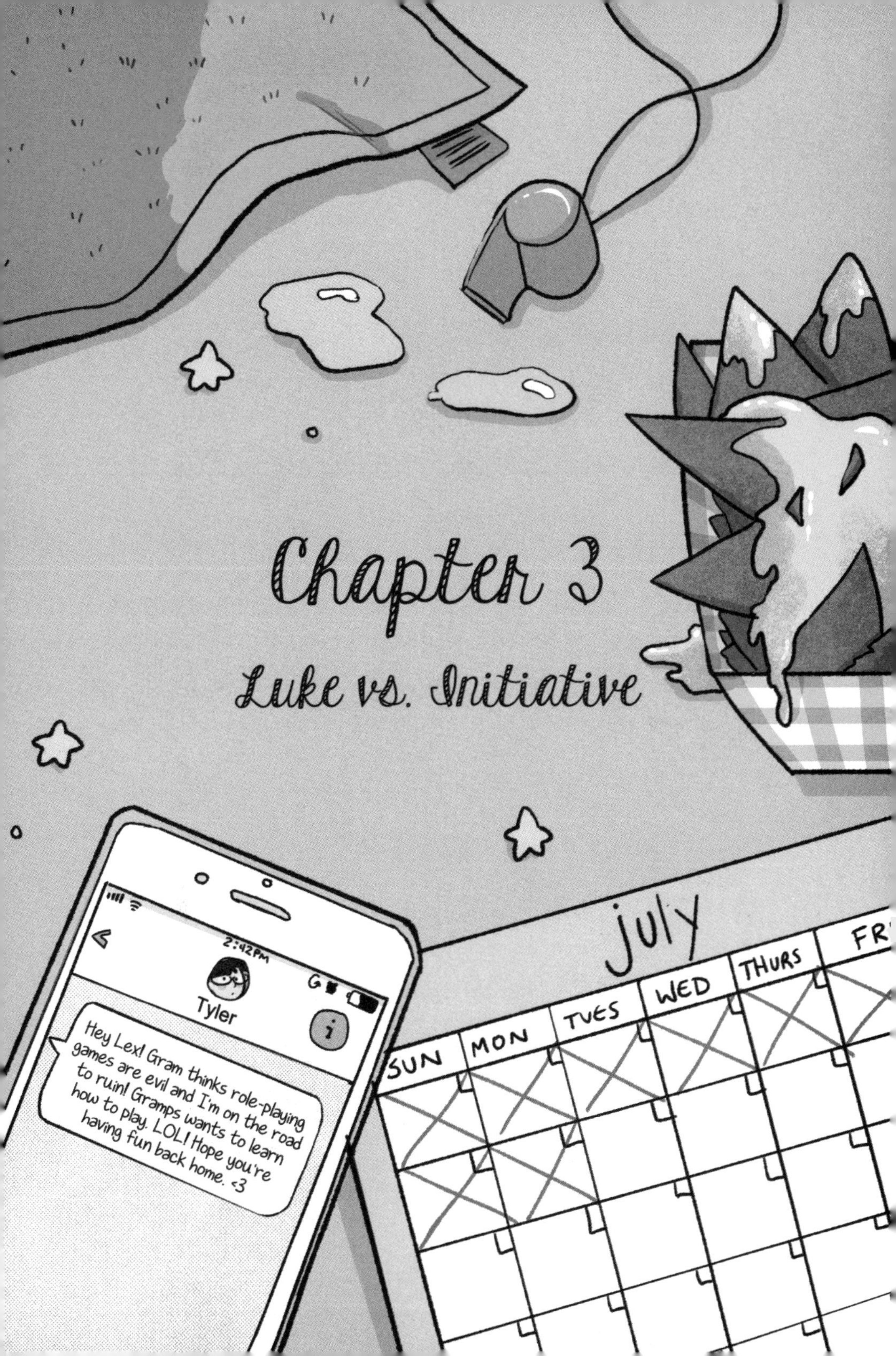
2:42PM
Tyler
Hey Lex! Gram thinks role-playing games are evil and I'm on the road to ruin! Gramps wants to learn how to play. LOL! Hope you're having fun back home. <3
july
SUN
MON
TUES
WED
THURS

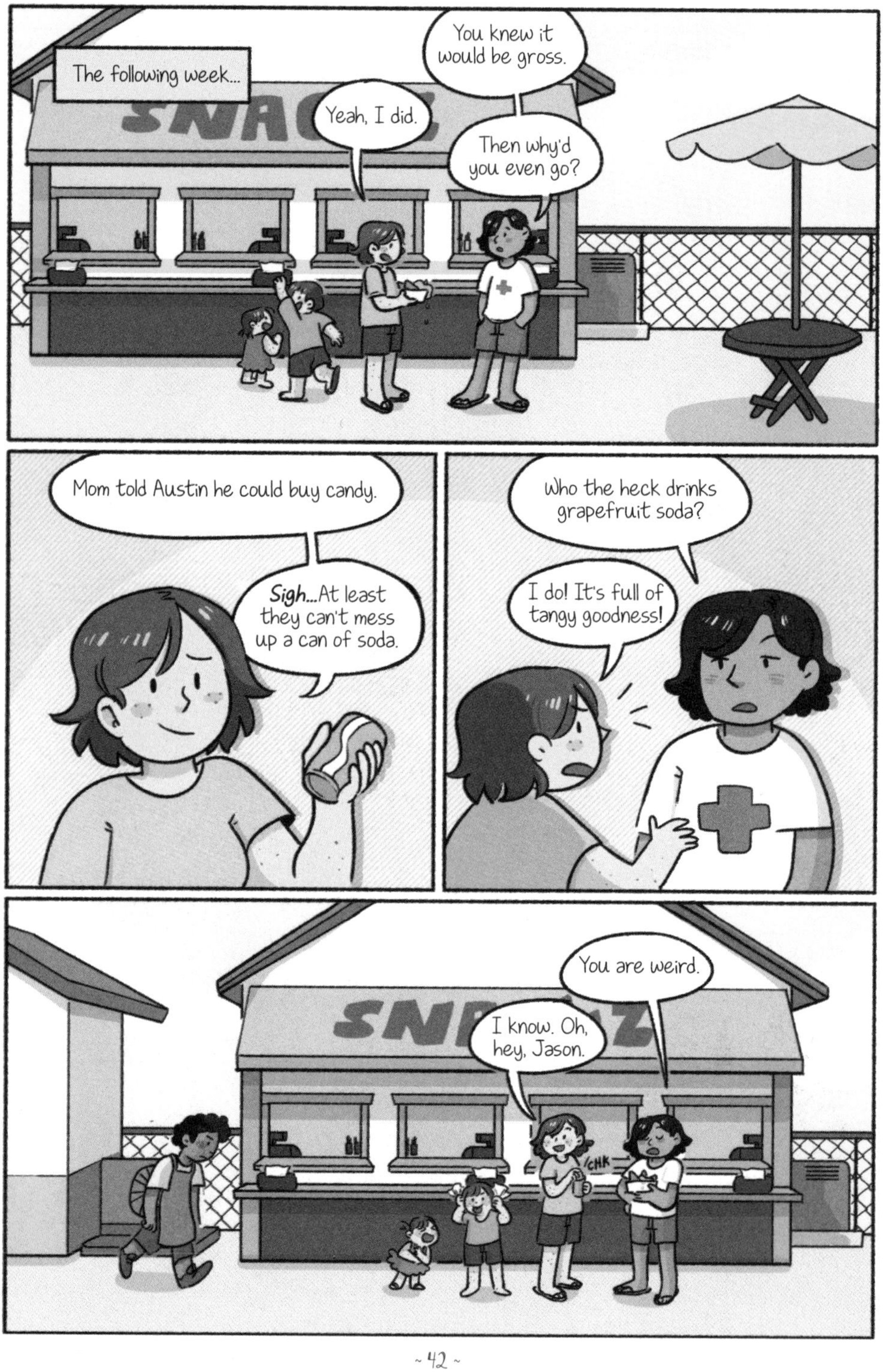
The following week...
SNACK
You knew it would be gross.
Yeah, I did.
Then why'd you even go?
Mom told Austin he could buy candy.
Sigh...At least they can't mess up a can of soda.
Who the heck drinks grapefruit soda?
I do! It's full of tangy goodness!
You are weird.
I know. Oh, hey, Jason.
CHK

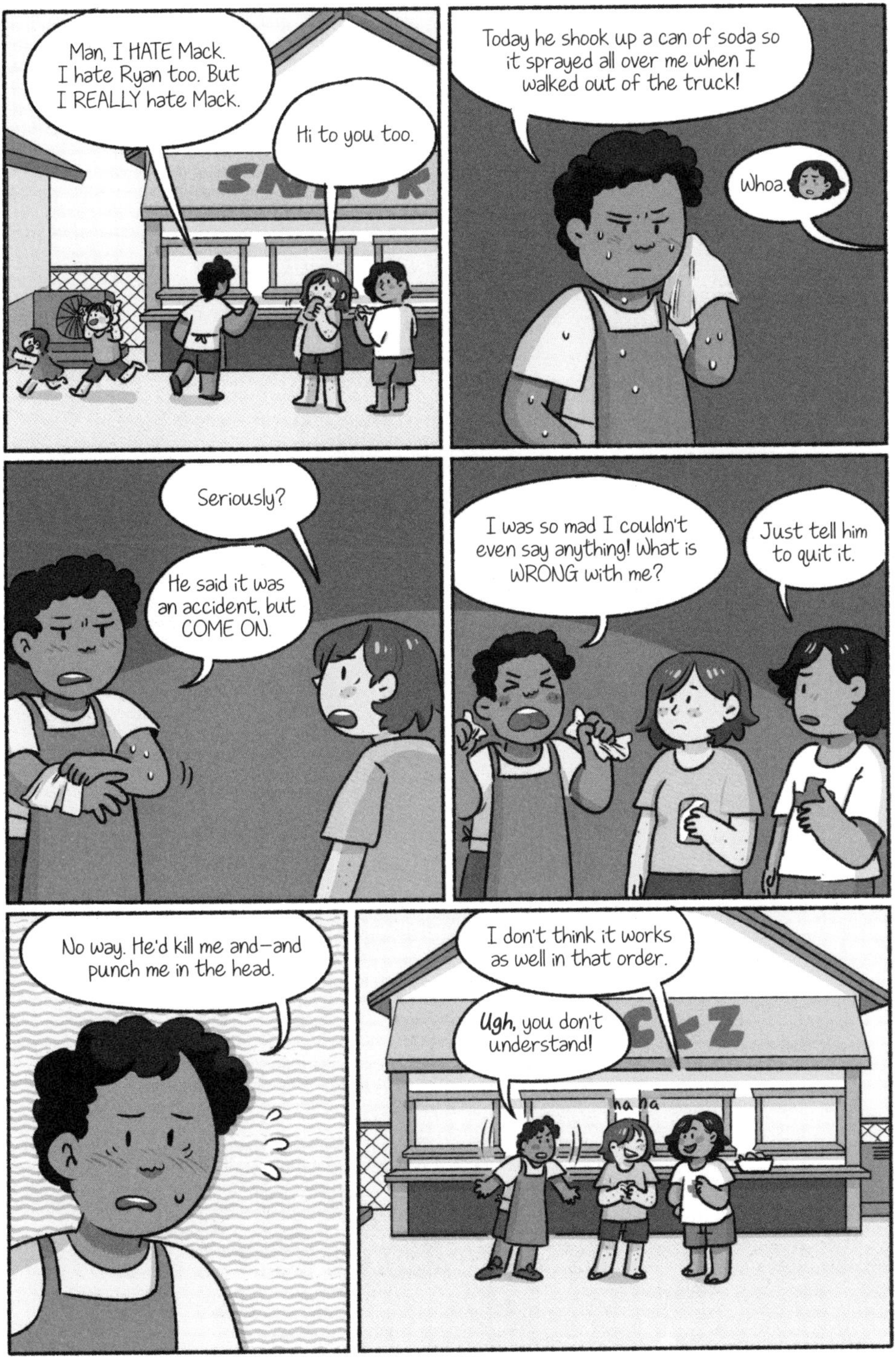
Man, I HATE Mack. I hate Ryan too. But I REALLY hate Mack.
Hi to you too.
SNACK
Today he shook up a can of soda so it sprayed all over me when I walked out of the truck!
Whoa.
Seriously?
He said it was an accident, but COME ON.
I was so mad I couldn't even say anything! What is WRONG with me?
Just tell him to quit it.
No way. He'd kill me and—and punch me in the head.
I don't think it works as well in that order.
Ugh, you don't understand!
ha ha

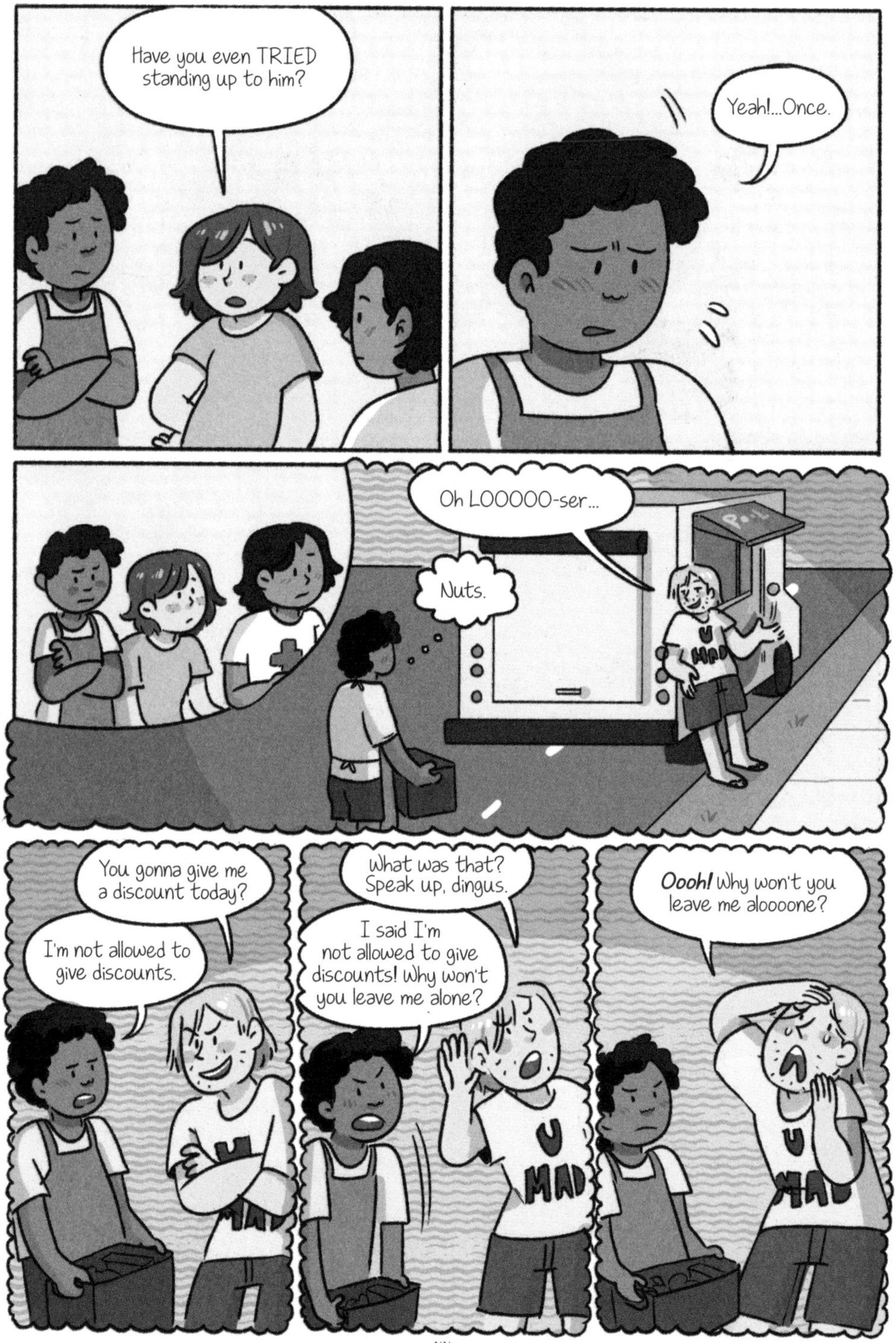
Have you even TRIED standing up to him?
Yeah!...Once.
Oh LOOOOO-ser...
Nuts.
You gonna give me a discount today?
I'm not allowed to give discounts.
What was that? Speak up, dingus.
I said I'm not allowed to give discounts! Why won't you leave me alone?
Oooh! Why won't you leave me aloooone?

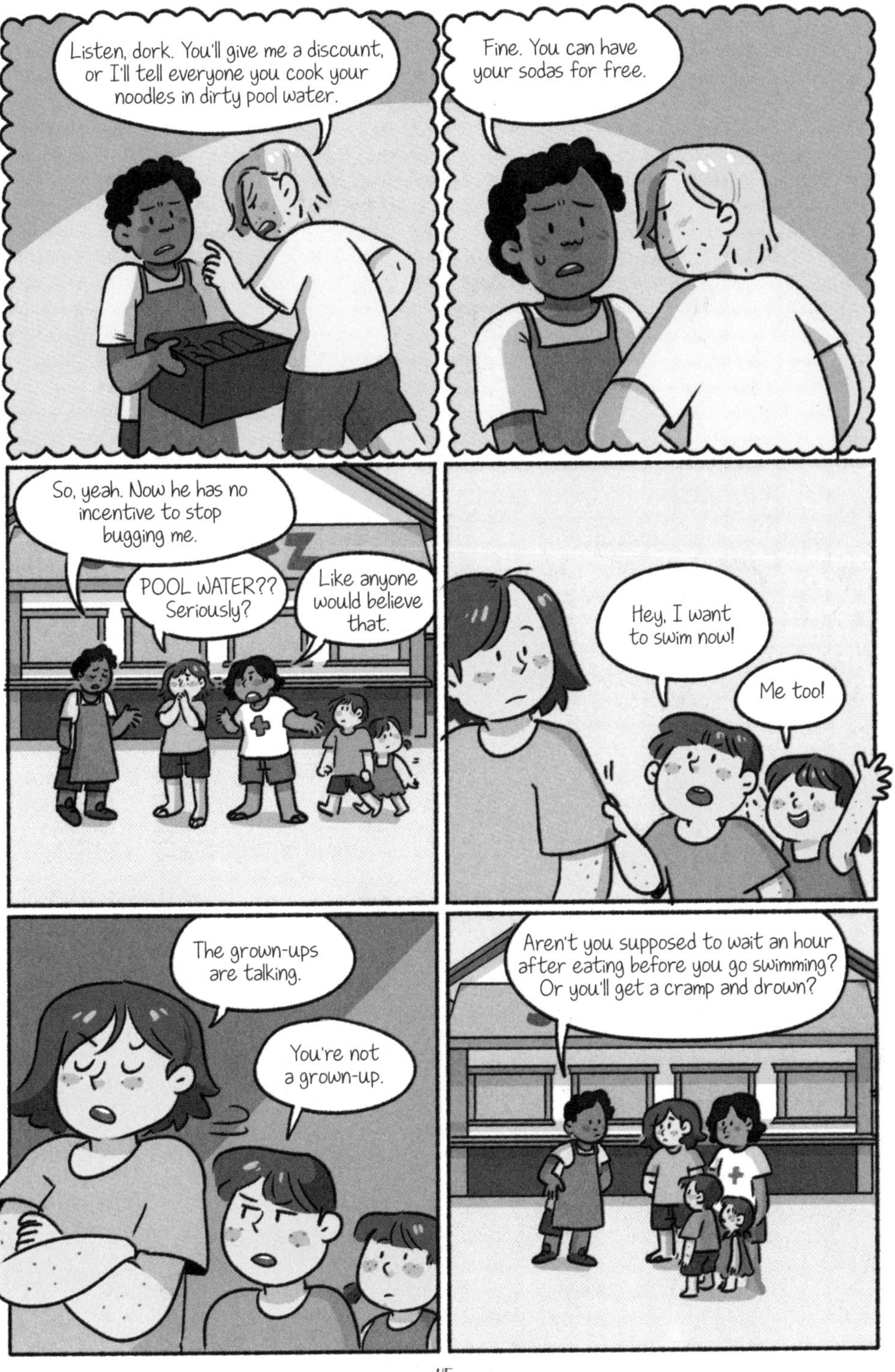
Listen, dork. You'll give me a discount, or I'll tell everyone you cook your noodles in dirty pool water.
Fine. You can have your sodas for free.
So, yeah. Now he has no incentive to stop bugging me.
POOL WATER?? Seriously?
Like anyone would believe that.
Hey, I want to swim now!
Me too!
The grown-ups are talking.
You're not a grown-up.
Aren't you supposed to wait an hour after eating before you go swimming? Or you'll get a cramp and drown?

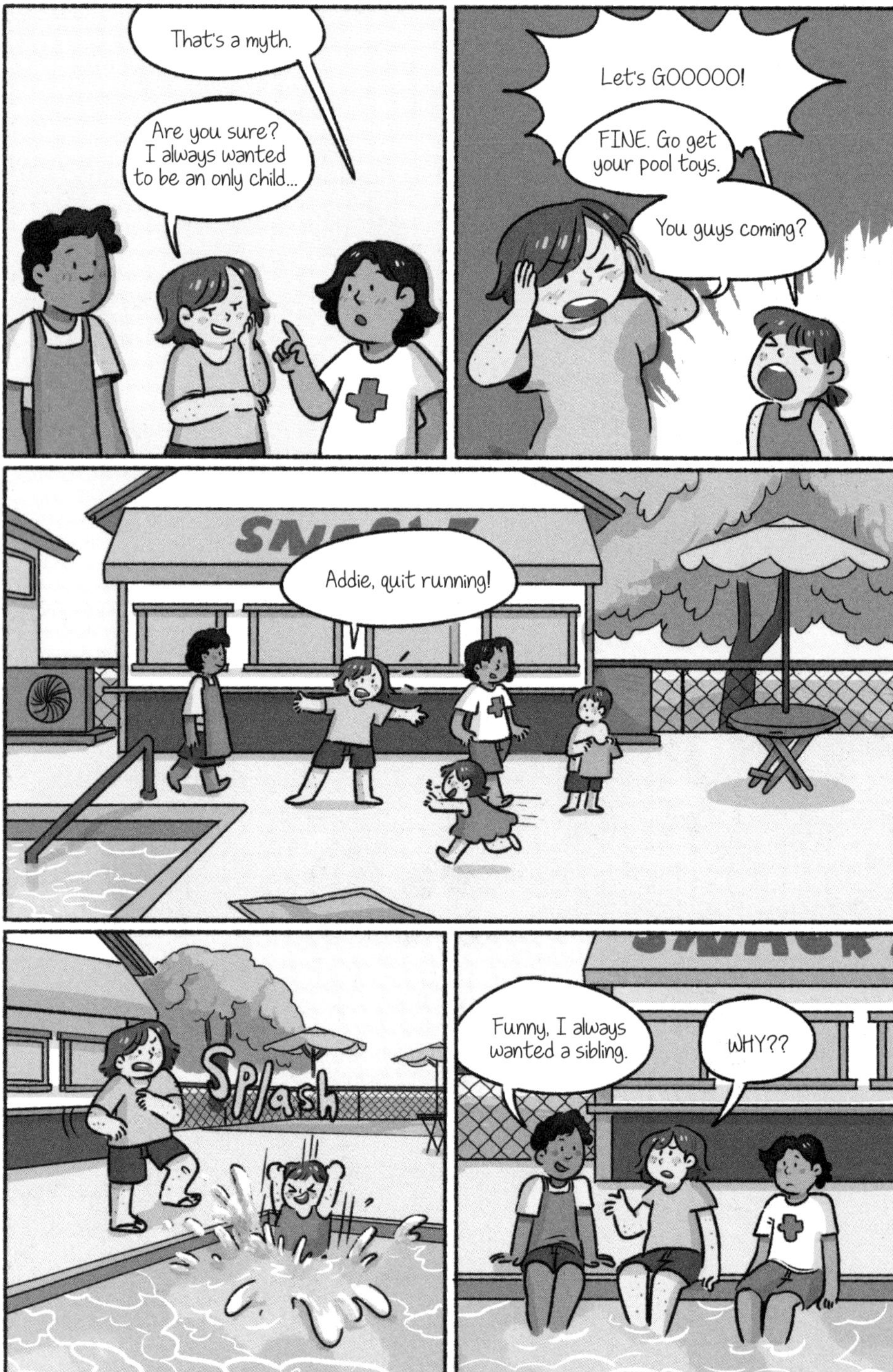
That's a myth.
Are you sure? I always wanted to be an only child...
Let's GOOOOO!
FINE. Go get your pool toys.
You guys coming?
Addie, quit running!
Splash
Funny, I always wanted a sibling.
WHY??

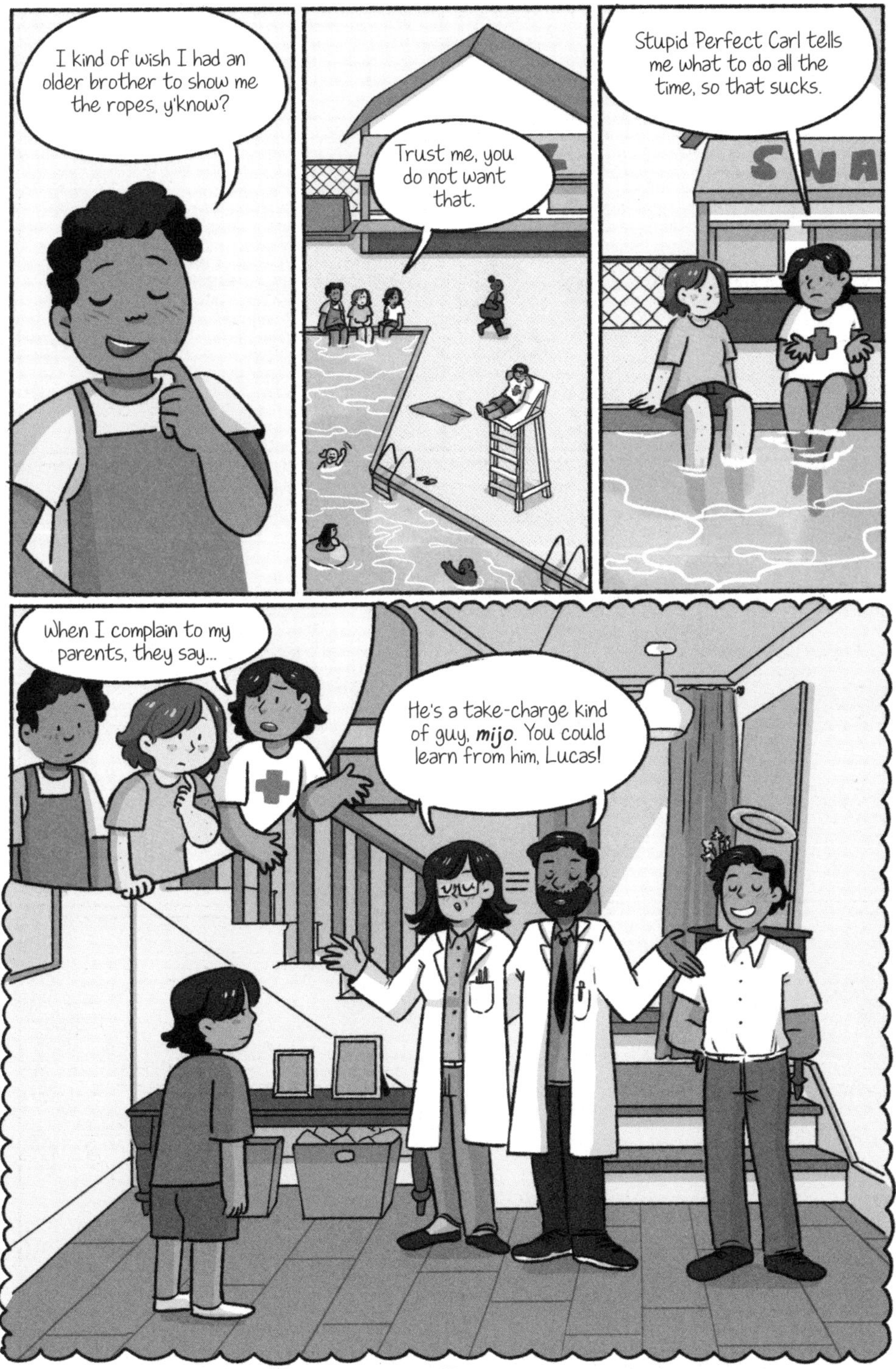
I kind of wish I had an older brother to show me the ropes, y'know?
Trust me, you do not want that.
Stupid Perfect Carl tells me what to do all the time, so that sucks.
When I complain to my parents, they say...
He's a take-charge kind of guy, ***mijo***. You could learn from him, Lucas!

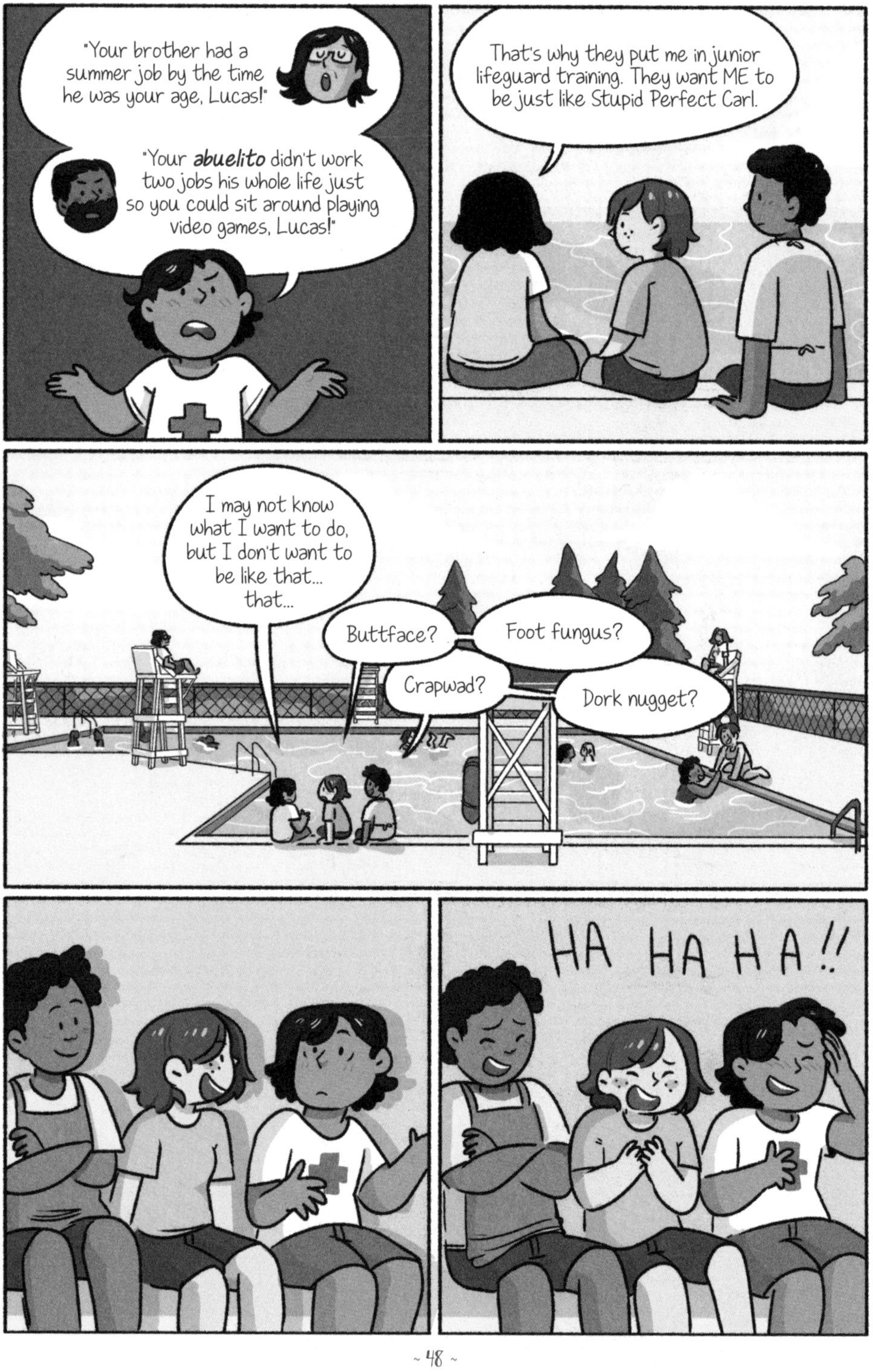
"Your brother had a summer job by the time he was your age, Lucas!"
"Your **abuelito** didn't work two jobs his whole life just so you could sit around playing video games, Lucas!"
That's why they put me in junior lifeguard training. They want ME to be just like Stupid Perfect Carl.
I may not know what I want to do, but I don't want to be like that... that...
Buttface?
Foot fungus?
Crapwad?
Dork nugget?
HA HA HA!!

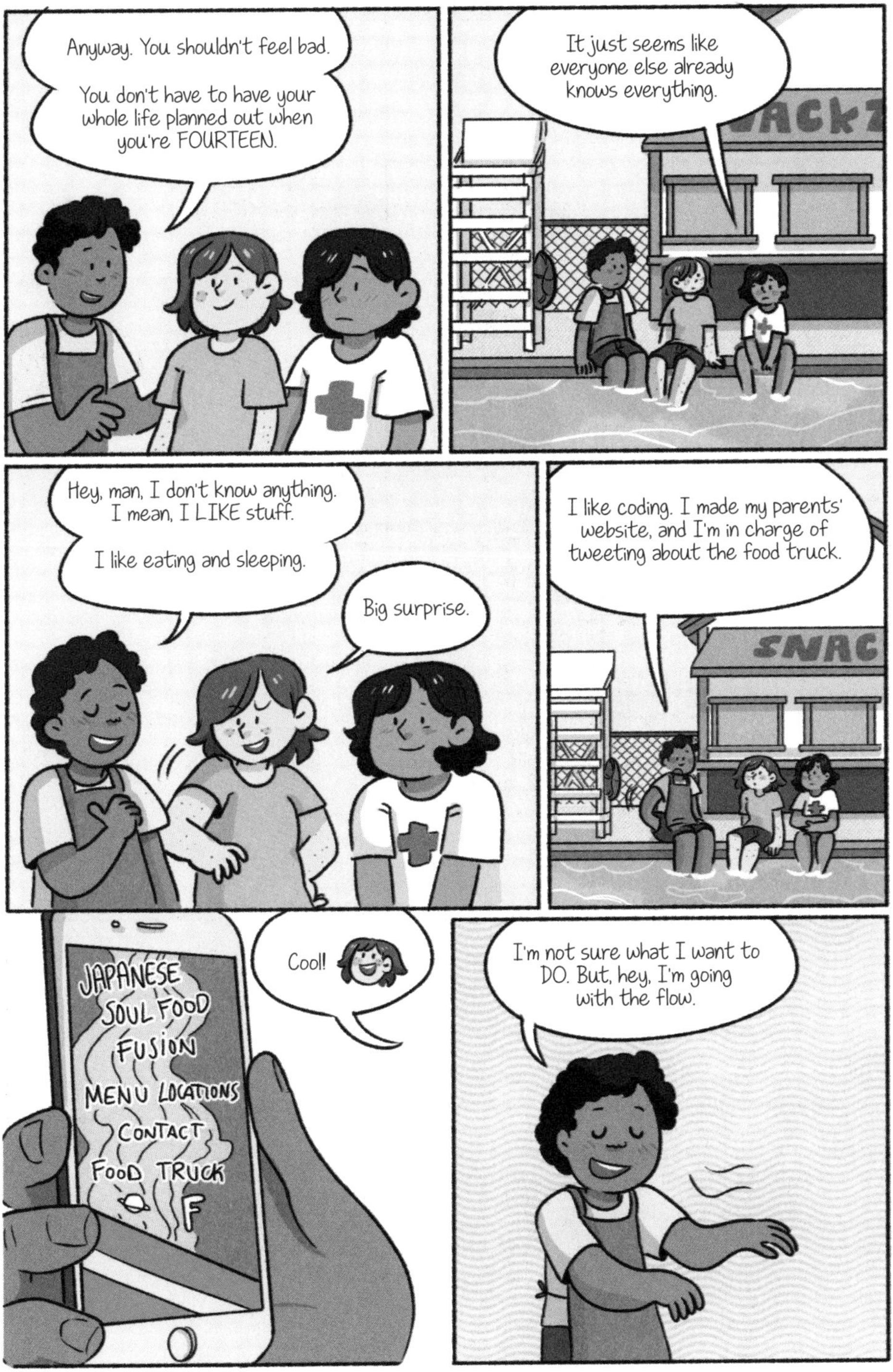
Anyway. You shouldn't feel bad.
You don't have to have your whole life planned out when you're FOURTEEN.
It just seems like everyone else already knows everything.
Hey, man, I don't know anything. I mean, I LIKE stuff.
I like eating and sleeping.
Big surprise.
I like coding. I made my parents' website, and I'm in charge of tweeting about the food truck.
JAPANESE SOUL FOOD FUSION
MENU LOCATIONS
CONTACT
FOOD TRUCK
Cool!
I'm not sure what I want to DO. But, hey, I'm going with the flow.

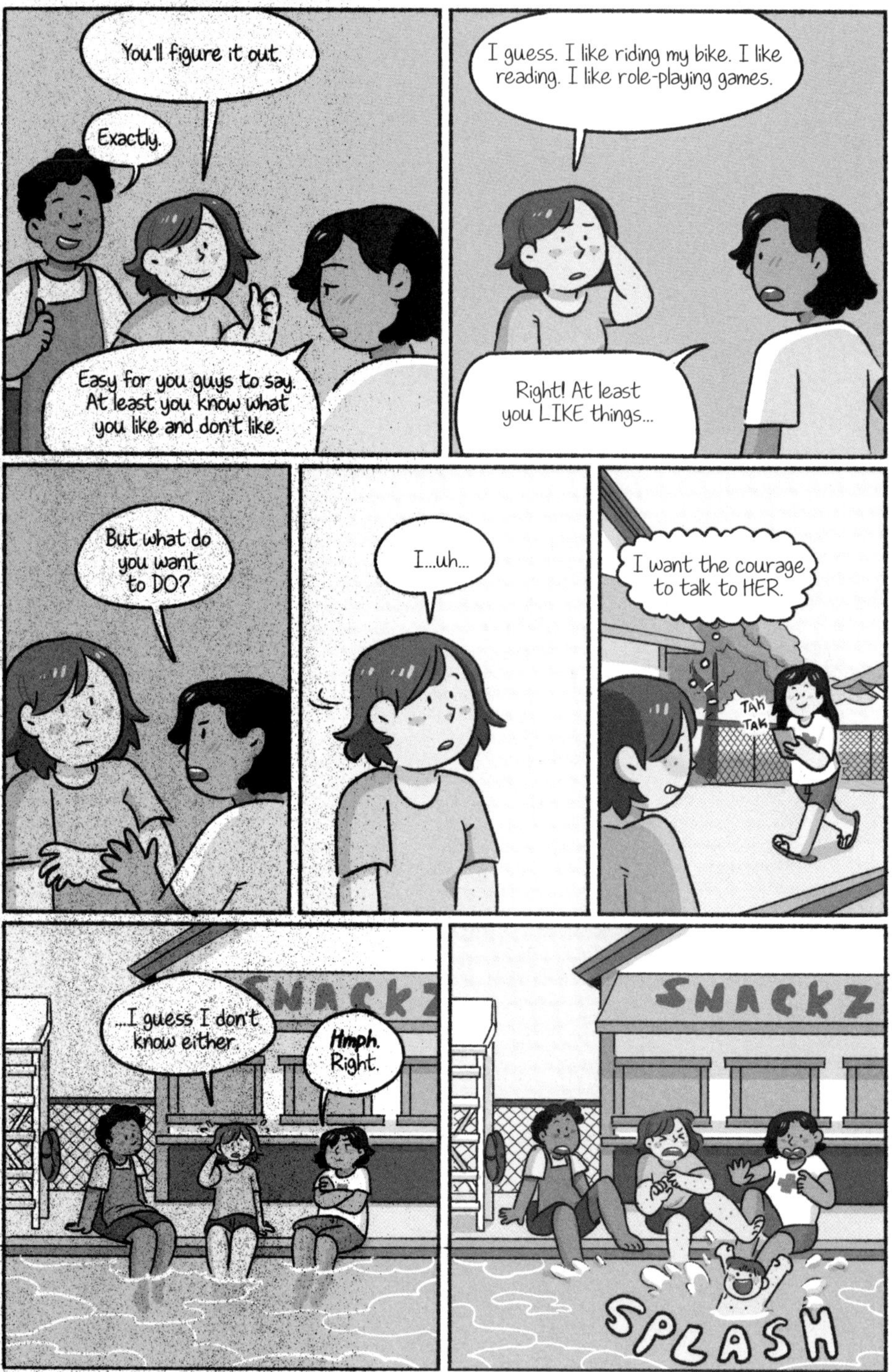
You'll figure it out.
Exactly.
Easy for you guys to say. At least you know what you like and don't like.
I guess. I like riding my bike. I like reading. I like role-playing games.
Right! At least you LIKE things...
But what do you want to DO?
I...uh...
I want the courage to talk to HER.
TAK TAK
...I guess I don't know either.
Hmph. Right.
SNACKZ
SNACKZ
SPLASH

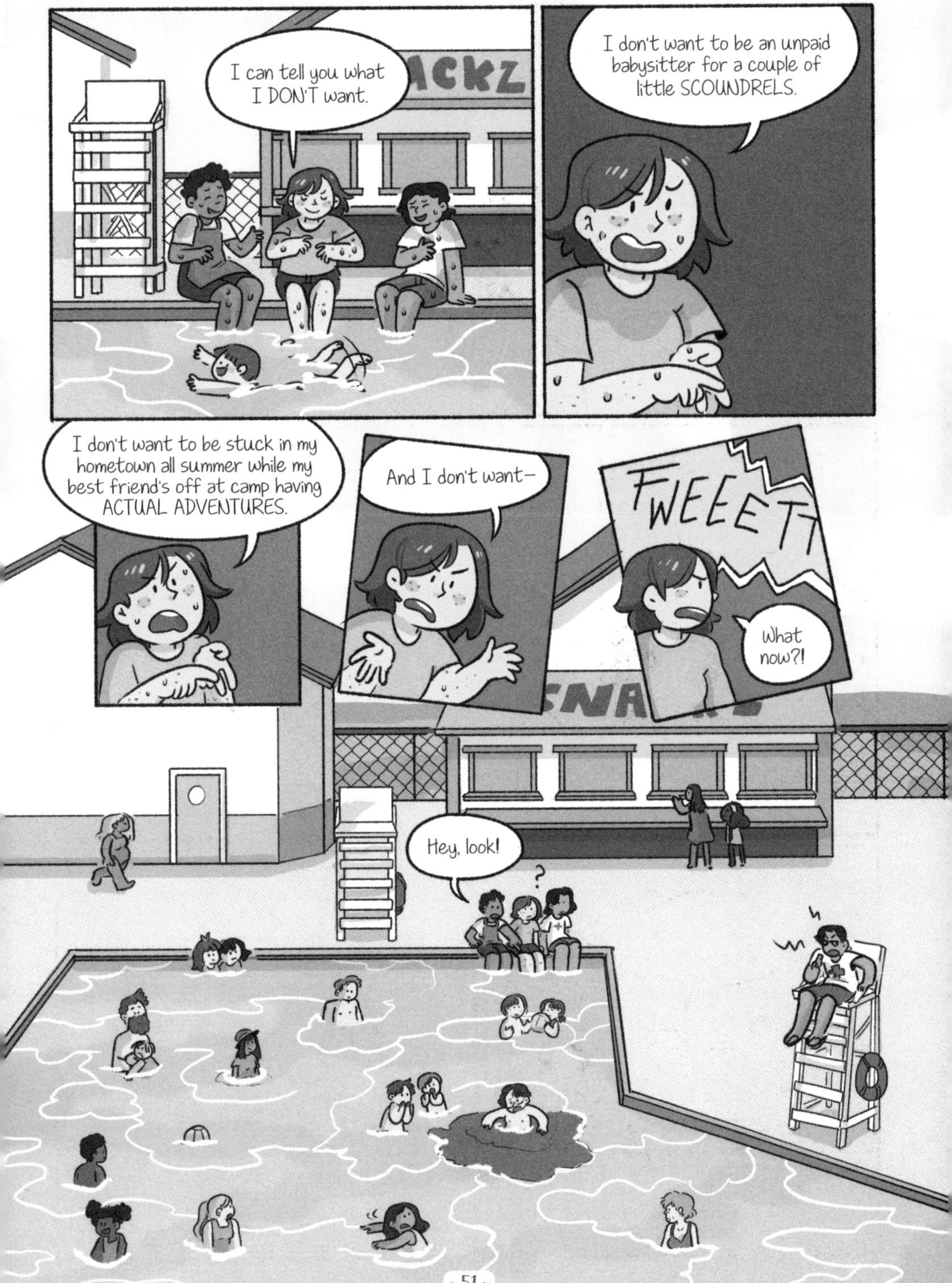

ACKZ
I can tell you what I DON'T want.
I don't want to be an unpaid babysitter for a couple of little SCOUNDRELS.
I don't want to be stuck in my hometown all summer while my best friend's off at camp having ACTUAL ADVENTURES.
And I don't want—
FWEEETT
What now?!
Hey, look!
?

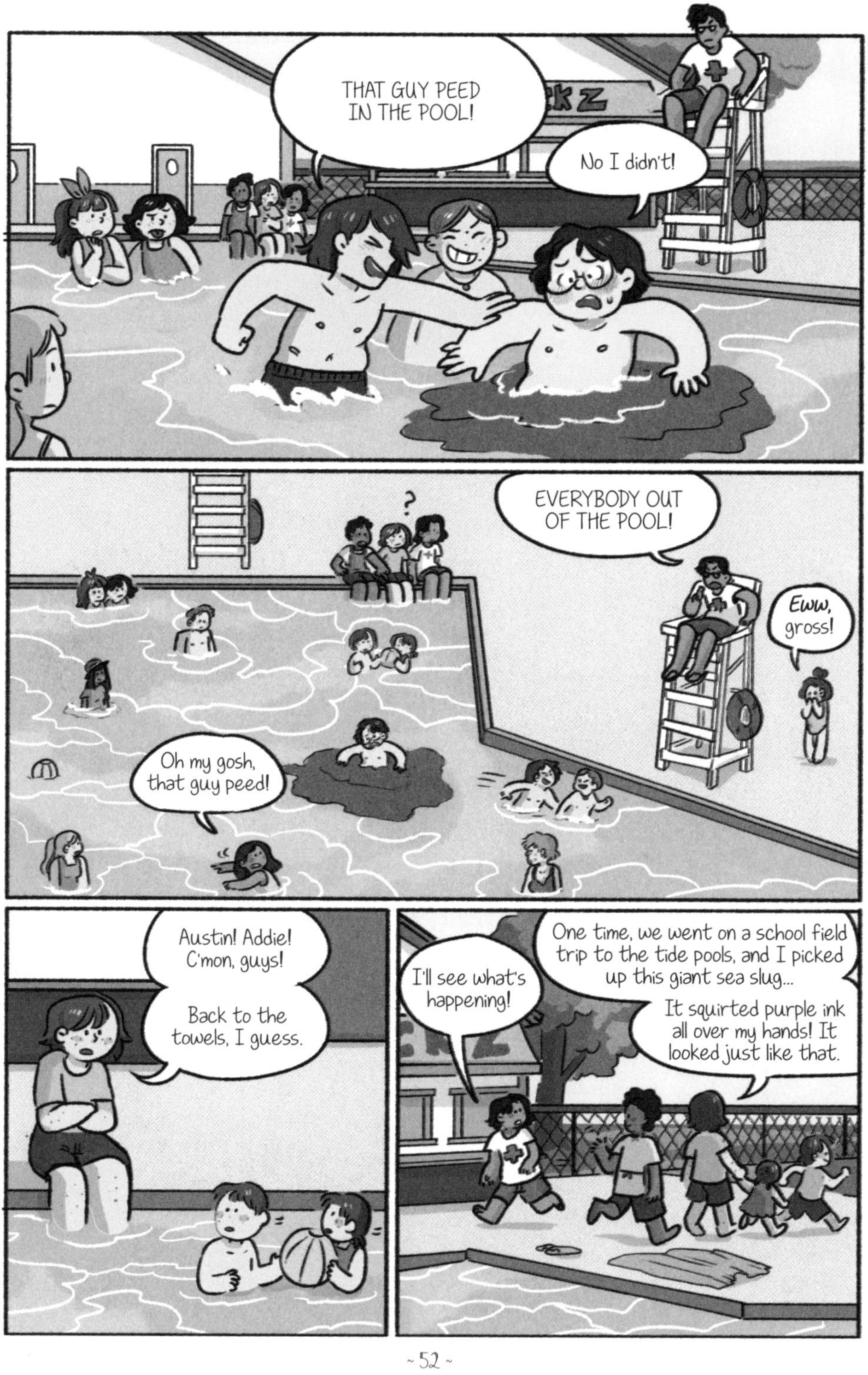
THAT GUY PEED IN THE POOL!
No I didn't!
EVERYBODY OUT OF THE POOL!
Eww, gross!
Oh my gosh, that guy peed!
Austin! Addie! C'mon, guys!
Back to the towels, I guess.
I'll see what's happening!
One time, we went on a school field trip to the tide pools, and I picked up this giant sea slug...
It squirted purple ink all over my hands! It looked just like that.

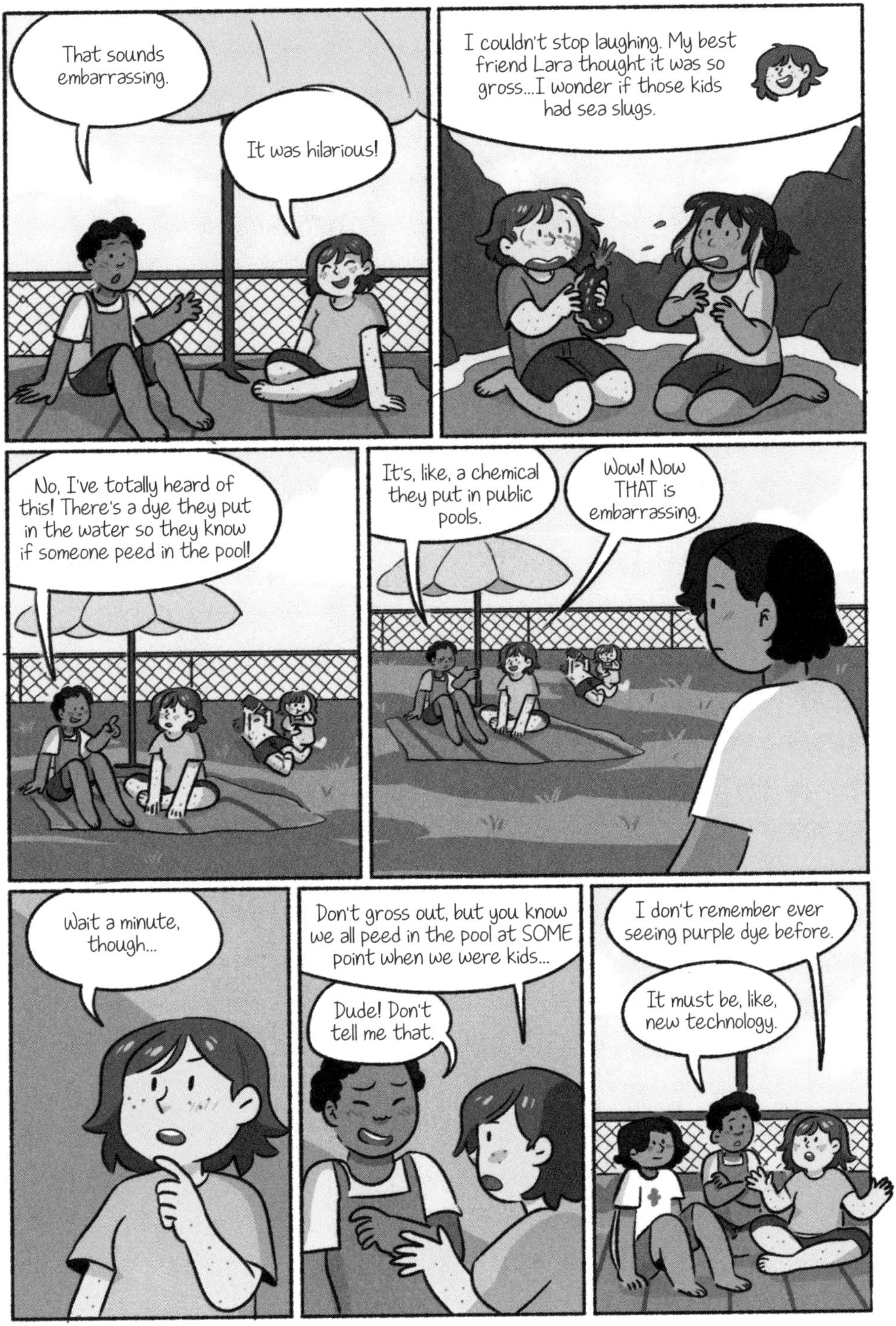
That sounds embarrassing.
It was hilarious!
I couldn't stop laughing. My best friend Lara thought it was so gross...I wonder if those kids had sea slugs.
No, I've totally heard of this! There's a dye they put in the water so they know if someone peed in the pool!
It's, like, a chemical they put in public pools.
Wow! Now THAT is embarrassing.
Wait a minute, though...
Don't gross out, but you know we all peed in the pool at SOME point when we were kids...
Dude! Don't tell me that.
I don't remember ever seeing purple dye before.
It must be, like, new technology.

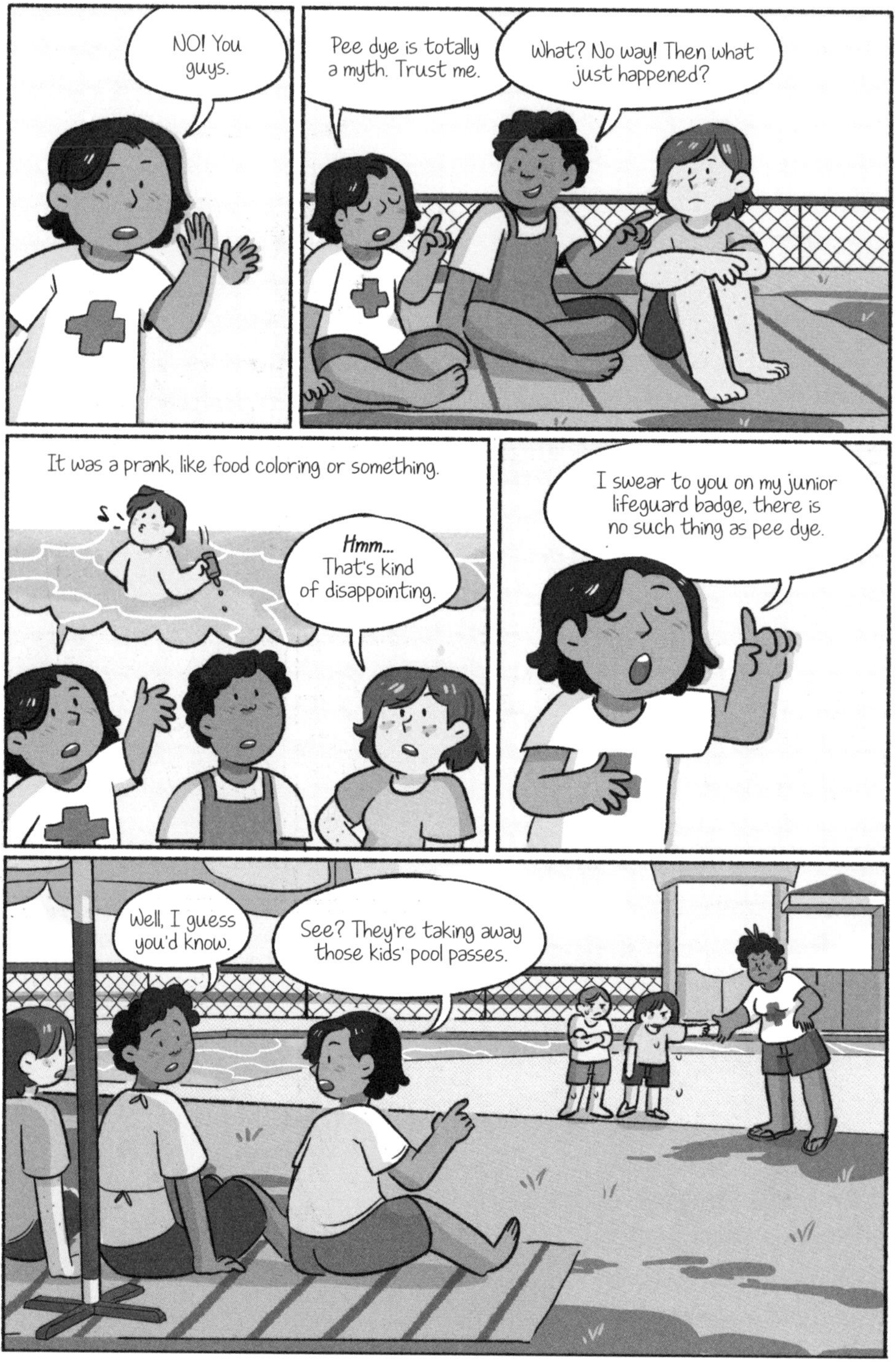
NO! You guys.
Pee dye is totally a myth. Trust me.
What? No way! Then what just happened?
It was a prank, like food coloring or something.
Hmm... That's kind of disappointing.
I swear to you on my junior lifeguard badge, there is no such thing as pee dye.
Well, I guess you'd know.
See? They're taking away those kids' pool passes.

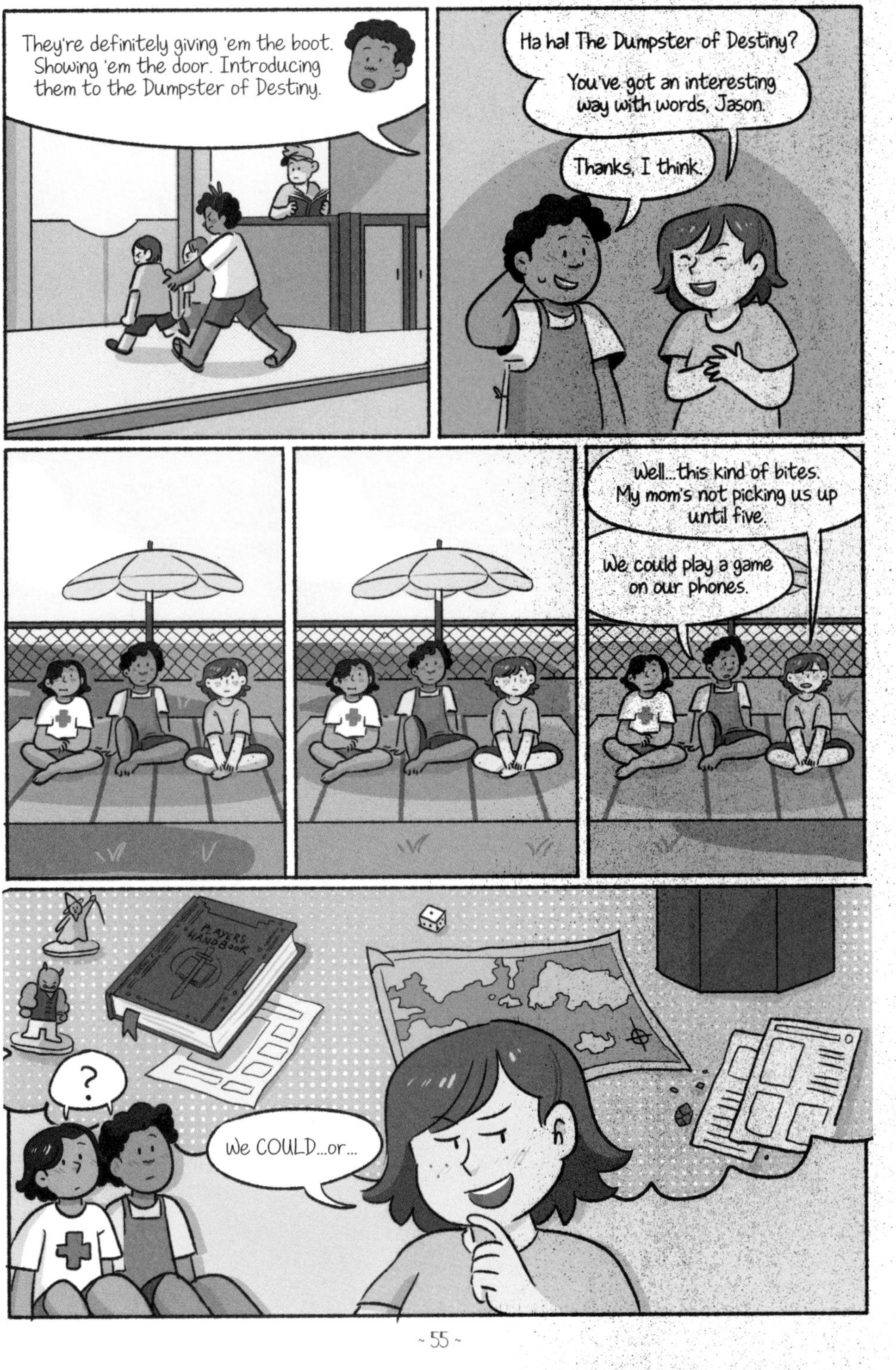
They're definitely giving 'em the boot. Showing 'em the door. Introducing them to the Dumpster of Destiny.
Ha ha! The Dumpster of Destiny?
You've got an interesting way with words, Jason.
Thanks, I think.
Well...this kind of bites. My mom's not picking us up until five.
We could play a game on our phones.
PLAYERS HANDBOOK
?
We COULD...or...

Chapter 4

Alexis vs. the Noobs

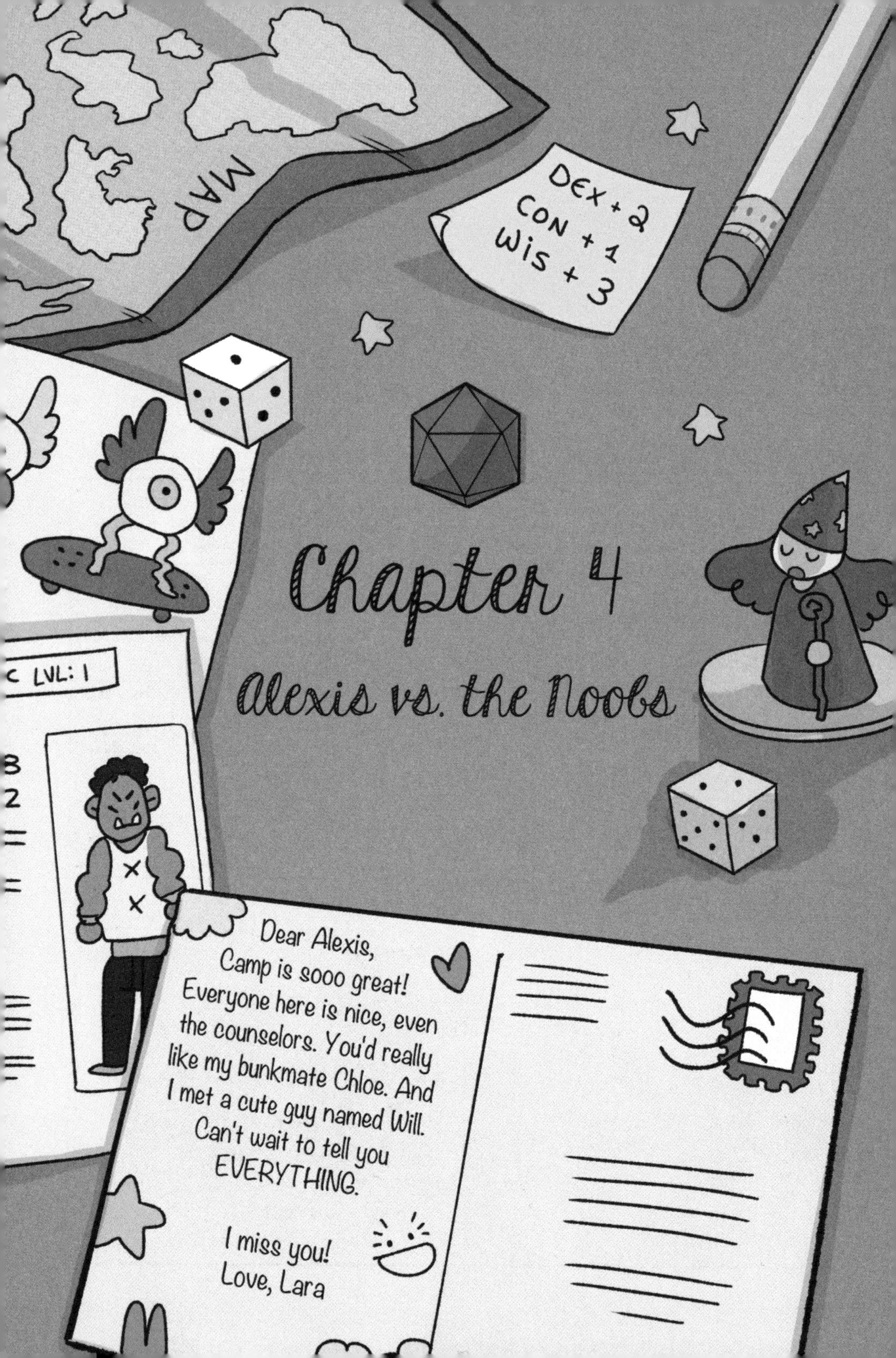

MAP
DEX + 2
CON + 1
WIS + 3
C LVL: 1
Dear Alexis,
Camp is sooo great!
Everyone here is nice, even
the counselors. You'd really
like my bunkmate Chloe. And
I met a cute guy named Will.
Can't wait to tell you
EVERYTHING.
I miss you!
Love, Lara

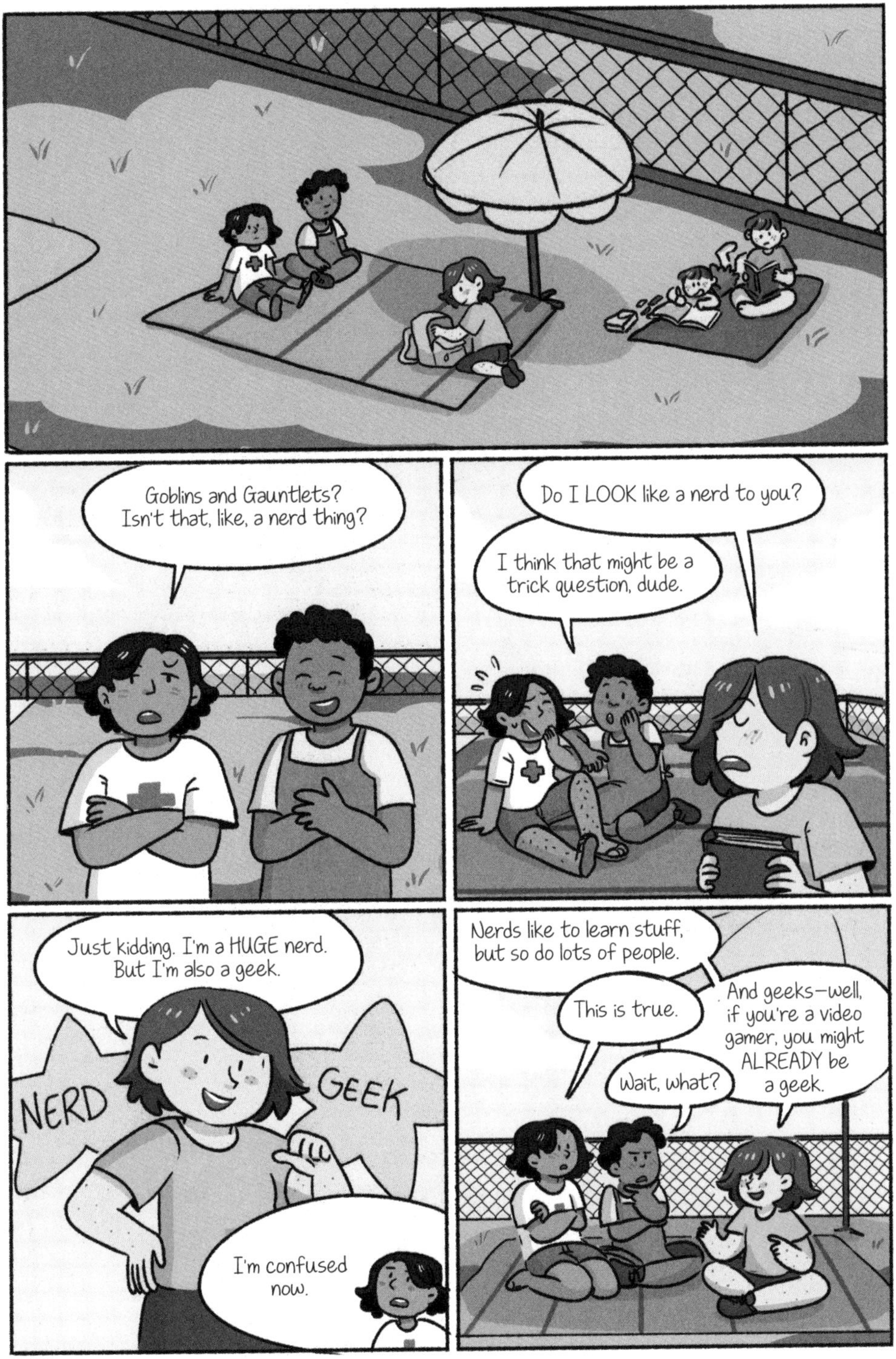
Goblins and Gauntlets? Isn't that, like, a nerd thing?
Do I LOOK like a nerd to you?
I think that might be a trick question, dude.
Just kidding. I'm a HUGE nerd. But I'm also a geek.
NERD
GEEK
I'm confused now.
Nerds like to learn stuff, but so do lots of people.
This is true.
And geeks—well, if you're a video gamer, you might ALREADY be a geek.
Wait, what?

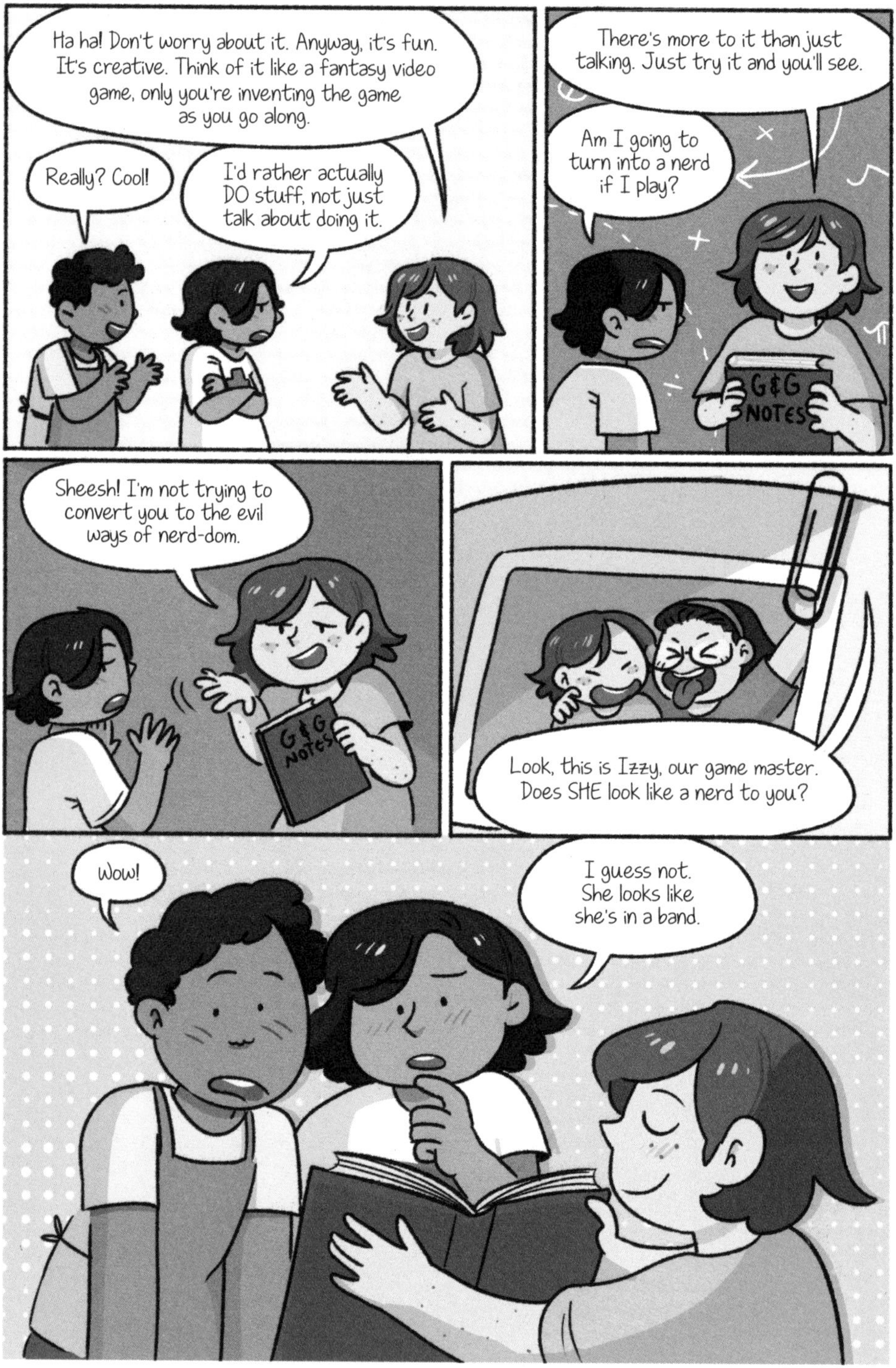

Ha ha! Don't worry about it. Anyway, it's fun. It's creative. Think of it like a fantasy video game, only you're inventing the game as you go along.
Really? Cool!
I'd rather actually DO stuff, not just talk about doing it.
There's more to it than just talking. Just try it and you'll see.
Am I going to turn into a nerd if I play?
G&G NOTES
Sheesh! I'm not trying to convert you to the evil ways of nerd-dom.
G&G NOTES
Look, this is Izzy, our game master. Does SHE look like a nerd to you?
Wow!
I guess not. She looks like she's in a band.

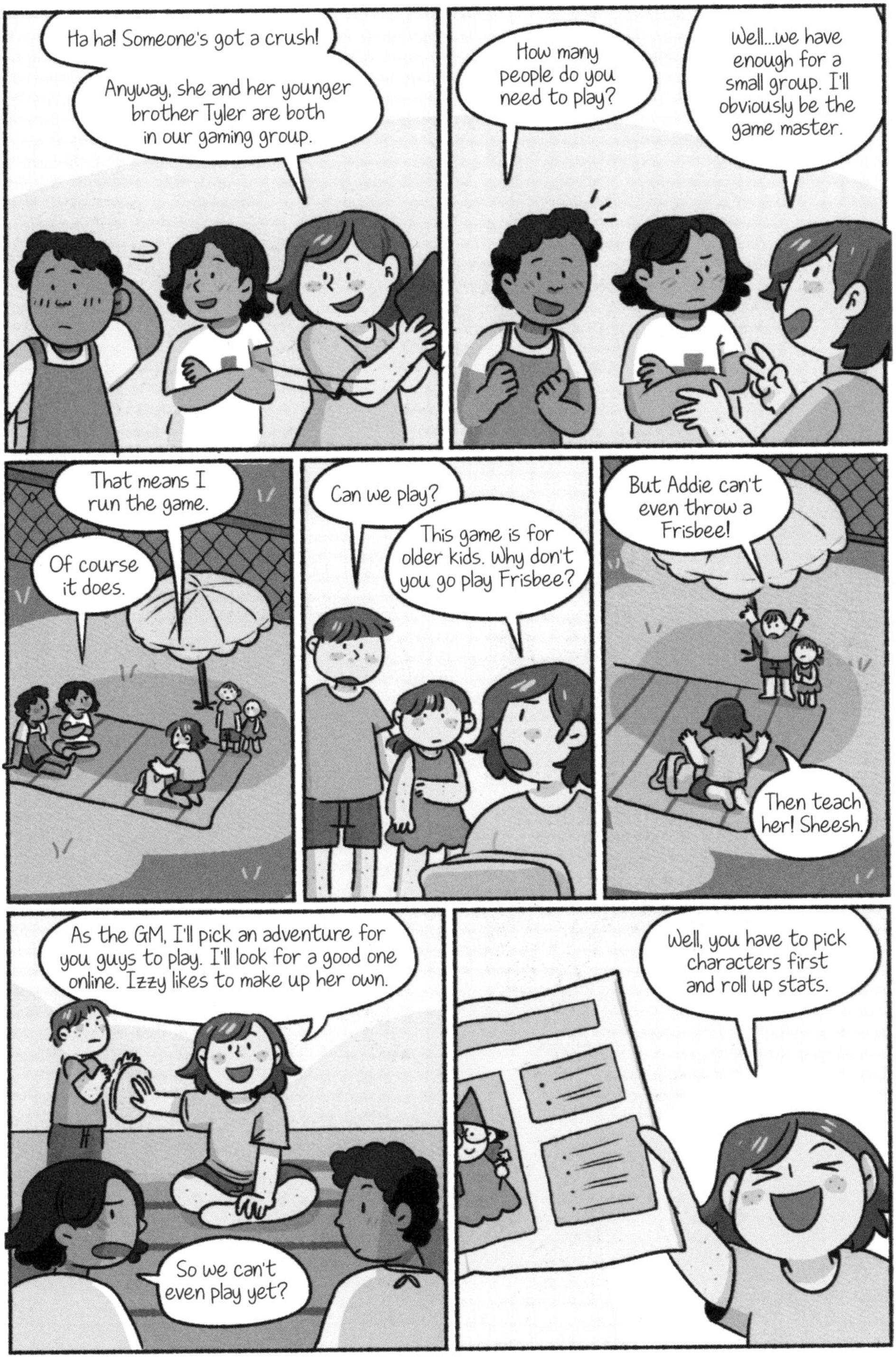
Ha ha! Someone's got a crush!
Anyway, she and her younger brother Tyler are both in our gaming group.
How many people do you need to play?
Well...we have enough for a small group. I'll obviously be the game master.
That means I run the game.
Of course it does.
Can we play?
This game is for older kids. Why don't you go play Frisbee?
But Addie can't even throw a Frisbee!
Then teach her! Sheesh.
As the GM, I'll pick an adventure for you guys to play. I'll look for a good one online. Izzy likes to make up her own.
So we can't even play yet?
Well, you have to pick characters first and roll up stats.

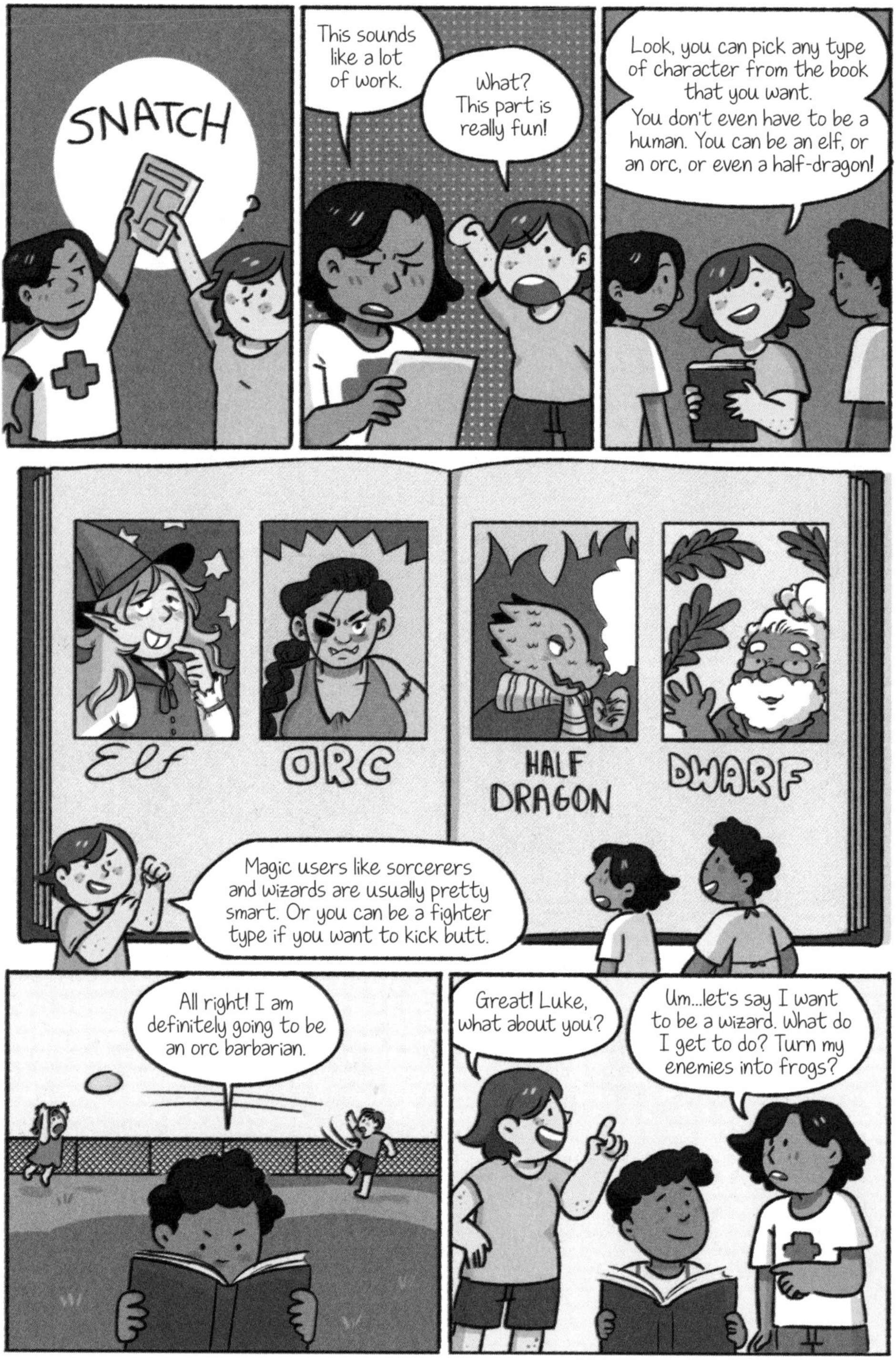
SNATCH
?
This sounds like a lot of work.
What? This part is really fun!
Look, you can pick any type of character from the book that you want. You don't even have to be a human. You can be an elf, or an orc, or even a half-dragon!
Elf
ORC
HALF DRAGON
DWARF
Magic users like sorcerers and wizards are usually pretty smart. Or you can be a fighter type if you want to kick butt.
All right! I am definitely going to be an orc barbarian.
Great! Luke, what about you?
Um...let's say I want to be a wizard. What do I get to do? Turn my enemies into frogs?

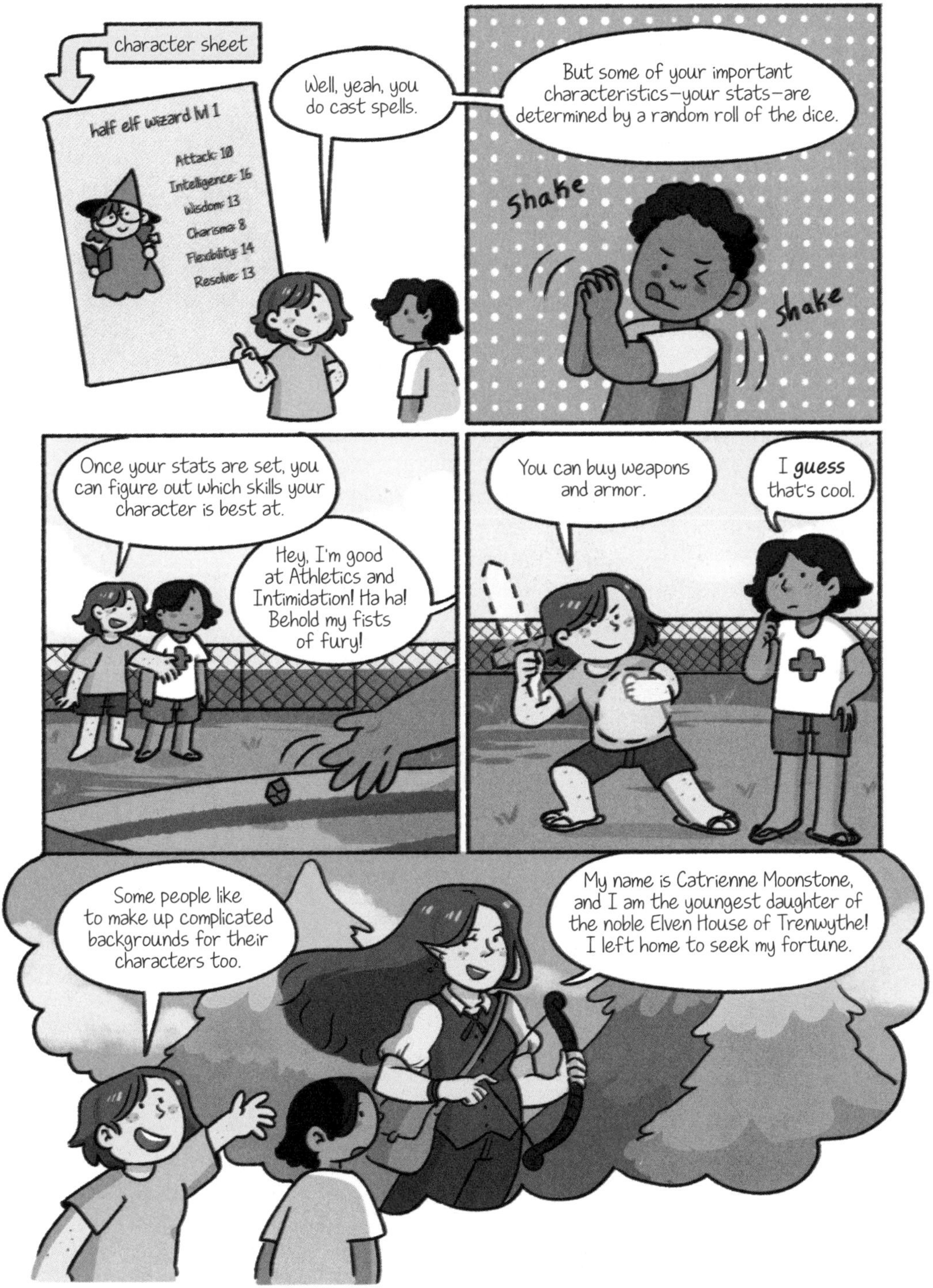
character sheet
half elf wizard lvl 1
Attack: 10
Intelligence: 16
Wisdom: 13
Charisma: 8
Flexibility: 14
Resolve: 13
Well, yeah, you do cast spells.
But some of your important characteristics—your stats—are determined by a random roll of the dice.
Shake
Shake
Once your stats are set, you can figure out which skills your character is best at.
Hey, I'm good at Athletics and Intimidation! Ha ha! Behold my fists of fury!
You can buy weapons and armor.
I **guess** that's cool.
Some people like to make up complicated backgrounds for their characters too.
My name is Catrienne Moonstone, and I am the youngest daughter of the noble Elven House of Trenwythe! I left home to seek my fortune.

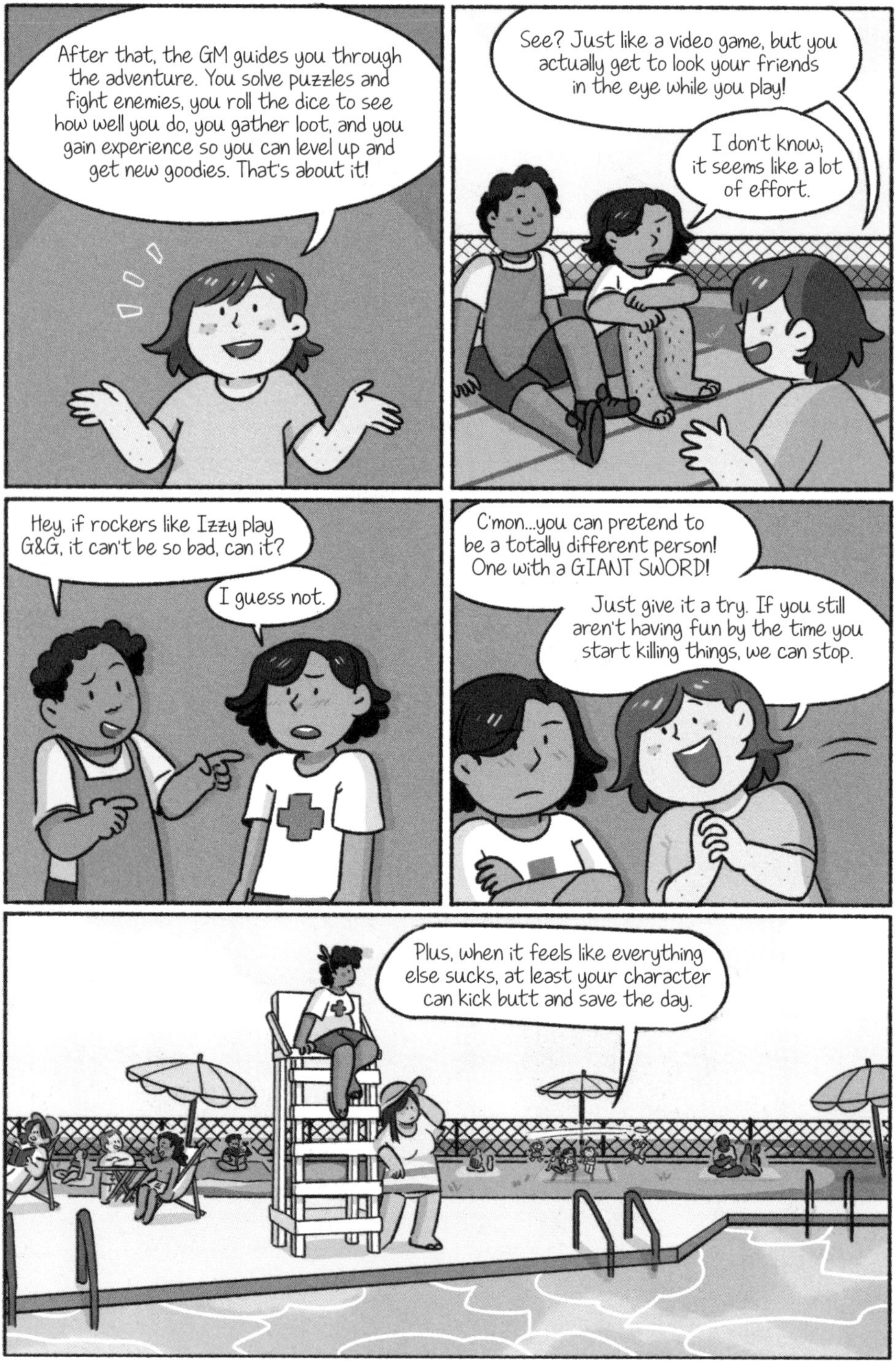
After that, the GM guides you through the adventure. You solve puzzles and fight enemies, you roll the dice to see how well you do, you gather loot, and you gain experience so you can level up and get new goodies. That's about it!
See? Just like a video game, but you actually get to look your friends in the eye while you play!
I don't know; it seems like a lot of effort.
Hey, if rockers like Izzy play G&G, it can't be so bad, can it?
I guess not.
C'mon...you can pretend to be a totally different person! One with a GIANT SWORD!
Just give it a try. If you still aren't having fun by the time you start killing things, we can stop.
Plus, when it feels like everything else sucks, at least your character can kick butt and save the day.

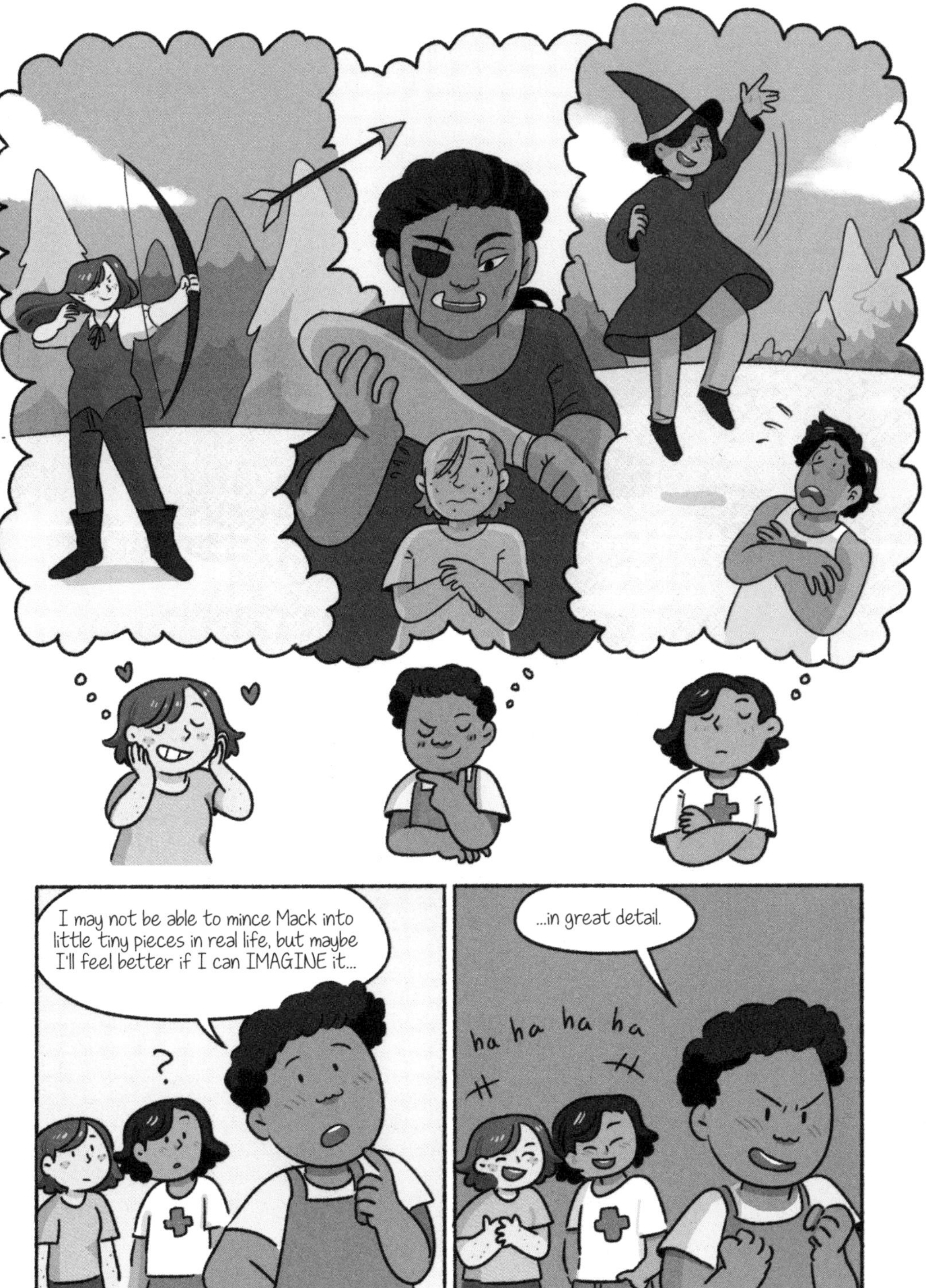

I may not be able to mince Mack into little tiny pieces in real life, but maybe I'll feel better if I can IMAGINE it...
?
...in great detail.
ha ha ha ha

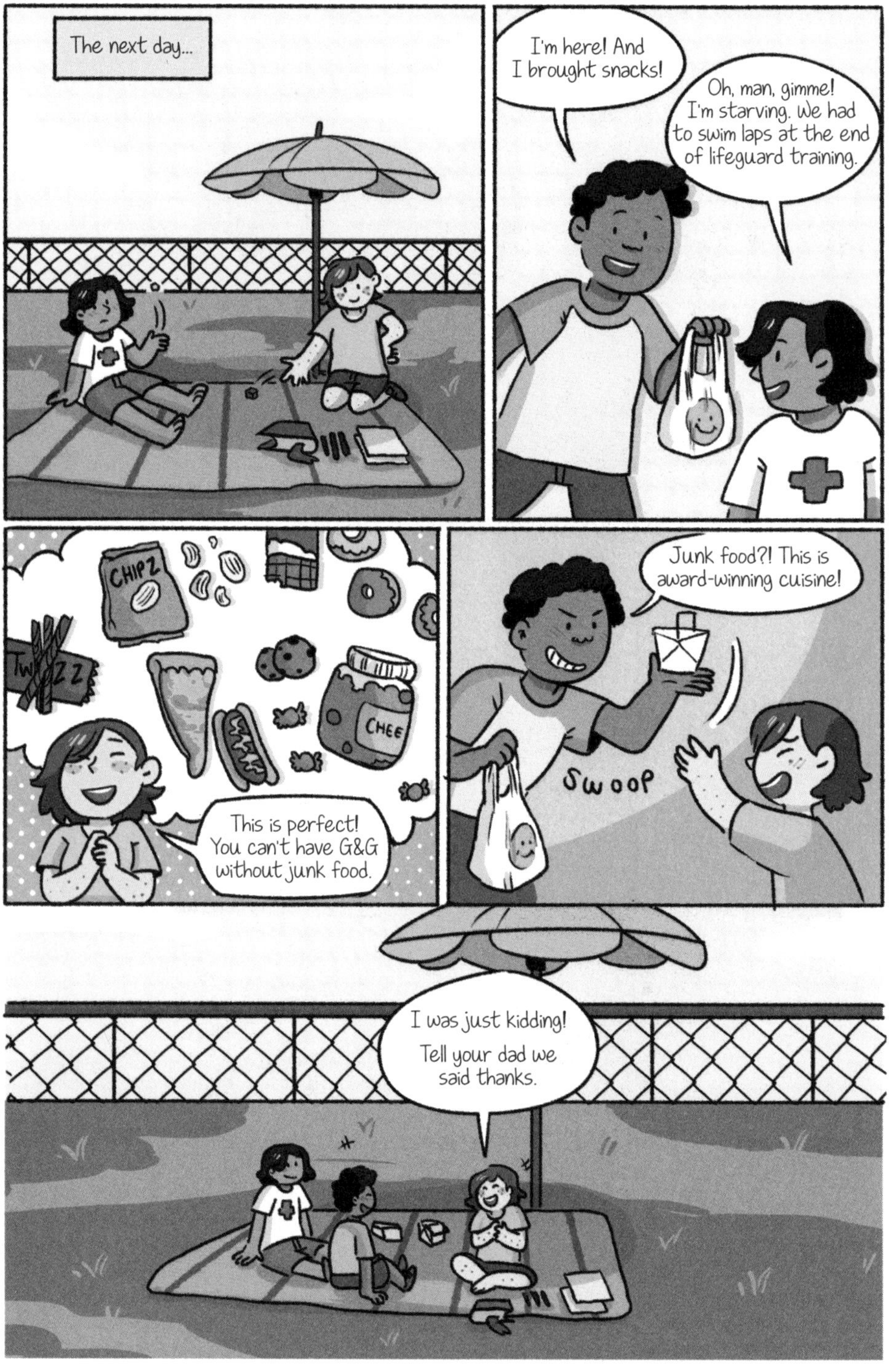
The next day...
I'm here! And I brought snacks!
Oh, man, gimme! I'm starving. We had to swim laps at the end of lifeguard training.
CHIPZ
TWIZZ
CHEE
This is perfect! You can't have G&G without junk food.
Junk food?! This is award-winning cuisine!
SWOOP
I was just kidding!
Tell your dad we said thanks.

Let's get down to business.

It was fun at first, but now things are starting to go wrong...

...like with Luke's wizard, Nicanor.

How come my Charisma is so low?

Ha ha! That's a good question.

You had to put your low dice roll SOMEWHERE.

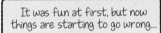

You won't need high Charisma anyway. Jason's fighter can be your party spokesperson.

hmph.

But what if I wanted to be the spokesperson?

Dude. Do you WANT to be the spokesperson?

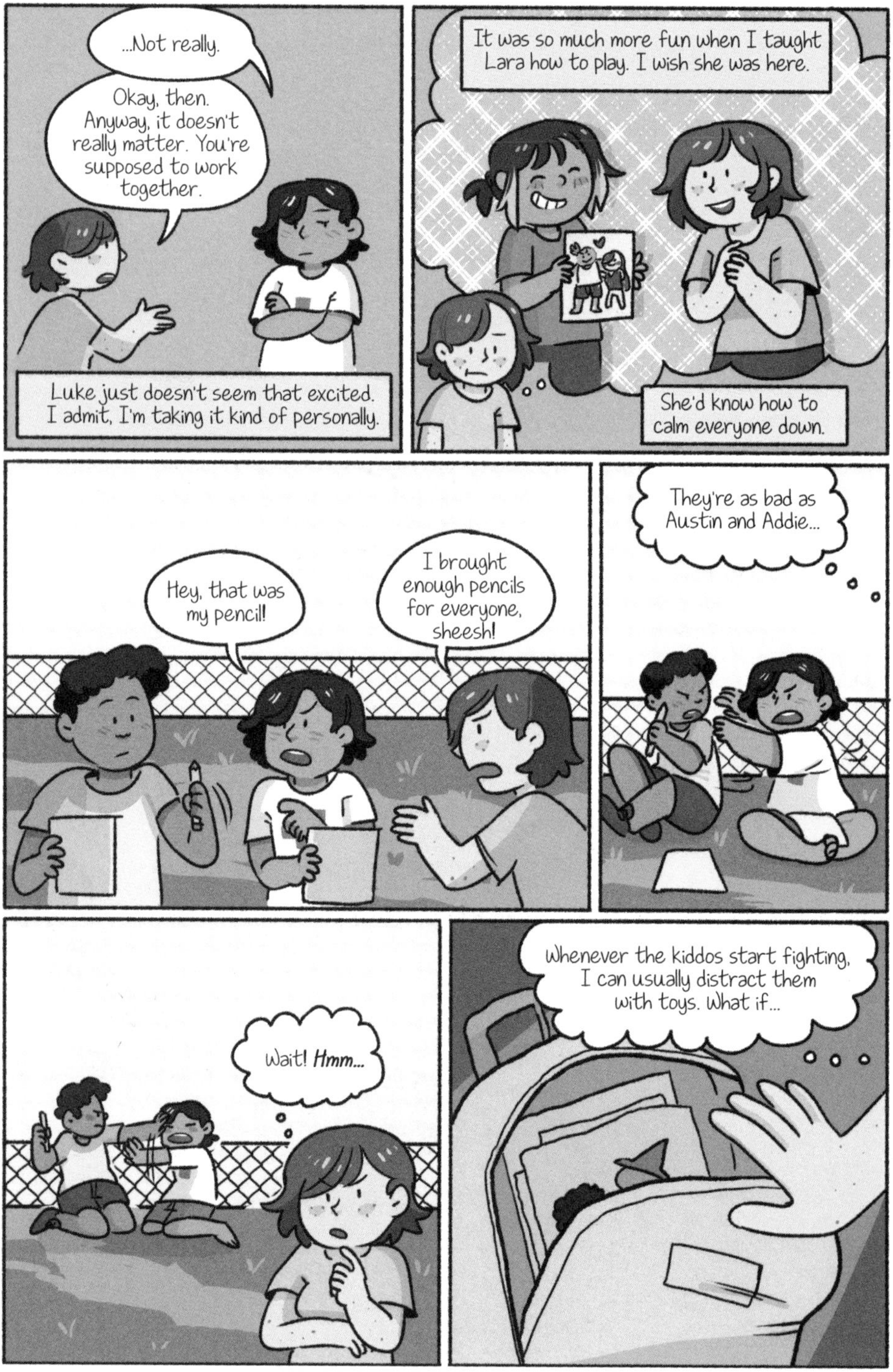
...Not really.
Okay, then. Anyway, it doesn't really matter. You're supposed to work together.
Luke just doesn't seem that excited. I admit, I'm taking it kind of personally.
It was so much more fun when I taught Lara how to play. I wish she was here.
She'd know how to calm everyone down.
Hey, that was my pencil!
I brought enough pencils for everyone, sheesh!
They're as bad as Austin and Addie...
Wait! Hmm...
Whenever the kiddos start fighting, I can usually distract them with toys. What if...

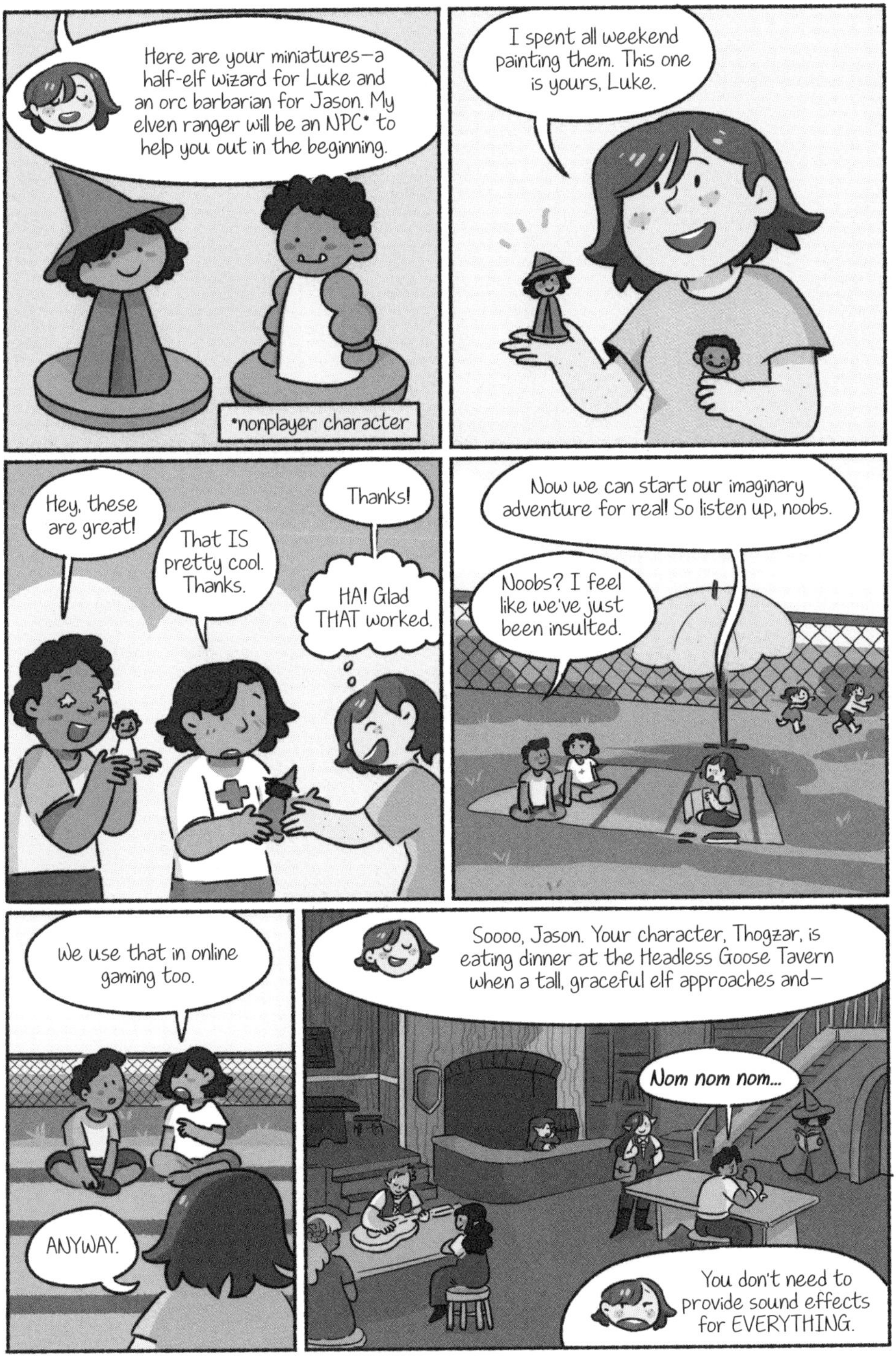
Here are your miniatures—a half-elf wizard for Luke and an orc barbarian for Jason. My elven ranger will be an NPC* to help you out in the beginning.
*nonplayer character
I spent all weekend painting them. This one is yours, Luke.
Hey, these are great!
That IS pretty cool. Thanks.
Thanks!
HA! Glad THAT worked.
Now we can start our imaginary adventure for real! So listen up, noobs.
Noobs? I feel like we've just been insulted.
We use that in online gaming too.
ANYWAY.
Soooo, Jason. Your character, Thogzar, is eating dinner at the Headless Goose Tavern when a tall, graceful elf approaches and—
Nom nom nom...
You don't need to provide sound effects for EVERYTHING.

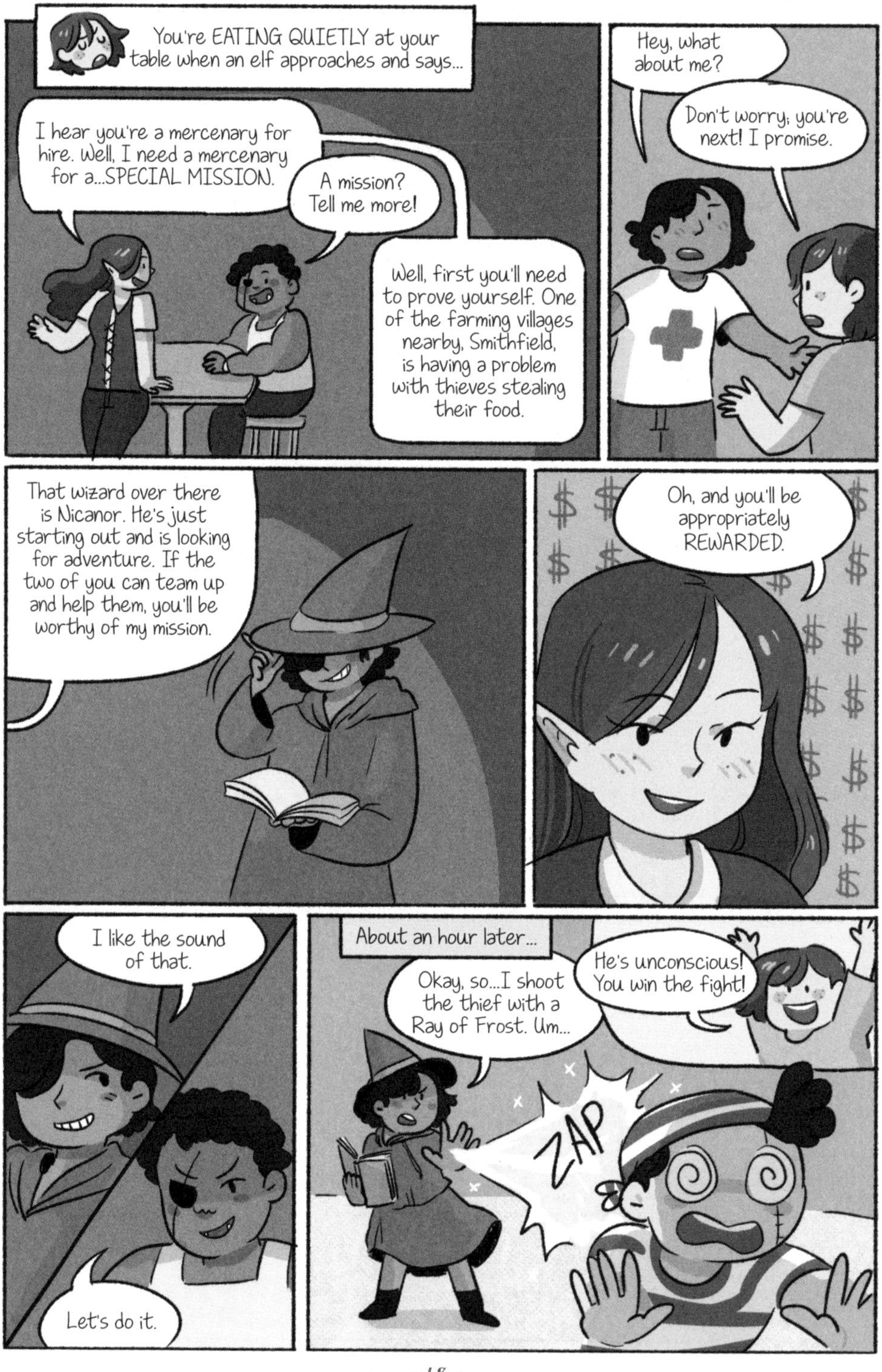
You're EATING QUIETLY at your table when an elf approaches and says...
I hear you're a mercenary for hire. Well, I need a mercenary for a...SPECIAL MISSION.
A mission? Tell me more!
Well, first you'll need to prove yourself. One of the farming villages nearby, Smithfield, is having a problem with thieves stealing their food.
Hey, what about me?
Don't worry; you're next! I promise.
That wizard over there is Nicanor. He's just starting out and is looking for adventure. If the two of you can team up and help them, you'll be worthy of my mission.
Oh, and you'll be appropriately REWARDED.
I like the sound of that.
Let's do it.
About an hour later...
Okay, so...I shoot the thief with a Ray of Frost. Um...
He's unconscious! You win the fight!
ZAP

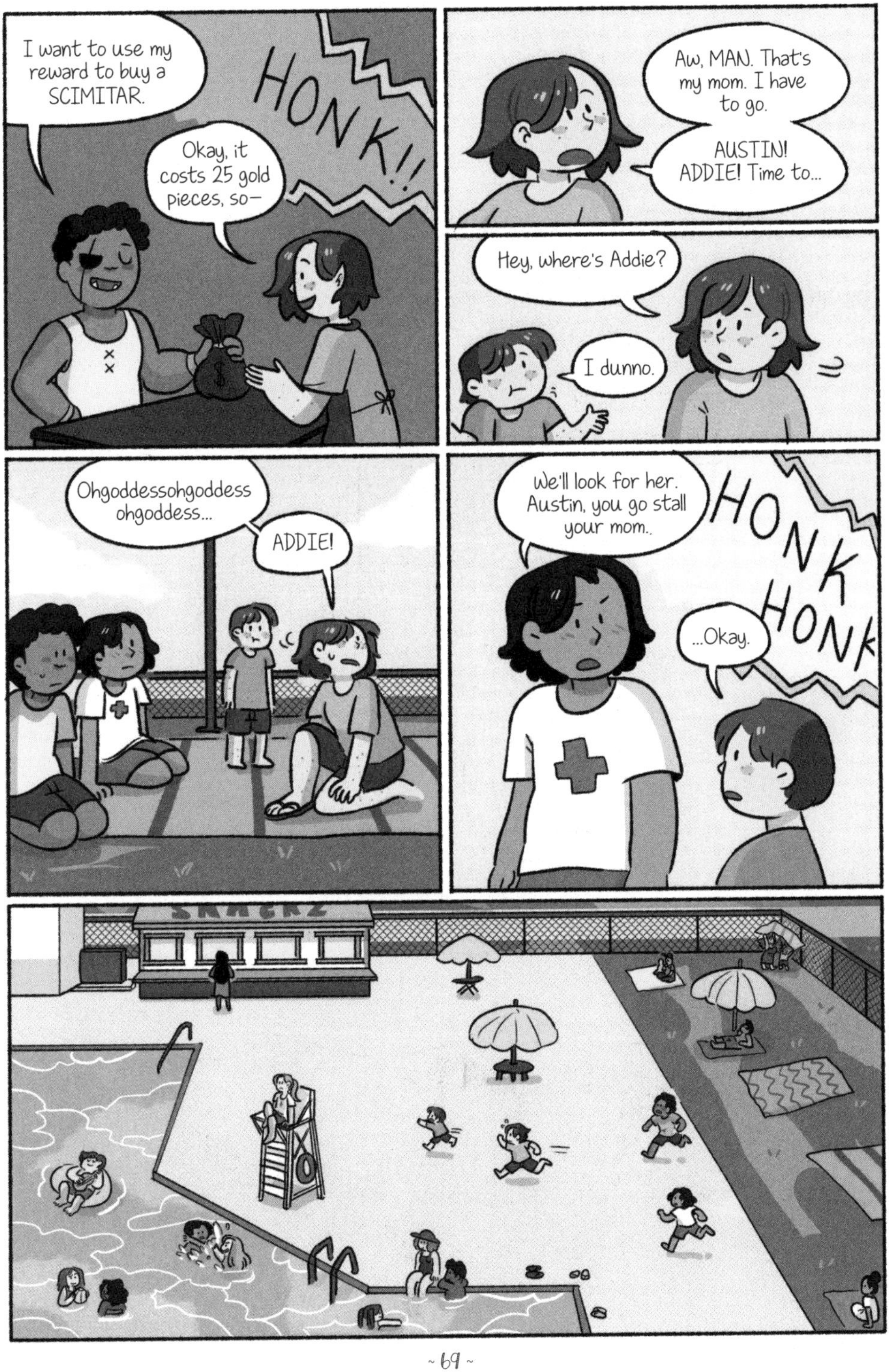
I want to use my reward to buy a SCIMITAR.
HONK!!
Okay, it costs 25 gold pieces, so—
Aw, MAN. That's my mom. I have to go.
AUSTIN! ADDIE! Time to...
Hey, where's Addie?
I dunno.
Ohgoddessohgoddess ohgoddess...
ADDIE!
We'll look for her. Austin, you go stall your mom..
HONK HONK
...Okay.

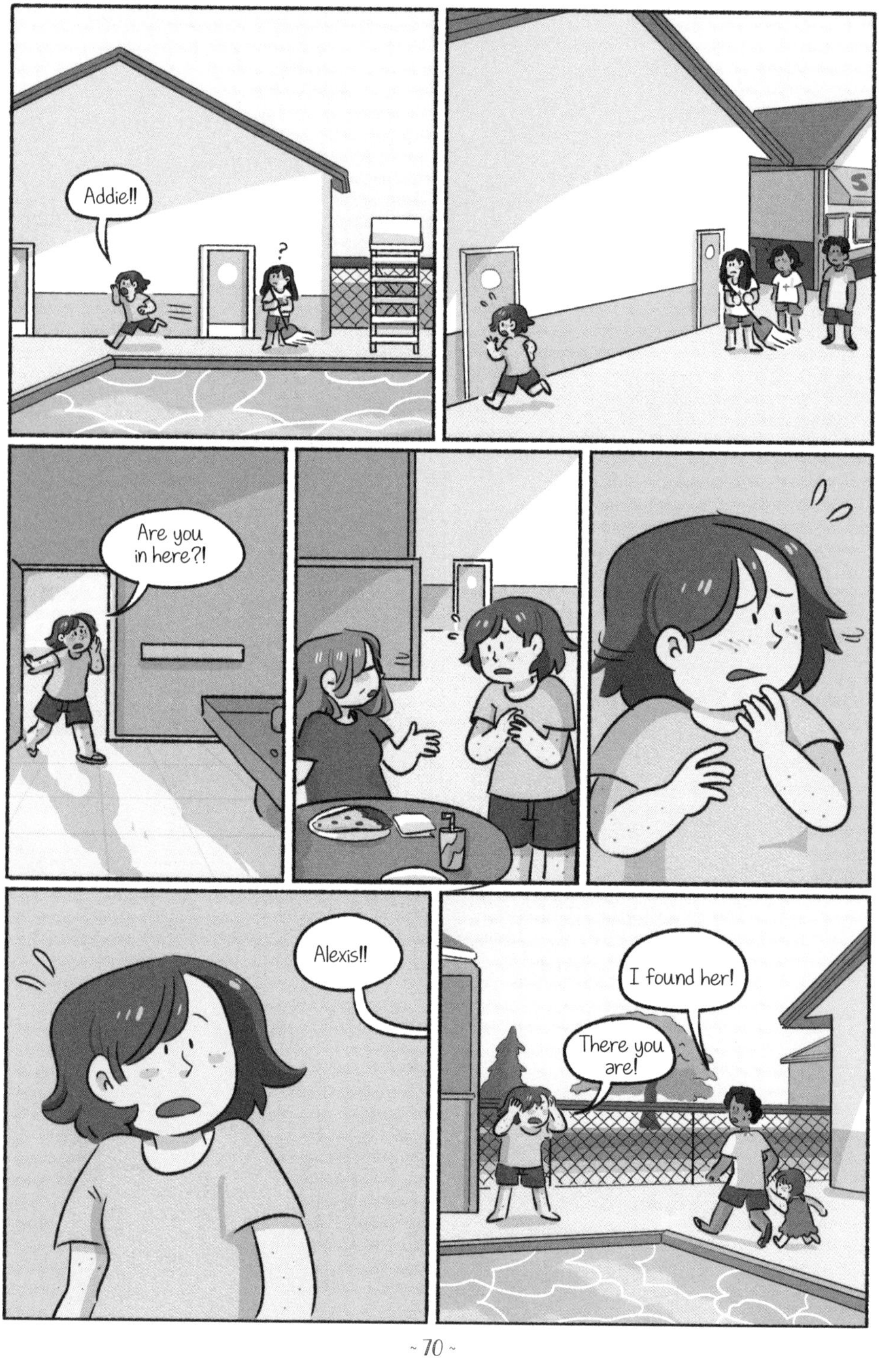
Addie!!
?
Are you
in here?!
Alexis!!
I found her!
There you
are!

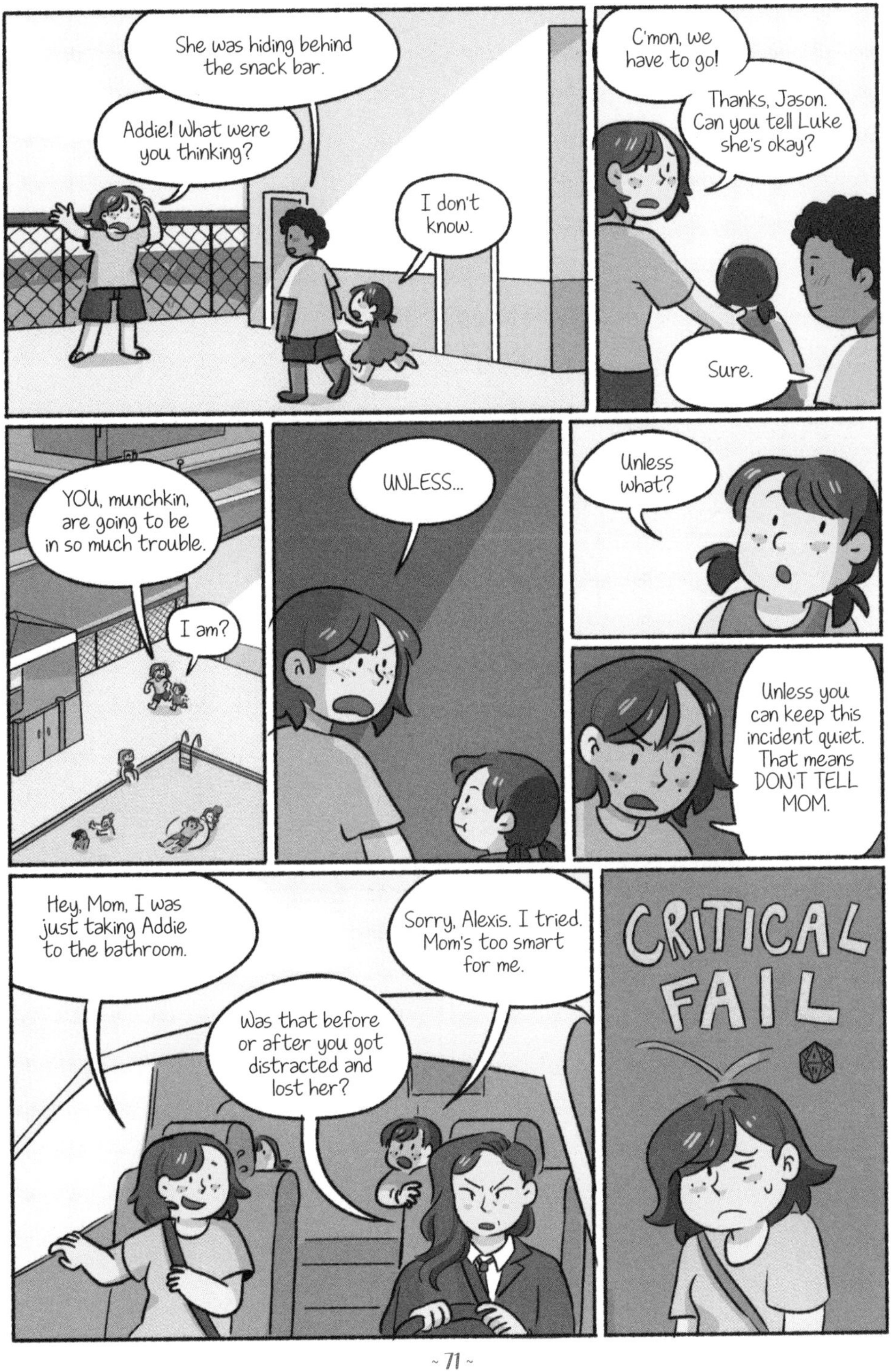
She was hiding behind the snack bar.
Addie! What were you thinking?
I don't know.
C'mon, we have to go!
Thanks, Jason. Can you tell Luke she's okay?
Sure.
YOU, munchkin, are going to be in so much trouble.
I am?
UNLESS...
Unless what?
Unless you can keep this incident quiet. That means DON'T TELL MOM.
Hey, Mom, I was just taking Addie to the bathroom.
Was that before or after you got distracted and lost her?
Sorry, Alexis. I tried. Mom's too smart for me.
CRITICAL FAIL

Chapter 5

Alexis vs. Life

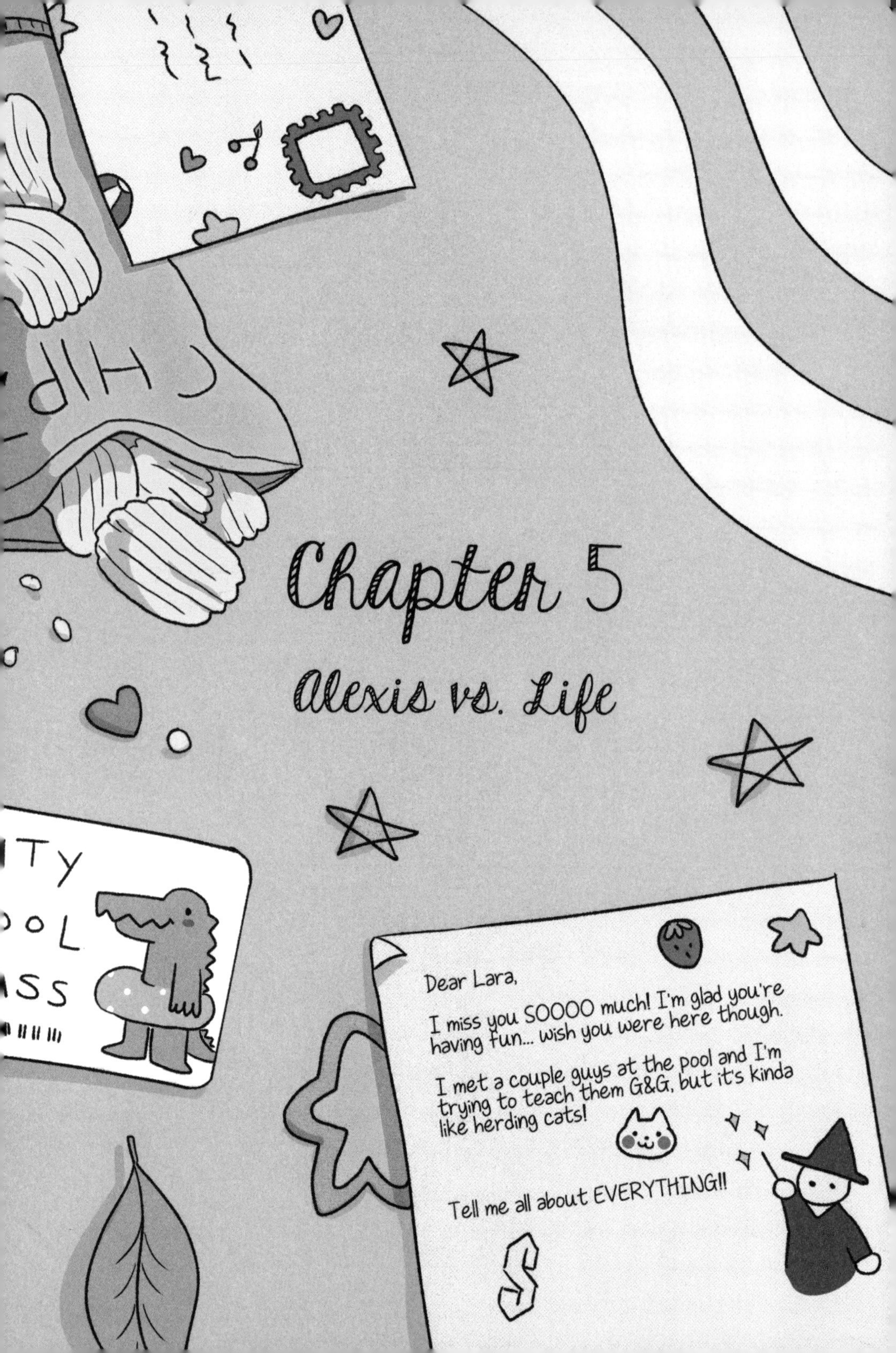
Dear Lara,
I miss you SOOOO much! I'm glad you're having fun... wish you were here though.
I met a couple guys at the pool and I'm trying to teach them G&G, but it's kinda like herding cats!
Tell me all about EVERYTHING!!
S

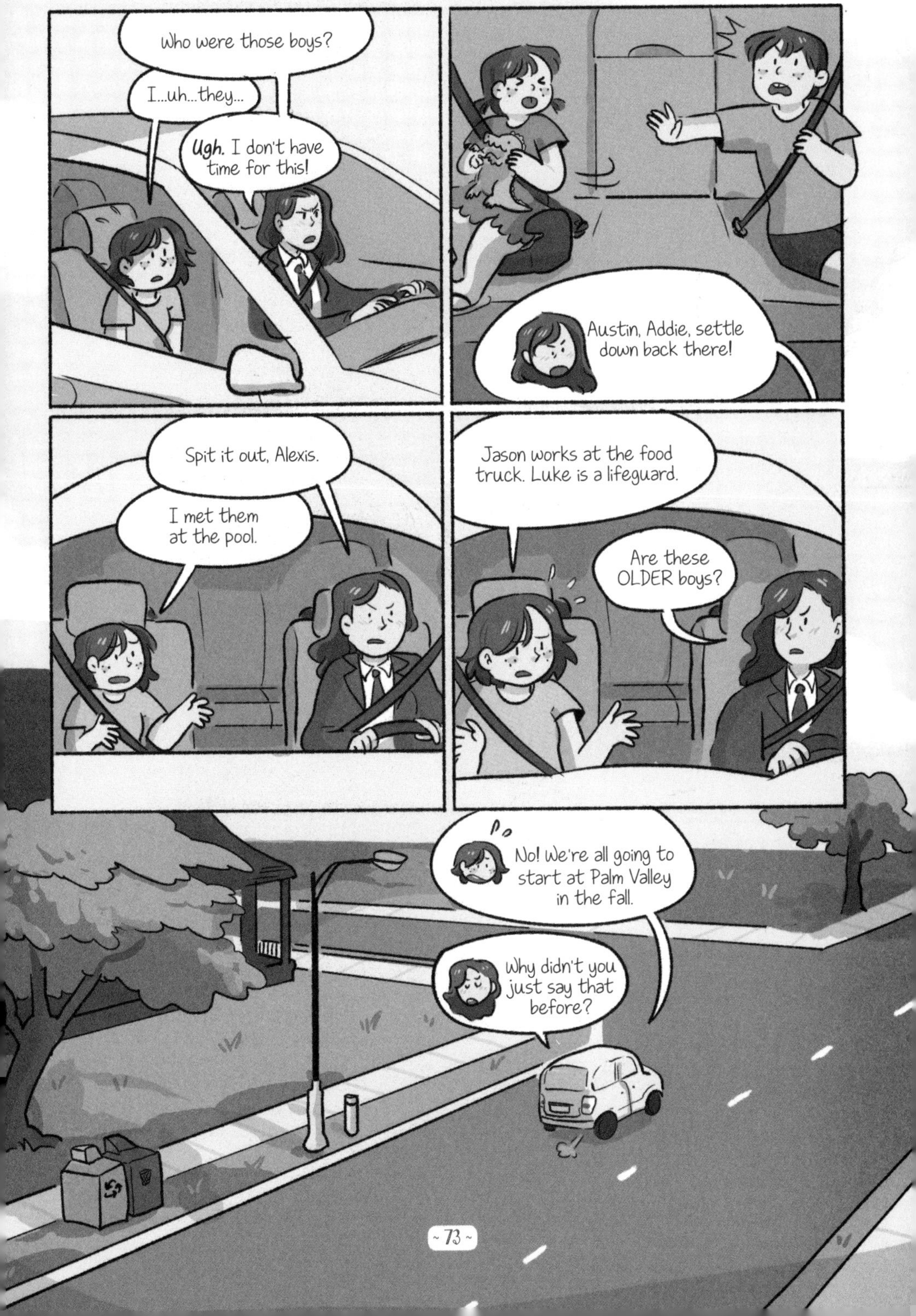
Who were those boys?
I...uh...they...
Ugh. I don't have time for this!
Austin, Addie, settle down back there!
Spit it out, Alexis.
I met them at the pool.
Jason works at the food truck. Luke is a lifeguard.
Are these OLDER boys?
No! We're all going to start at Palm Valley in the fall.
Why didn't you just say that before?

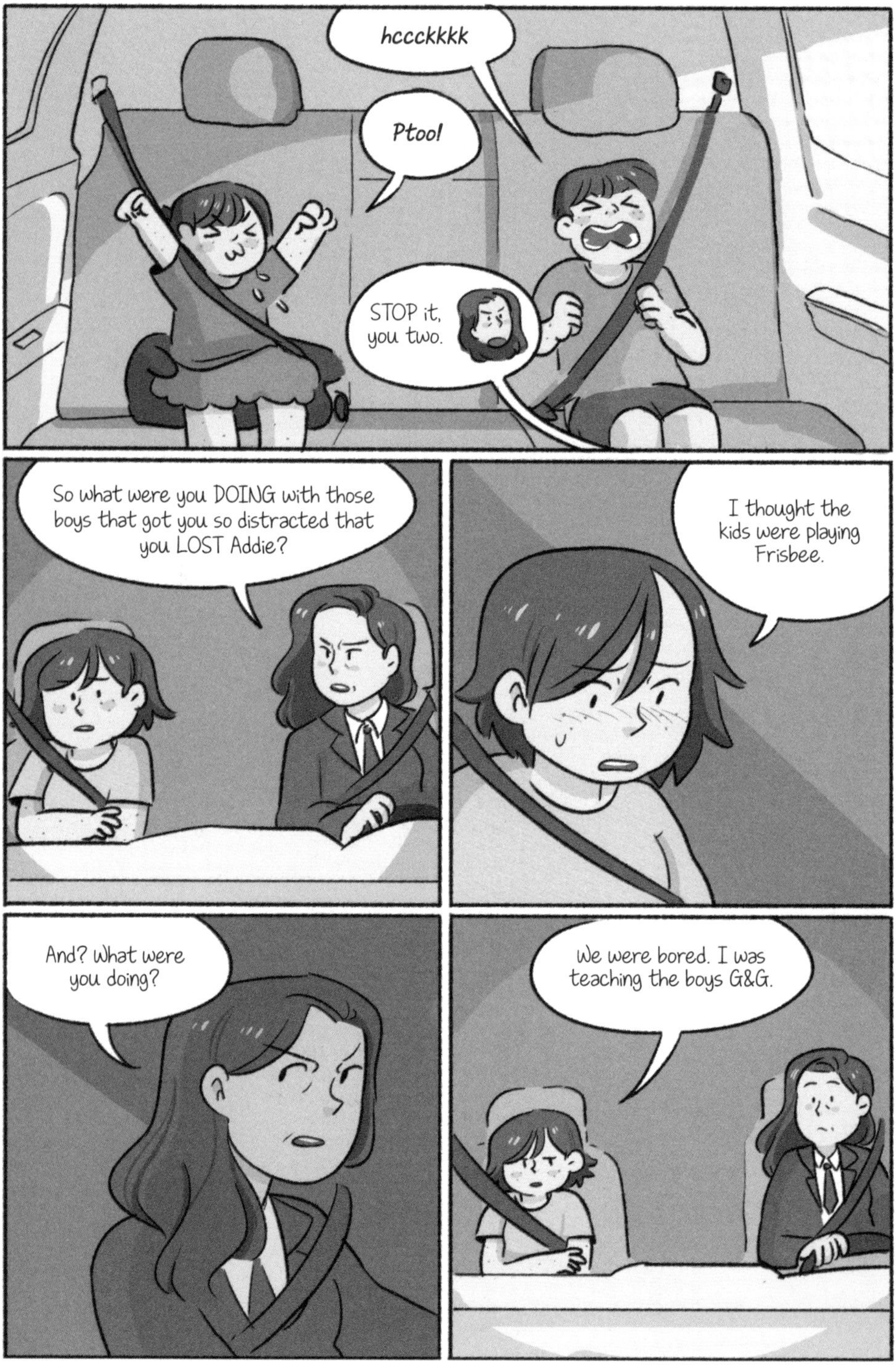
hccckkkk
Ptoo!
STOP it, you two.
So what were you DOING with those boys that got you so distracted that you LOST Addie?
I thought the kids were playing Frisbee.
And? What were you doing?
We were bored. I was teaching the boys G&G.

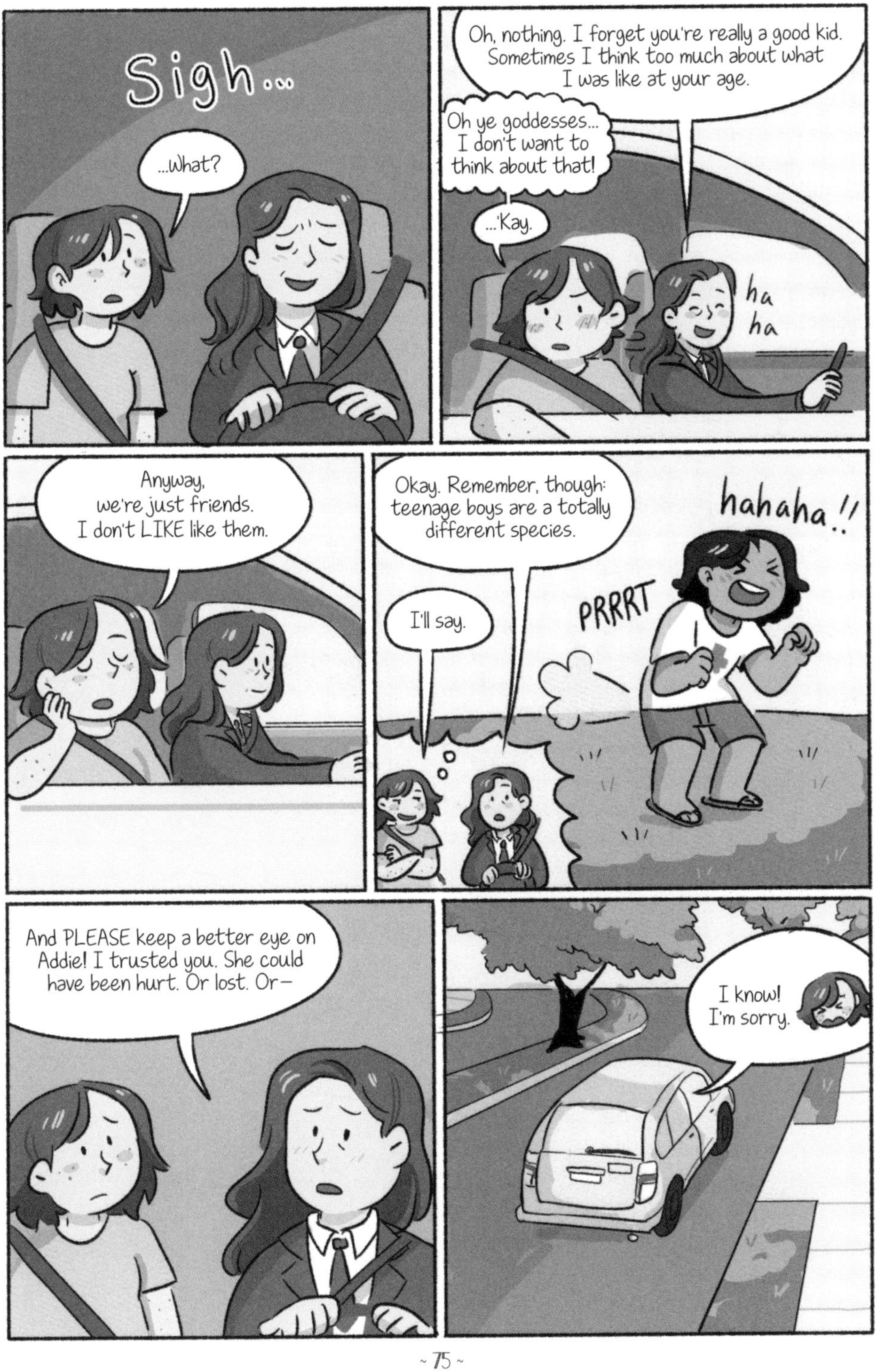

Sigh...
...What?
Oh, nothing. I forget you're really a good kid. Sometimes I think too much about what I was like at your age.
Oh ye goddesses... I don't want to think about that!
...'Kay.
ha ha
Anyway, we're just friends. I don't LIKE like them.
Okay. Remember, though: teenage boys are a totally different species.
I'll say.
hahaha!!
PRRRT
And PLEASE keep a better eye on Addie! I trusted you. She could have been hurt. Or lost. Or—
I know! I'm sorry.

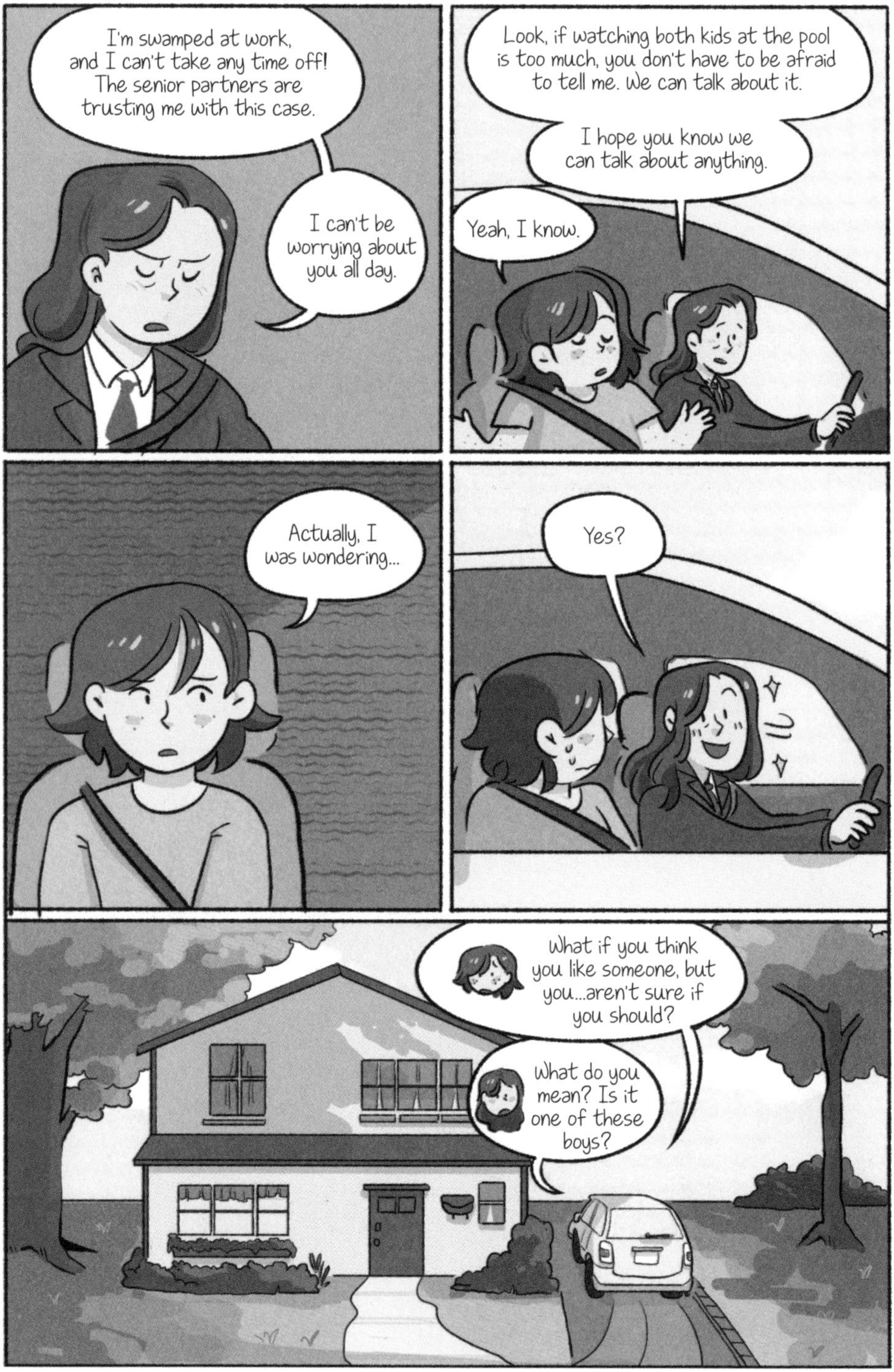
I'm swamped at work, and I can't take any time off! The senior partners are trusting me with this case.
I can't be worrying about you all day.
Look, if watching both kids at the pool is too much, you don't have to be afraid to tell me. We can talk about it.
I hope you know we can talk about anything.
Yeah, I know.
Actually, I was wondering...
Yes?
What if you think you like someone, but you...aren't sure if you should?
What do you mean? Is it one of these boys?

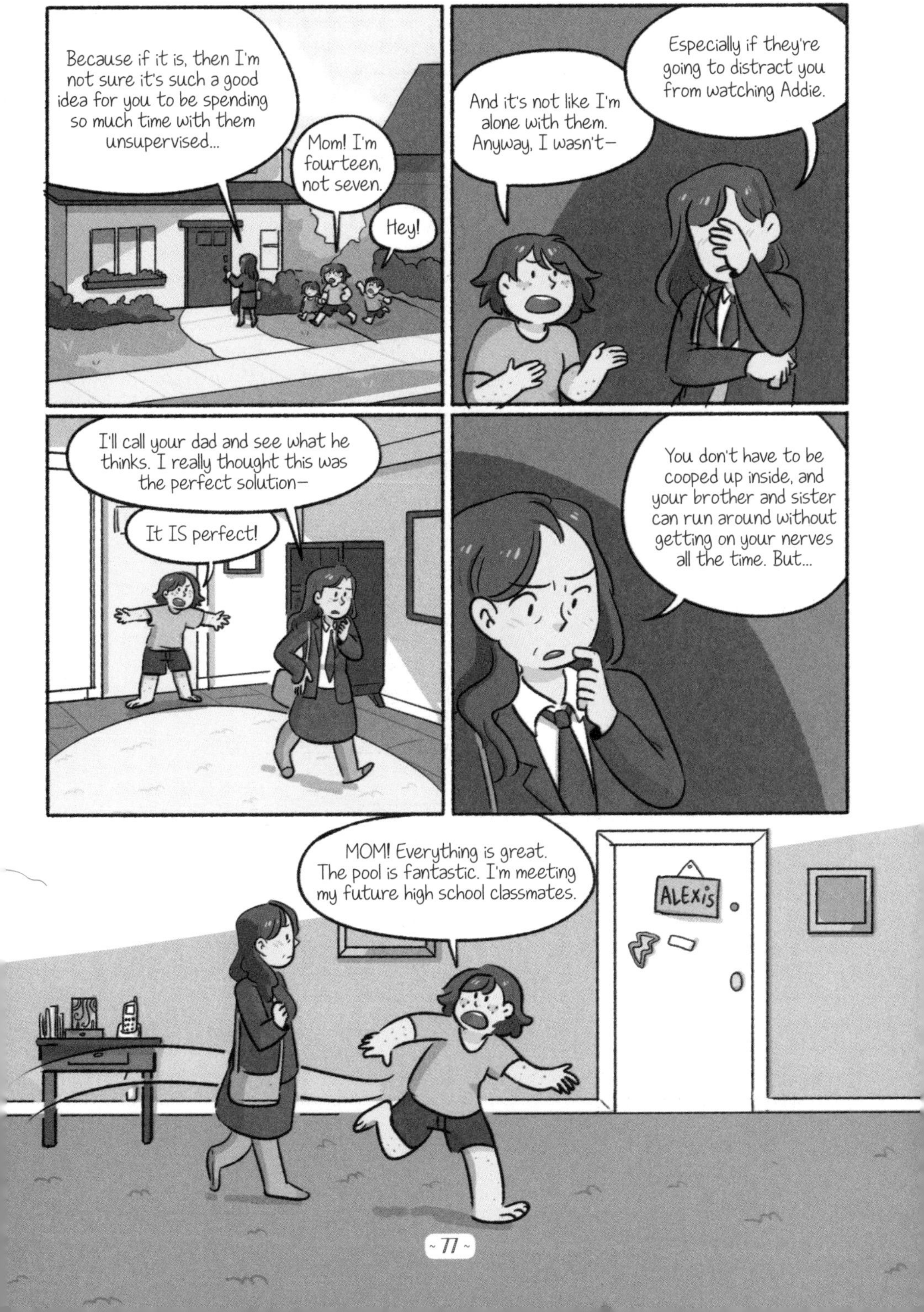

Because if it is, then I'm not sure it's such a good idea for you to be spending so much time with them unsupervised...
Mom! I'm fourteen, not seven.
Hey!
And it's not like I'm alone with them. Anyway, I wasn't—
Especially if they're going to distract you from watching Addie.
I'll call your dad and see what he thinks. I really thought this was the perfect solution—
It IS perfect!
You don't have to be cooped up inside, and your brother and sister can run around without getting on your nerves all the time. But...
MOM! Everything is great. The pool is fantastic. I'm meeting my future high school classmates.
ALEXis

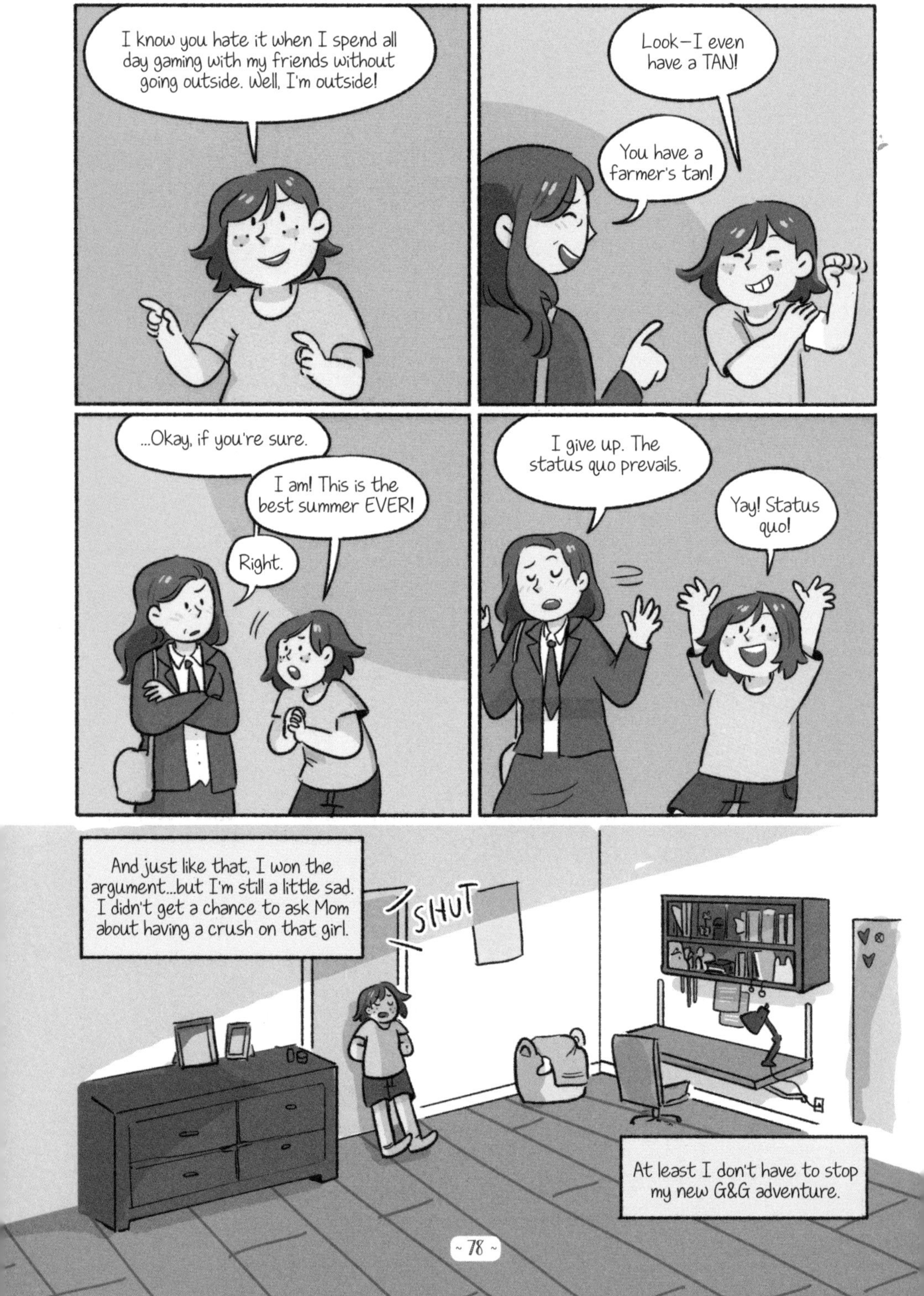
I know you hate it when I spend all day gaming with my friends without going outside. Well, I'm outside!
Look—I even have a TAN!
You have a farmer's tan!
...Okay, if you're sure.
I am! This is the best summer EVER!
Right.
I give up. The status quo prevails.
Yay! Status quo!
And just like that, I won the argument...but I'm still a little sad. I didn't get a chance to ask Mom about having a crush on that girl.
SHUT
At least I don't have to stop my new G&G adventure.

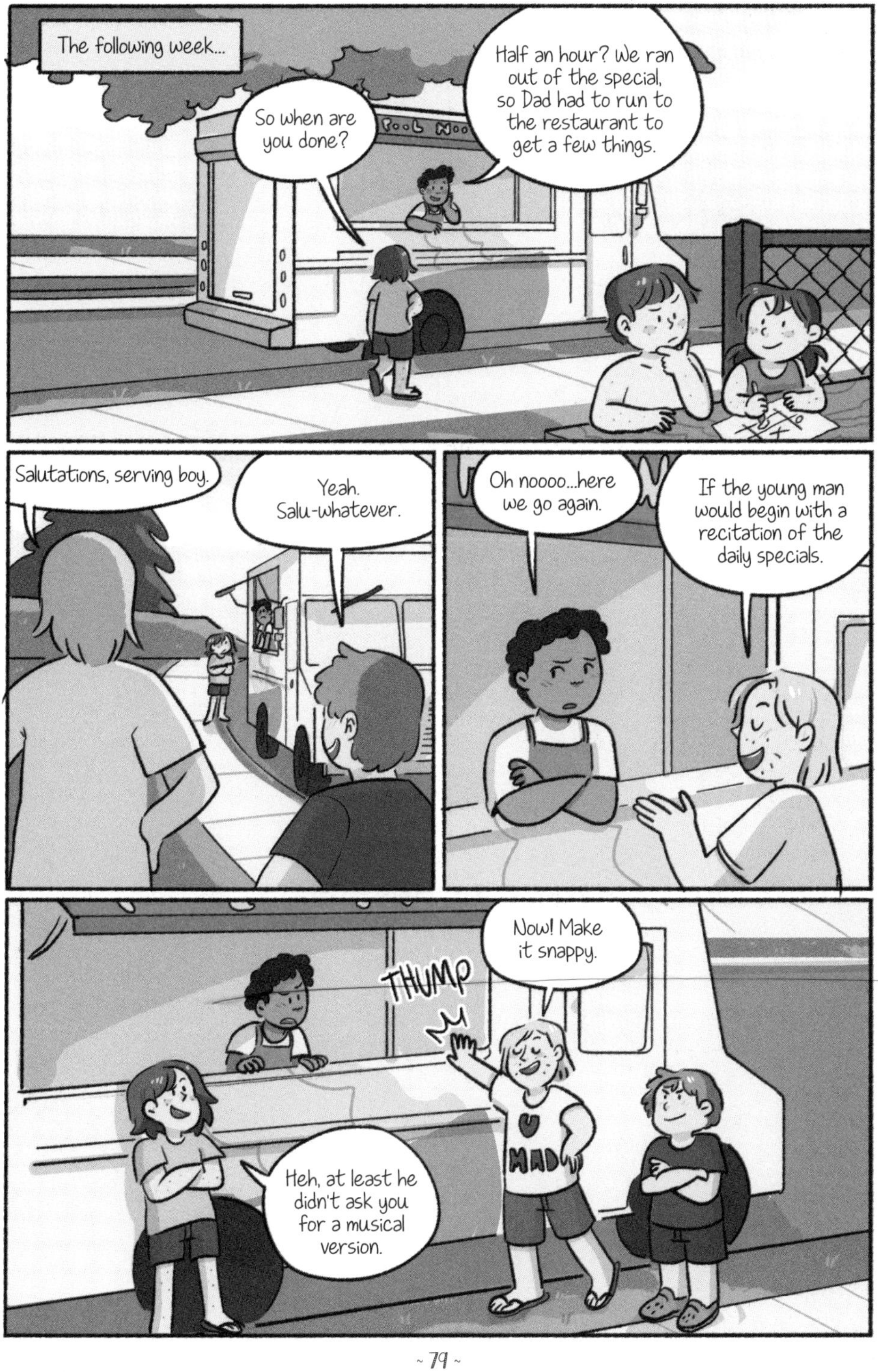
The following week...
So when are you done?
Half an hour? We ran out of the special, so Dad had to run to the restaurant to get a few things.
Salutations, serving boy.
Yeah. Salu-whatever.
Oh noooo...here we go again.
If the young man would begin with a recitation of the daily specials.
Now! Make it snappy.
THUMP
Heh, at least he didn't ask you for a musical version.
U MAD

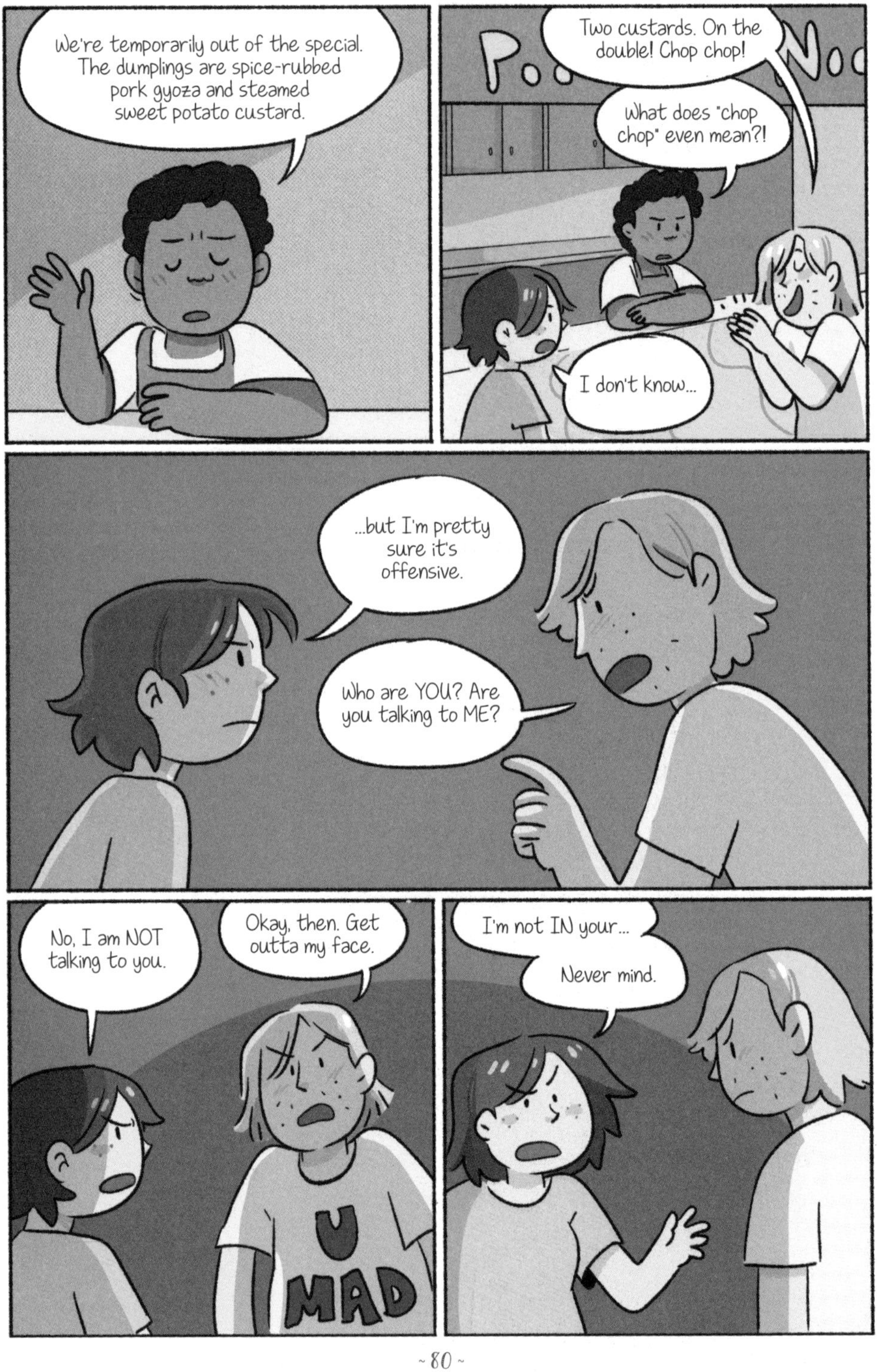
We're temporarily out of the special. The dumplings are spice-rubbed pork gyoza and steamed sweet potato custard.
Two custards. On the double! Chop chop!
What does "chop chop" even mean?!
I don't know...
...but I'm pretty sure it's offensive.
Who are YOU? Are you talking to ME?
No, I am NOT talking to you.
Okay, then. Get outta my face.
U MAD
I'm not IN your...
Never mind.

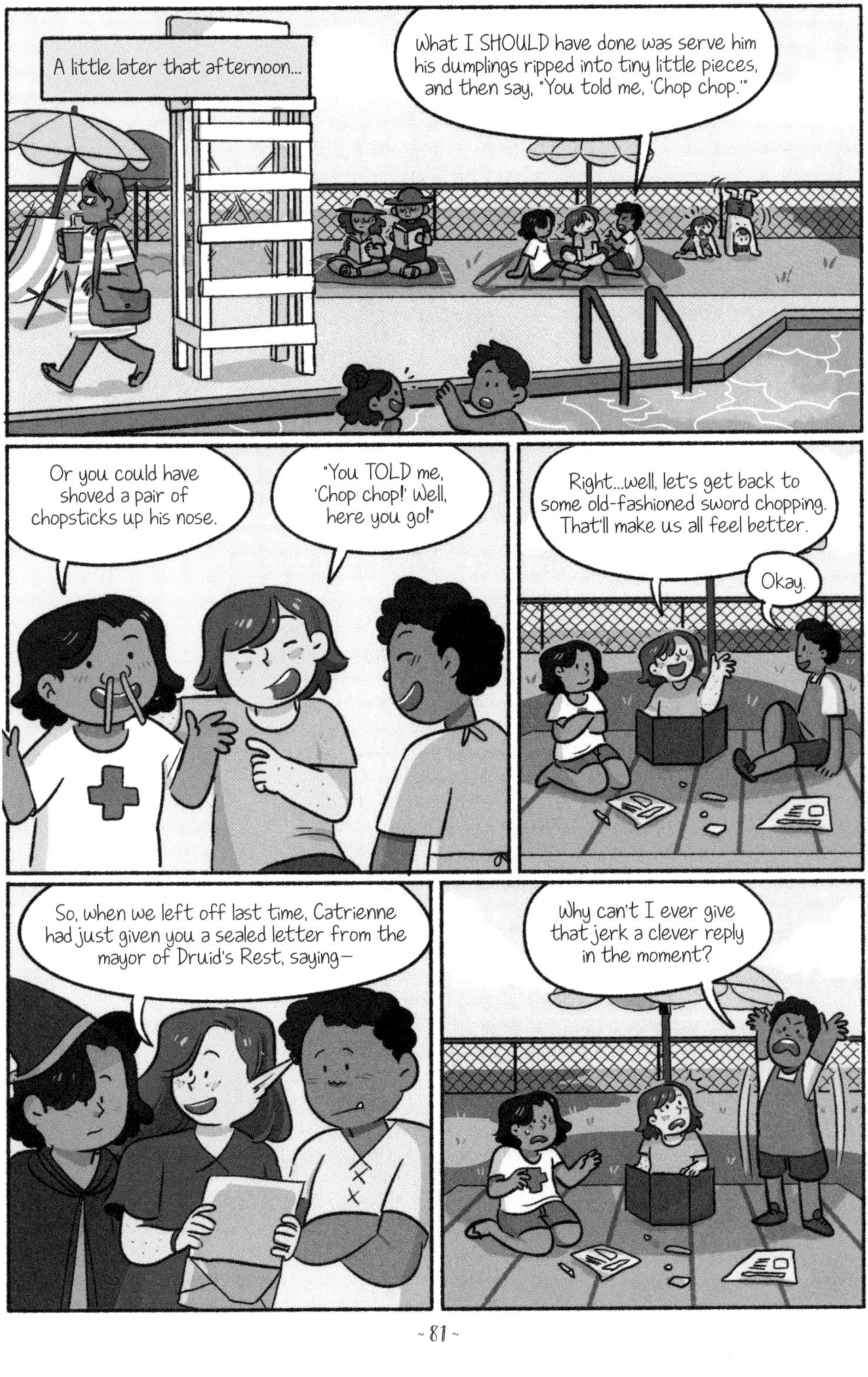

A little later that afternoon...
What I SHOULD have done was serve him his dumplings ripped into tiny little pieces, and then say, "You told me, 'Chop chop.'"
Or you could have shoved a pair of chopsticks up his nose.
"You TOLD me, 'Chop chop!' Well, here you go!"
Right...well, let's get back to some old-fashioned sword chopping. That'll make us all feel better.
Okay.
So, when we left off last time, Catrienne had just given you a sealed letter from the mayor of Druid's Rest, saying—
Why can't I ever give that jerk a clever reply in the moment?

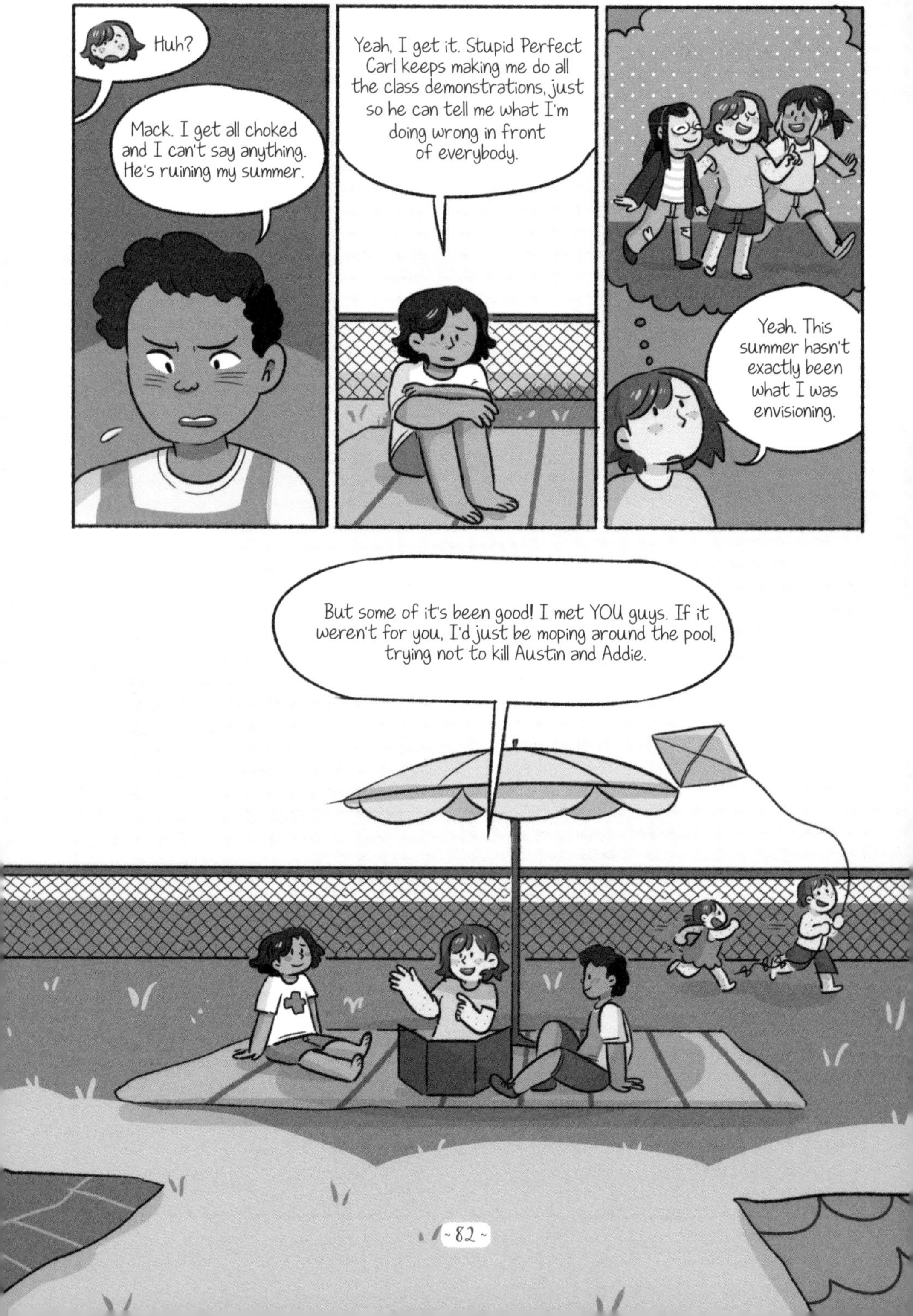
Huh?
Mack. I get all choked and I can't say anything. He's ruining my summer.
Yeah, I get it. Stupid Perfect Carl keeps making me do all the class demonstrations, just so he can tell me what I'm doing wrong in front of everybody.
Yeah. This summer hasn't exactly been what I was envisioning.
But some of it's been good! I met YOU guys. If it weren't for you, I'd just be moping around the pool, trying not to kill Austin and Addie.

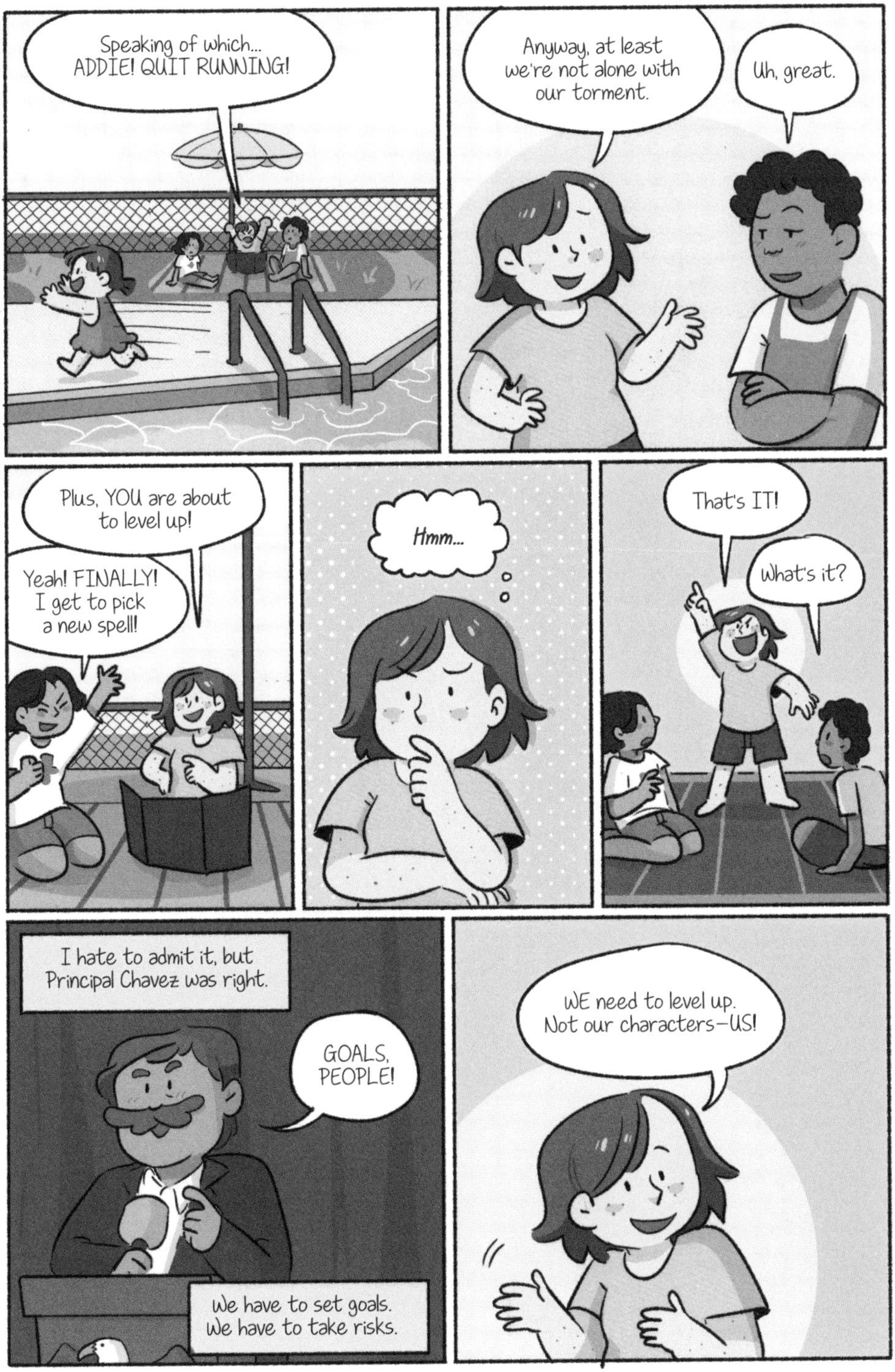

Speaking of which... ADDIE! QUIT RUNNING!
Anyway, at least we're not alone with our torment.
Uh, great.
Plus, YOU are about to level up!
Yeah! FINALLY! I get to pick a new spell!
Hmm...
That's IT!
What's it?
I hate to admit it, but Principal Chavez was right.
GOALS, PEOPLE!
We have to set goals. We have to take risks.
WE need to level up. Not our characters—US!

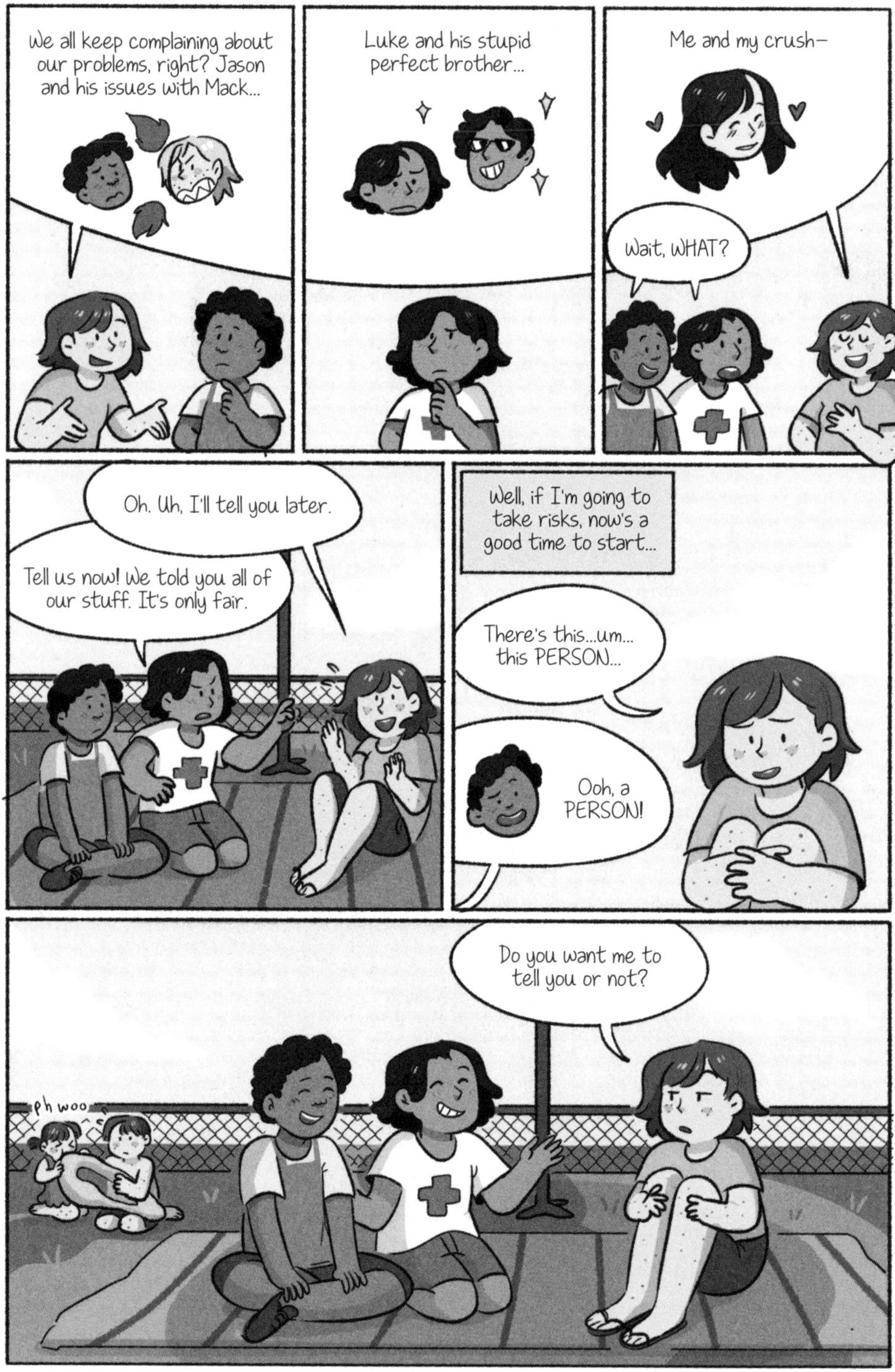
We all keep complaining about our problems, right? Jason and his issues with Mack...
Luke and his stupid perfect brother...
Me and my crush–
Wait, WHAT?
Oh. Uh, I'll tell you later.
Tell us now! We told you all of our stuff. It's only fair.
Well, if I'm going to take risks, now's a good time to start...
There's this...um... this PERSON...
Ooh, a PERSON!
Do you want me to tell you or not?
phwoo

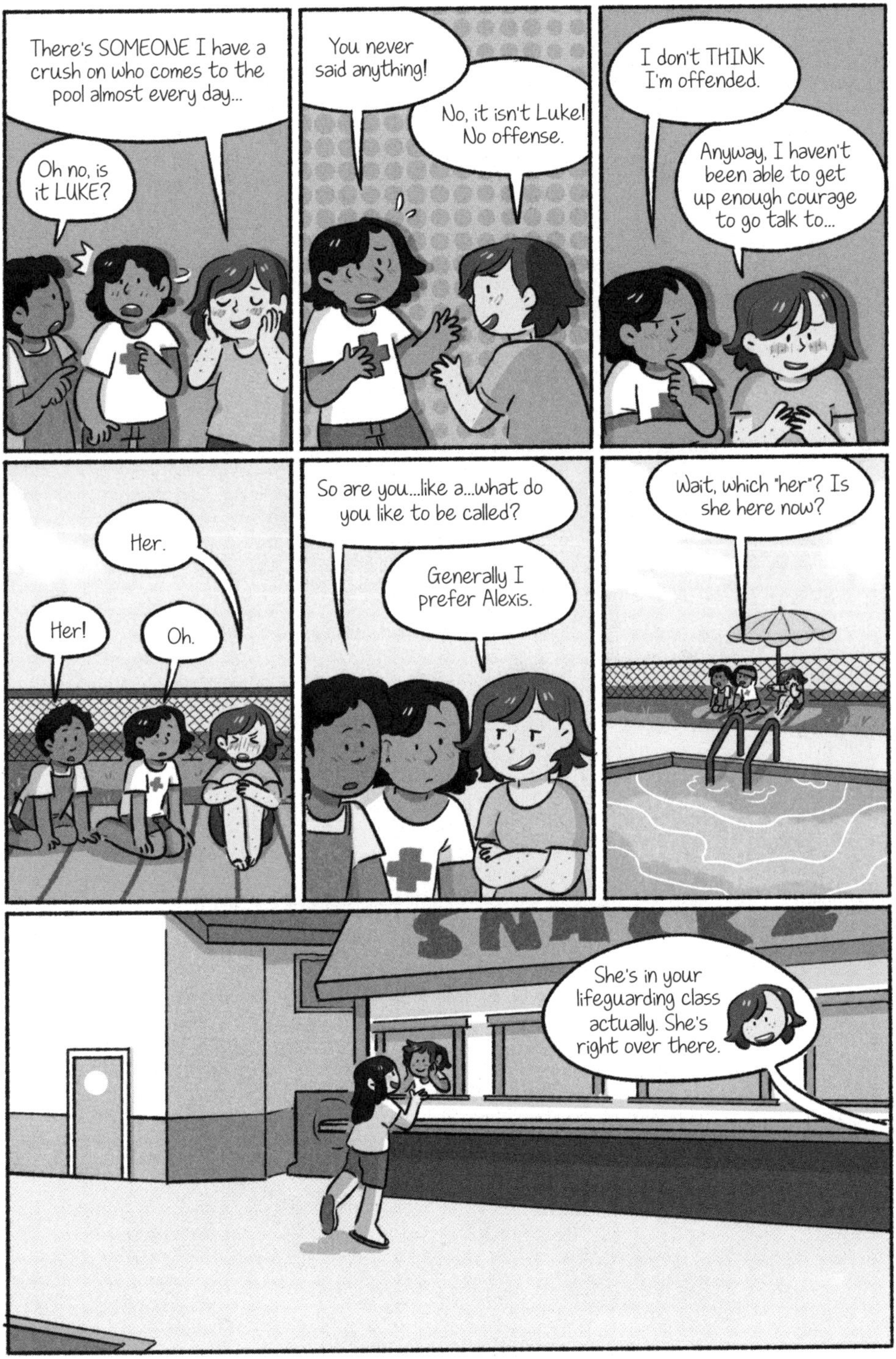
There's SOMEONE I have a crush on who comes to the pool almost every day...
Oh no, is it LUKE?
You never said anything!
No, it isn't Luke! No offense.
I don't THINK I'm offended.
Anyway, I haven't been able to get up enough courage to go talk to...
Her.
Her!
Oh.
So are you...like a...what do you like to be called?
Generally I prefer Alexis.
Wait, which "her"? Is she here now?
SNACKS
She's in your lifeguarding class actually. She's right over there.

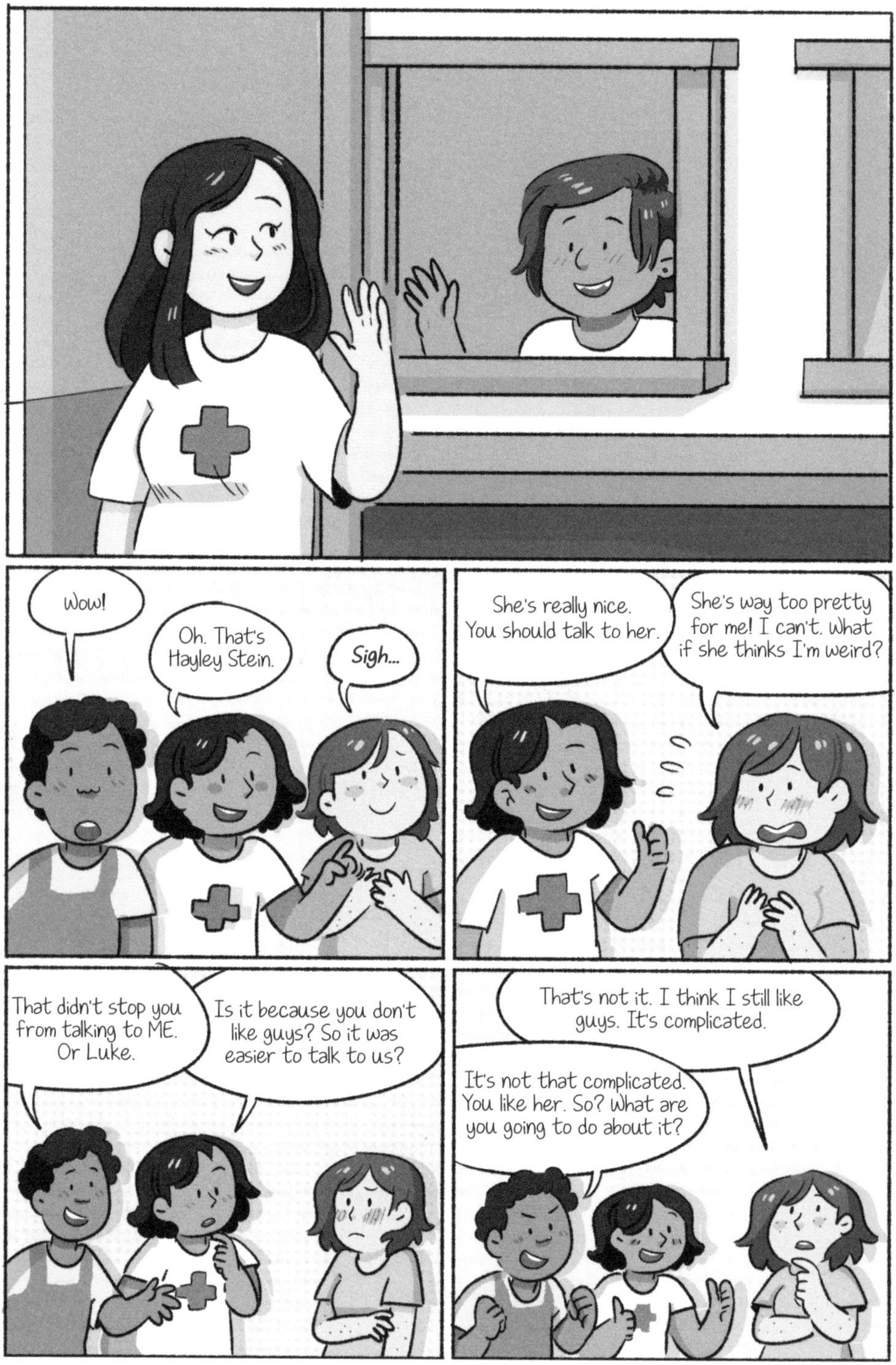
Wow!
Oh. That's Hayley Stein.
Sigh...
She's really nice. You should talk to her.
She's way too pretty for me! I can't. What if she thinks I'm weird?
That didn't stop you from talking to ME. Or Luke.
Is it because you don't like guys? So it was easier to talk to us?
That's not it. I think I still like guys. It's complicated.
It's not that complicated. You like her. So? What are you going to do about it?

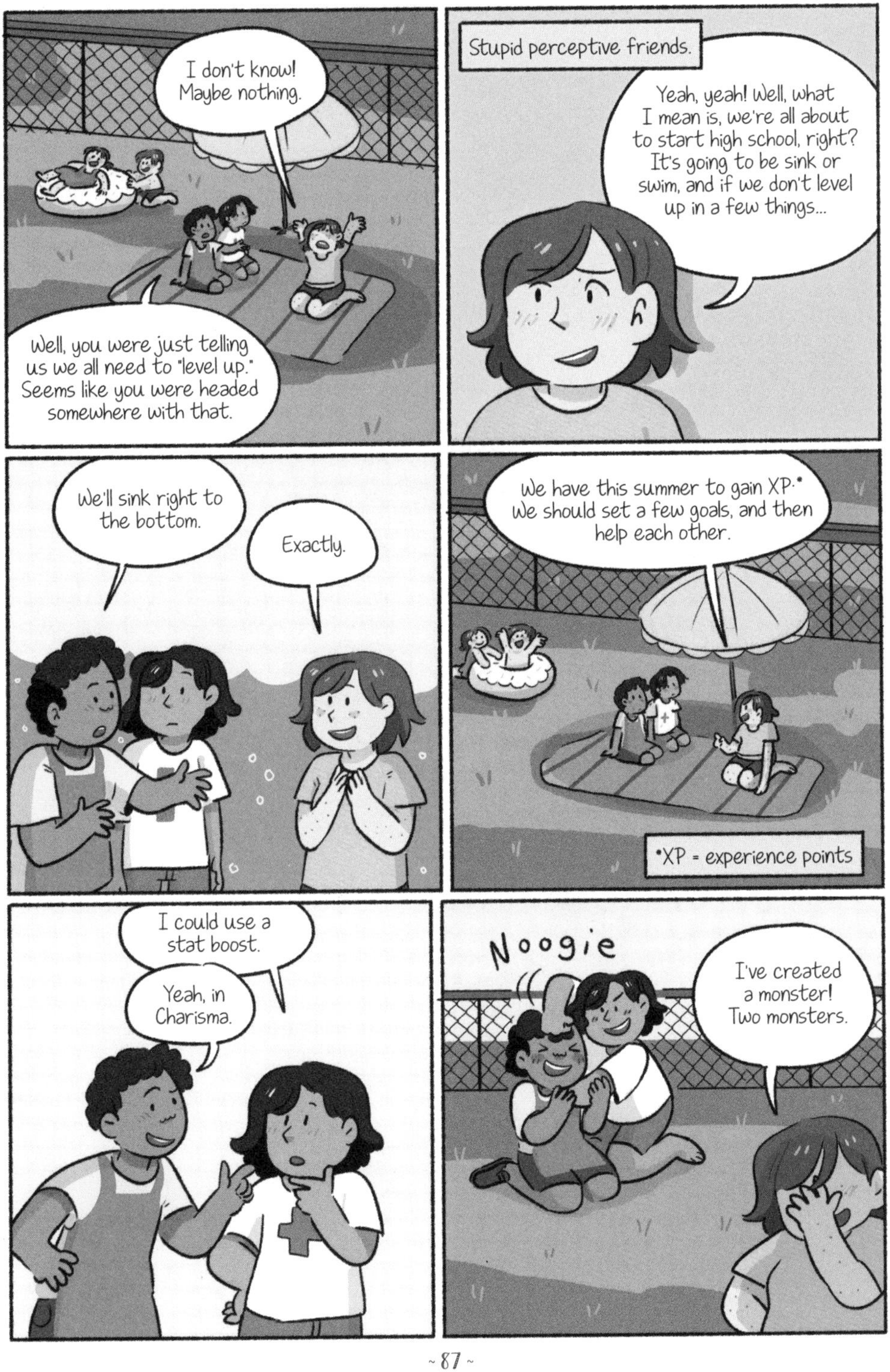
I don't know! Maybe nothing.
Well, you were just telling us we all need to "level up." Seems like you were headed somewhere with that.
Stupid perceptive friends.
Yeah, yeah! Well, what I mean is, we're all about to start high school, right? It's going to be sink or swim, and if we don't level up in a few things...
We'll sink right to the bottom.
Exactly.
We have this summer to gain XP.* We should set a few goals, and then help each other.
*XP = experience points
I could use a stat boost.
Yeah, in Charisma.
Noogie
I've created a monster! Two monsters.

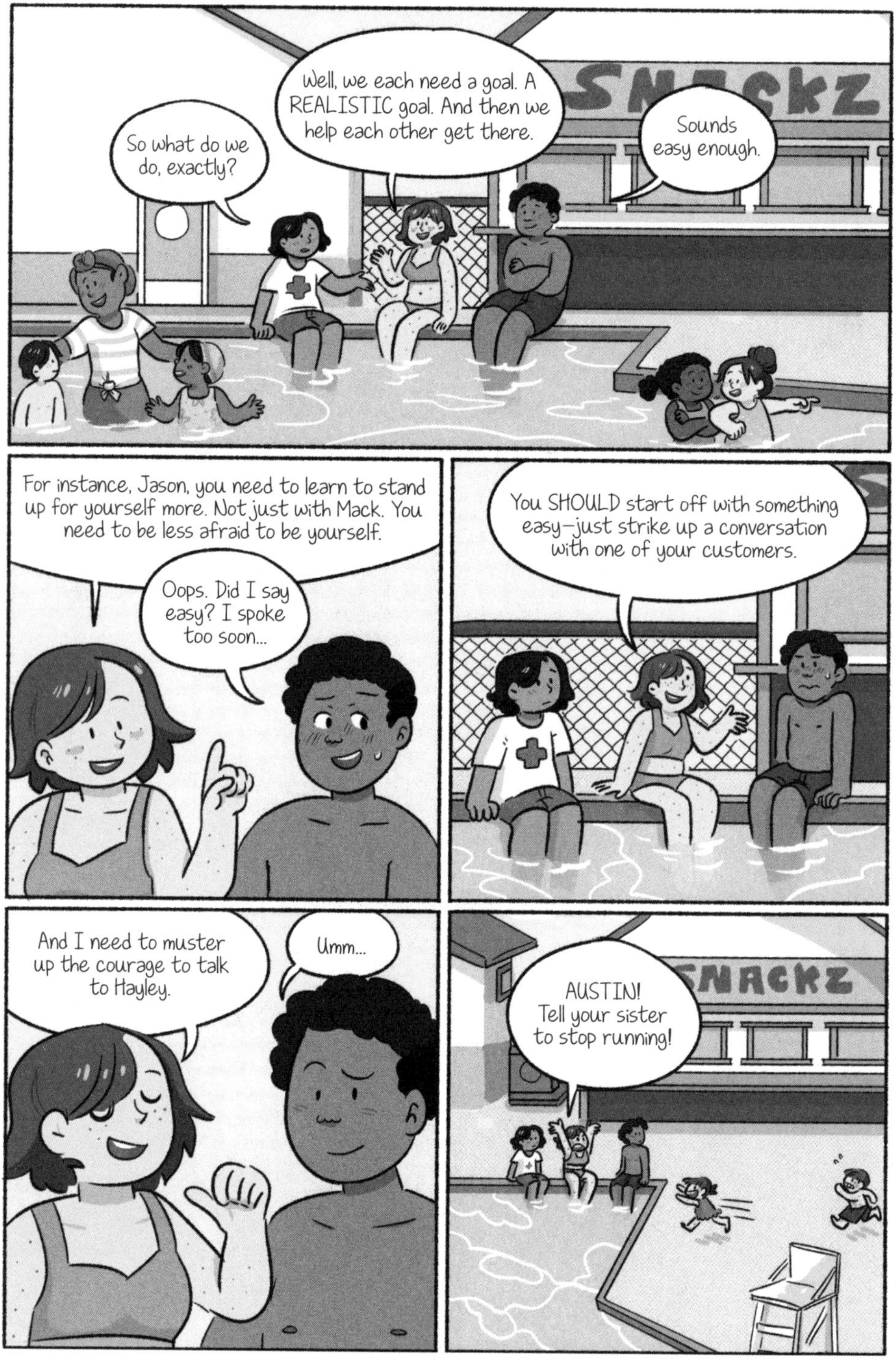
SNACKZ
So what do we do, exactly?
Well, we each need a goal. A REALISTIC goal. And then we help each other get there.
Sounds easy enough.
For instance, Jason, you need to learn to stand up for yourself more. Not just with Mack. You need to be less afraid to be yourself.
Oops. Did I say easy? I spoke too soon...
You SHOULD start off with something easy—just strike up a conversation with one of your customers.
And I need to muster up the courage to talk to Hayley.
Umm...
SNACKZ
AUSTIN! Tell your sister to stop running!

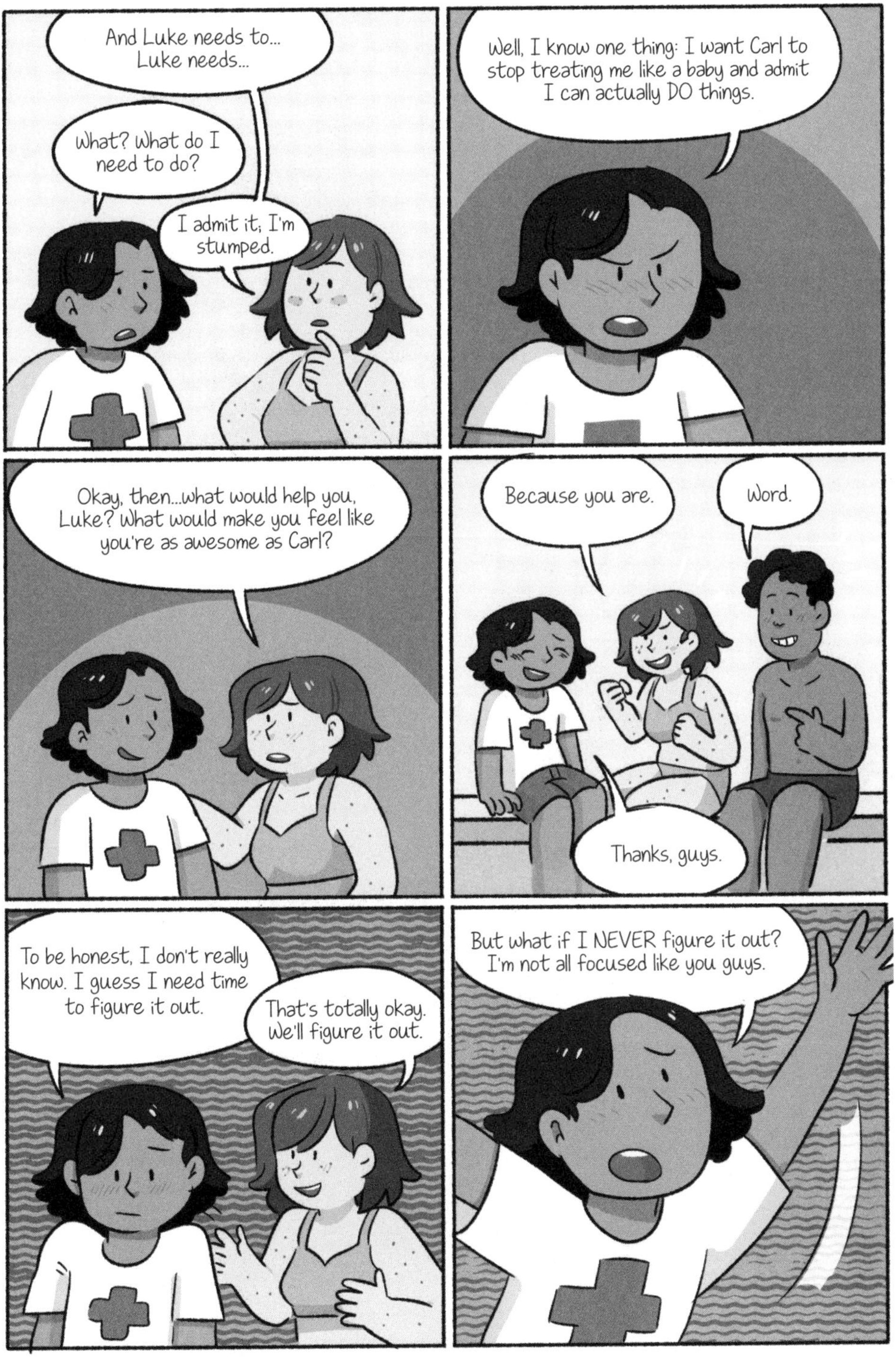
And Luke needs to... Luke needs...
What? What do I need to do?
I admit it; I'm stumped.
Well, I know one thing: I want Carl to stop treating me like a baby and admit I can actually DO things.
Okay, then...what would help you, Luke? What would make you feel like you're as awesome as Carl?
Because you are.
Word.
Thanks, guys.
To be honest, I don't really know. I guess I need time to figure it out.
That's totally okay. We'll figure it out.
But what if I NEVER figure it out? I'm not all focused like you guys.

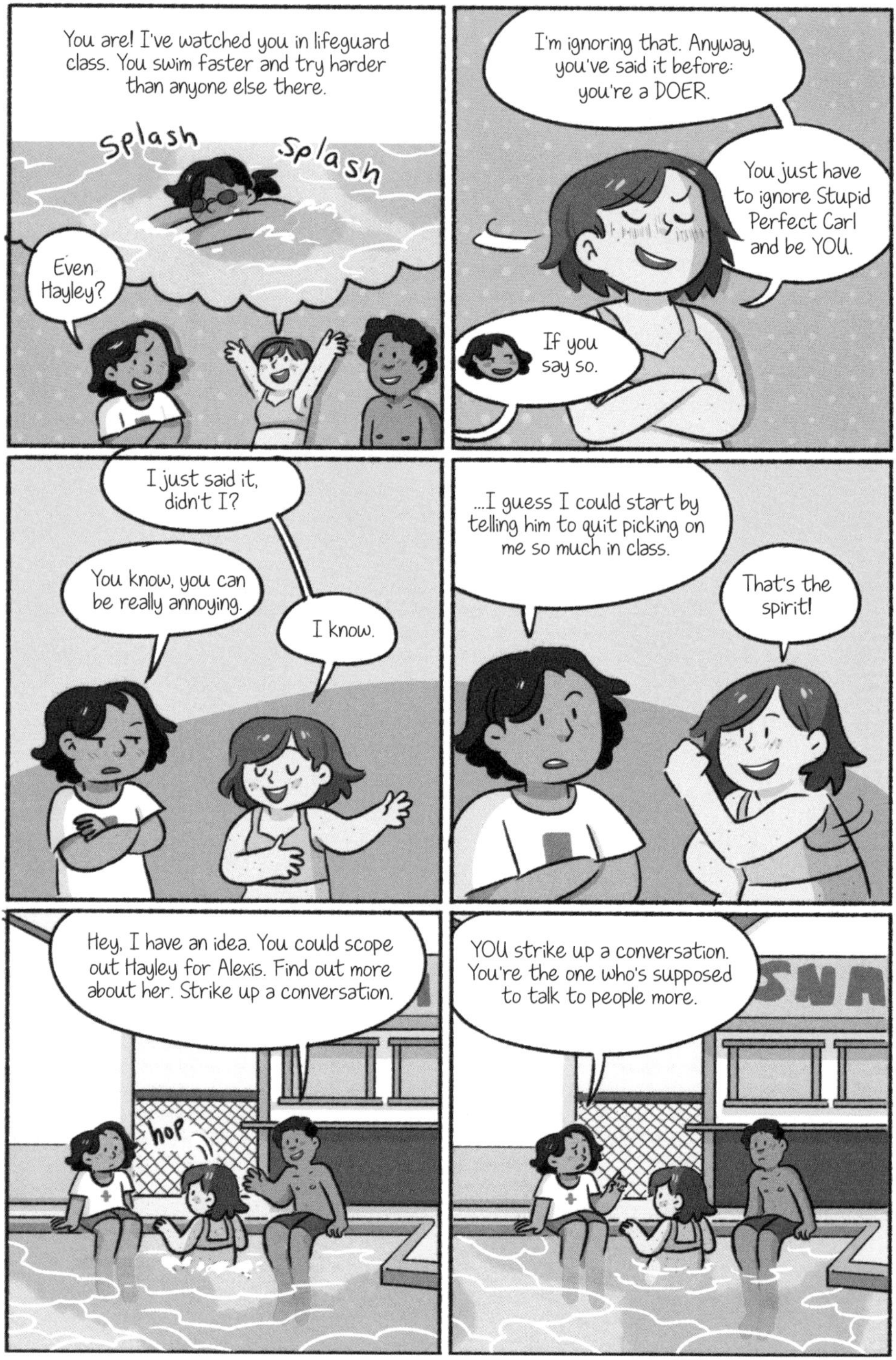
You are! I've watched you in lifeguard class. You swim faster and try harder than anyone else there.
Splash
Splash
Even Hayley?
I'm ignoring that. Anyway, you've said it before: you're a DOER.
You just have to ignore Stupid Perfect Carl and be YOU.
If you say so.
I just said it, didn't I?
You know, you can be really annoying.
I know.
...I guess I could start by telling him to quit picking on me so much in class.
That's the spirit!
Hey, I have an idea. You could scope out Hayley for Alexis. Find out more about her. Strike up a conversation.
hop
YOU strike up a conversation. You're the one who's supposed to talk to people more.

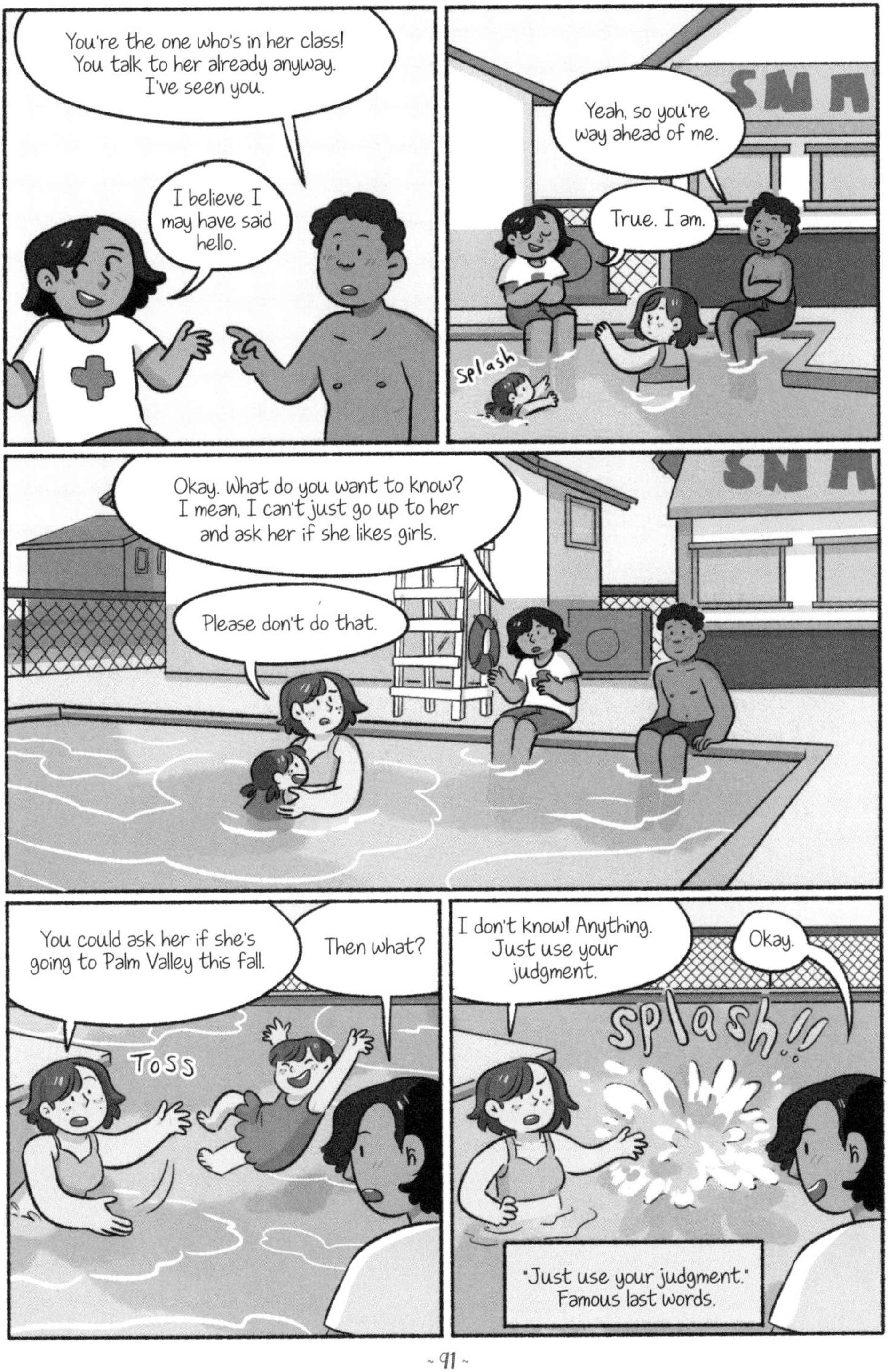
You're the one who's in her class! You talk to her already anyway. I've seen you.
I believe I may have said hello.
Yeah, so you're way ahead of me.
True. I am.
splash
Okay. What do you want to know? I mean, I can't just go up to her and ask her if she likes girls.
Please don't do that.
You could ask her if she's going to Palm Valley this fall.
Then what?
TOSS
I don't know! Anything. Just use your judgment.
Okay.
splash!!
"Just use your judgment." Famous last words.

Chapter 6

Alexis vs. Love

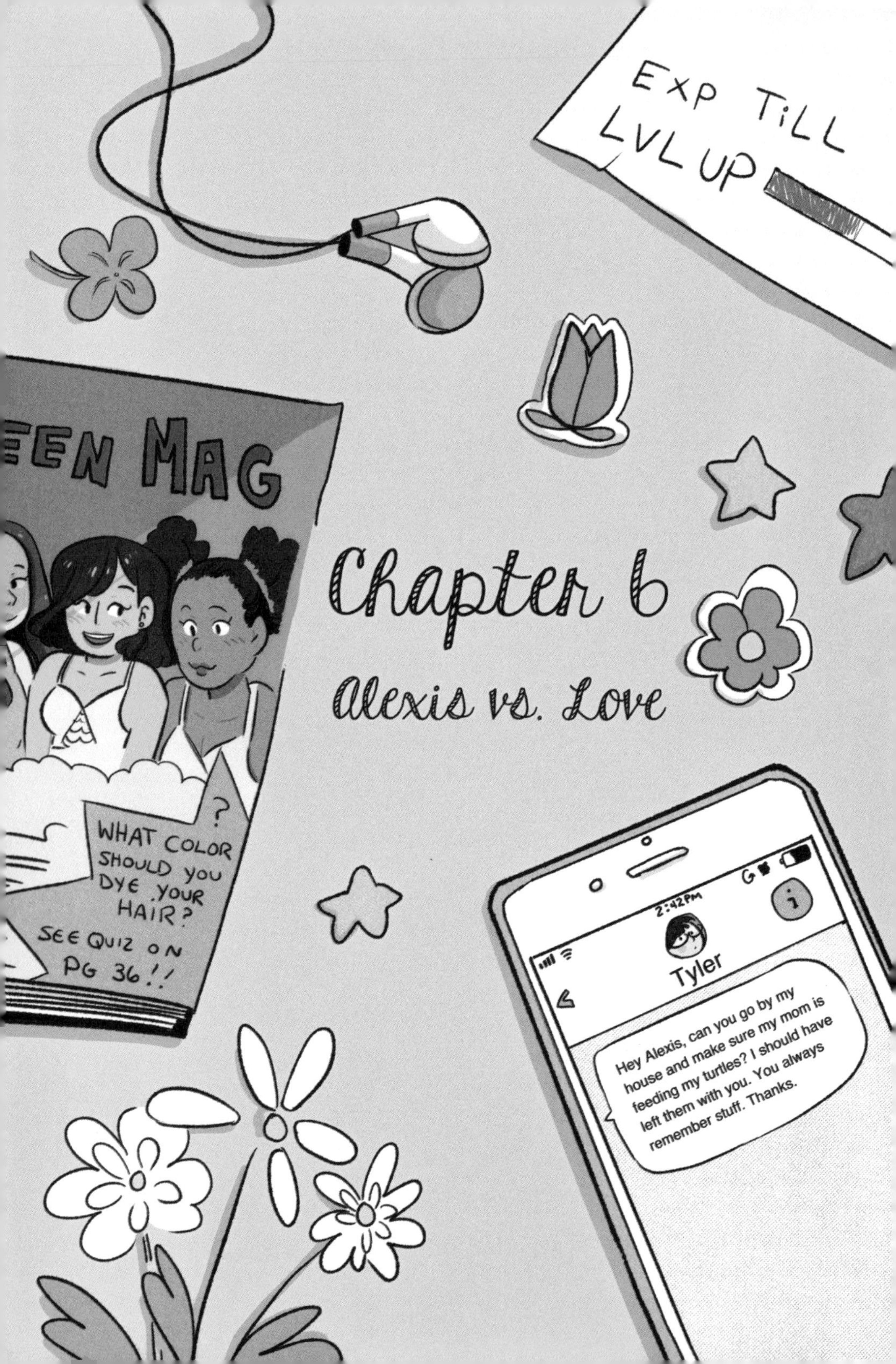
EXP TILL LVL UP
EEN MAG
?
WHAT COLOR SHOULD YOU DYE YOUR HAIR?
SEE QUIZ ON PG 36!!
2:42PM
Tyler
Hey Alexis, can you go by my house and make sure my mom is feeding my turtles? I should have left them with you. You always remember stuff. Thanks.

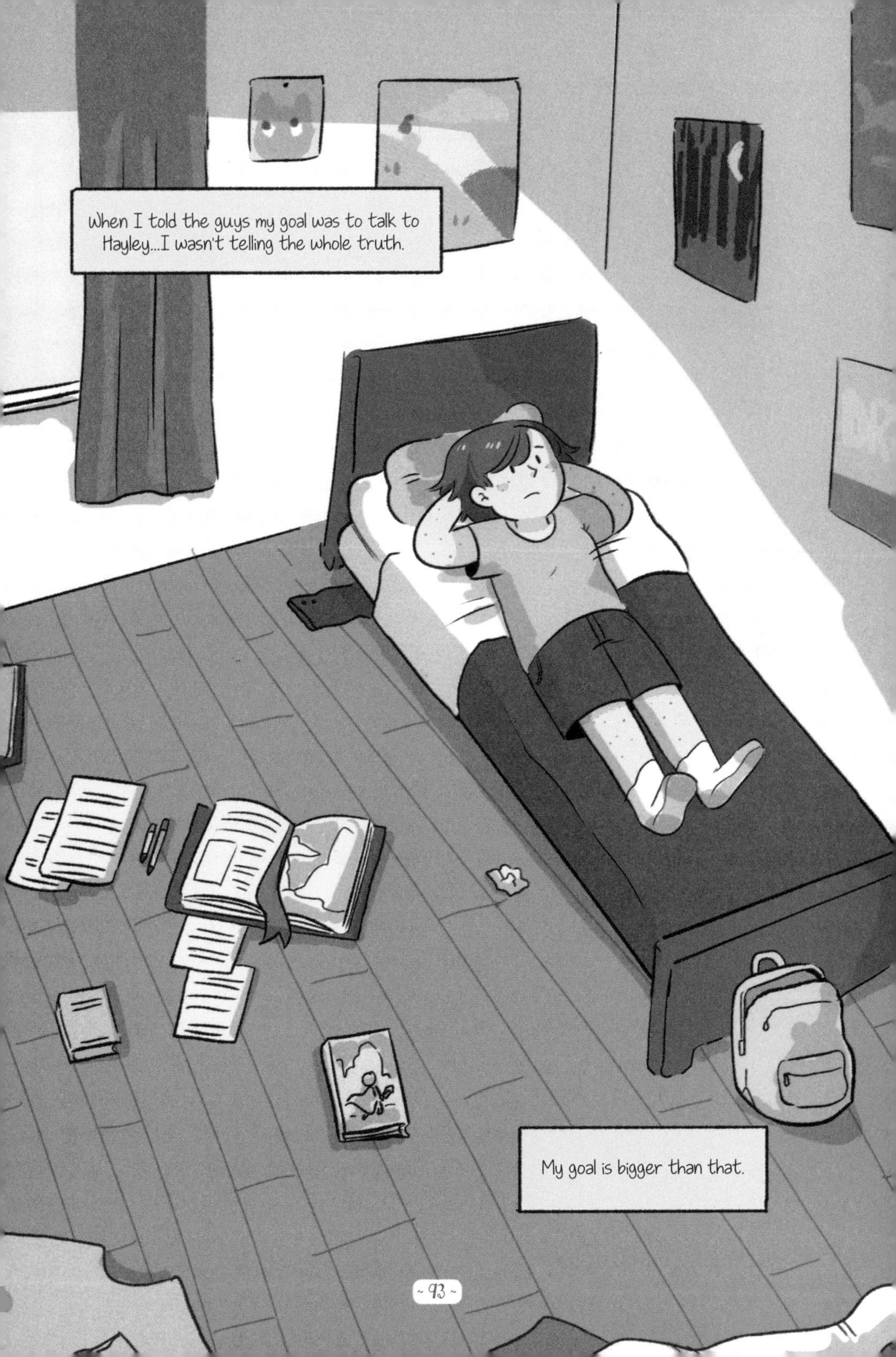
When I told the guys my goal was to talk to Hayley...I wasn't telling the whole truth.
My goal is bigger than that.

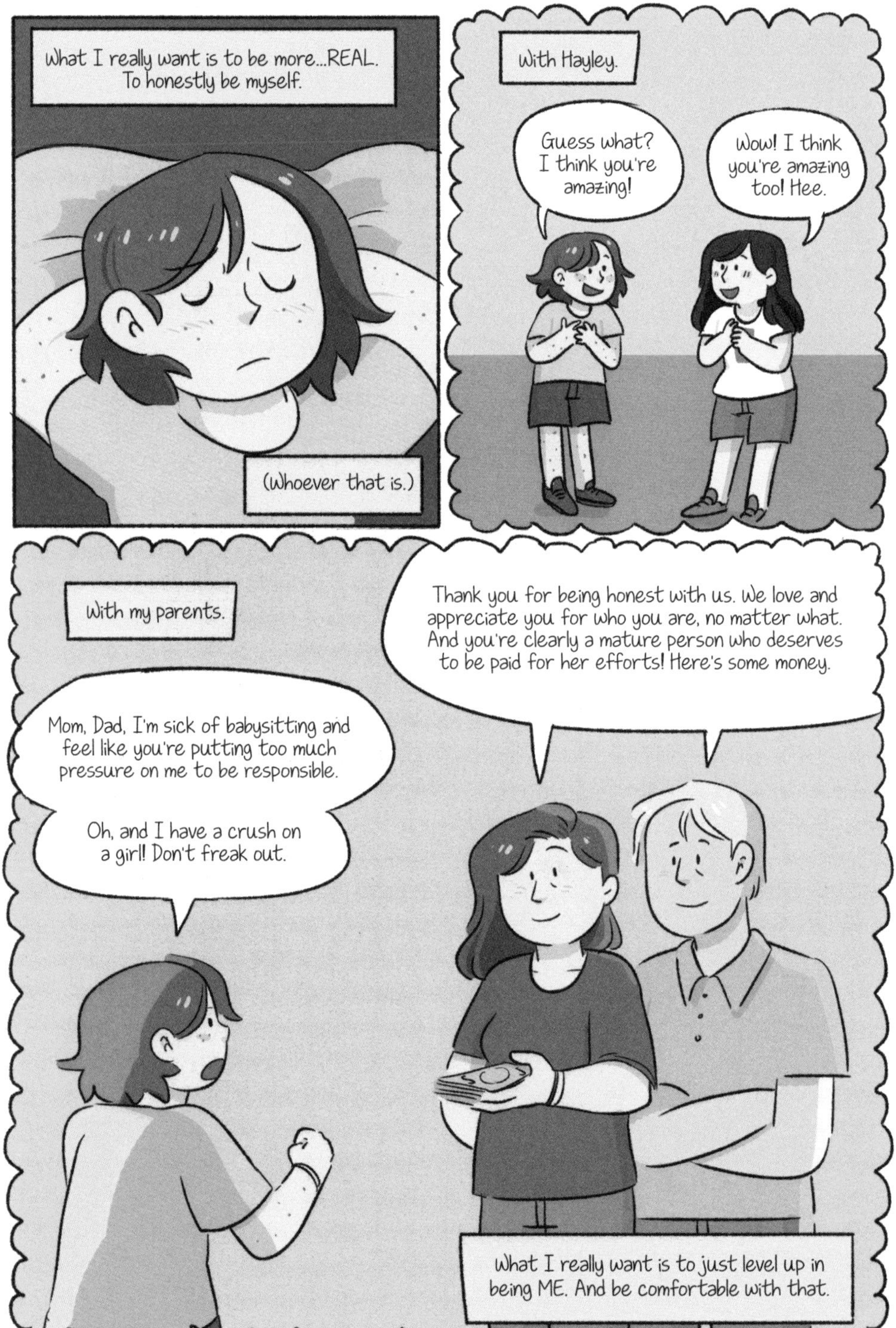
What I really want is to be more...REAL. To honestly be myself.
(Whoever that is.)
With Hayley.
Guess what? I think you're amazing!
Wow! I think you're amazing too! Hee.
With my parents.
Mom, Dad, I'm sick of babysitting and feel like you're putting too much pressure on me to be responsible.
Oh, and I have a crush on a girl! Don't freak out.
Thank you for being honest with us. We love and appreciate you for who you are, no matter what. And you're clearly a mature person who deserves to be paid for her efforts! Here's some money.
What I really want is to just level up in being ME. And be comfortable with that.

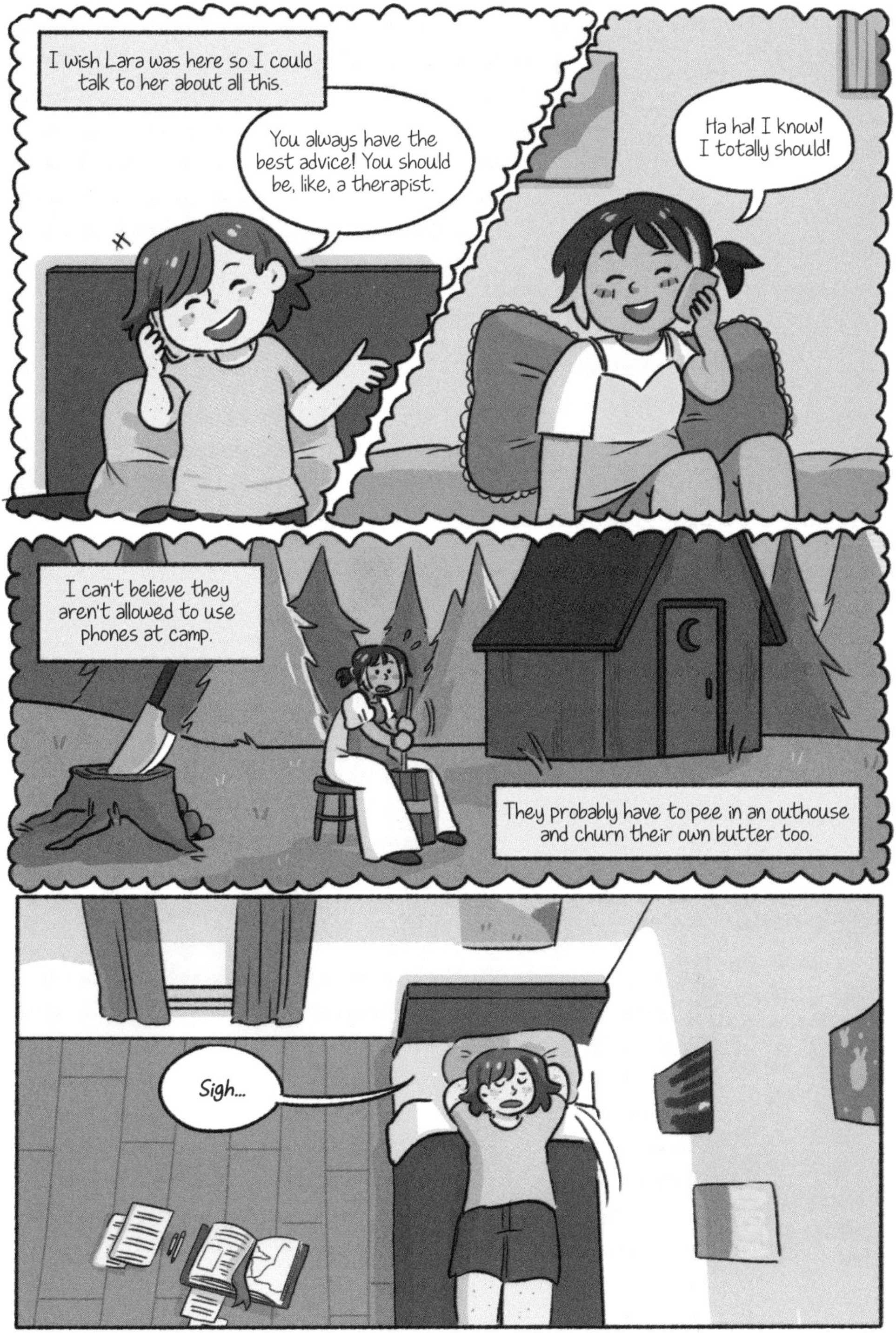

I wish Lara was here so I could talk to her about all this.
You always have the best advice! You should be, like, a therapist.
Ha ha! I know! I totally should!
I can't believe they aren't allowed to use phones at camp.
They probably have to pee in an outhouse and churn their own butter too.
Sigh...

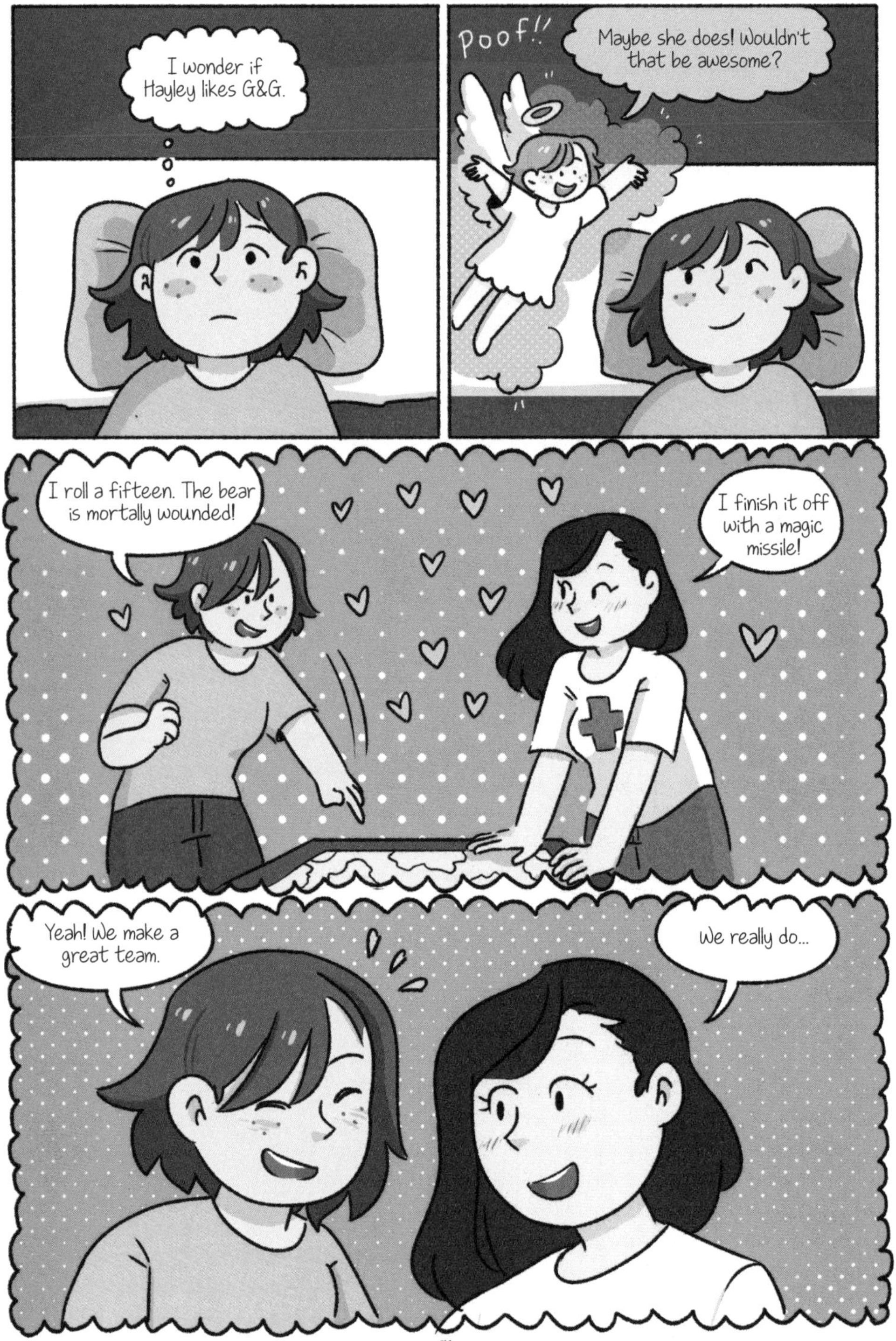
I wonder if Hayley likes G&G.
POOF!!
Maybe she does! Wouldn't that be awesome?
I roll a fifteen. The bear is mortally wounded!
I finish it off with a magic missile!
Yeah! We make a great team.
We really do...

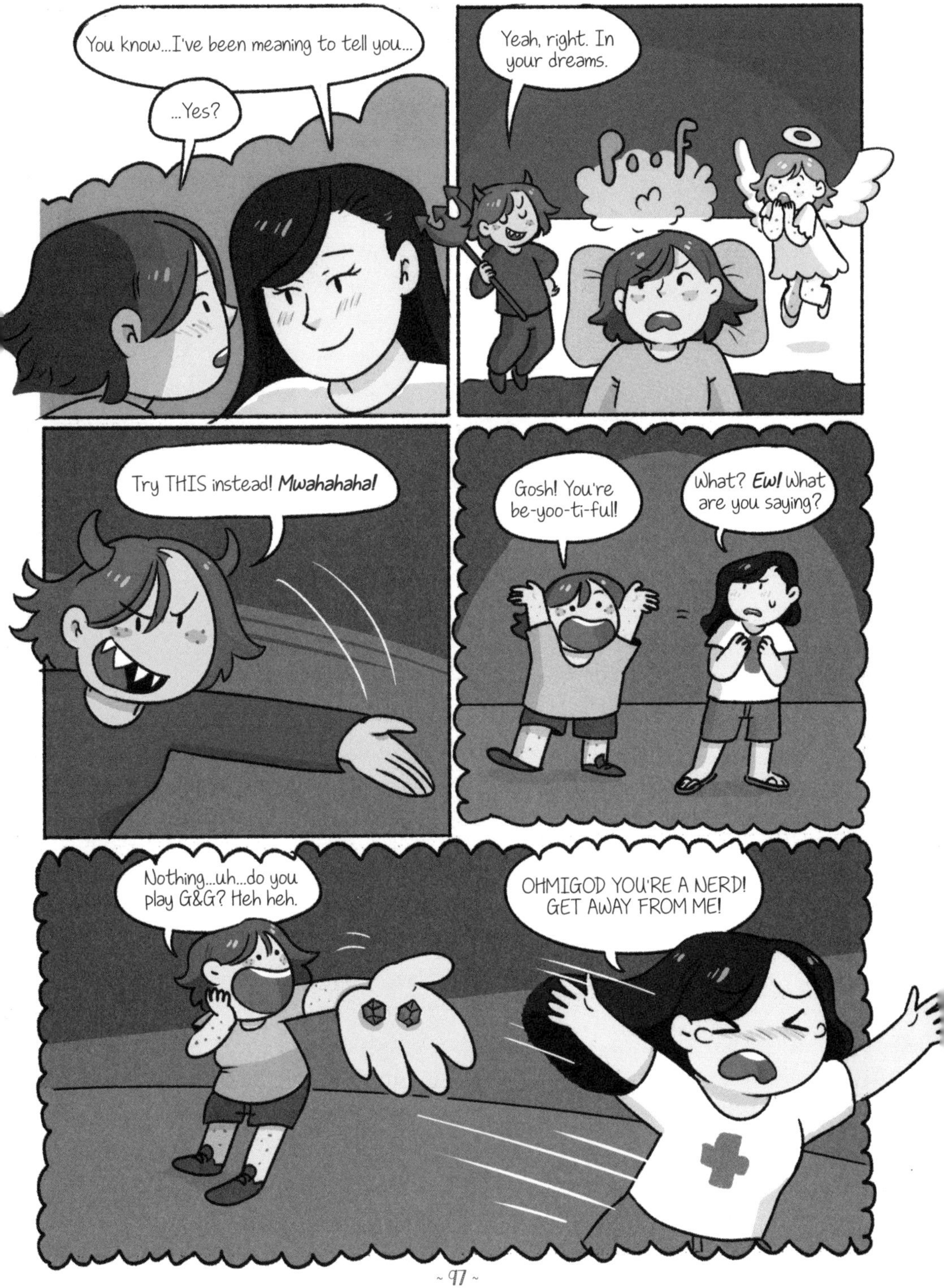
You know...I've been meaning to tell you...
...Yes?
Yeah, right. In your dreams.
POOF
Try THIS instead! **Mwahahaha!**
Gosh! You're be-yoo-ti-ful!
What? **Ew!** What are you saying?
Nothing...uh...do you play G&G? Heh heh.
OHMIGOD YOU'RE A NERD! GET AWAY FROM ME!

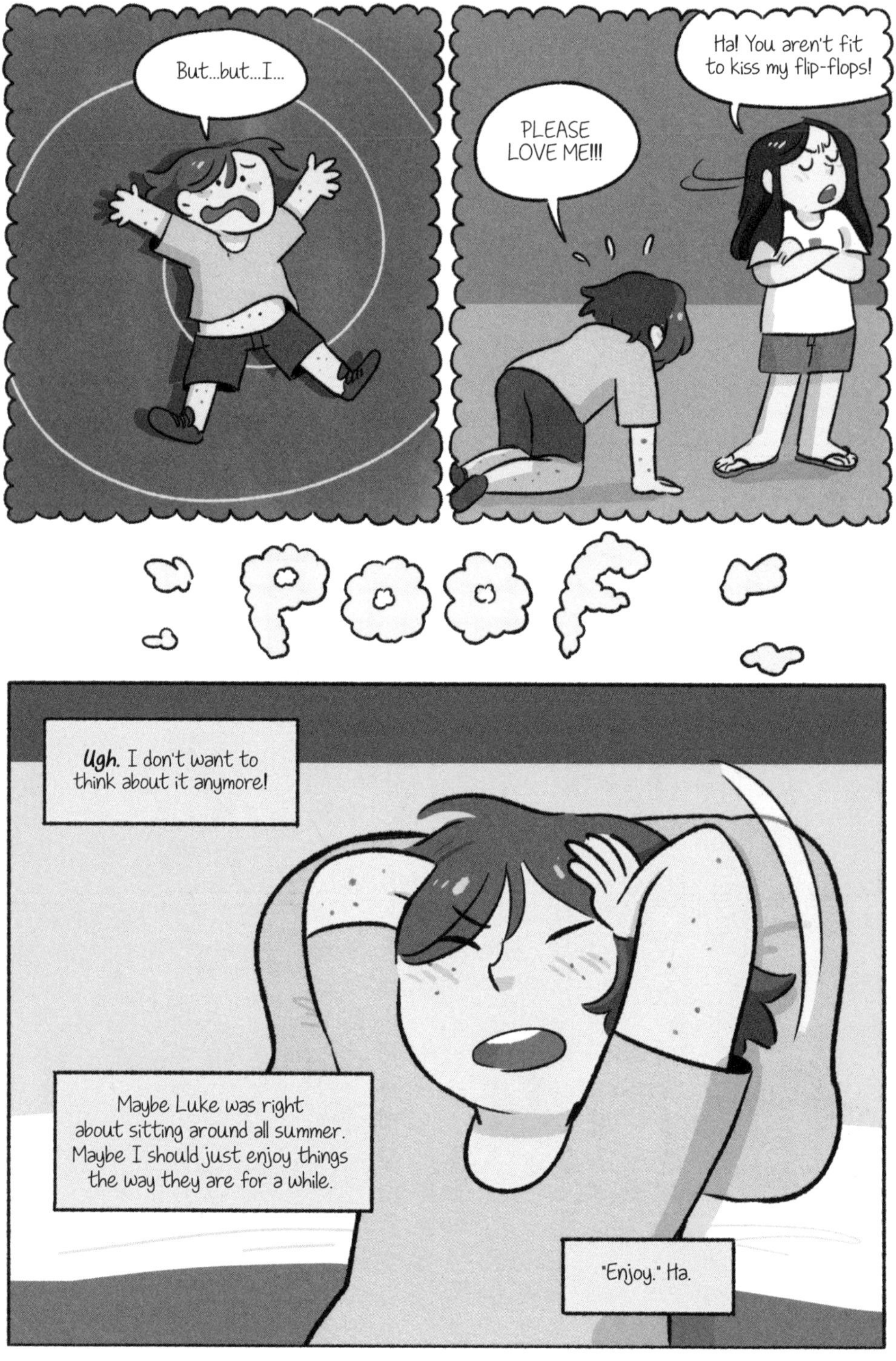
But...but...I...
PLEASE LOVE ME!!!
Ha! You aren't fit to kiss my flip-flops!
POOF
Ugh. I don't want to think about it anymore!
Maybe Luke was right about sitting around all summer. Maybe I should just enjoy things the way they are for a while.
"Enjoy." Ha.

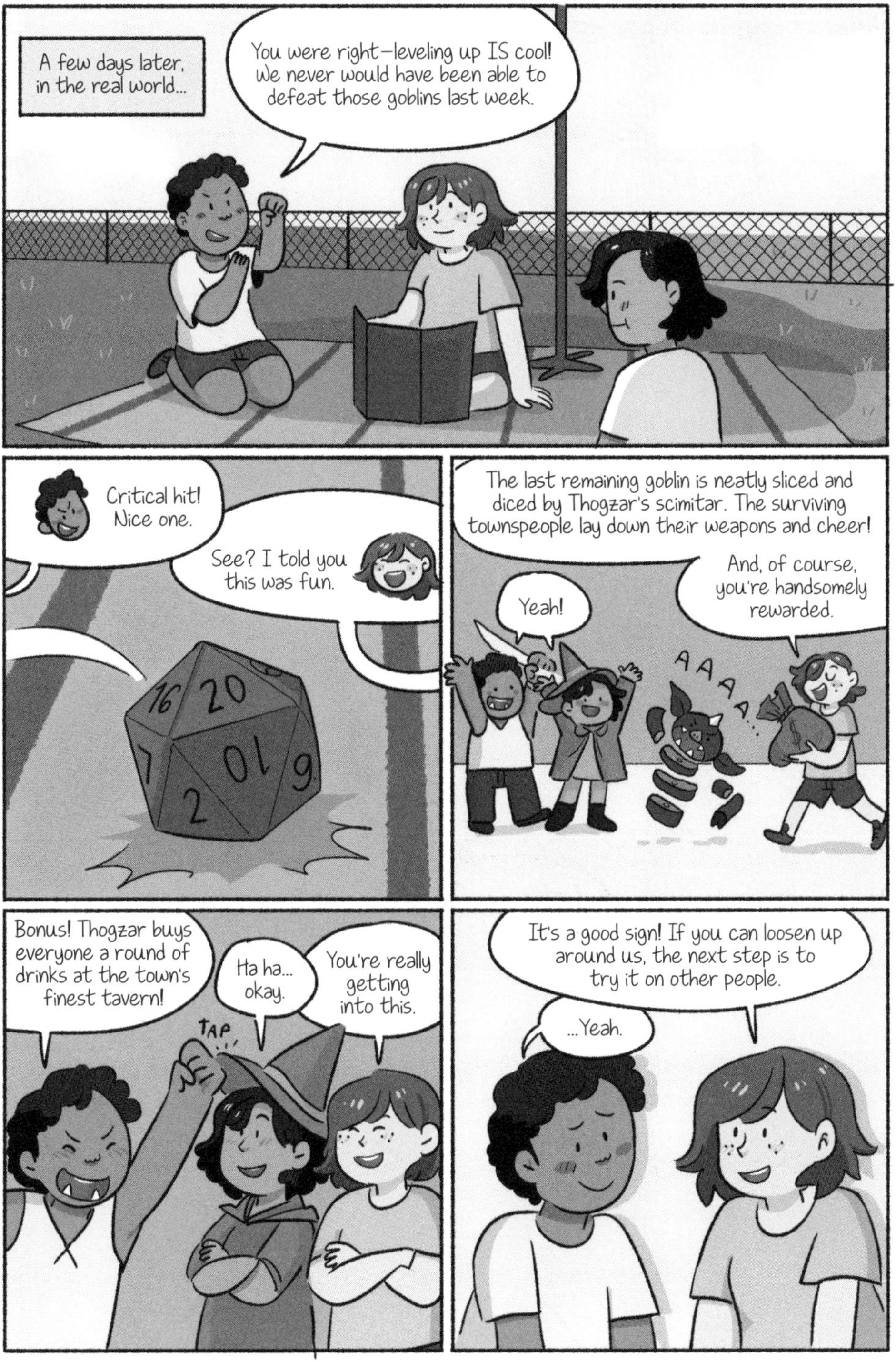
A few days later, in the real world...
You were right—leveling up IS cool! We never would have been able to defeat those goblins last week.
Critical hit! Nice one.
See? I told you this was fun.
16
20
7
10
9
2
The last remaining goblin is neatly sliced and diced by Thogzar's scimitar. The surviving townspeople lay down their weapons and cheer!
And, of course, you're handsomely rewarded.
Yeah!
AAAAA...
Bonus! Thogzar buys everyone a round of drinks at the town's finest tavern!
Ha ha... okay.
You're really getting into this.
TAP
It's a good sign! If you can loosen up around us, the next step is to try it on other people.
...Yeah.

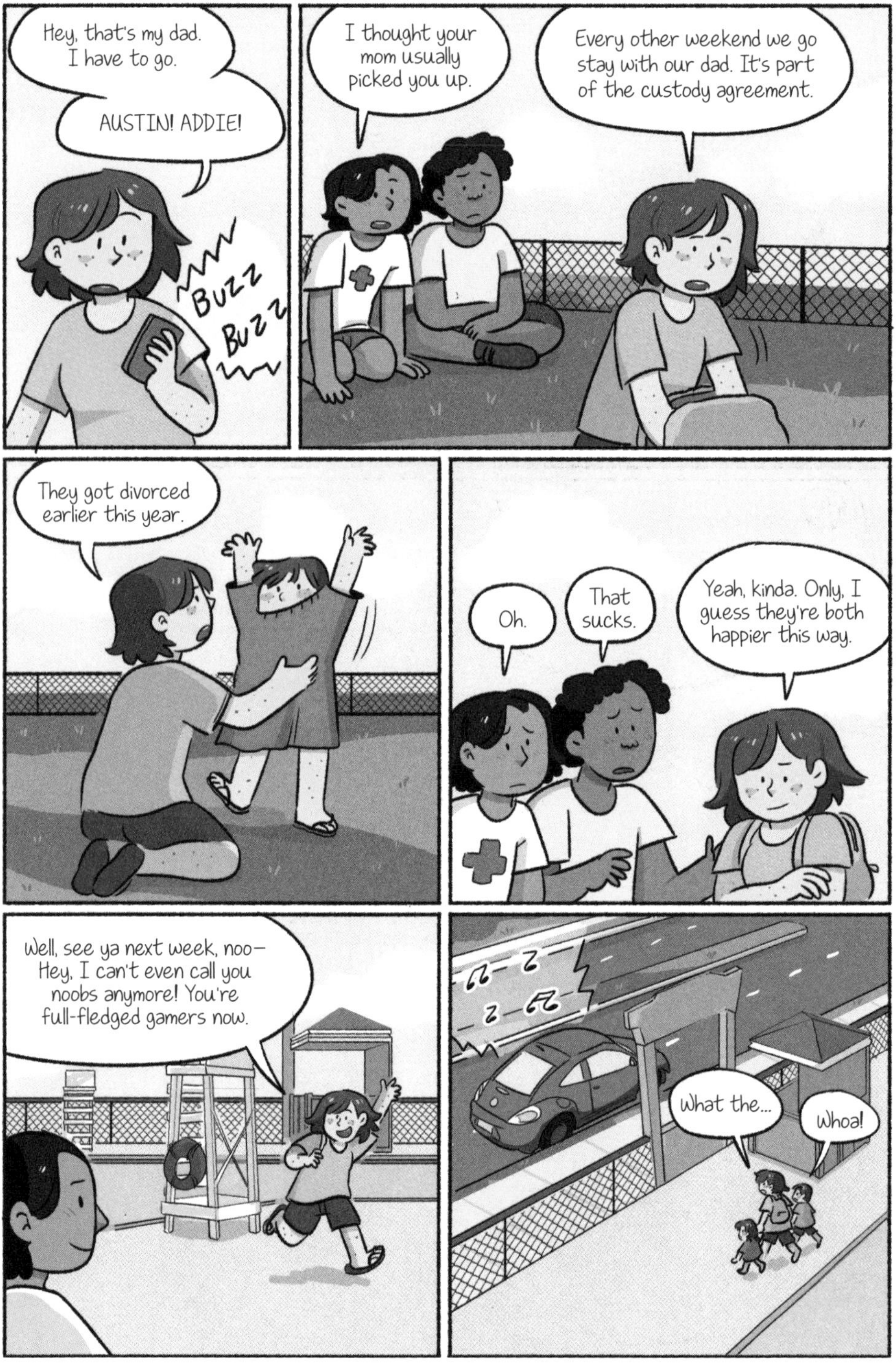
Hey, that's my dad. I have to go.
AUSTIN! ADDIE!
BUZZ
BUZZ
I thought your mom usually picked you up.
Every other weekend we go stay with our dad. It's part of the custody agreement.
They got divorced earlier this year.
Oh.
That sucks.
Yeah, kinda. Only, I guess they're both happier this way.
Well, see ya next week, noo— Hey, I can't even call you noobs anymore! You're full-fledged gamers now.
What the...
Whoa!

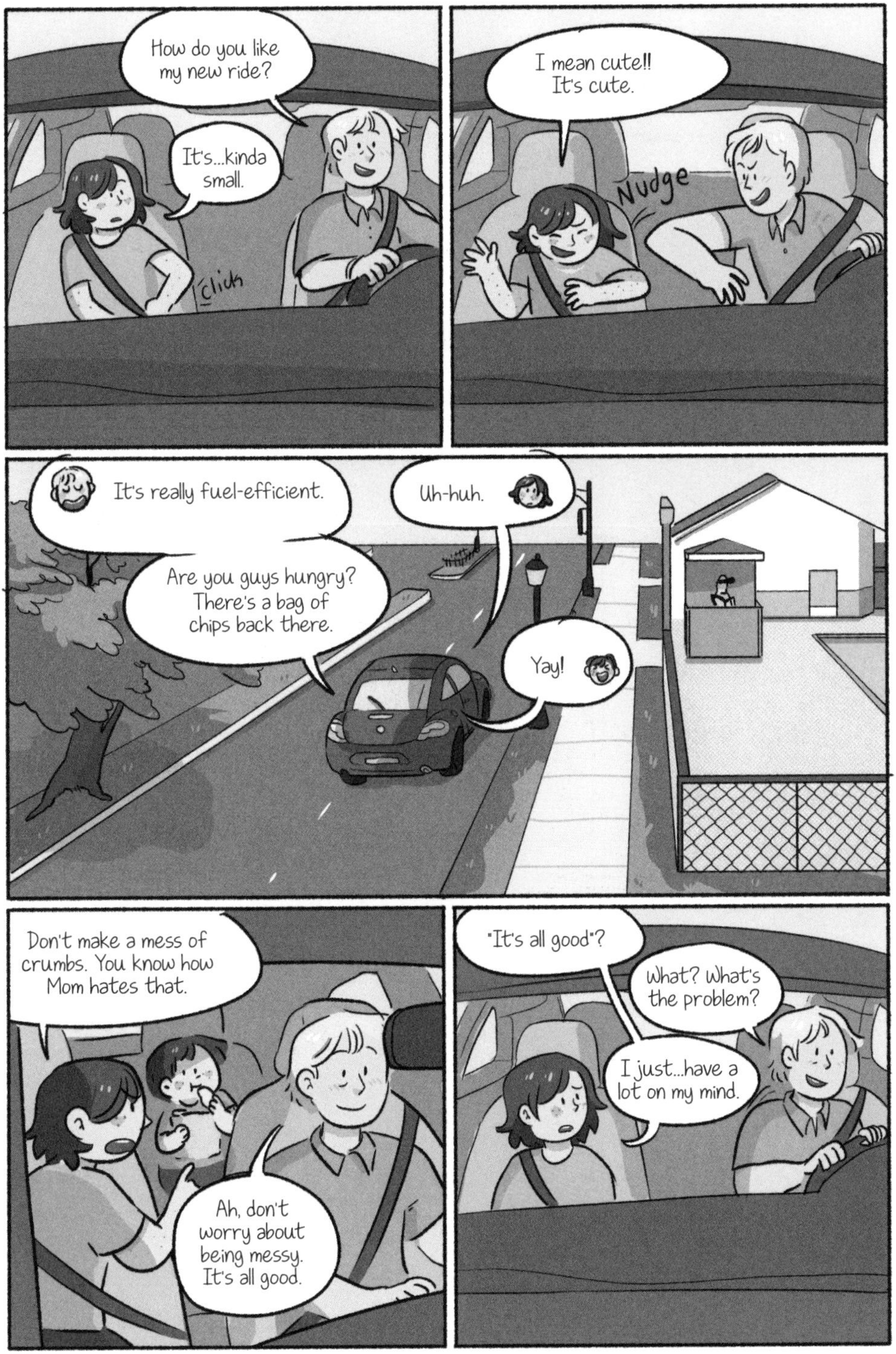
How do you like my new ride?
It's...kinda small.
click
I mean cute!! It's cute.
Nudge
It's really fuel-efficient.
Uh-huh.
Are you guys hungry? There's a bag of chips back there.
Yay!
Don't make a mess of crumbs. You know how Mom hates that.
Ah, don't worry about being messy. It's all good.
"It's all good"?
What? What's the problem?
I just...have a lot on my mind.

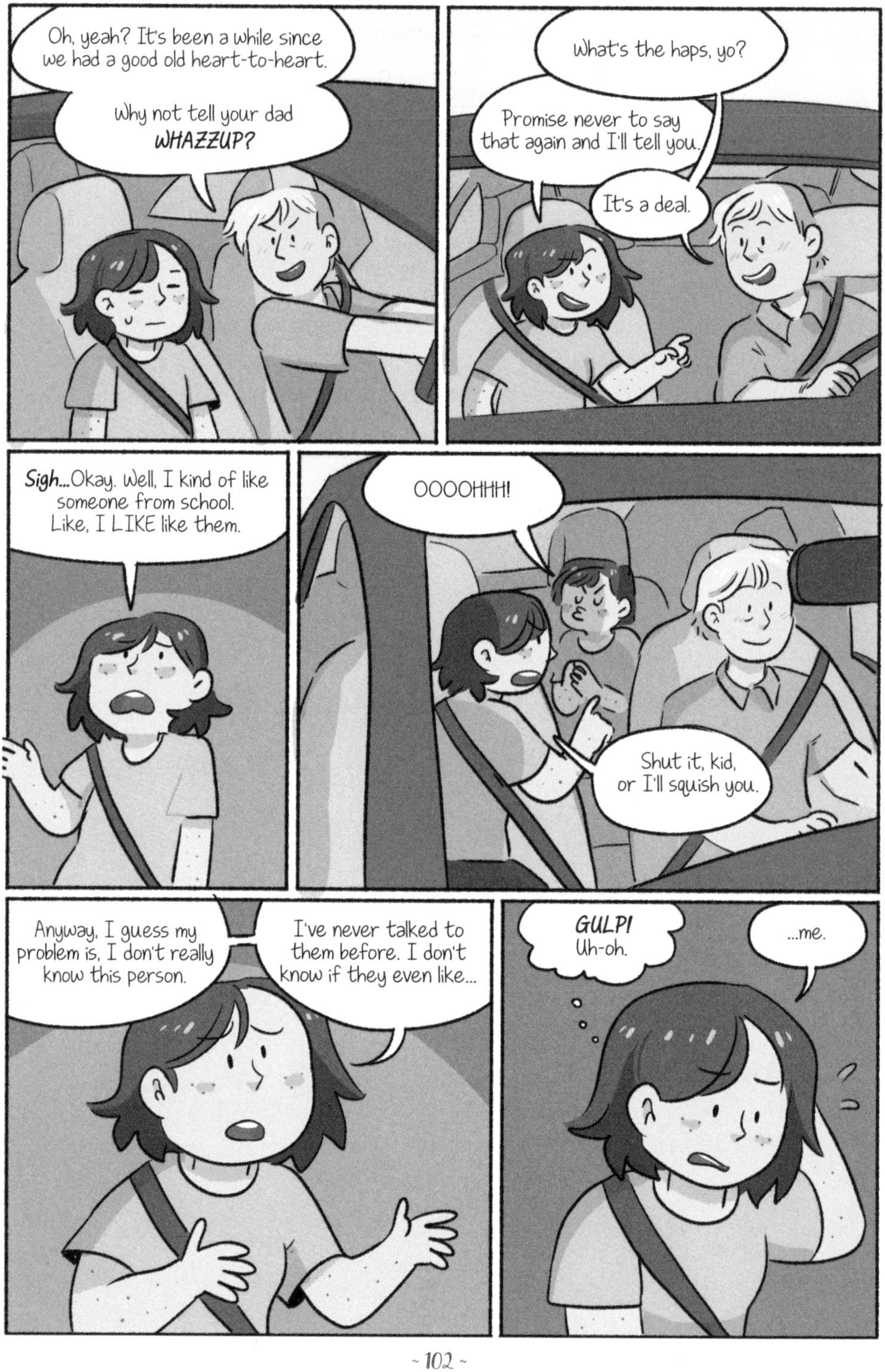
Oh, yeah? It's been a while since we had a good old heart-to-heart.
Why not tell your dad WHAZZUP?
What's the haps, yo?
Promise never to say that again and I'll tell you.
It's a deal.
Sigh...Okay. Well, I kind of like someone from school. Like, I LIKE like them.
OOOOHHH!
Shut it, kid, or I'll squish you.
Anyway, I guess my problem is, I don't really know this person.
I've never talked to them before. I don't know if they even like...
GULP! Uh-oh.
...me.

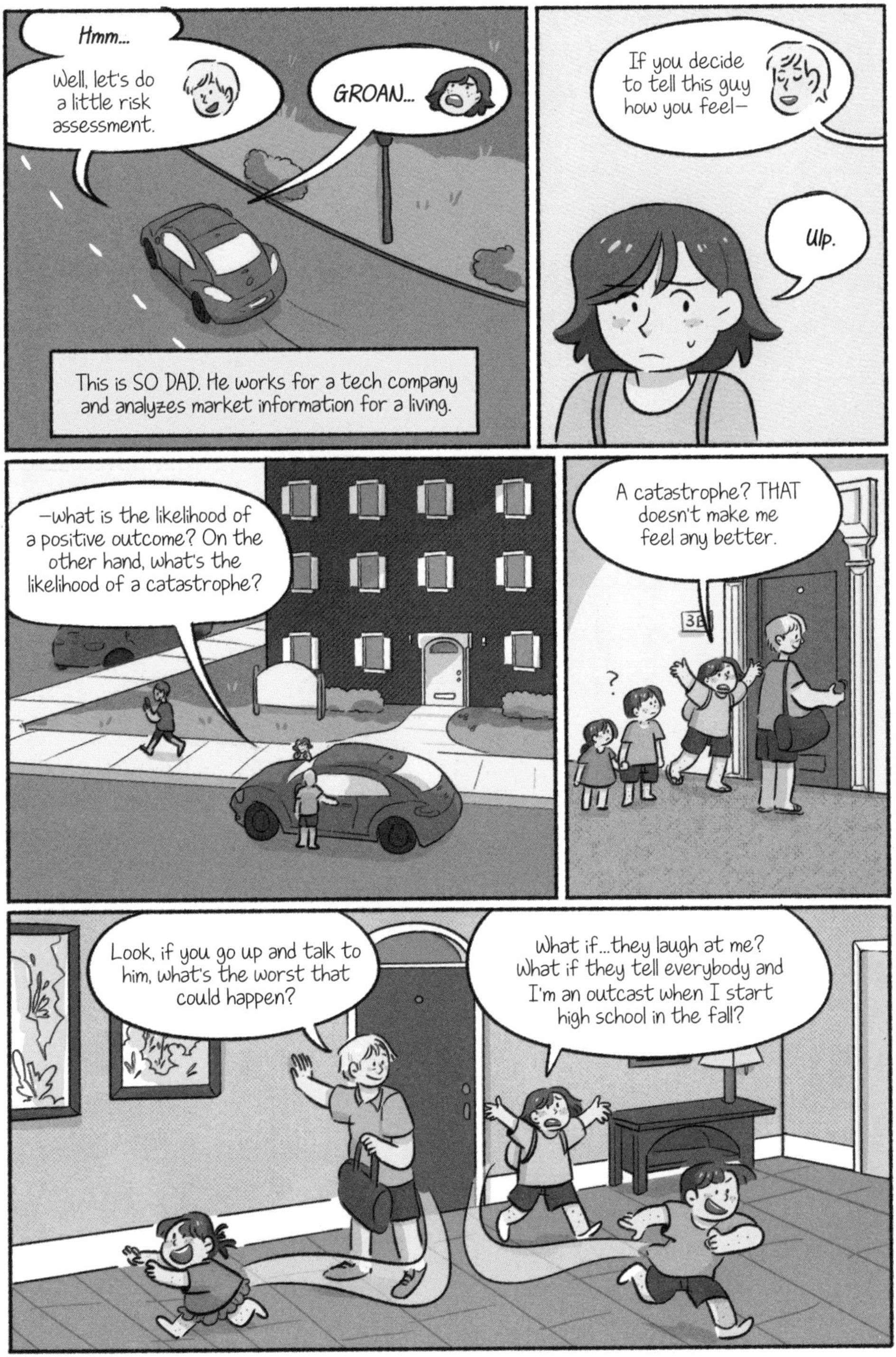
Hmm...
Well, let's do a little risk assessment.
GROAN...
This is SO DAD. He works for a tech company and analyzes market information for a living.
If you decide to tell this guy how you feel—
Ulp.
—what is the likelihood of a positive outcome? On the other hand, what's the likelihood of a catastrophe?
A catastrophe? THAT doesn't make me feel any better.
3B
?
Look, if you go up and talk to him, what's the worst that could happen?
What if...they laugh at me? What if they tell everybody and I'm an outcast when I start high school in the fall?

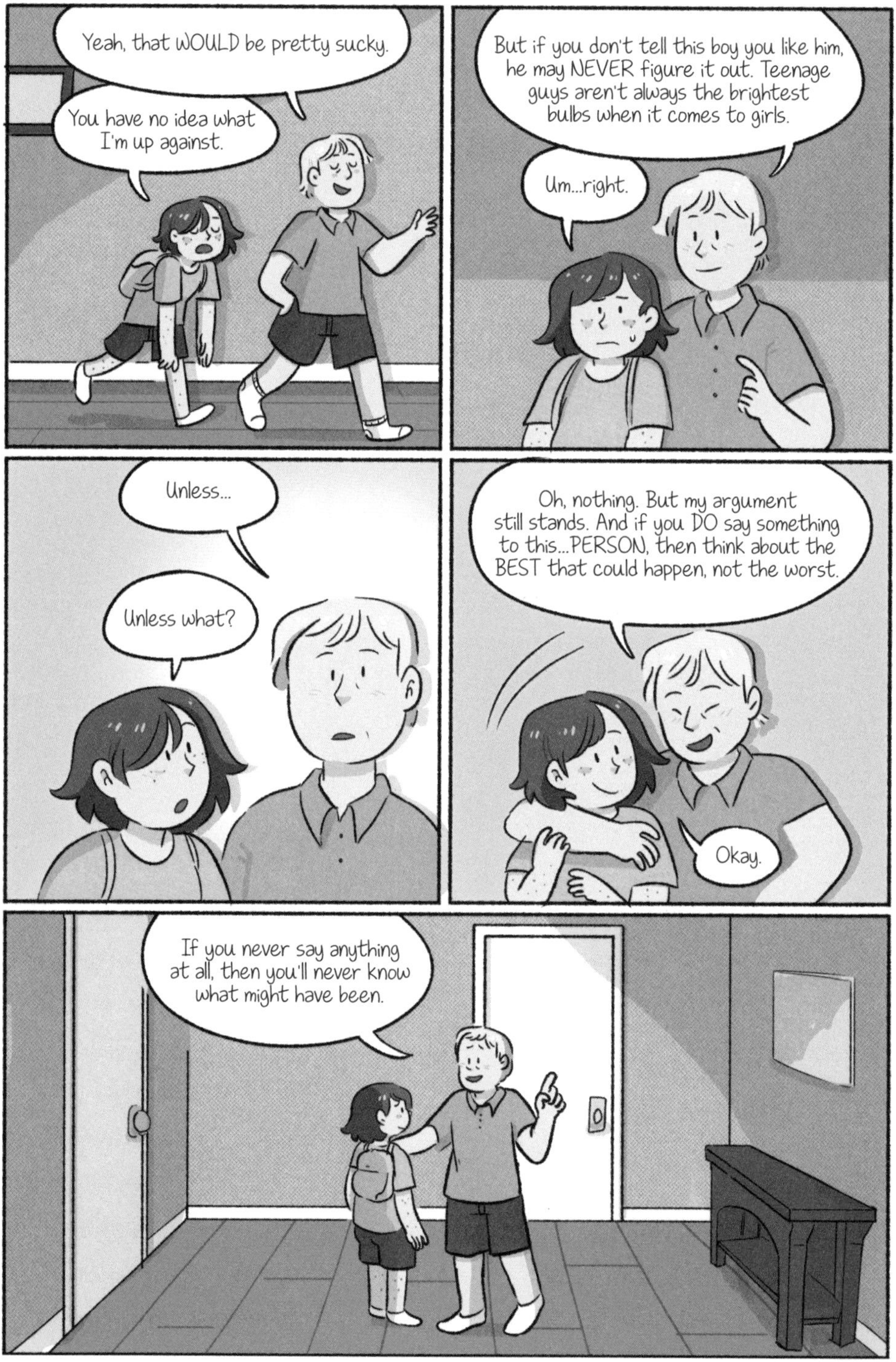
Yeah, that WOULD be pretty sucky.
You have no idea what I'm up against.
But if you don't tell this boy you like him, he may NEVER figure it out. Teenage guys aren't always the brightest bulbs when it comes to girls.
Um...right.
Unless...
Unless what?
Oh, nothing. But my argument still stands. And if you DO say something to this...PERSON, then think about the BEST that could happen, not the worst.
Okay.
If you never say anything at all, then you'll never know what might have been.

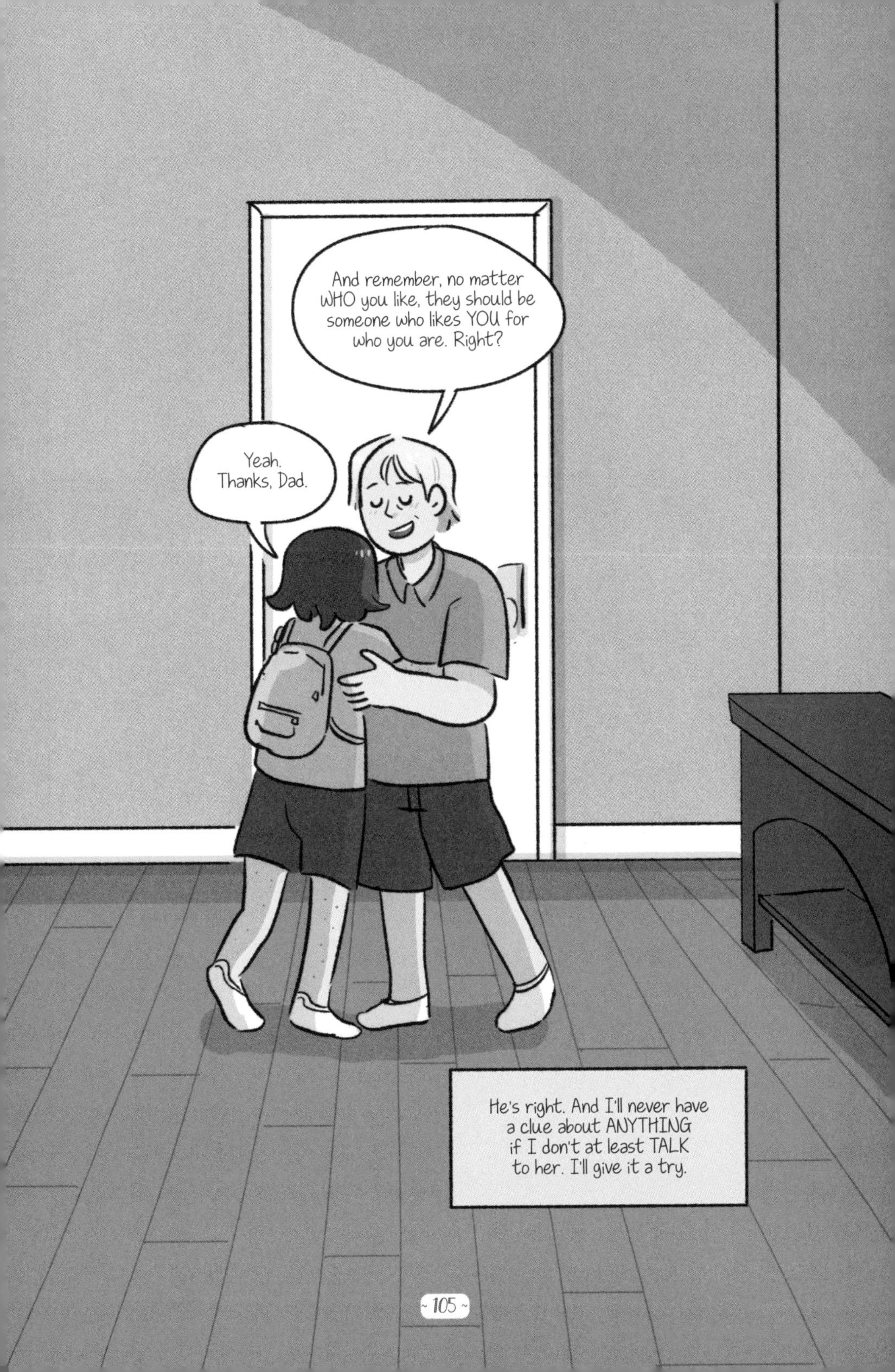
And remember, no matter WHO you like, they should be someone who likes YOU for who you are. Right?
Yeah. Thanks, Dad.
He's right. And I'll never have a clue about ANYTHING if I don't at least TALK to her. I'll give it a try.

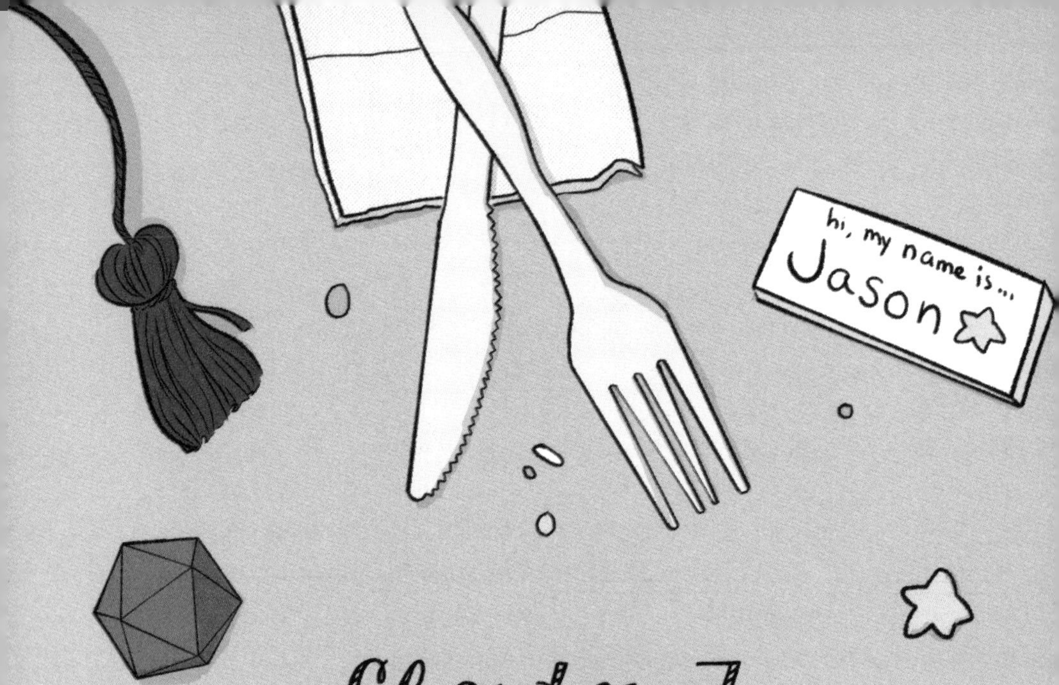
hi, my name is...
Jason

Chapter 7

Jason vs. the Game Master

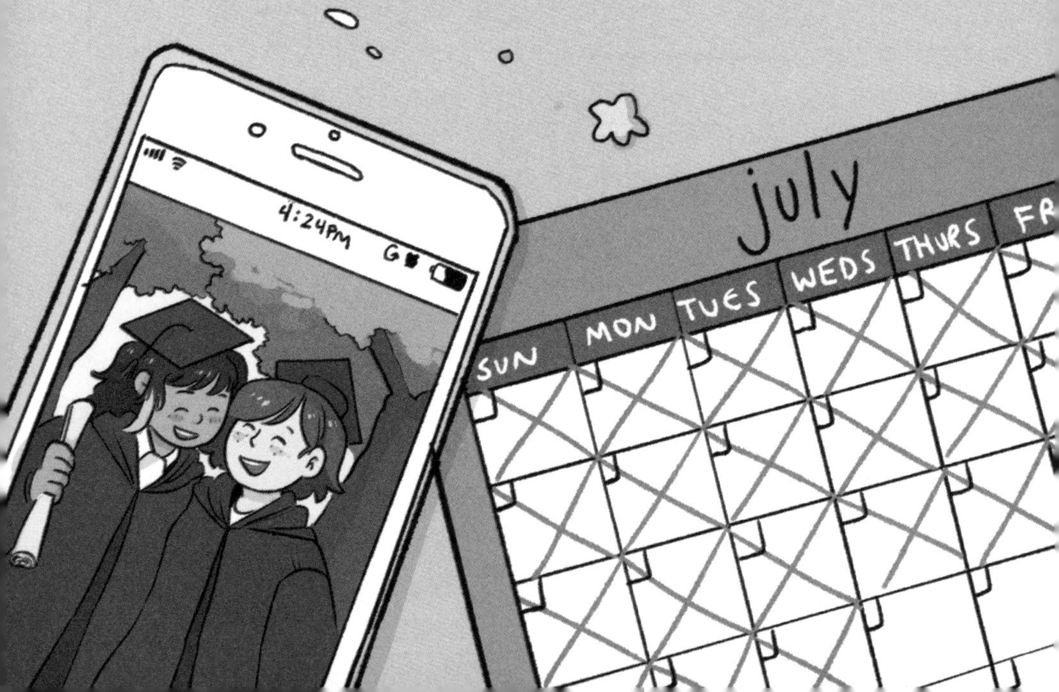
4:24PM
july
SUN
MON
TUES
WEDS
THURS
FR

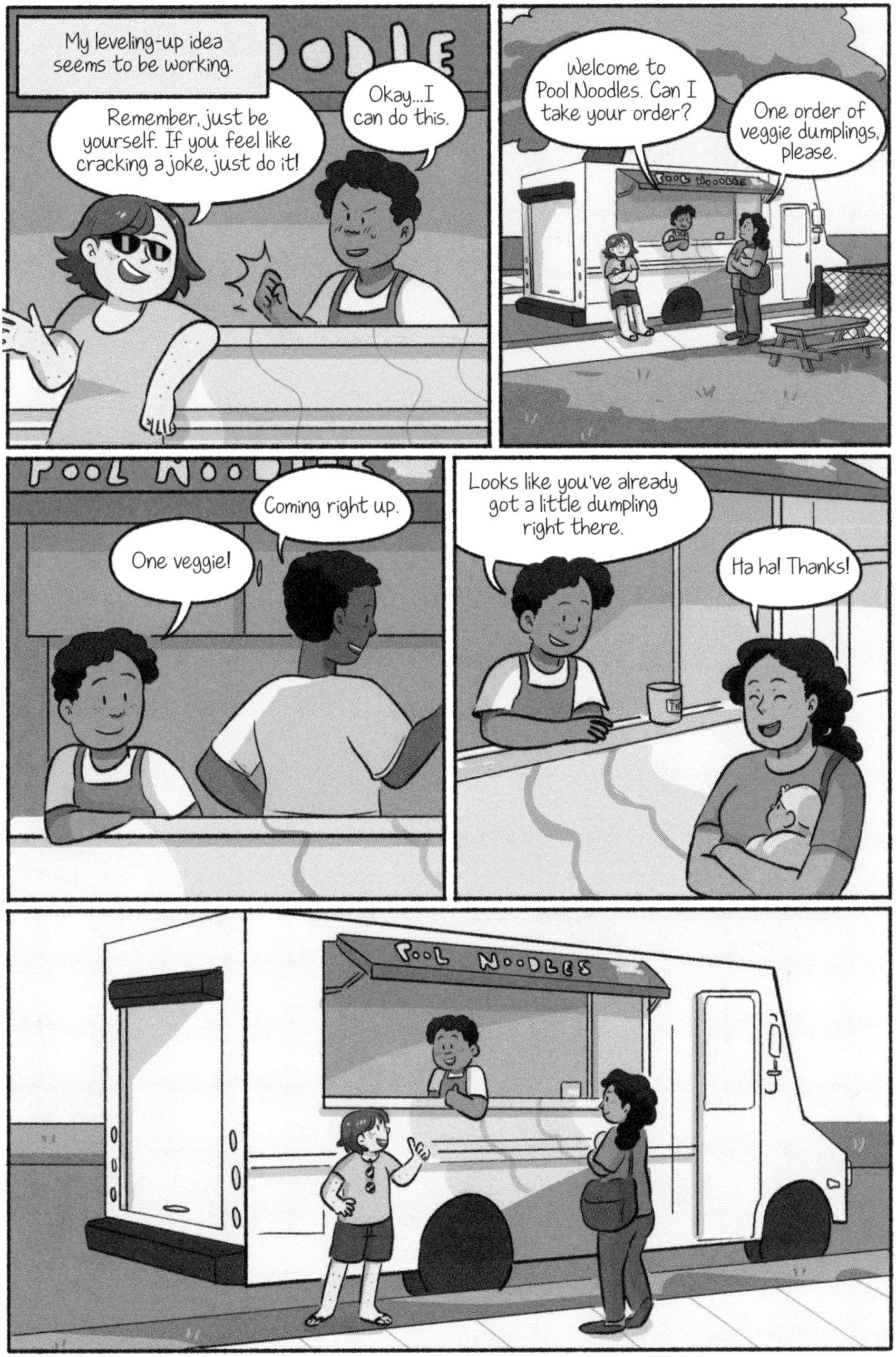
My leveling-up idea seems to be working.
Remember, just be yourself. If you feel like cracking a joke, just do it!
Okay...I can do this.
Welcome to Pool Noodles. Can I take your order?
One order of veggie dumplings, please.
POOL NOODLES
Coming right up.
One veggie!
Looks like you've already got a little dumpling right there.
Ha ha! Thanks!
POOL NOODLES

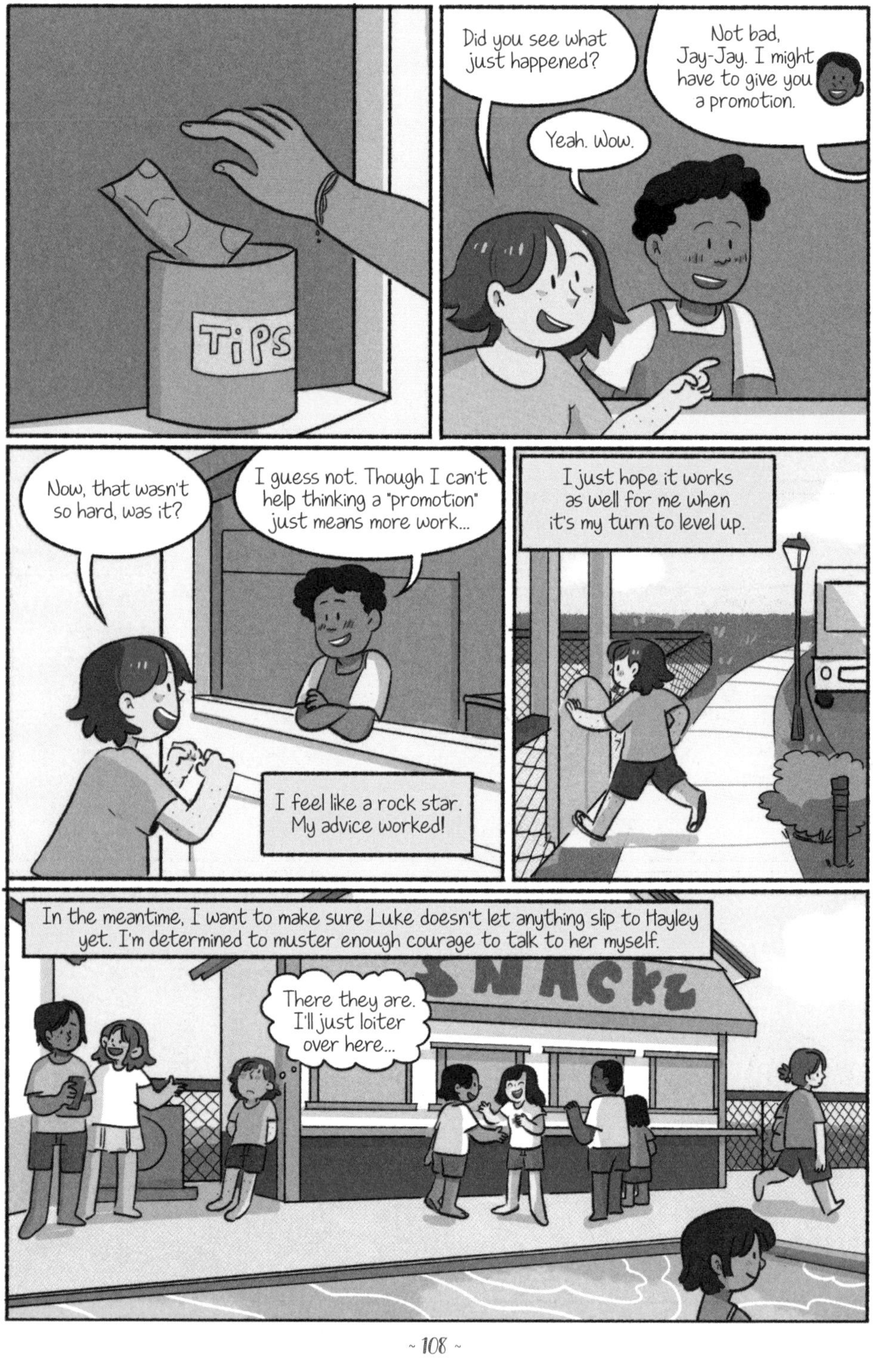
Tips
Did you see what just happened?
Yeah. Wow.
Not bad, Jay-Jay. I might have to give you a promotion.
Now, that wasn't so hard, was it?
I guess not. Though I can't help thinking a "promotion" just means more work...
I feel like a rock star. My advice worked!
I just hope it works as well for me when it's my turn to level up.
In the meantime, I want to make sure Luke doesn't let anything slip to Hayley yet. I'm determined to muster enough courage to talk to her myself.
SNACKS
There they are. I'll just loiter over here...

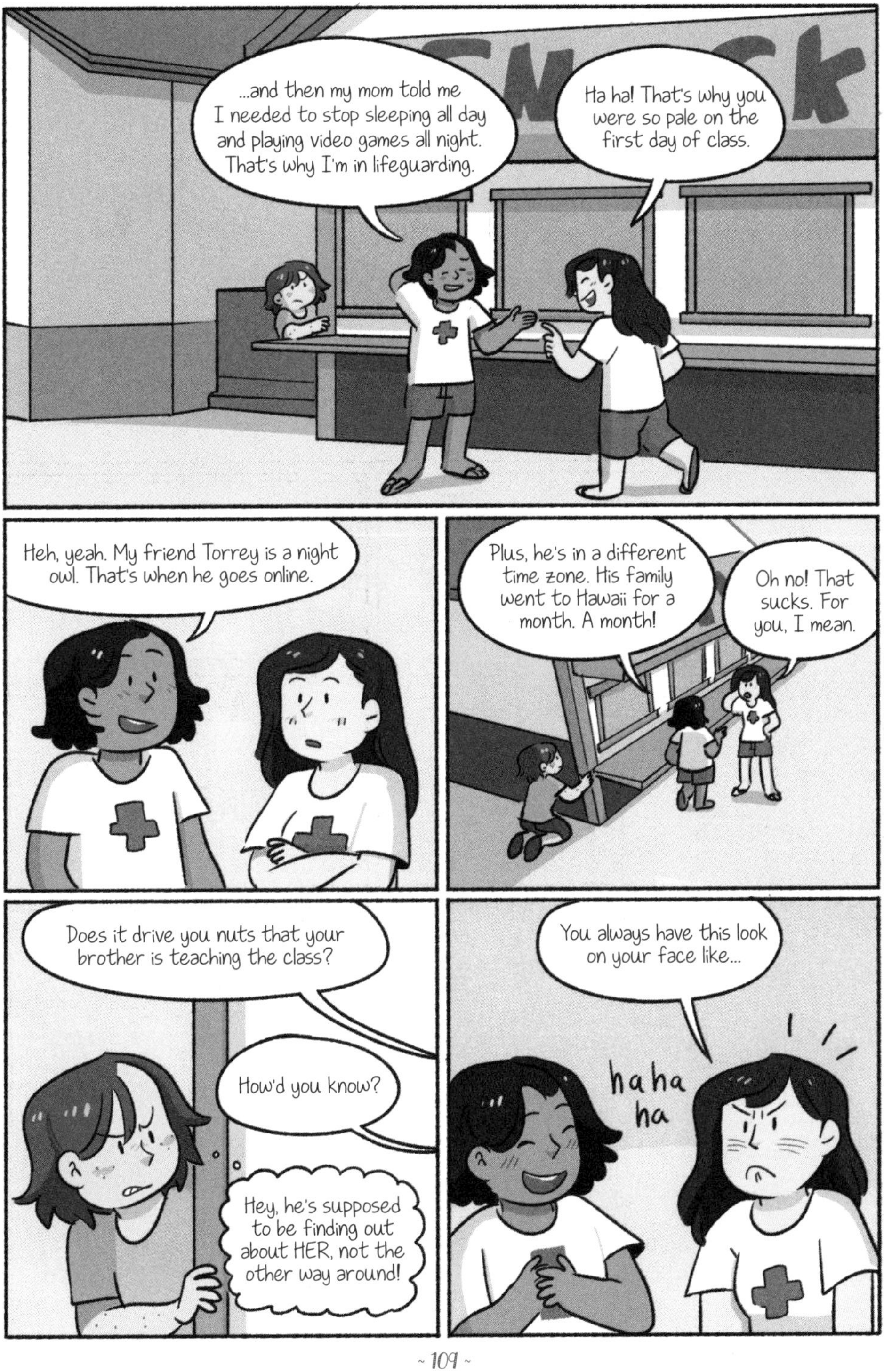
SNACK
...and then my mom told me I needed to stop sleeping all day and playing video games all night. That's why I'm in lifeguarding.
Ha ha! That's why you were so pale on the first day of class.
Heh, yeah. My friend Torrey is a night owl. That's when he goes online.
Plus, he's in a different time zone. His family went to Hawaii for a month. A month!
Oh no! That sucks. For you, I mean.
Does it drive you nuts that your brother is teaching the class?
How'd you know?
Hey, he's supposed to be finding out about HER, not the other way around!
You always have this look on your face like...
ha ha ha

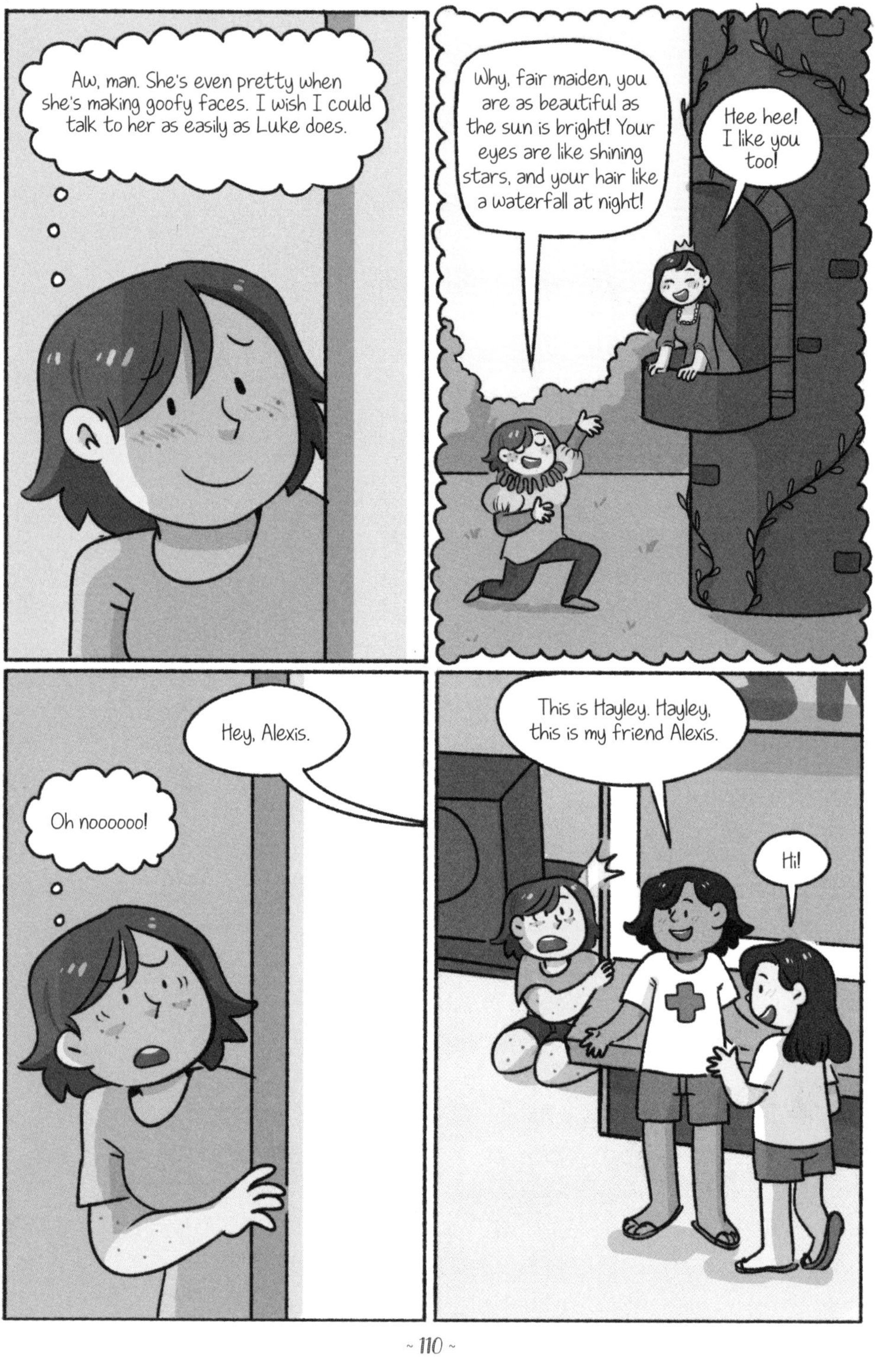
Aw, man. She's even pretty when she's making goofy faces. I wish I could talk to her as easily as Luke does.
Why, fair maiden, you are as beautiful as the sun is bright! Your eyes are like shining stars, and your hair like a waterfall at night!
Hee hee! I like you too!
Hey, Alexis.
Oh noooooo!
This is Hayley. Hayley, this is my friend Alexis.
Hi!

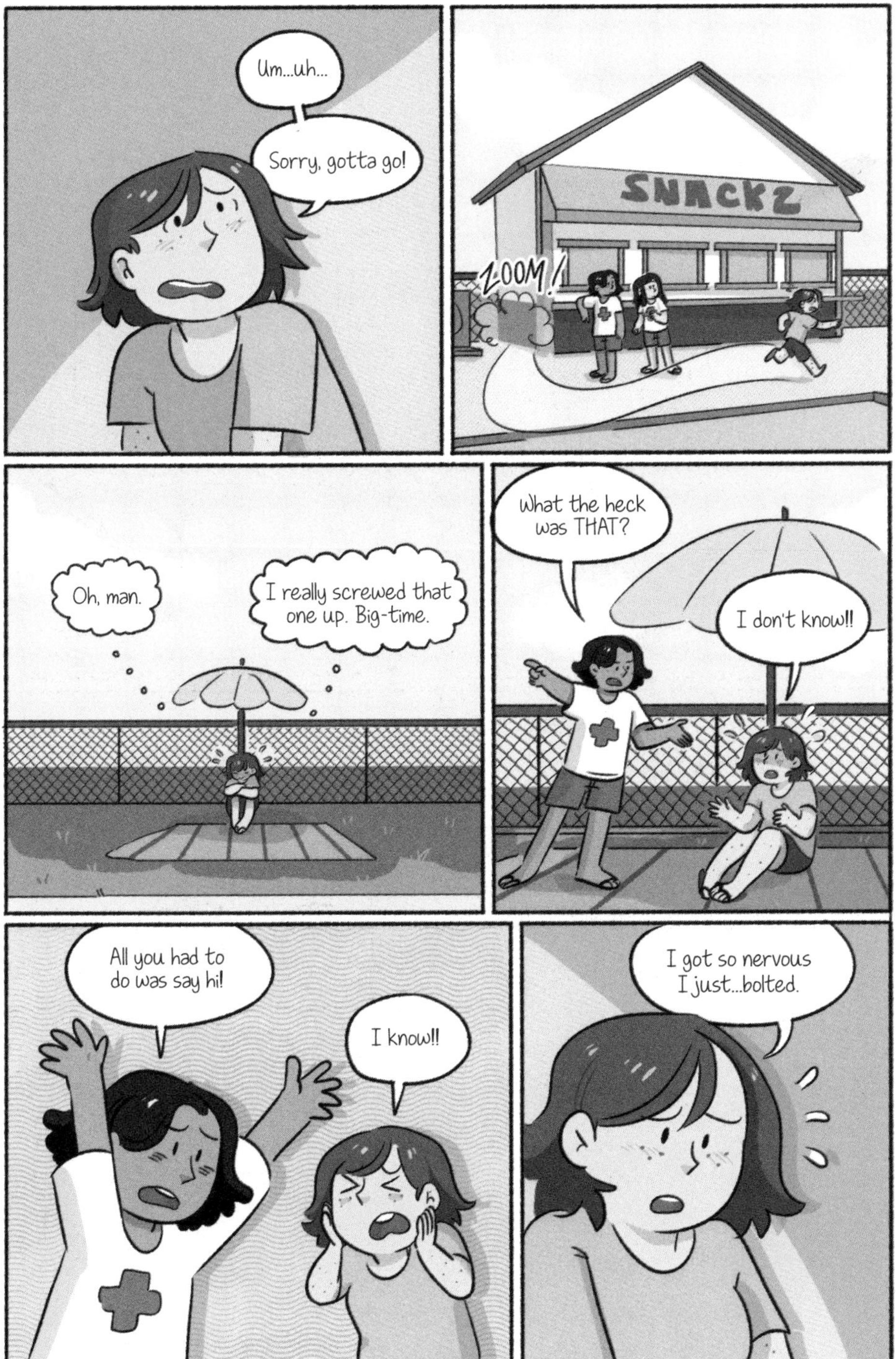
Um...uh...
Sorry, gotta go!
SNACKZ
ZOOM!
Oh, man.
I really screwed that one up. Big-time.
What the heck was THAT?
I don't know!!
All you had to do was say hi!
I know!!
I got so nervous I just...bolted.

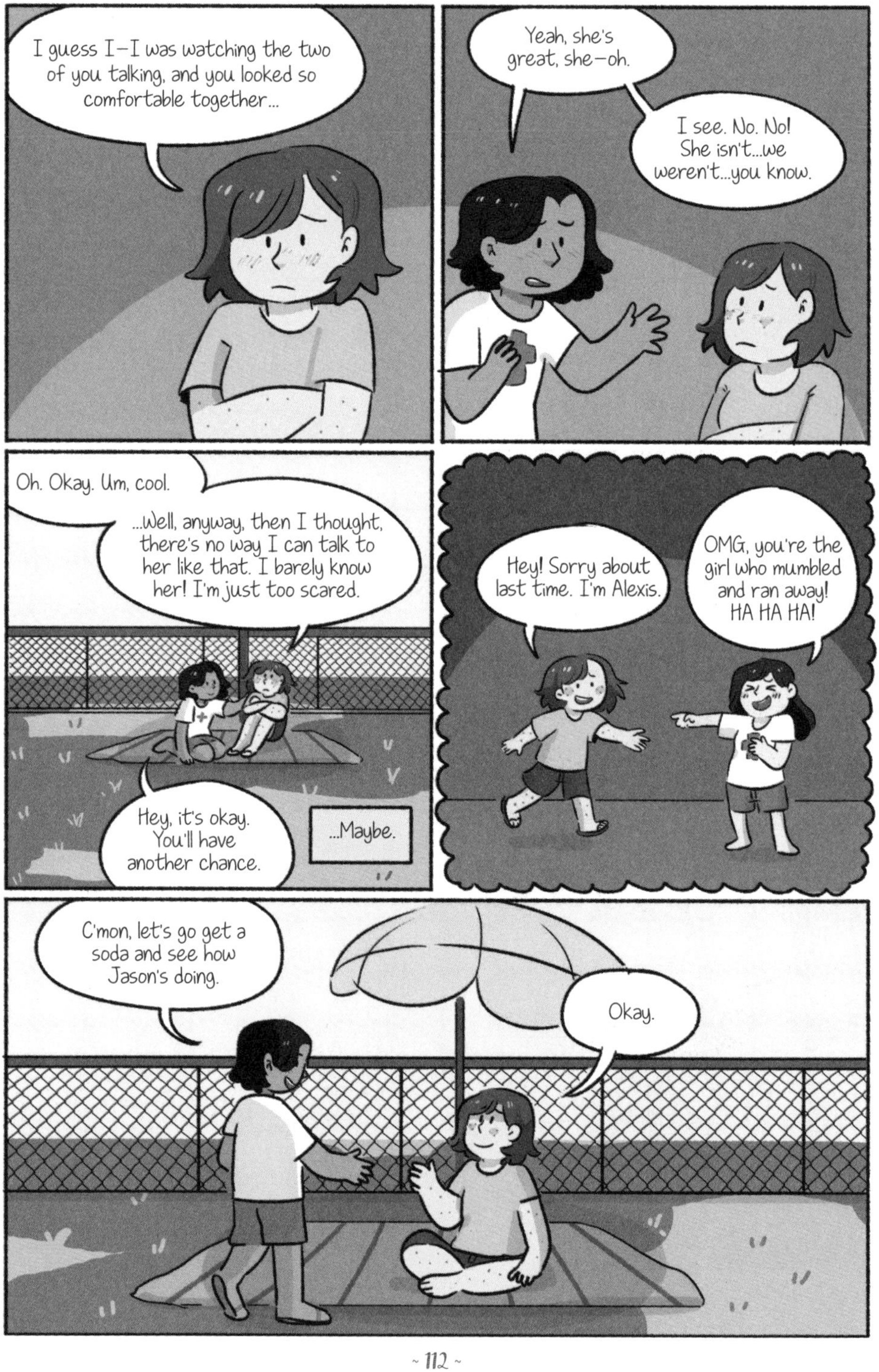

I guess I—I was watching the two of you talking, and you looked so comfortable together...
Yeah, she's great, she—oh.
I see. No. No! She isn't...we weren't...you know.
Oh. Okay. Um, cool.
...Well, anyway, then I thought, there's no way I can talk to her like that. I barely know her! I'm just too scared.
Hey, it's okay. You'll have another chance.
...Maybe.
Hey! Sorry about last time. I'm Alexis.
OMG, you're the girl who mumbled and ran away! HA HA HA!
C'mon, let's go get a soda and see how Jason's doing.
Okay.

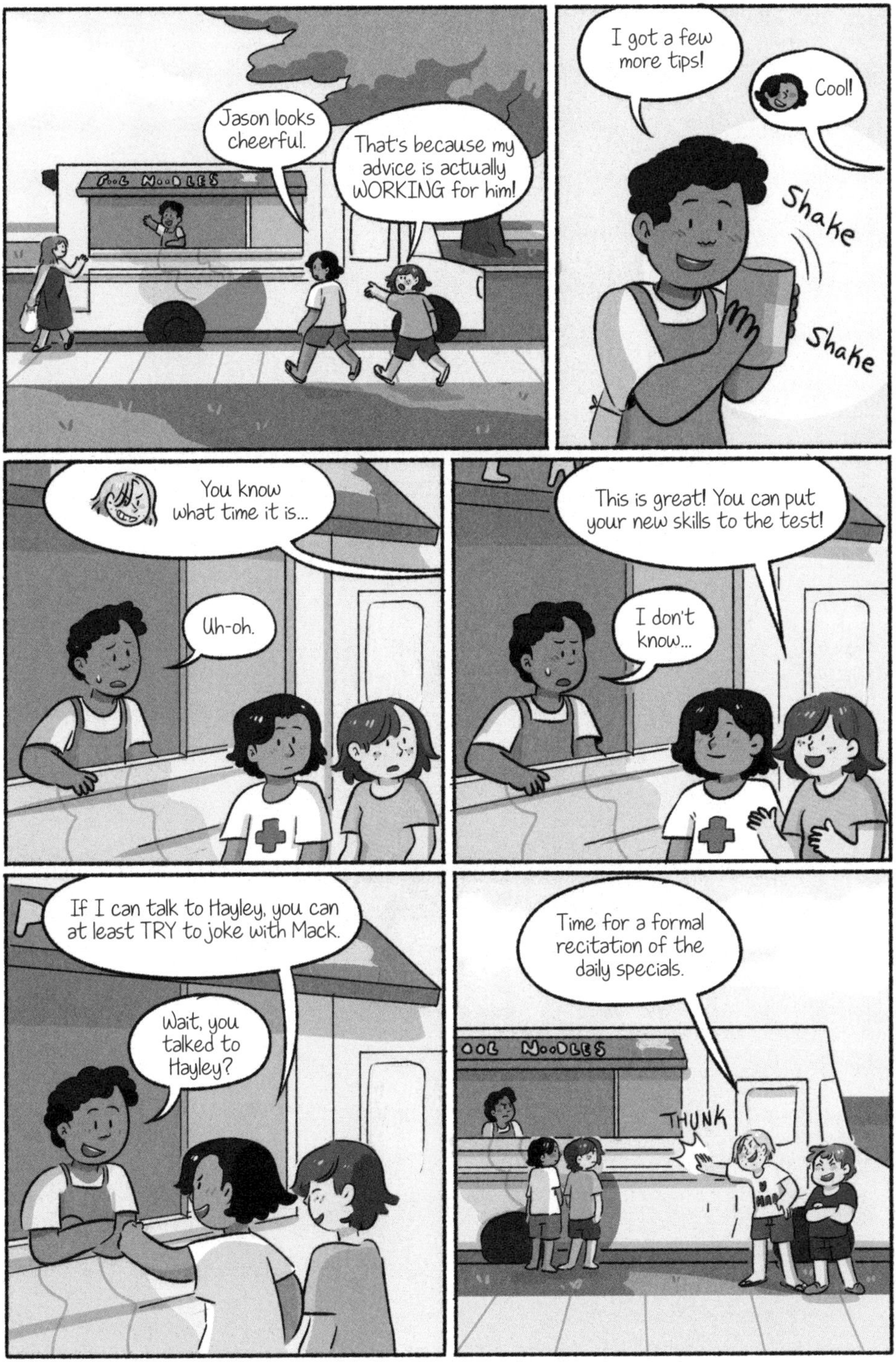
Jason looks cheerful.
That's because my advice is actually WORKING for him!
I got a few more tips!
Cool!
Shake
Shake
You know what time it is...
Uh-oh.
This is great! You can put your new skills to the test!
I don't know...
If I can talk to Hayley, you can at least TRY to joke with Mack.
Wait, you talked to Hayley?
Time for a formal recitation of the daily specials.
THUNK

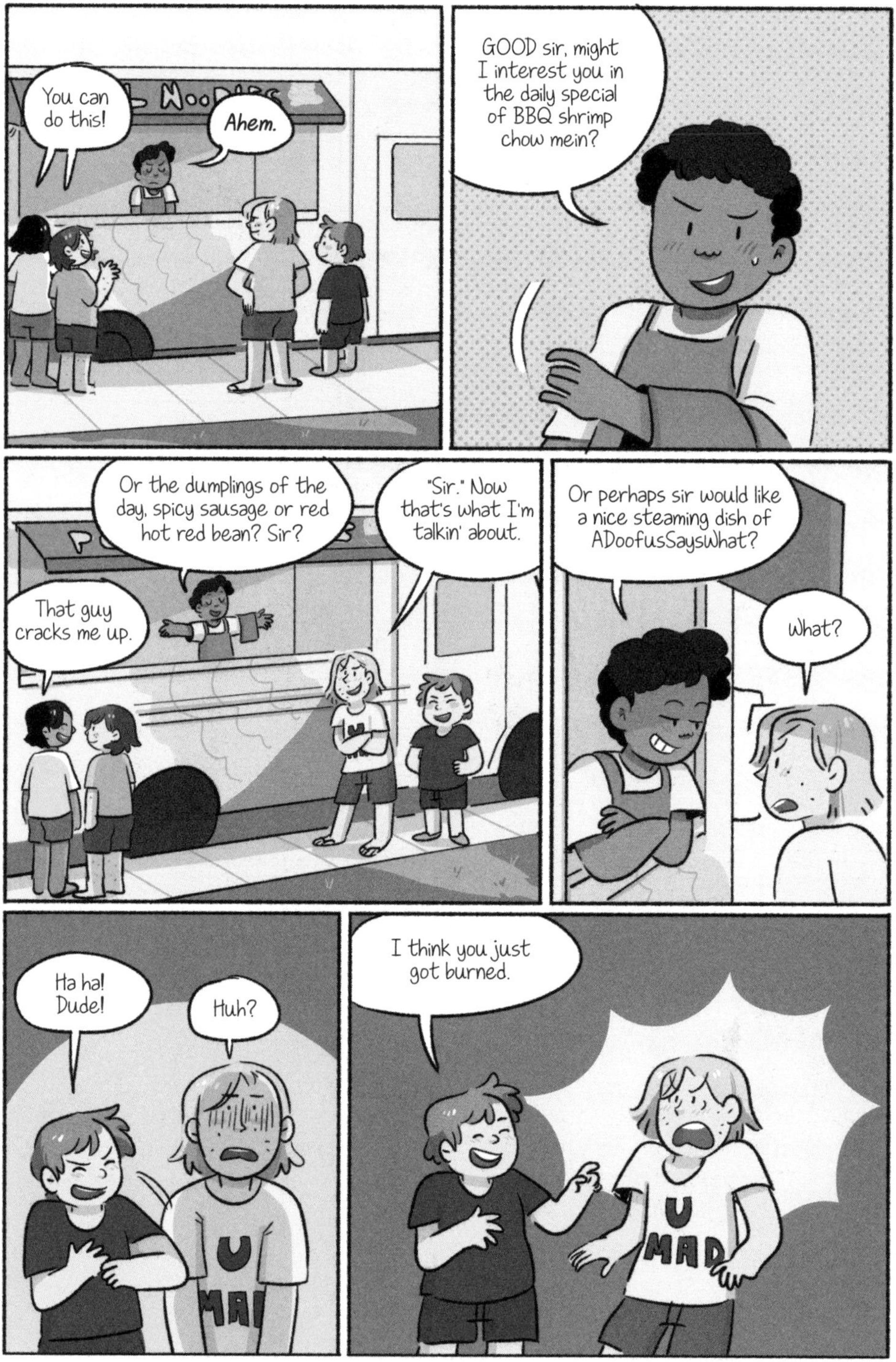
You can do this!
Ahem.
GOOD sir, might I interest you in the daily special of BBQ shrimp chow mein?
Or the dumplings of the day, spicy sausage or red hot red bean? Sir?
"Sir." Now that's what I'm talkin' about.
That guy cracks me up.
Or perhaps sir would like a nice steaming dish of ADoofusSaysWhat?
What?
Ha ha! Dude!
Huh?
U MAD
I think you just got burned.
U MAD

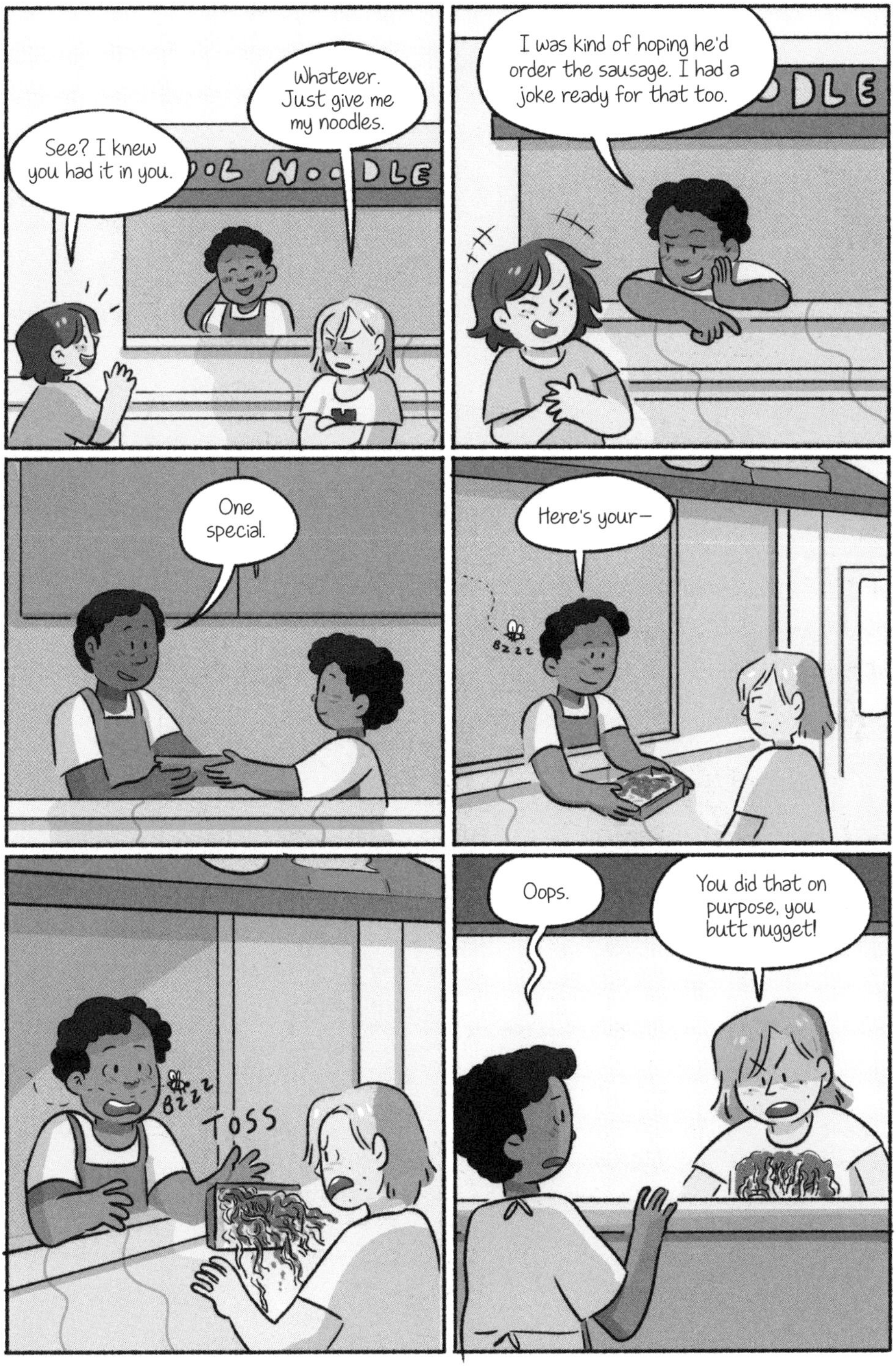
Whatever. Just give me my noodles.
See? I knew you had it in you.
I was kind of hoping he'd order the sausage. I had a joke ready for that too.
One special.
Here's your—
Bzzz
Bzzz
TOSS
Oops.
You did that on purpose, you butt nugget!

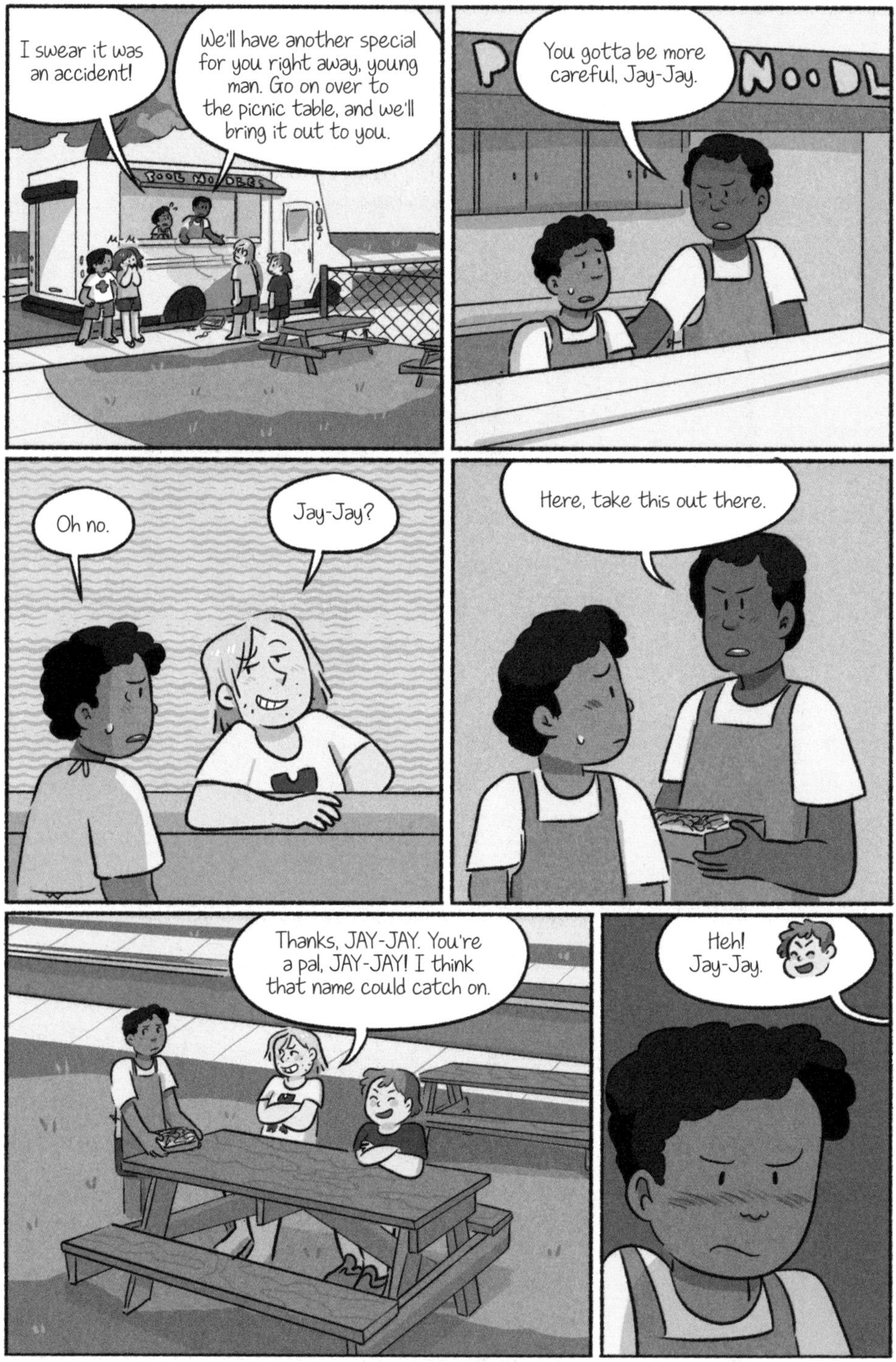
I swear it was an accident!
We'll have another special for you right away, young man. Go on over to the picnic table, and we'll bring it out to you.
You gotta be more careful, Jay-Jay.
Oh no.
Jay-Jay?
Here, take this out there.
Thanks, JAY-JAY. You're a pal, JAY-JAY! I think that name could catch on.
Heh! Jay-Jay.

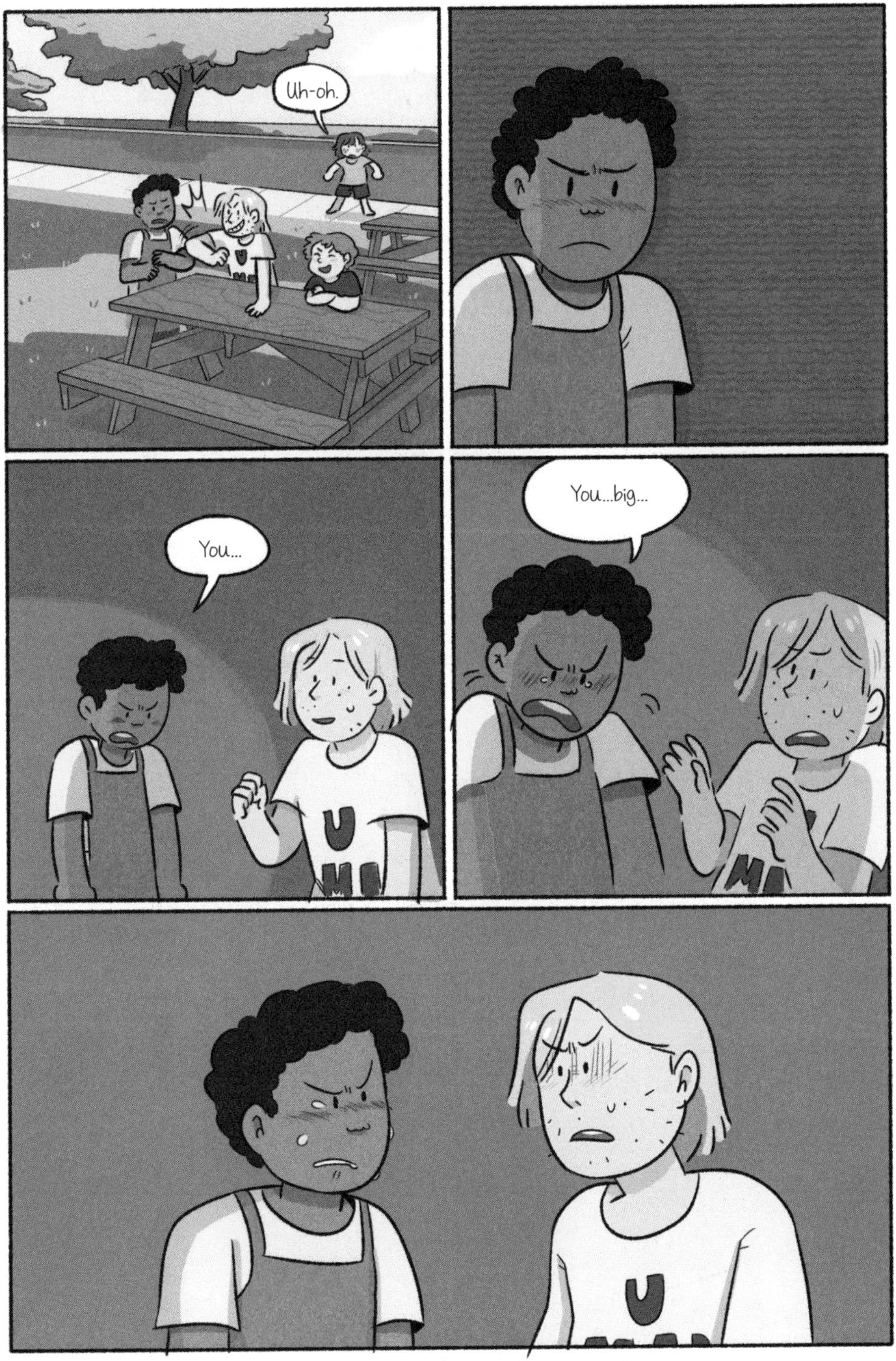
Uh-oh.
You...
You...big...

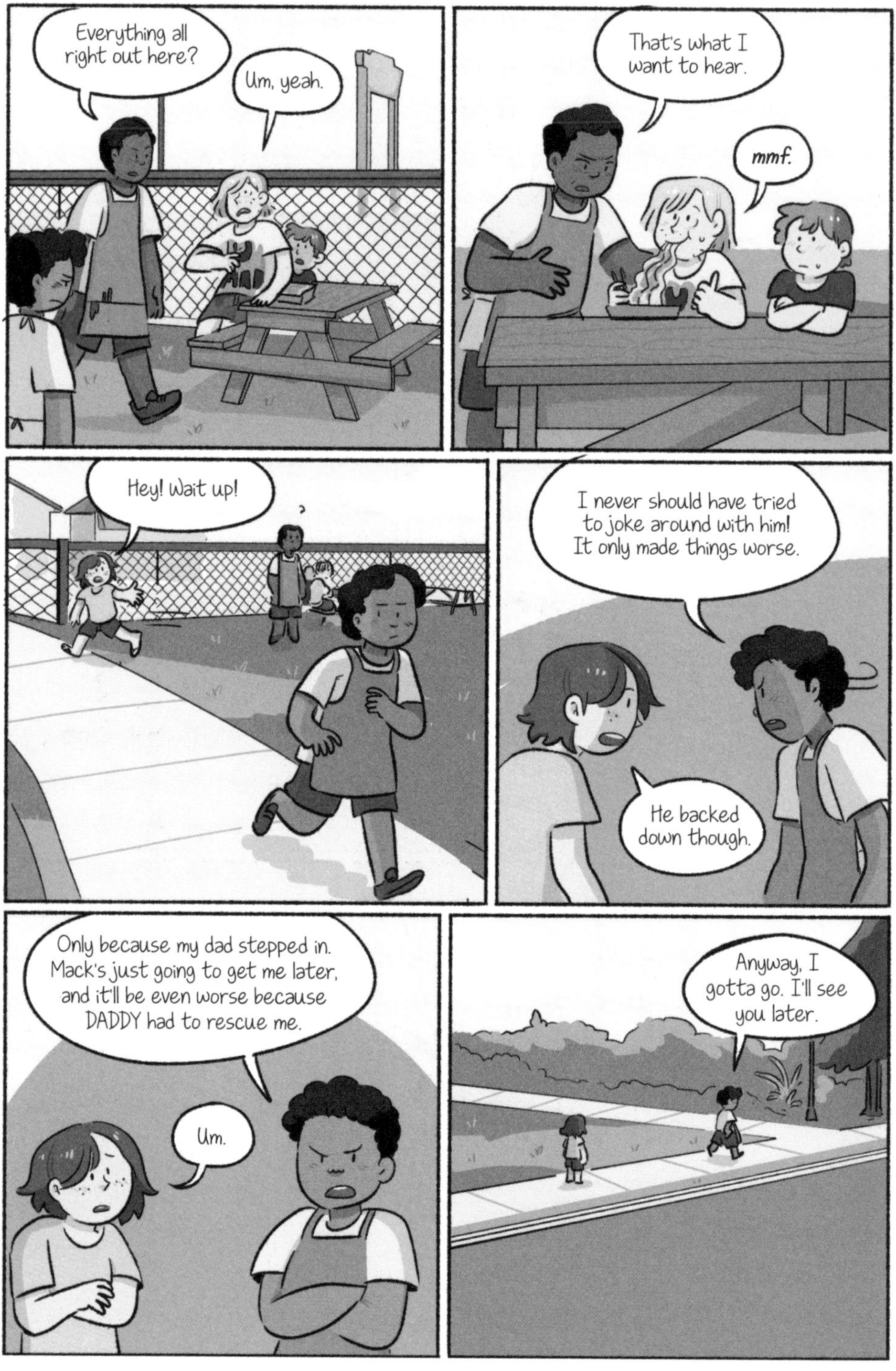

Everything all right out here?
Um, yeah.
That's what I want to hear.
mmf.
Hey! Wait up!
?
I never should have tried to joke around with him! It only made things worse.
He backed down though.
Only because my dad stepped in. Mack's just going to get me later, and it'll be even worse because DADDY had to rescue me.
Um.
Anyway, I gotta go. I'll see you later.

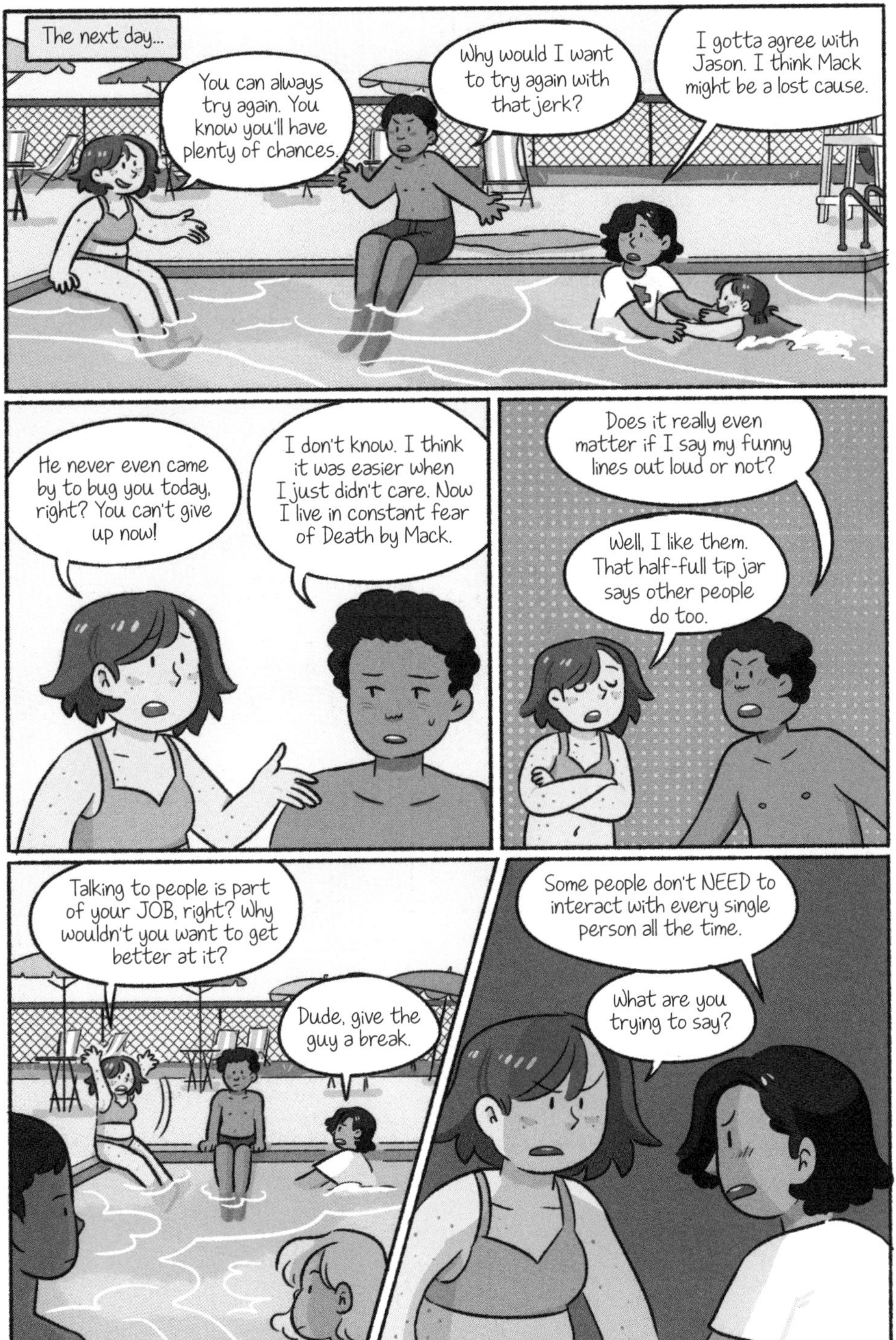
The next day...
You can always try again. You know you'll have plenty of chances.
Why would I want to try again with that jerk?
I gotta agree with Jason. I think Mack might be a lost cause.
He never even came by to bug you today, right? You can't give up now!
I don't know. I think it was easier when I just didn't care. Now I live in constant fear of Death by Mack.
Does it really even matter if I say my funny lines out loud or not?
Well, I like them. That half-full tip jar says other people do too.
Talking to people is part of your JOB, right? Why wouldn't you want to get better at it?
Dude, give the guy a break.
Some people don't NEED to interact with every single person all the time.
What are you trying to say?

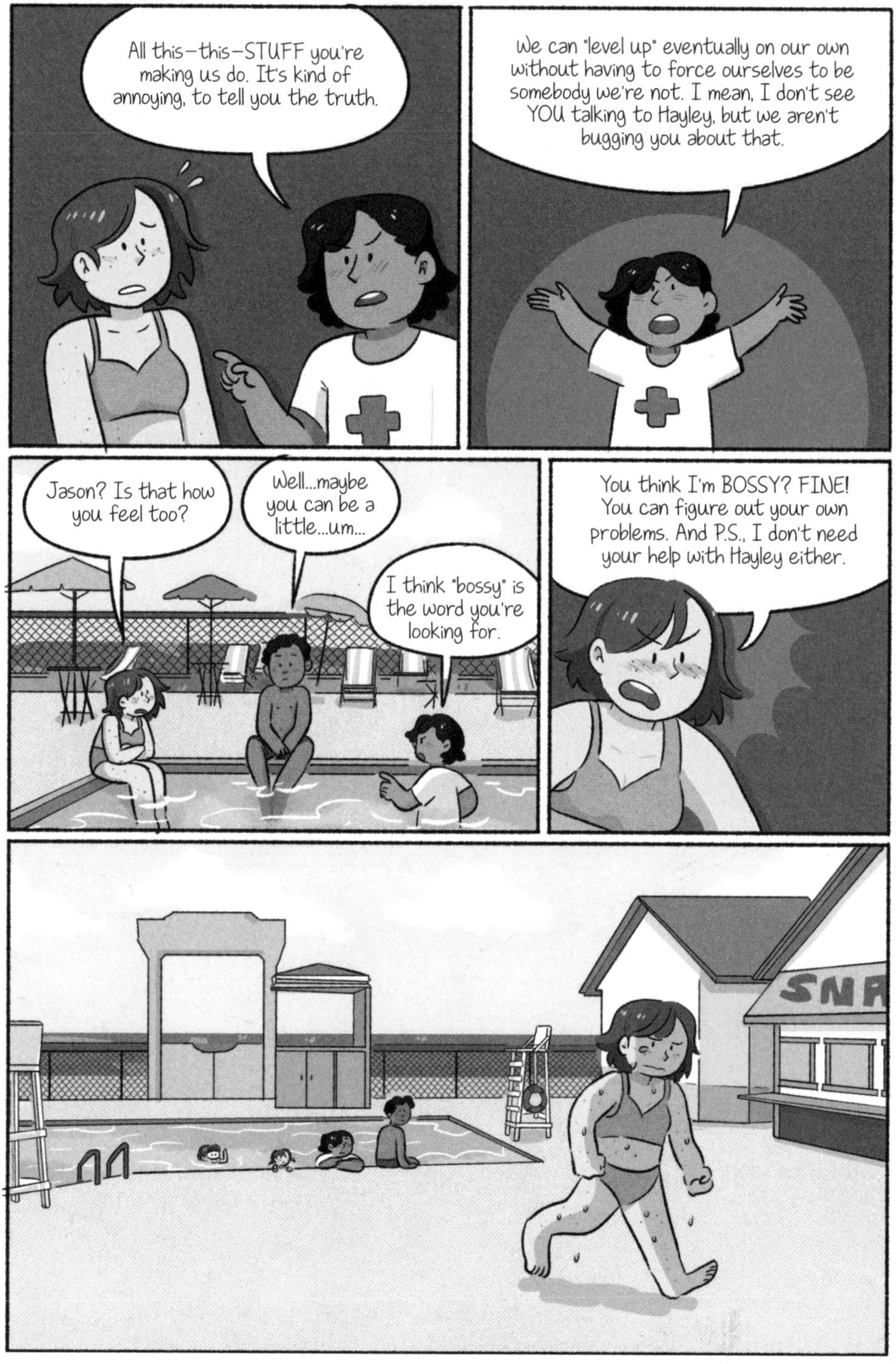
All this—this—STUFF you're making us do. It's kind of annoying, to tell you the truth.
We can "level up" eventually on our own without having to force ourselves to be somebody we're not. I mean, I don't see YOU talking to Hayley, but we aren't bugging you about that.
Jason? Is that how you feel too?
Well...maybe you can be a little...um...
I think "bossy" is the word you're looking for.
You think I'm BOSSY? FINE! You can figure out your own problems. And P.S., I don't need your help with Hayley either.
SNA

Chapter 8

Luke vs. Stupid Perfect Carl

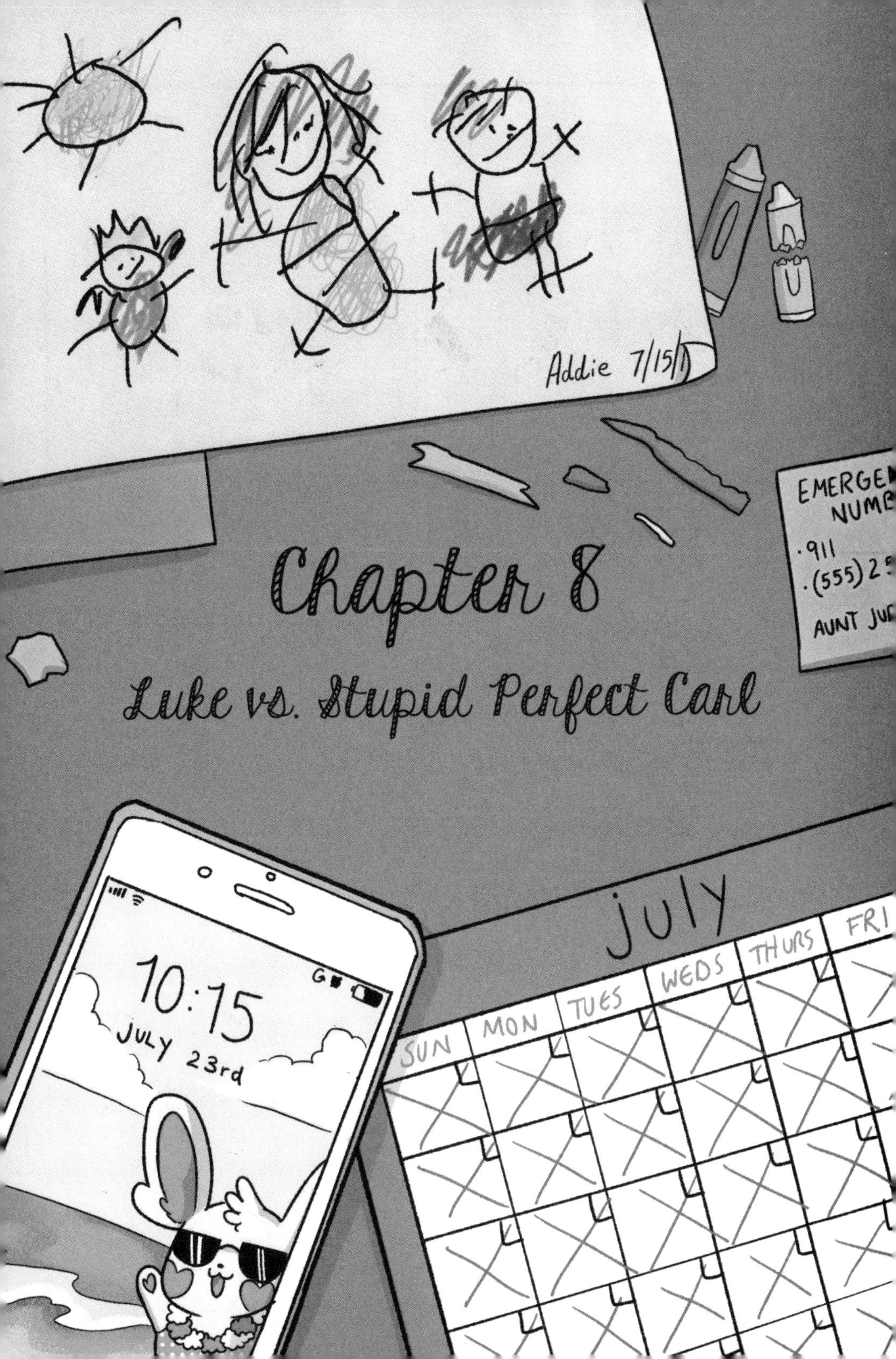
Addie 7/15
10:15
JULY 23rd
july
SUN
MON
TUES
WEDS
THURS

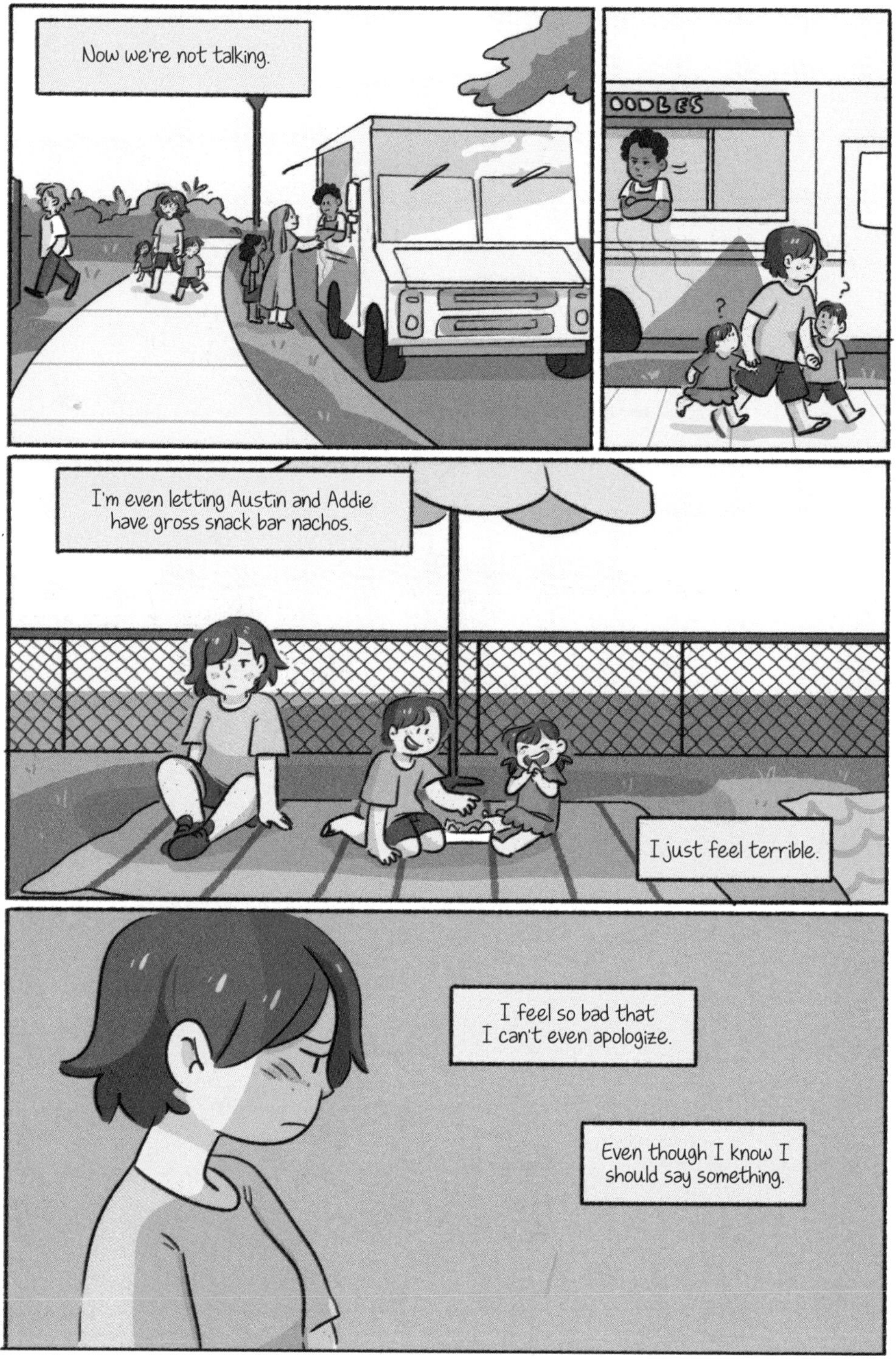
Now we're not talking.
OODLES
?
?
I'm even letting Austin and Addie have gross snack bar nachos.
I just feel terrible.
I feel so bad that I can't even apologize.
Even though I know I should say something.

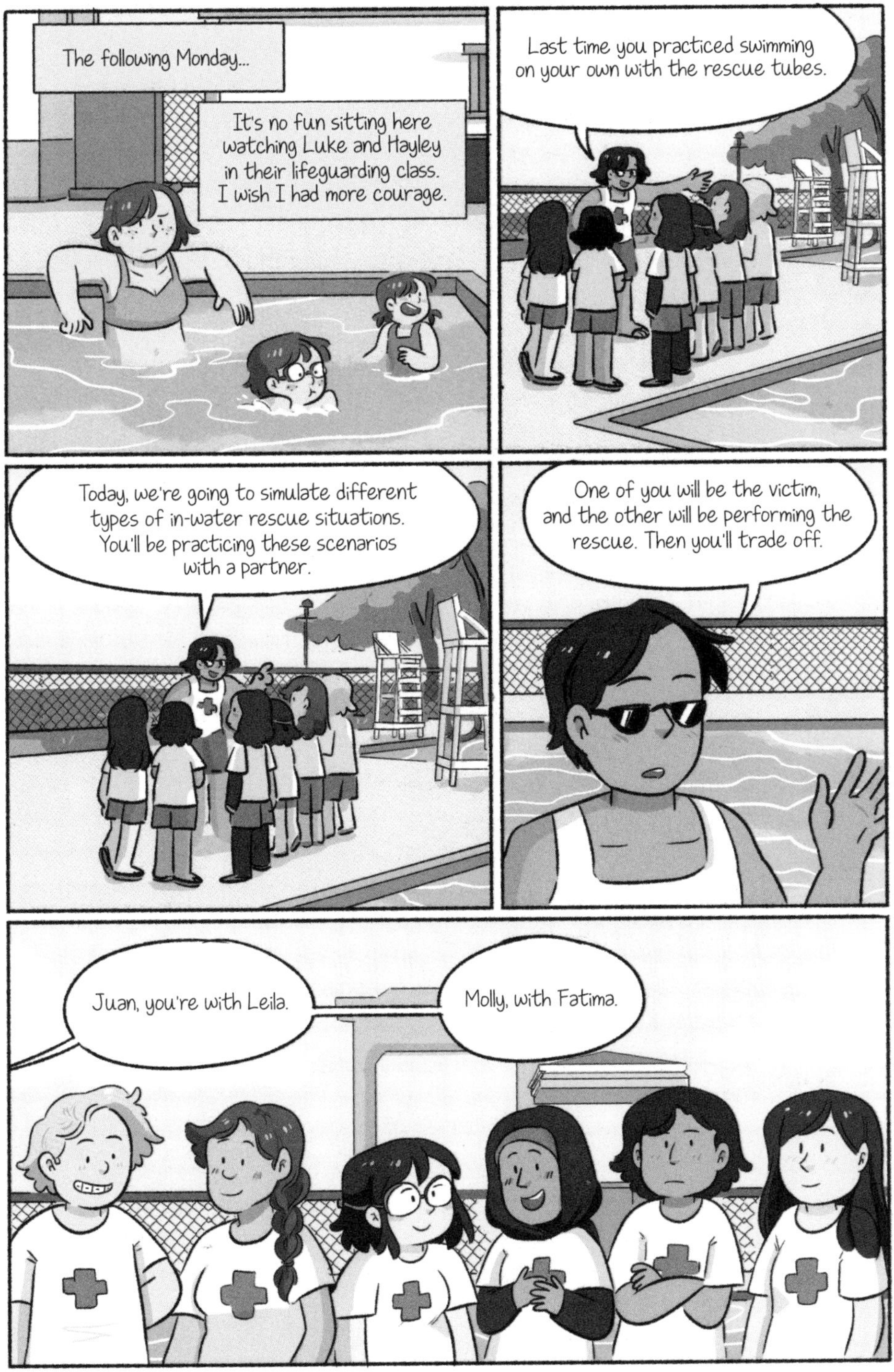
The following Monday...
It's no fun sitting here watching Luke and Hayley in their lifeguarding class. I wish I had more courage.
Last time you practiced swimming on your own with the rescue tubes.
Today, we're going to simulate different types of in-water rescue situations. You'll be practicing these scenarios with a partner.
One of you will be the victim, and the other will be performing the rescue. Then you'll trade off.
Juan, you're with Leila.
Molly, with Fatima.

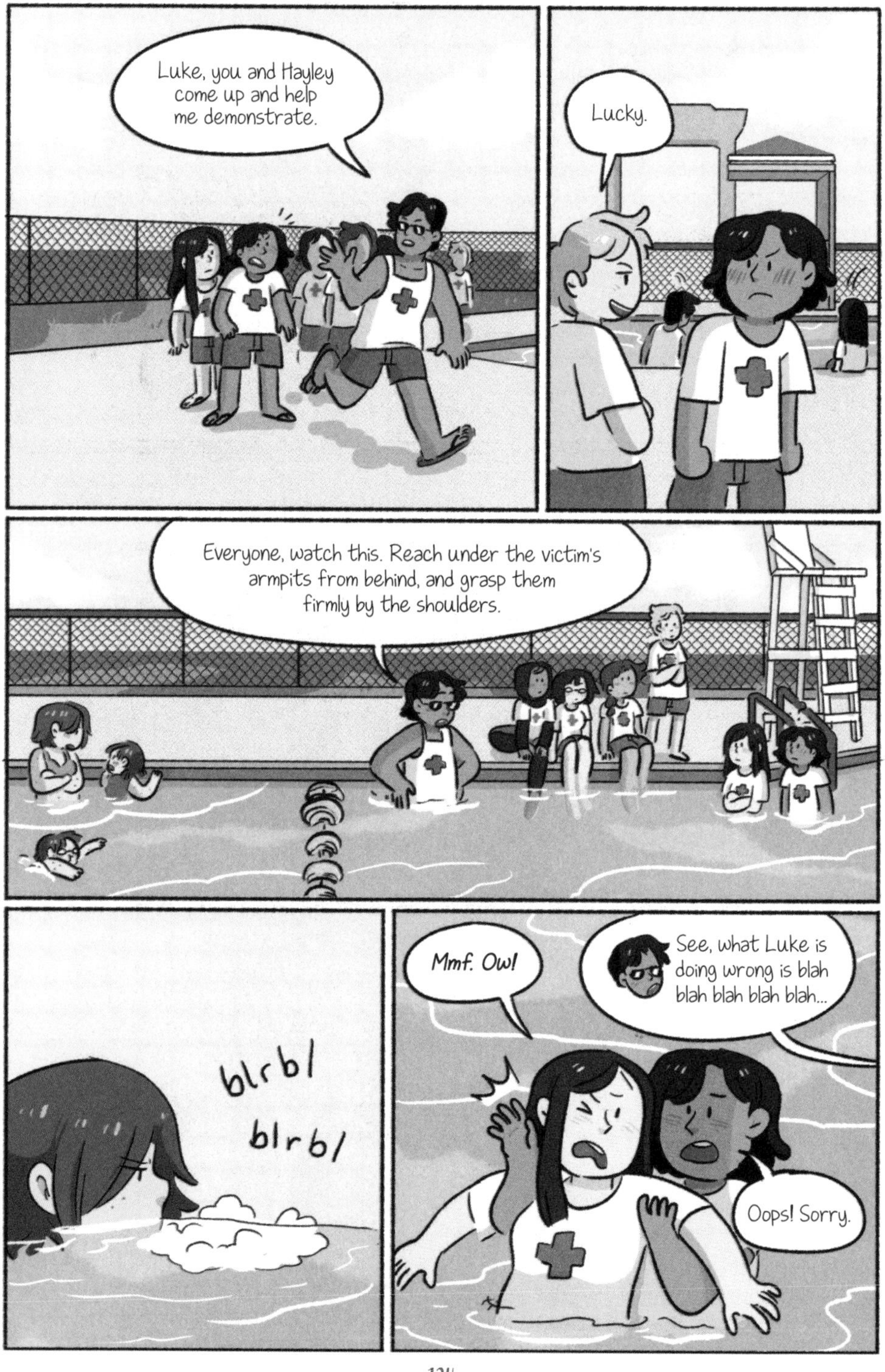
Luke, you and Hayley come up and help me demonstrate.
Lucky.
Everyone, watch this. Reach under the victim's armpits from behind, and grasp them firmly by the shoulders.
blrbl
blrbl
Mmf. Ow!
See, what Luke is doing wrong is blah blah blah blah blah...
Oops! Sorry.

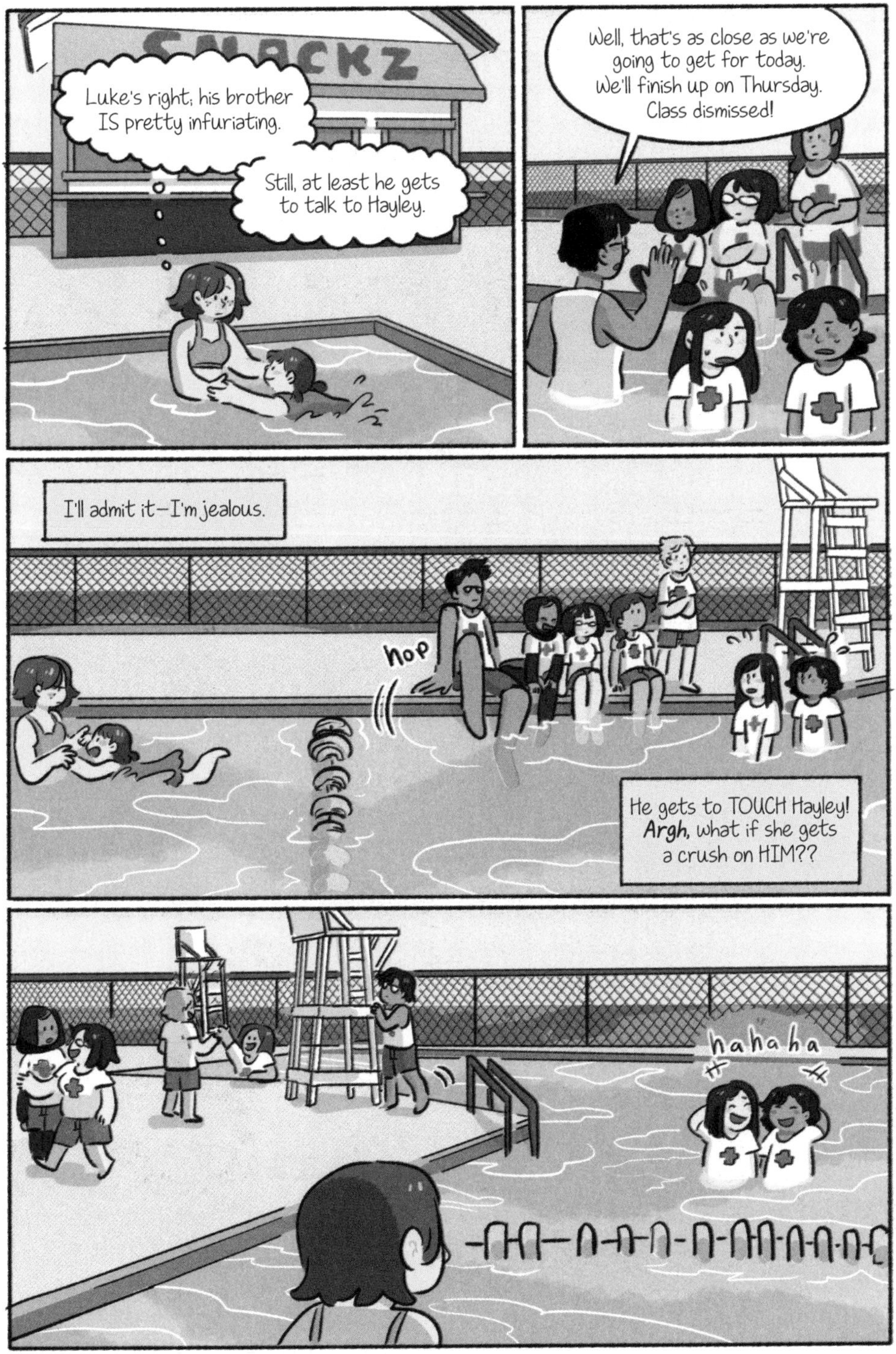
SNACKZ
Luke's right; his brother IS pretty infuriating.
Still, at least he gets to talk to Hayley.
Well, that's as close as we're going to get for today. We'll finish up on Thursday. Class dismissed!
I'll admit it—I'm jealous.
hop
He gets to TOUCH Hayley! **Argh,** what if she gets a crush on HIM??
hahaha

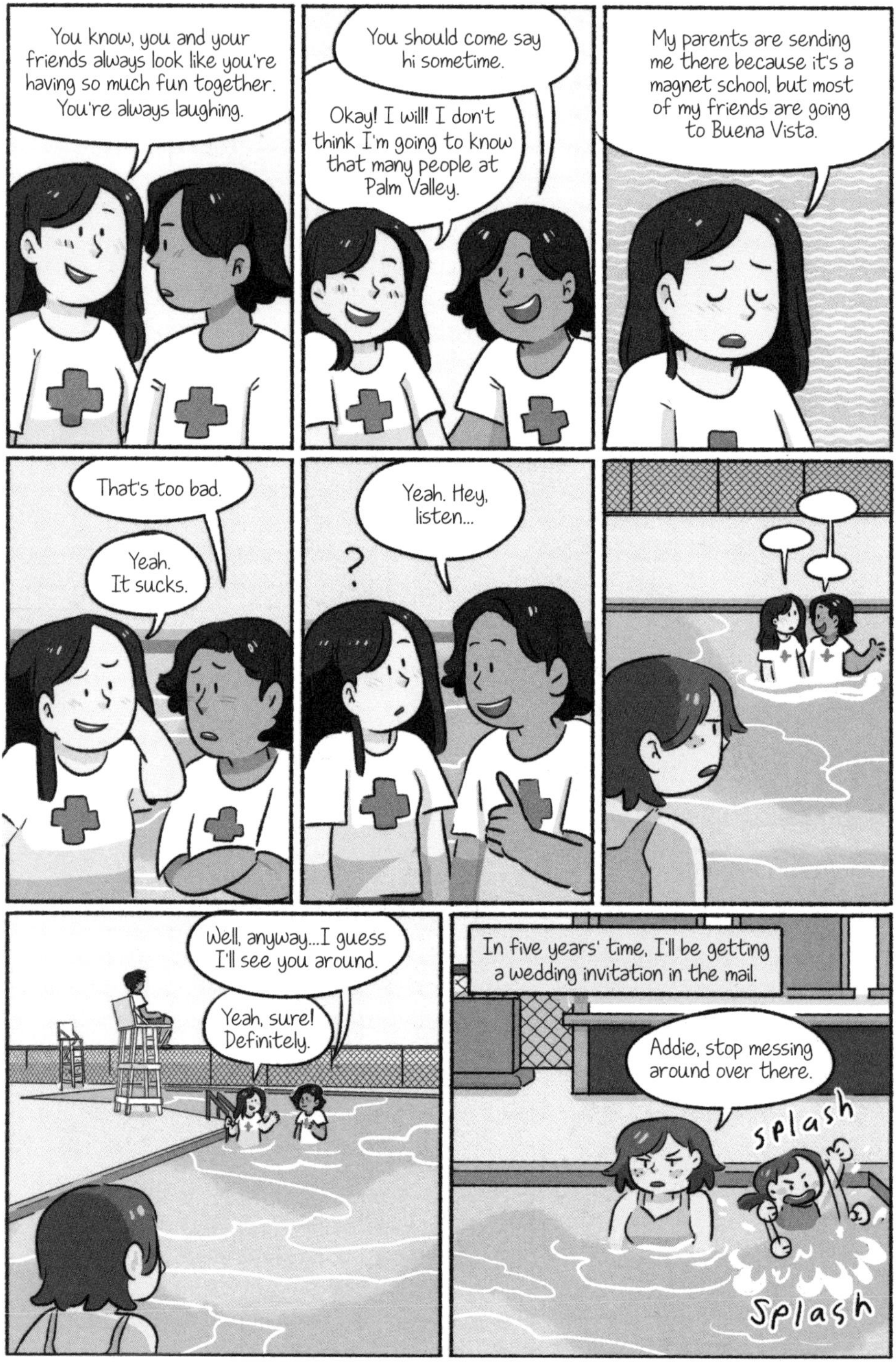
You know, you and your friends always look like you're having so much fun together. You're always laughing.
You should come say hi sometime.
Okay! I will! I don't think I'm going to know that many people at Palm Valley.
My parents are sending me there because it's a magnet school, but most of my friends are going to Buena Vista.
That's too bad.
Yeah. It sucks.
?
Yeah. Hey, listen...
Well, anyway...I guess I'll see you around.
Yeah, sure! Definitely.
In five years' time, I'll be getting a wedding invitation in the mail.
Addie, stop messing around over there.
splash
Splash

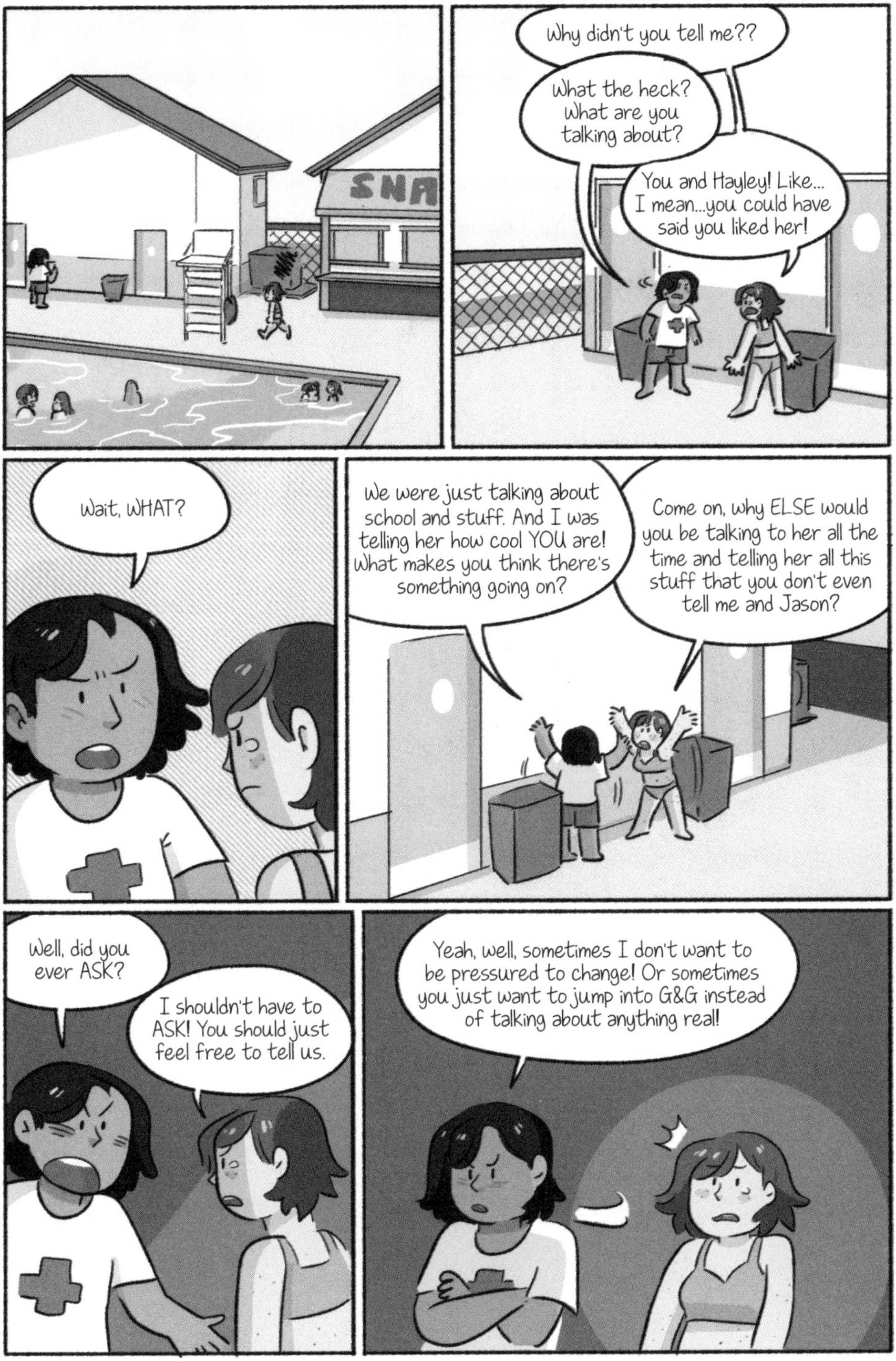
SNA
Why didn't you tell me??
What the heck? What are you talking about?
You and Hayley! Like... I mean...you could have said you liked her!
Wait, WHAT?
We were just talking about school and stuff. And I was telling her how cool YOU are! What makes you think there's something going on?
Come on, why ELSE would you be talking to her all the time and telling her all this stuff that you don't even tell me and Jason?
Well, did you ever ASK?
I shouldn't have to ASK! You should just feel free to tell us.
Yeah, well, sometimes I don't want to be pressured to change! Or sometimes you just want to jump into G&G instead of talking about anything real!

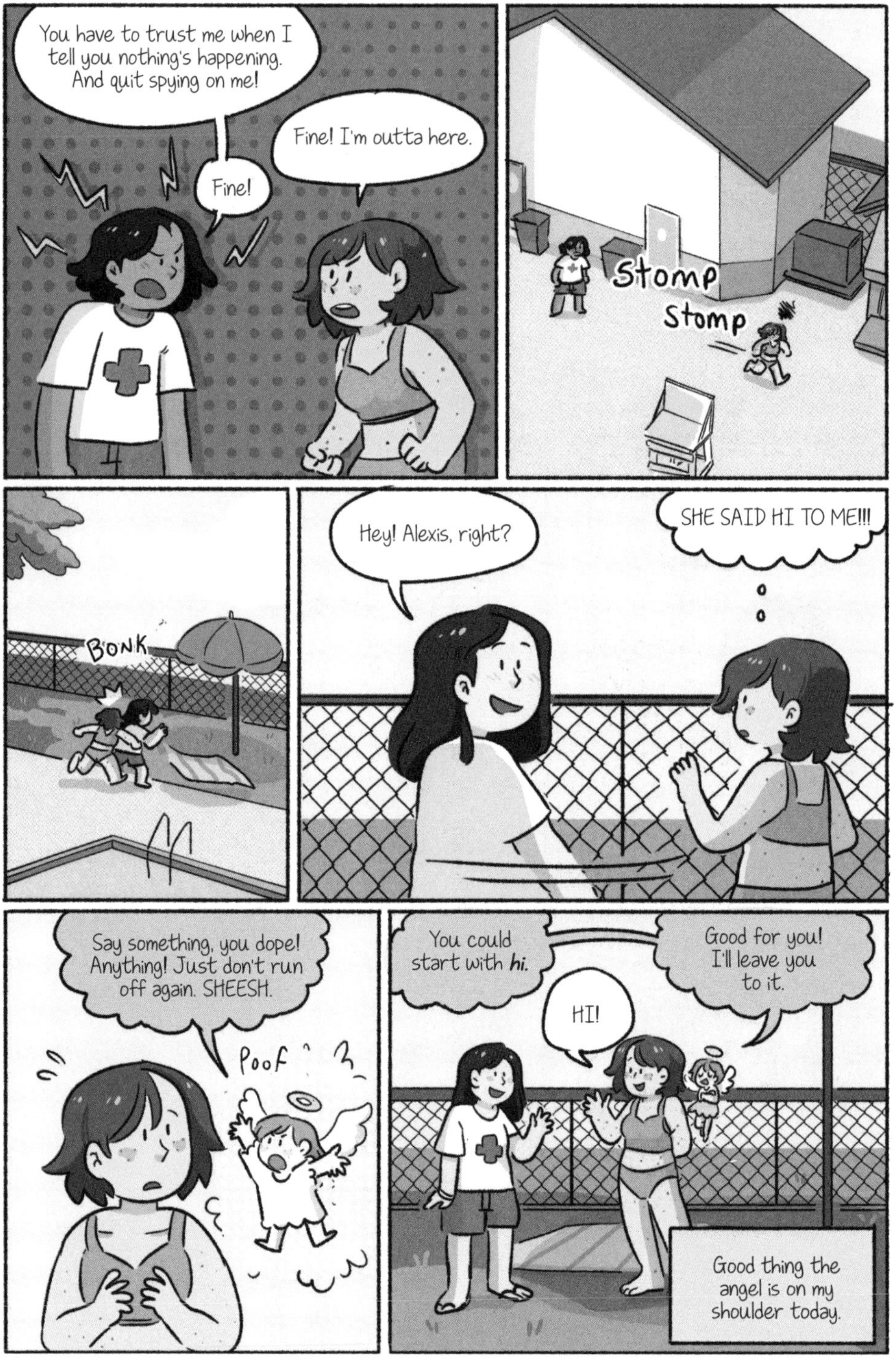
You have to trust me when I tell you nothing's happening. And quit spying on me!
Fine!
Fine! I'm outta here.
Stomp
Stomp
BONK
Hey! Alexis, right?
SHE SAID HI TO ME!!!
Say something, you dope! Anything! Just don't run off again. SHEESH.
Poof
You could start with *hi.*
Good for you! I'll leave you to it.
HI!
Good thing the angel is on my shoulder today.

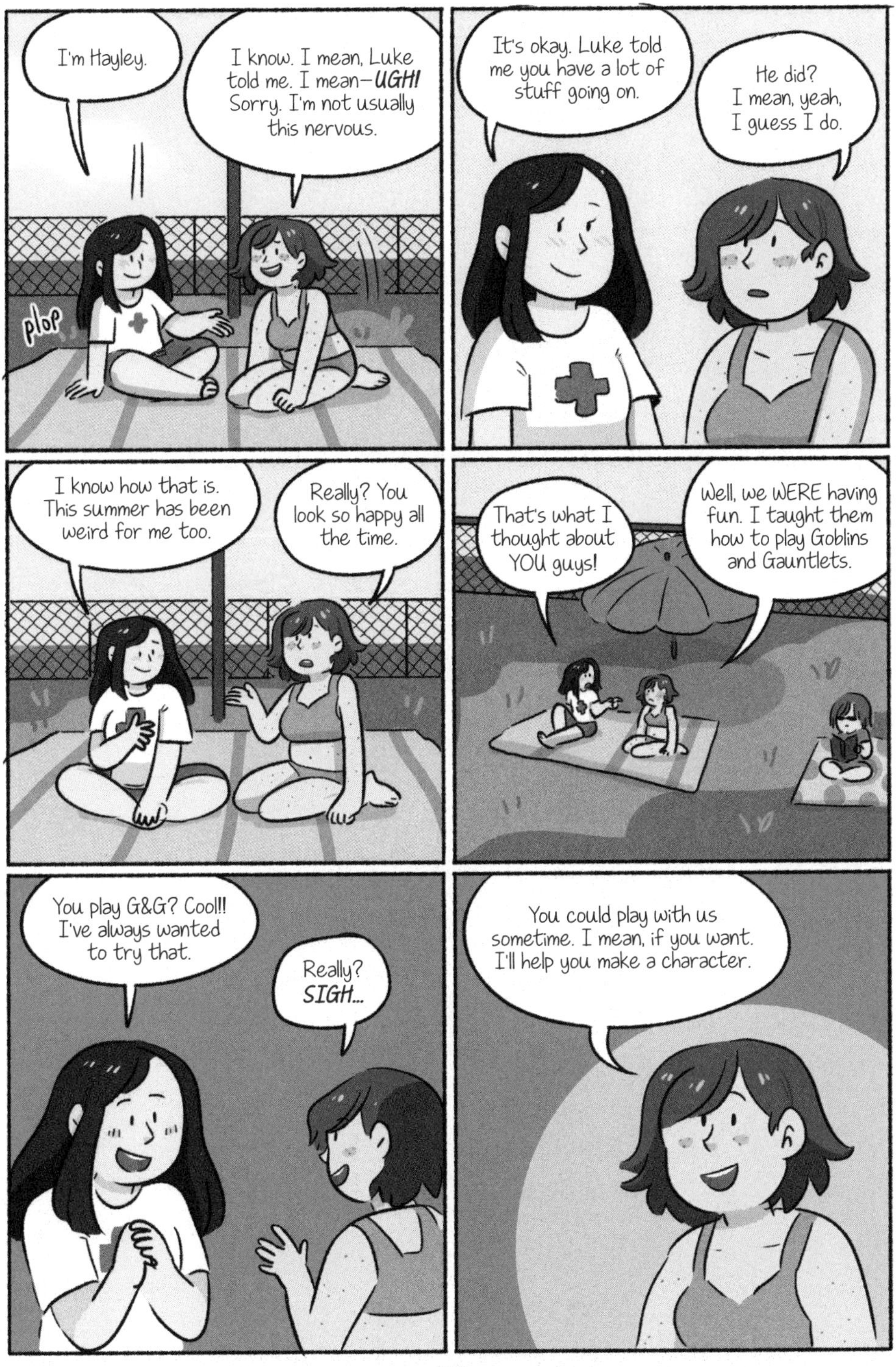
I'm Hayley.
I know. I mean, Luke told me. I mean—UGH! Sorry. I'm not usually this nervous.
plop
It's okay. Luke told me you have a lot of stuff going on.
He did? I mean, yeah, I guess I do.
I know how that is. This summer has been weird for me too.
Really? You look so happy all the time.
That's what I thought about YOU guys!
Well, we WERE having fun. I taught them how to play Goblins and Gauntlets.
You play G&G? Cool!! I've always wanted to try that.
Really? SIGH...
You could play with us sometime. I mean, if you want. I'll help you make a character.

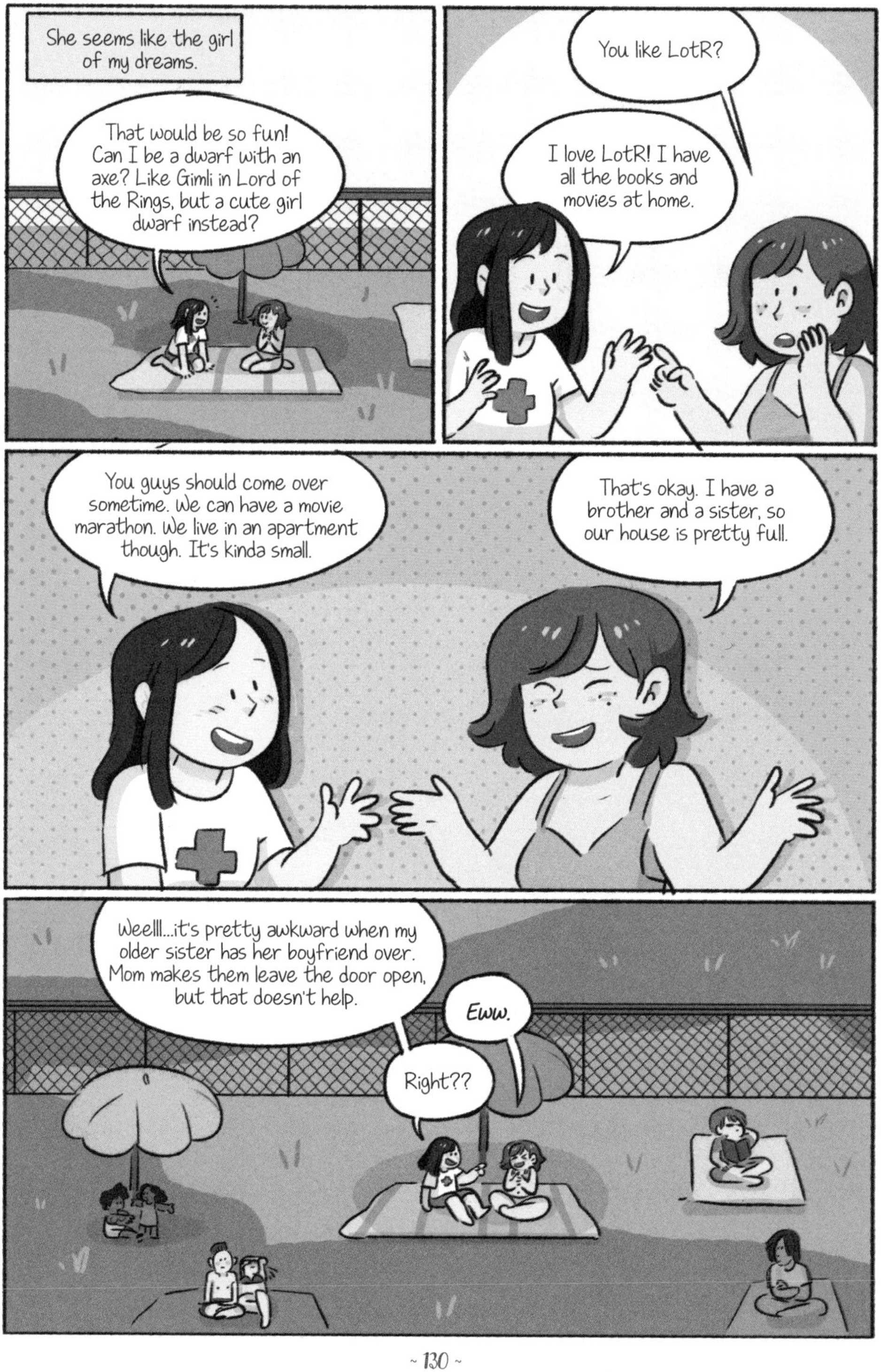

She seems like the girl of my dreams.
That would be so fun! Can I be a dwarf with an axe? Like Gimli in Lord of the Rings, but a cute girl dwarf instead?
You like LotR?
I love LotR! I have all the books and movies at home.
You guys should come over sometime. We can have a movie marathon. We live in an apartment though. It's kinda small.
That's okay. I have a brother and a sister, so our house is pretty full.
Weelll...it's pretty awkward when my older sister has her boyfriend over. Mom makes them leave the door open, but that doesn't help.
Eww.
Right??

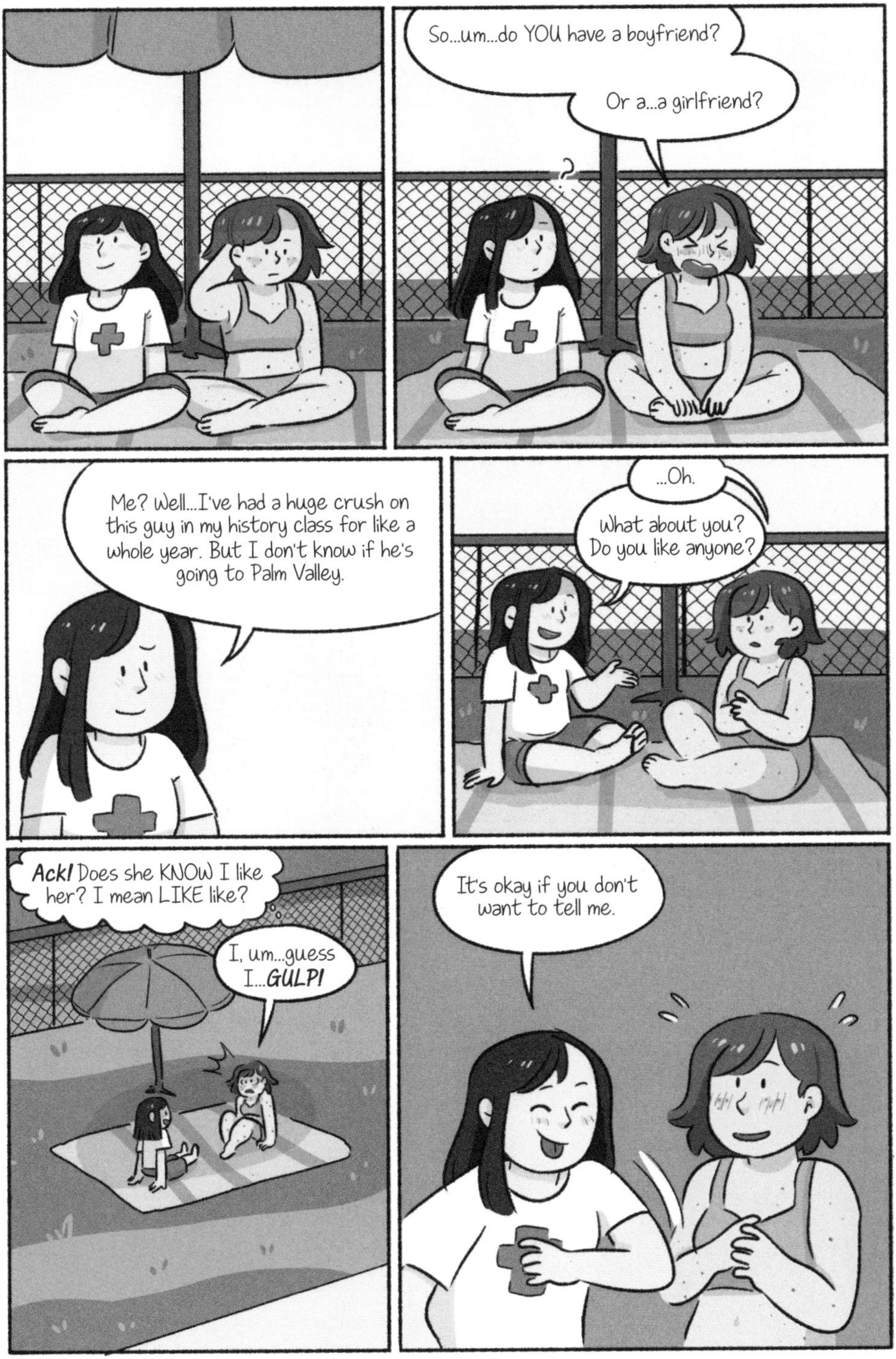
So...um...do YOU have a boyfriend?
Or a...a girlfriend?
Me? Well...I've had a huge crush on this guy in my history class for like a whole year. But I don't know if he's going to Palm Valley.
...Oh.
What about you? Do you like anyone?
Ack! Does she KNOW I like her? I mean LIKE like?
I, um...guess I...GULP!
It's okay if you don't want to tell me.

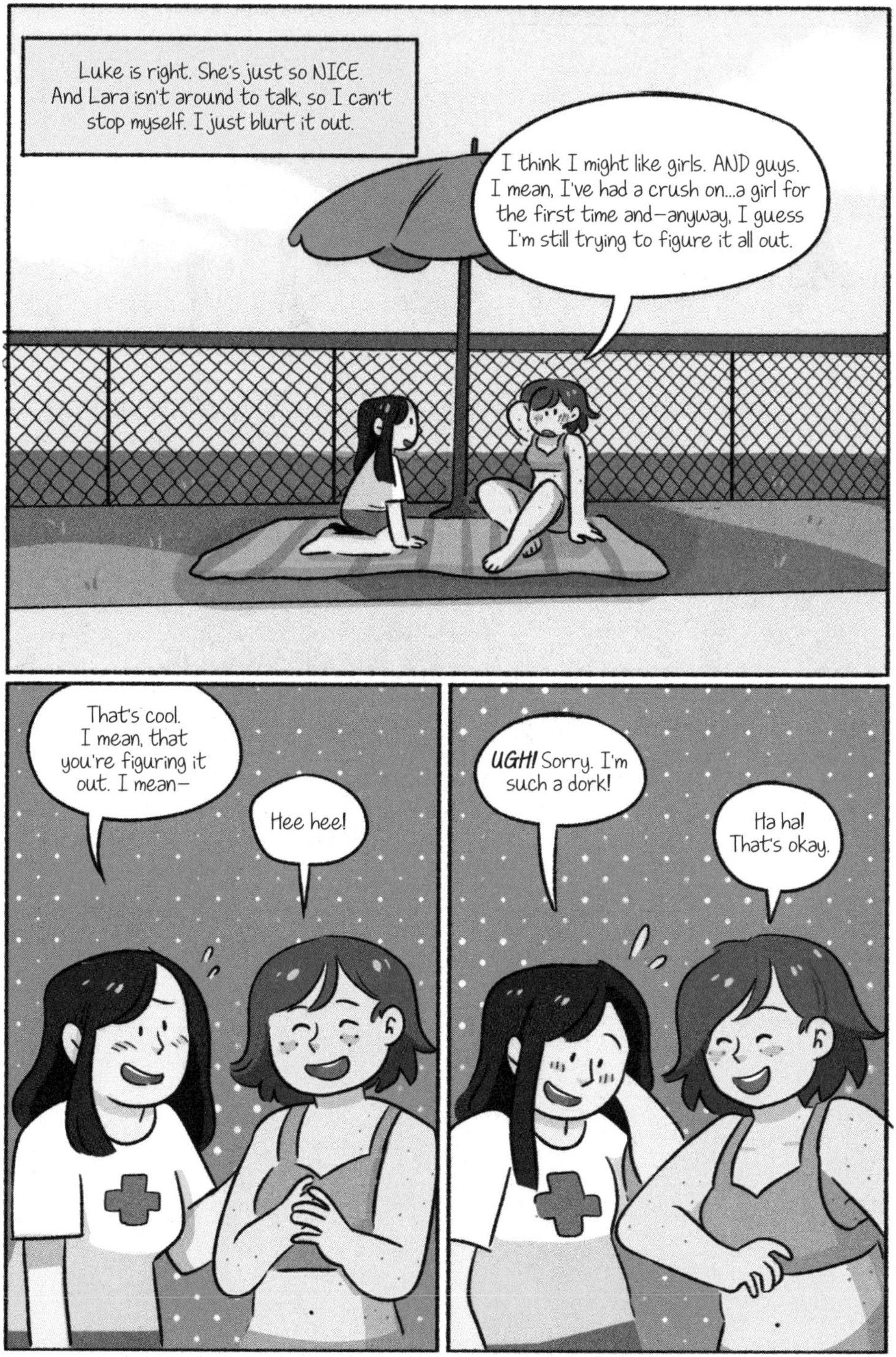
Luke is right. She's just so NICE. And Lara isn't around to talk, so I can't stop myself. I just blurt it out.
I think I might like girls. AND guys. I mean, I've had a crush on...a girl for the first time and—anyway, I guess I'm still trying to figure it all out.
That's cool. I mean, that you're figuring it out. I mean—
Hee hee!
UGH! Sorry. I'm such a dork!
Ha ha! That's okay.

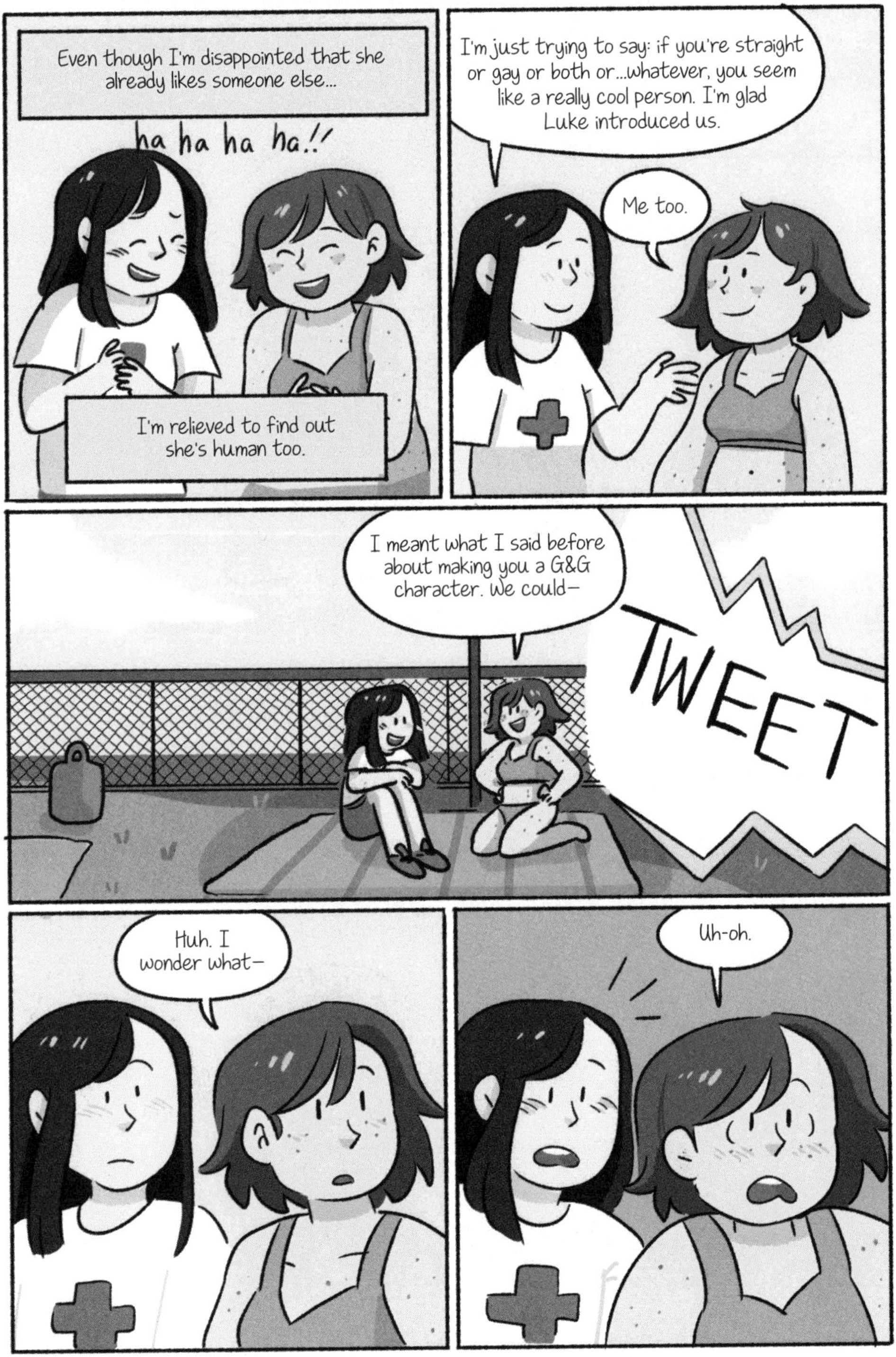
Even though I'm disappointed that she already likes someone else...
ha ha ha ha!!
I'm relieved to find out she's human too.
I'm just trying to say: if you're straight or gay or both or...whatever, you seem like a really cool person. I'm glad Luke introduced us.
Me too.
I meant what I said before about making you a G&G character. We could—
TWEET
Huh. I wonder what—
Uh-oh.

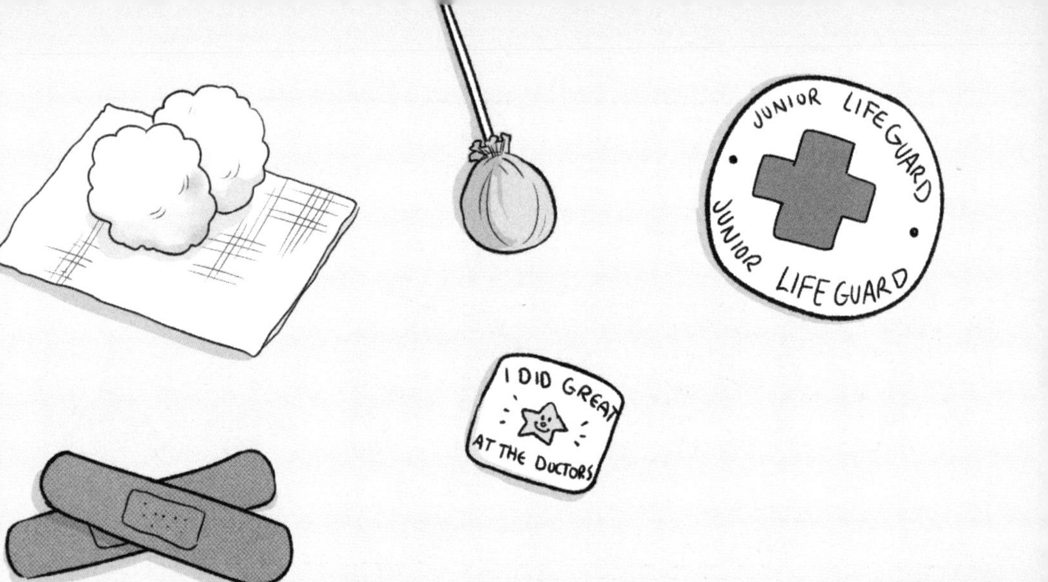
JUNIOR LIFEGUARD
JUNIOR LIFEGUARD
I DID GREAT
AT THE DOCTORS

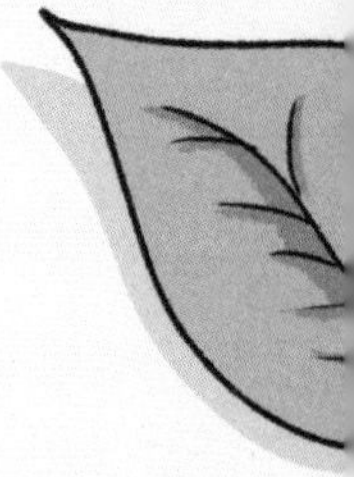

Chapter 9

Alexis vs. Leveling Up

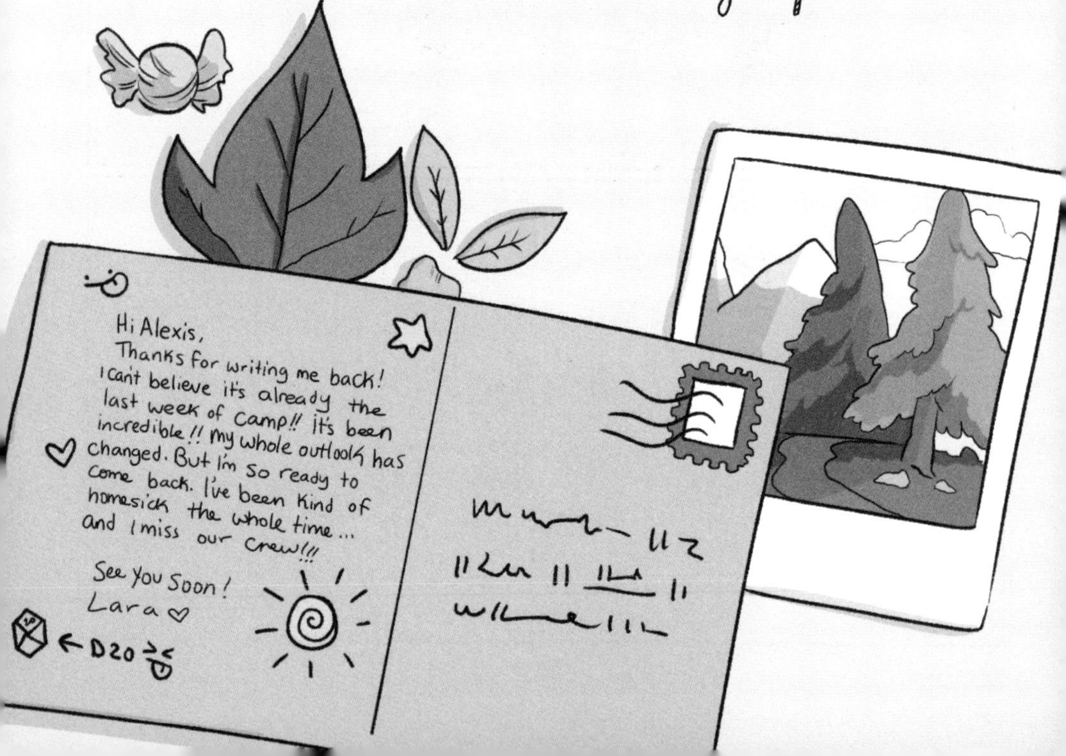
Hi Alexis,
Thanks for writing me back! I can't believe it's already the last week of camp!! It's been incredible!! My whole outlook has changed. But I'm so ready to come back. I've been kind of homesick the whole time... and I miss our crew!!!
See you soon!
Lara
D20

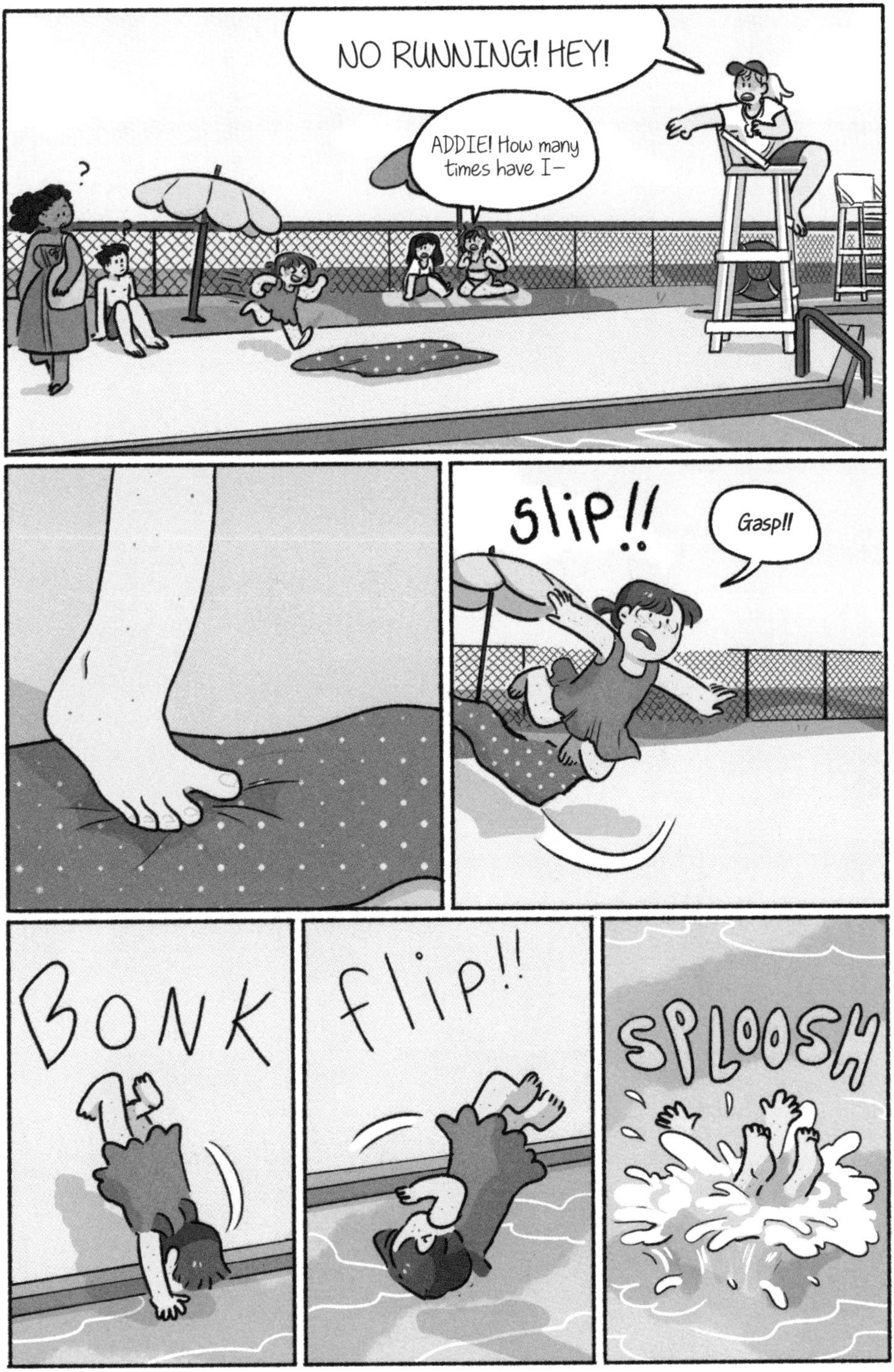
NO RUNNING! HEY!
ADDIE! How many times have I—
?
SLIP!!
Gasp!!
BONK
flip!!
SPLOOSH

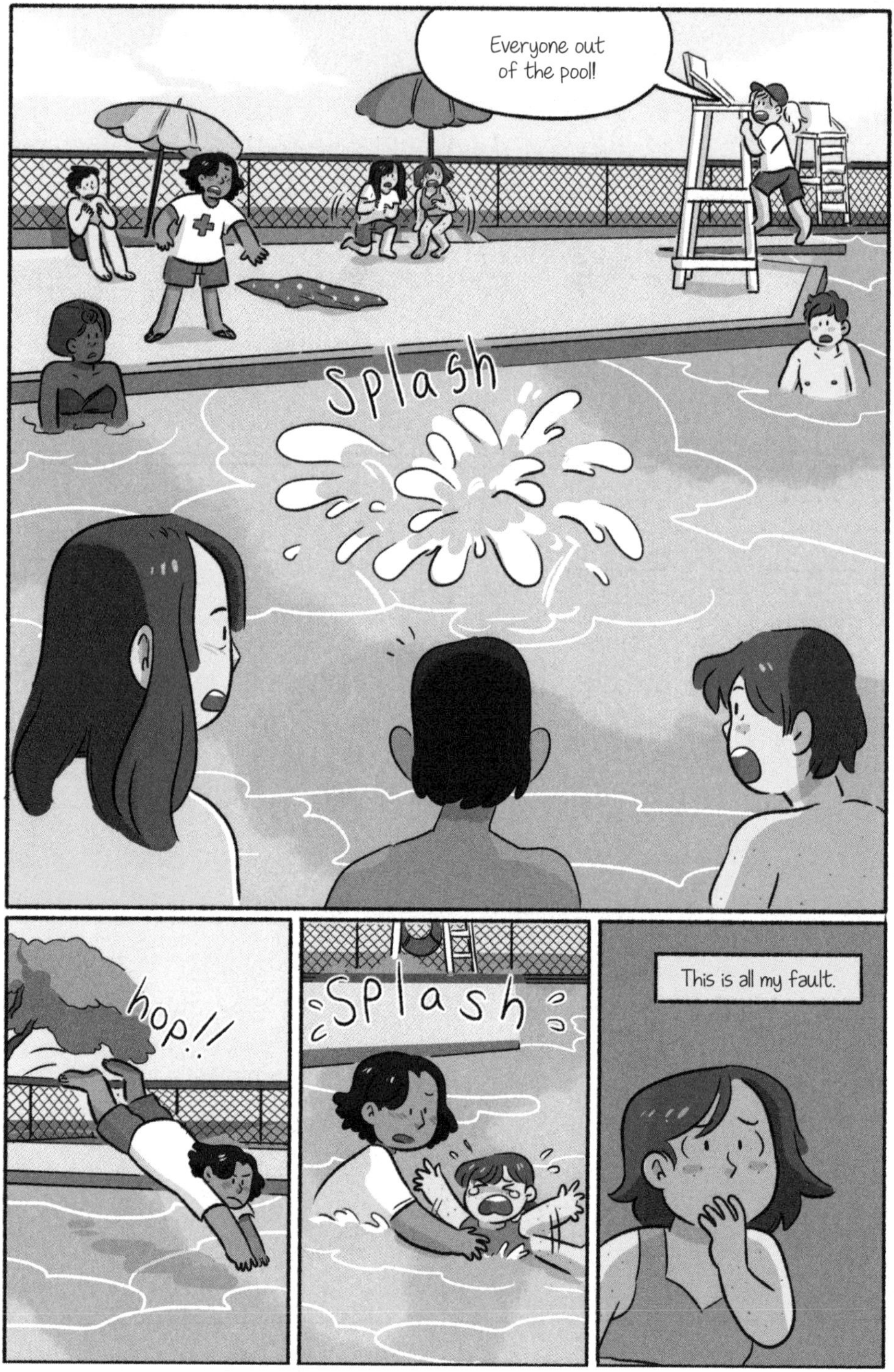
Everyone out of the pool!
Splash
hop!!
Splash
This is all my fault.

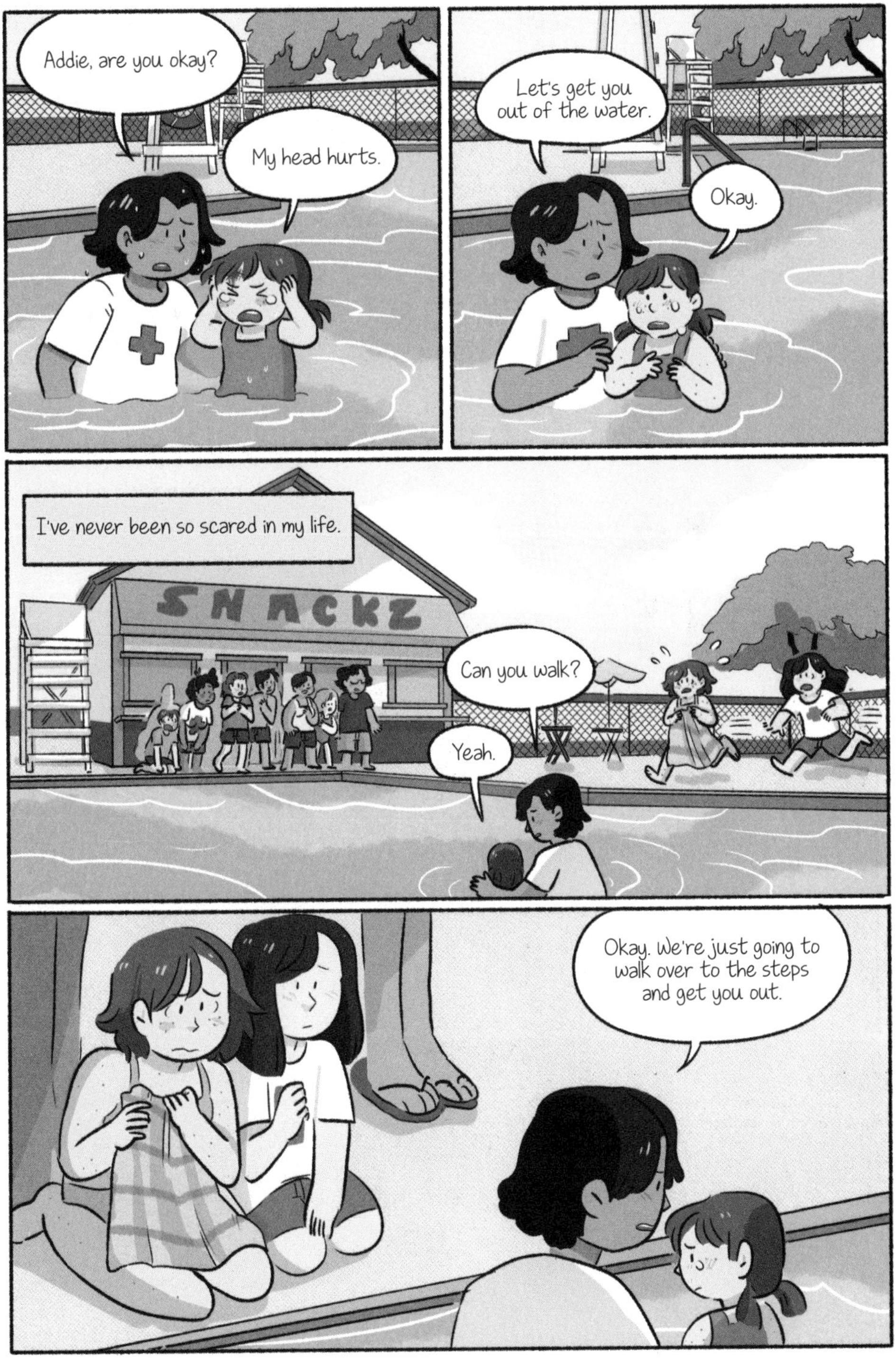
Addie, are you okay?
My head hurts.
Let's get you out of the water.
Okay.
I've never been so scared in my life.
SNACKZ
Can you walk?
Yeah.
Okay. We're just going to walk over to the steps and get you out.

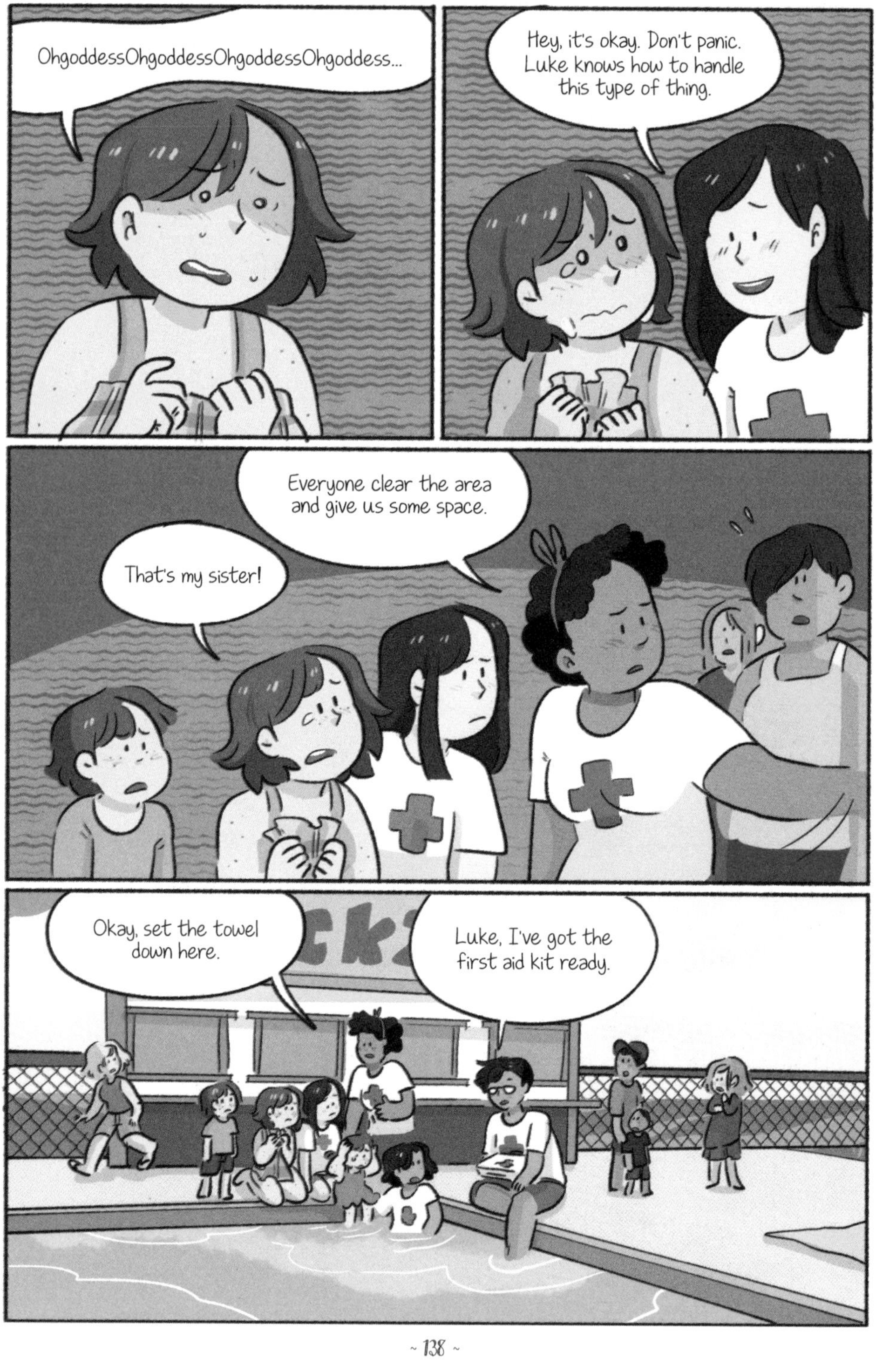
OhgoddessOhgoddessOhgoddessOhgoddess...
Hey, it's okay. Don't panic. Luke knows how to handle this type of thing.
That's my sister!
Everyone clear the area and give us some space.
Okay, set the towel down here.
Luke, I've got the first aid kit ready.

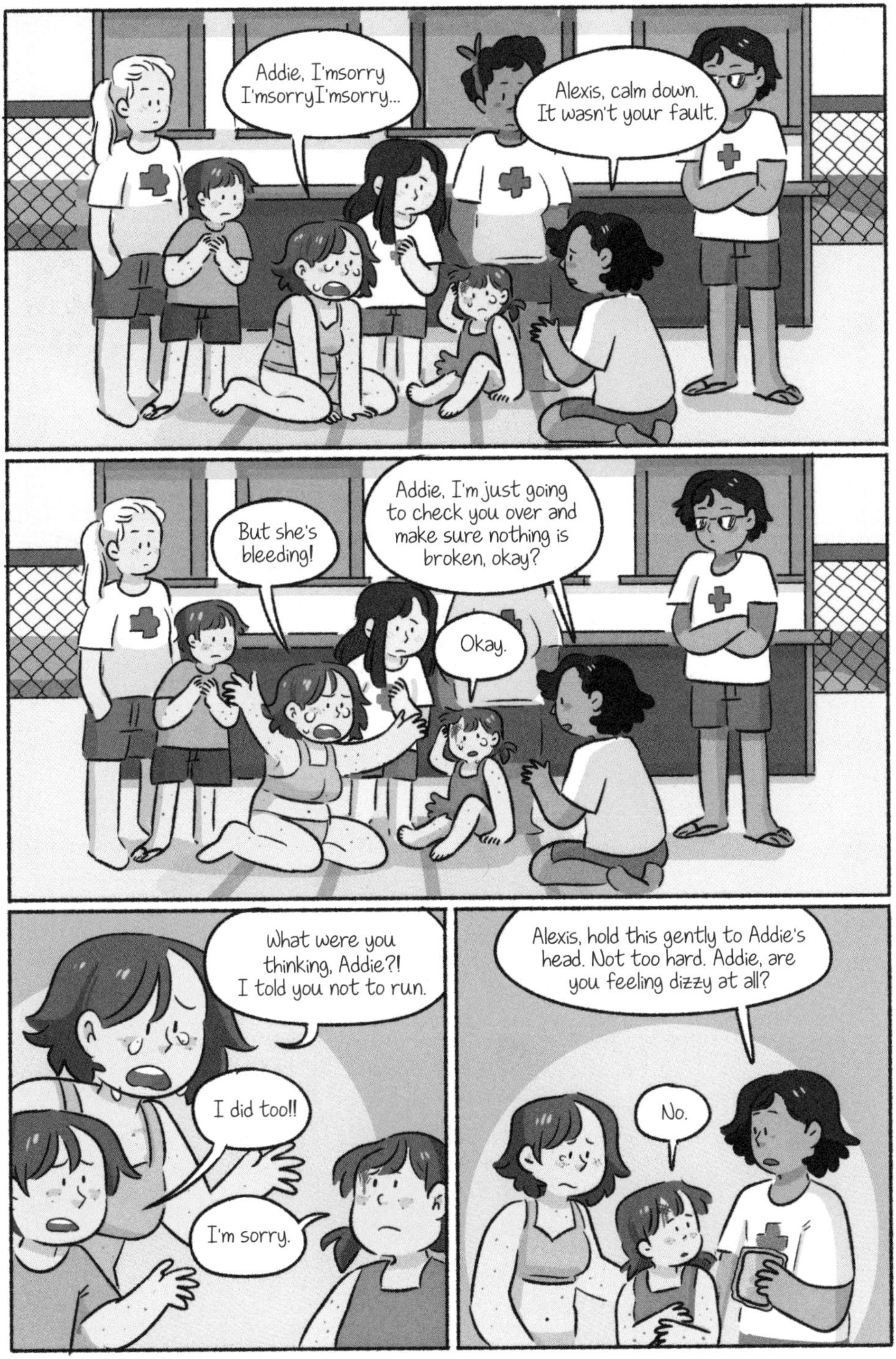

Addie, I'msorry I'msorryI'msorry...
Alexis, calm down. It wasn't your fault.
But she's bleeding!
Addie, I'm just going to check you over and make sure nothing is broken, okay?
Okay.
What were you thinking, Addie?! I told you not to run.
I did too!!
I'm sorry.
Alexis, hold this gently to Addie's head. Not too hard. Addie, are you feeling dizzy at all?
No.

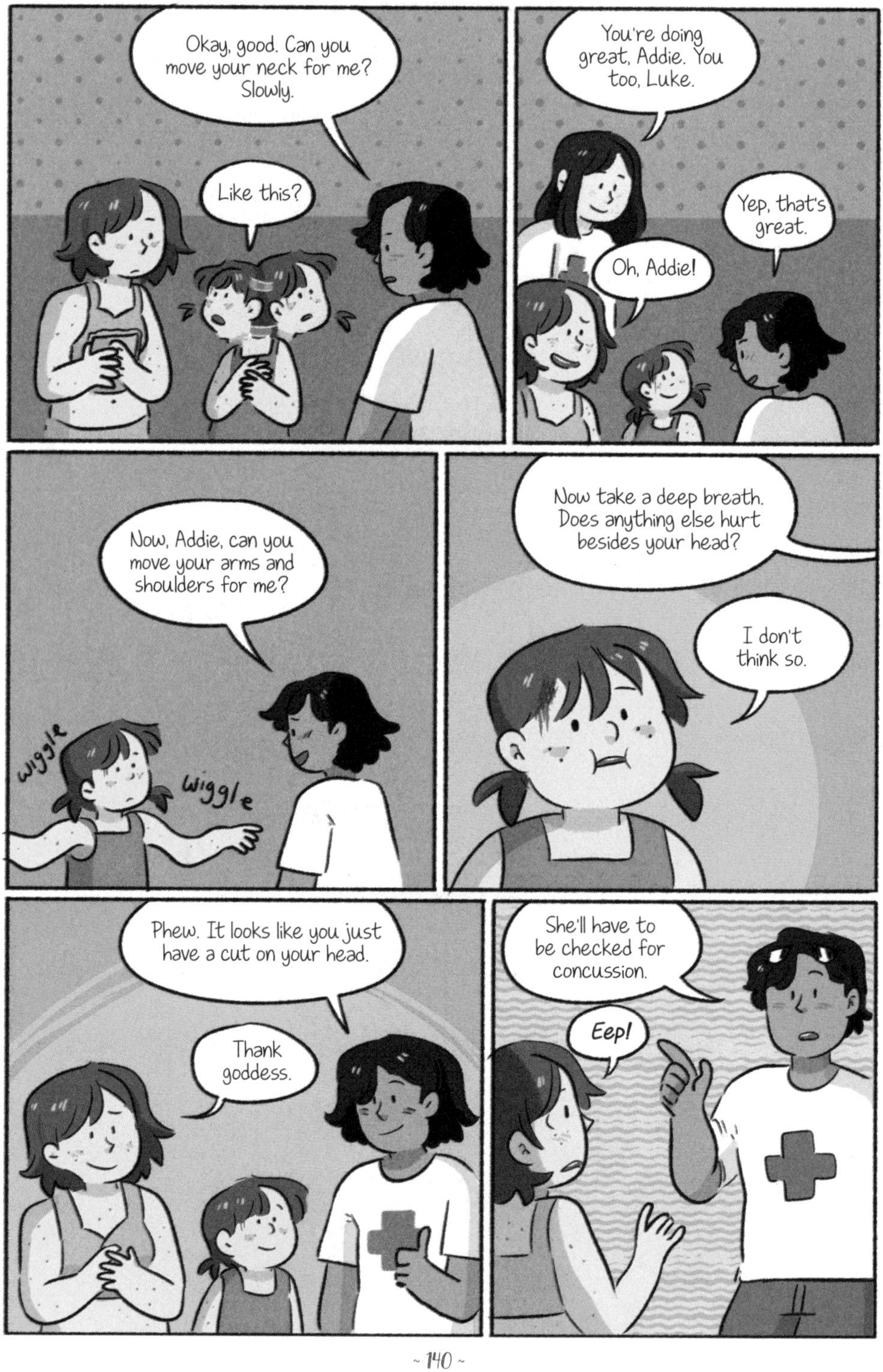
Okay, good. Can you move your neck for me? Slowly.
Like this?
You're doing great, Addie. You too, Luke.
Yep, that's great.
Oh, Addie!
Now, Addie, can you move your arms and shoulders for me?
wiggle
wiggle
Now take a deep breath. Does anything else hurt besides your head?
I don't think so.
Phew. It looks like you just have a cut on your head.
Thank goddess.
She'll have to be checked for concussion.
Eep!

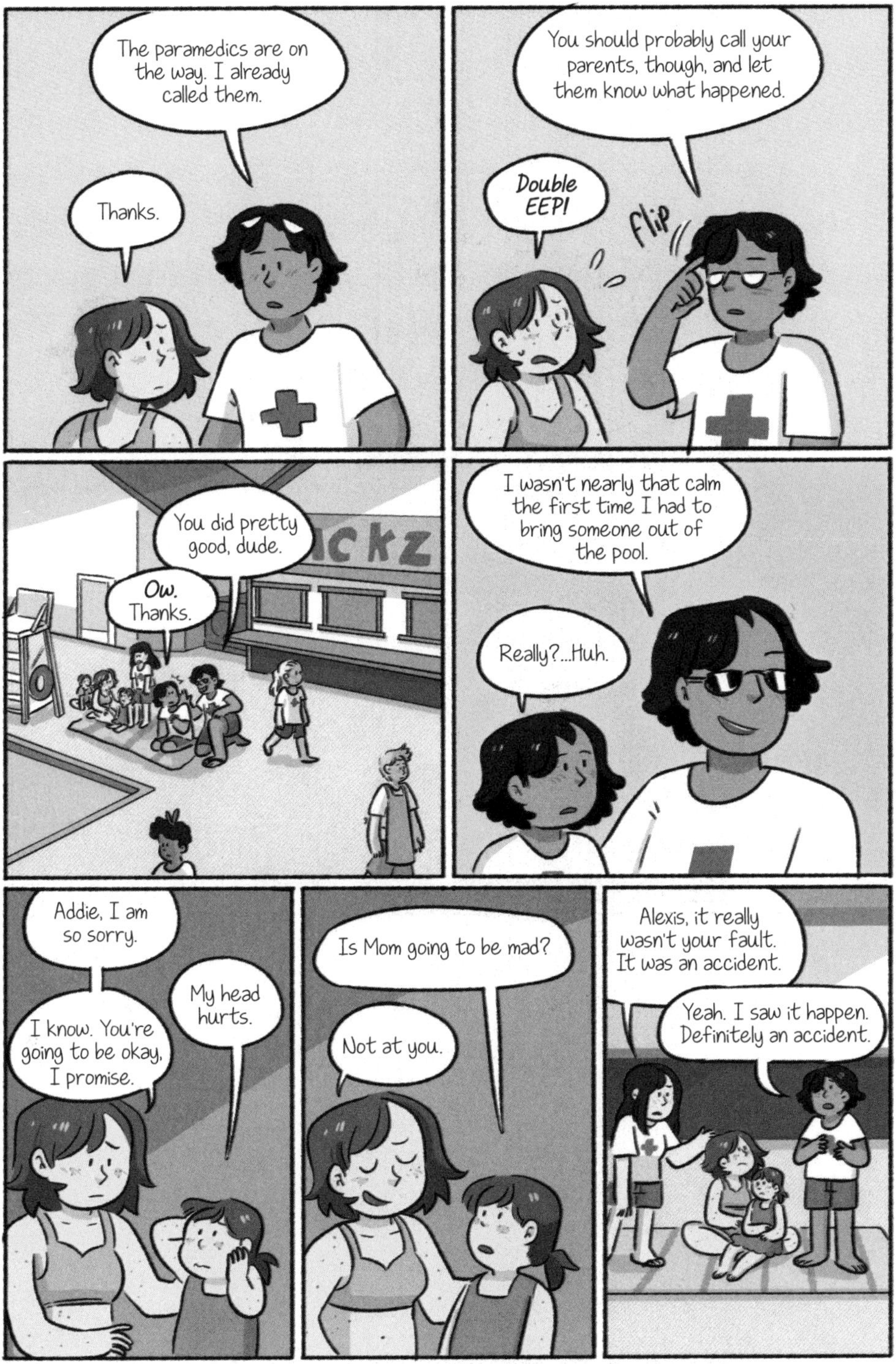

The paramedics are on the way. I already called them.
Thanks.
You should probably call your parents, though, and let them know what happened.
Double EEP!
Flip
You did pretty good, dude.
Ow. Thanks.
I wasn't nearly that calm the first time I had to bring someone out of the pool.
Really?...Huh.
Addie, I am so sorry.
My head hurts.
I know. You're going to be okay, I promise.
Is Mom going to be mad?
Not at you.
Alexis, it really wasn't your fault. It was an accident.
Yeah. I saw it happen. Definitely an accident.

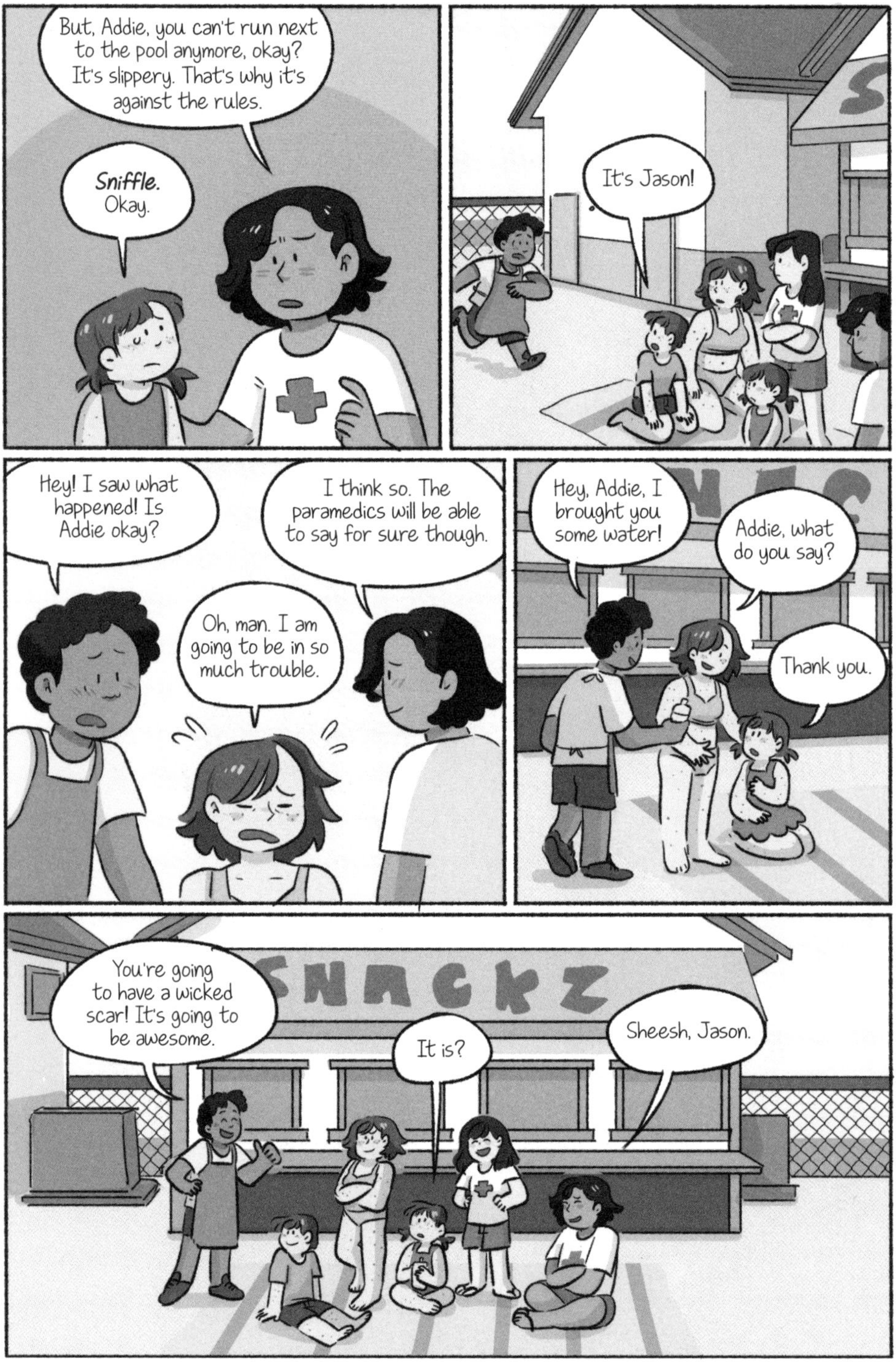
But, Addie, you can't run next to the pool anymore, okay? It's slippery. That's why it's against the rules.
Sniffle. Okay.
It's Jason!
Hey! I saw what happened! Is Addie okay?
I think so. The paramedics will be able to say for sure though.
Oh, man. I am going to be in so much trouble.
Hey, Addie, I brought you some water!
Addie, what do you say?
Thank you.
SNACKZ
You're going to have a wicked scar! It's going to be awesome.
It is?
Sheesh, Jason.

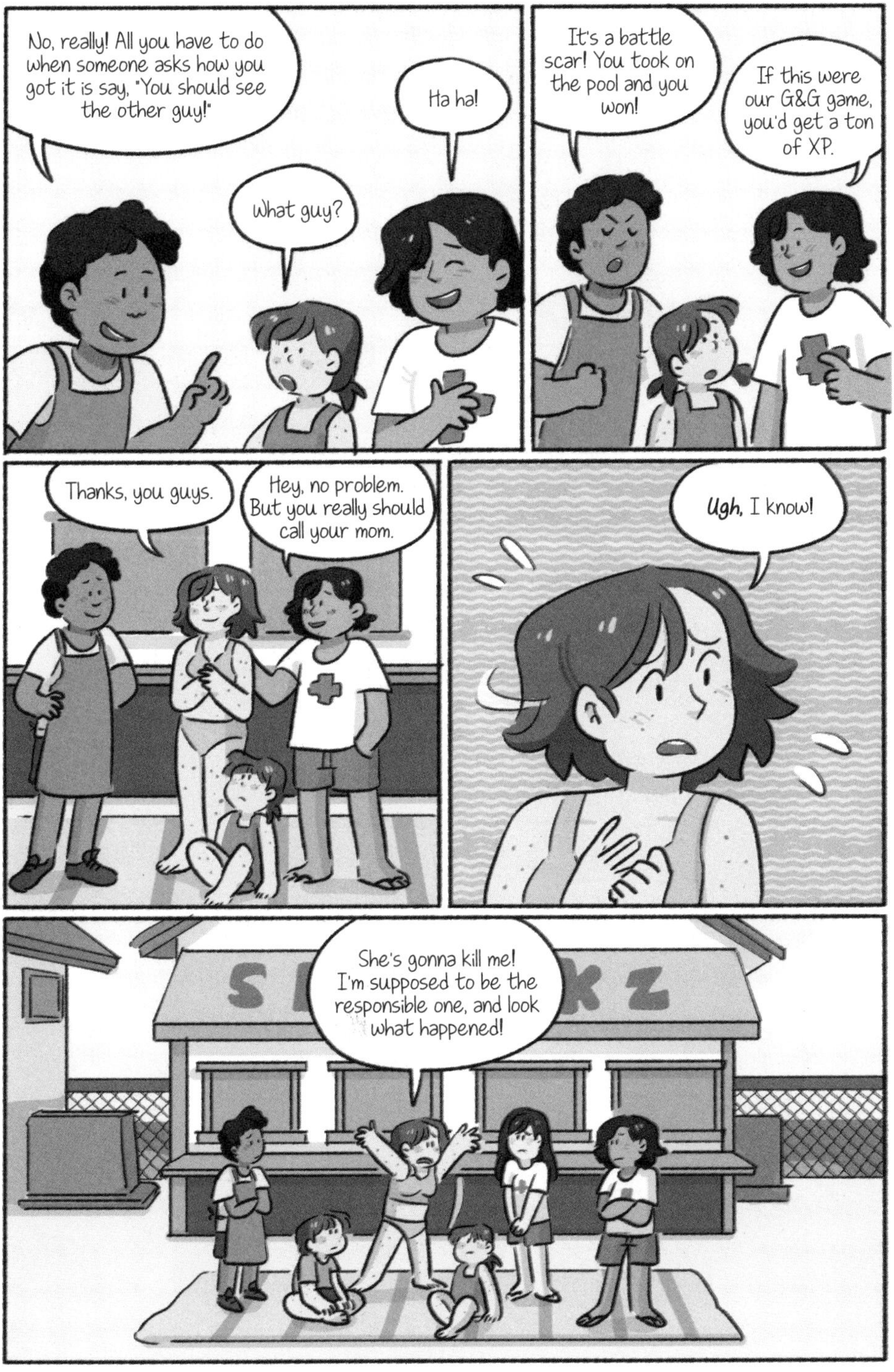
No, really! All you have to do when someone asks how you got it is say, "You should see the other guy!"
Ha ha!
What guy?
It's a battle scar! You took on the pool and you won!
If this were our G&G game, you'd get a ton of XP.
Thanks, you guys.
Hey, no problem. But you really should call your mom.
Ugh, I know!
She's gonna kill me! I'm supposed to be the responsible one, and look what happened!

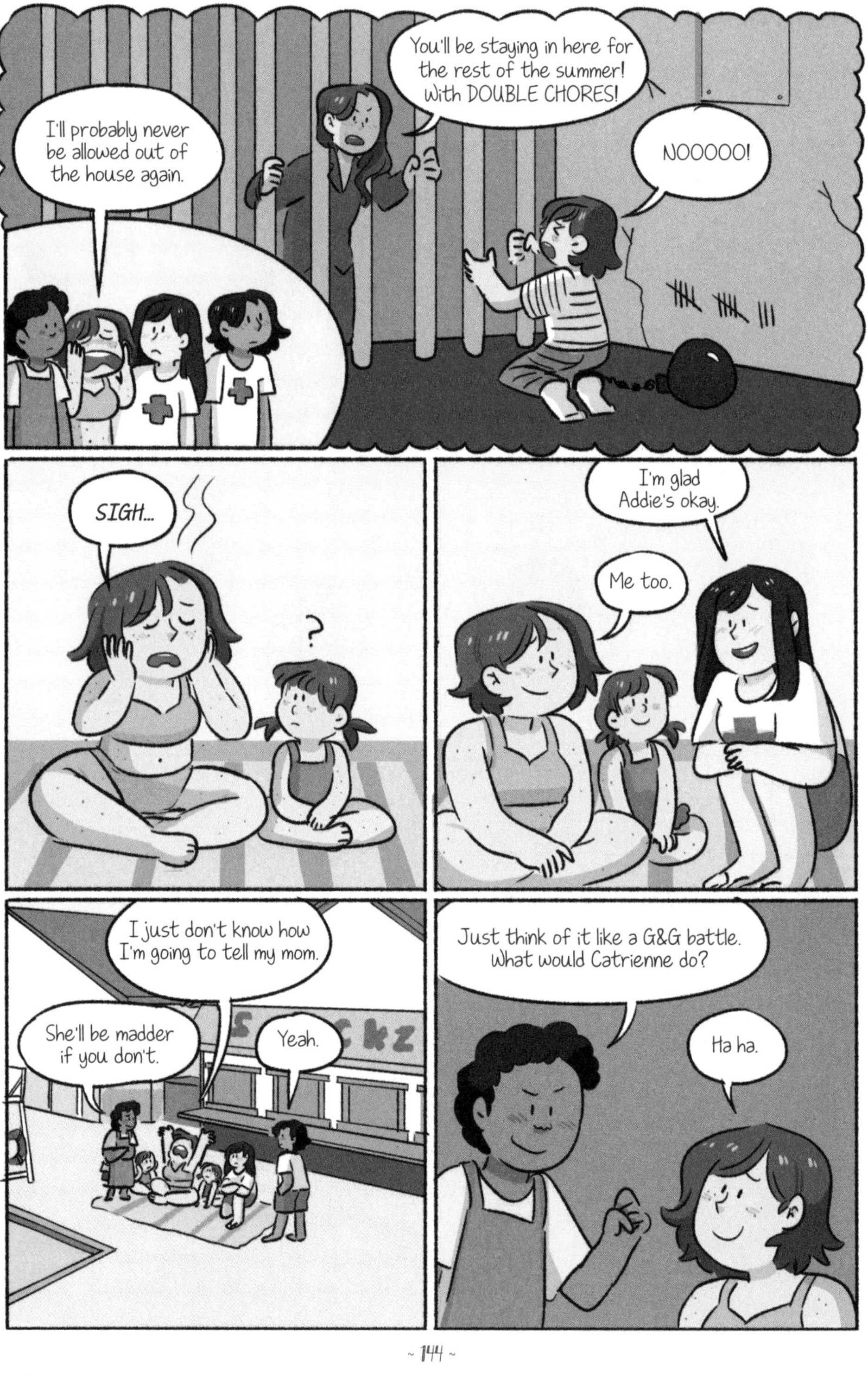
I'll probably never be allowed out of the house again.
You'll be staying in here for the rest of the summer! With DOUBLE CHORES!
NOOOOO!
SIGH...
?
I'm glad Addie's okay.
Me too.
I just don't know how I'm going to tell my mom.
She'll be madder if you don't.
Yeah.
Just think of it like a G&G battle. What would Catrienne do?
Ha ha.

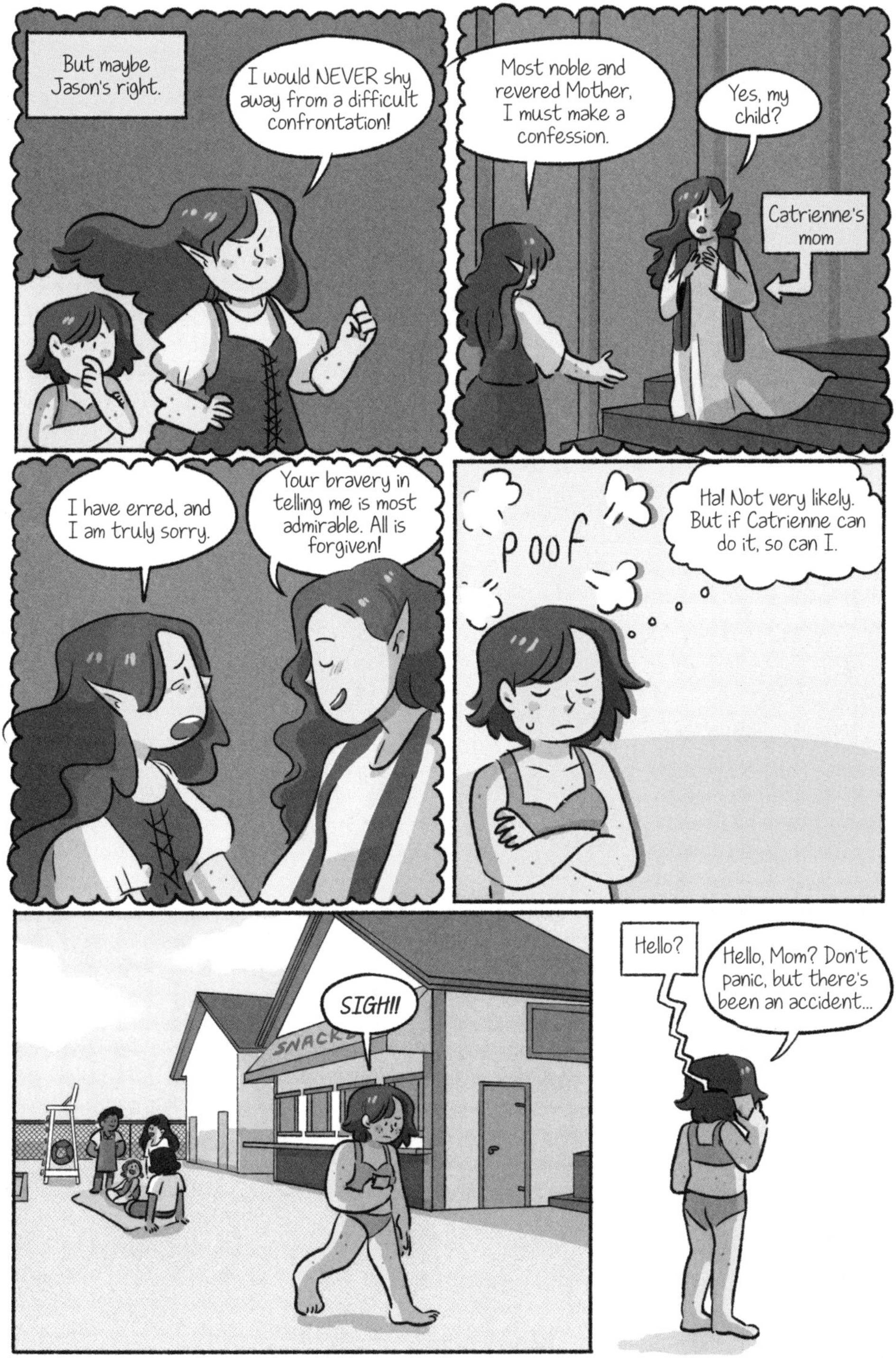

But maybe Jason's right.
I would NEVER shy away from a difficult confrontation!
Most noble and revered Mother, I must make a confession.
Yes, my child?
Catrienne's mom
I have erred, and I am truly sorry.
Your bravery in telling me is most admirable. All is forgiven!
poof
Ha! Not very likely. But if Catrienne can do it, so can I.
SIGH!!
SNACKS
Hello?
Hello, Mom? Don't panic, but there's been an accident...

Chapter 10

Alexis vs. Herself

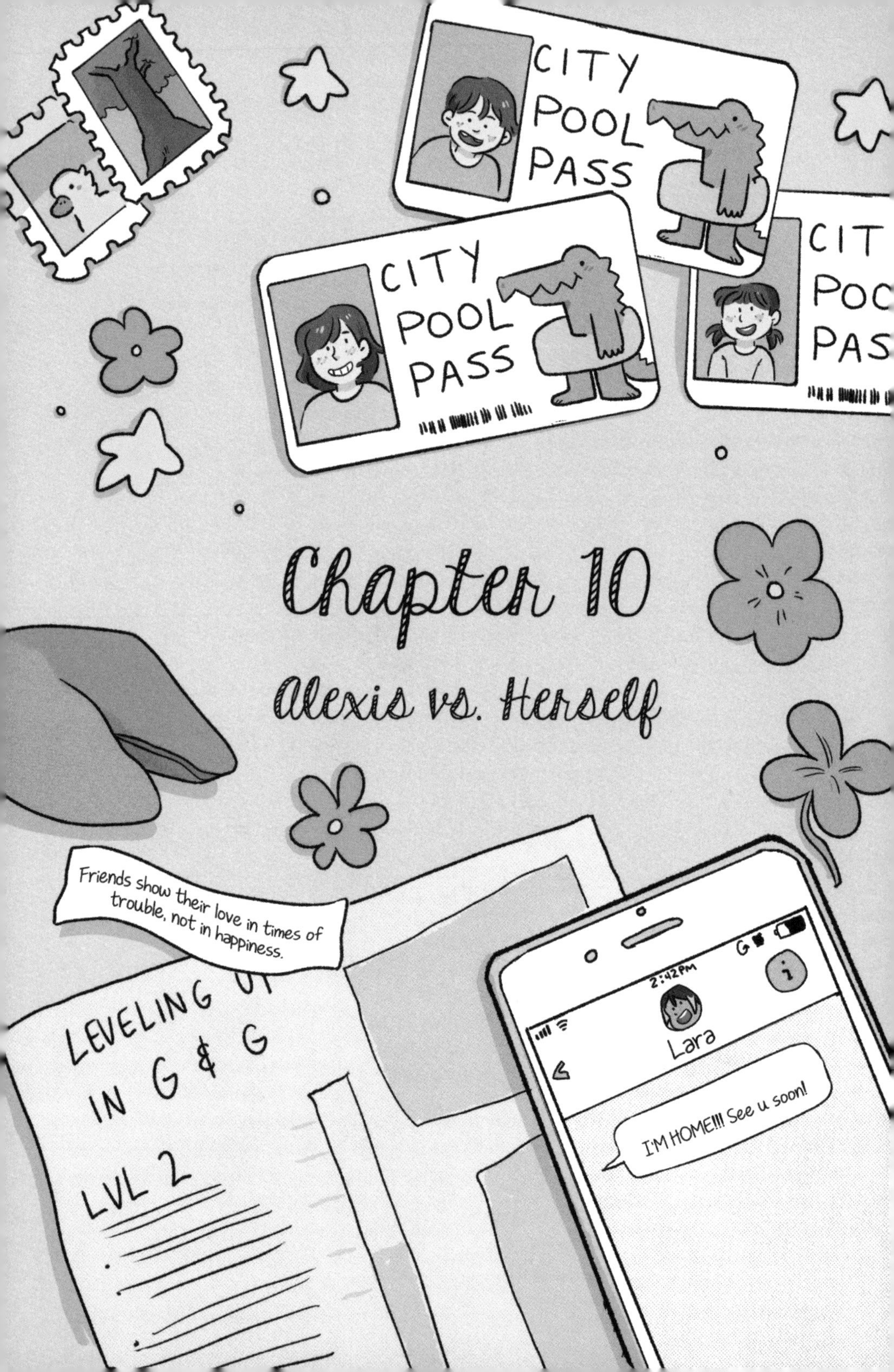
CITY POOL PASS
CITY POOL PASS
Friends show their love in times of trouble, not in happiness.
LEVELING
IN G & G
LVL 2
2:42 PM
Lara
I'M HOME!!! See u soon!

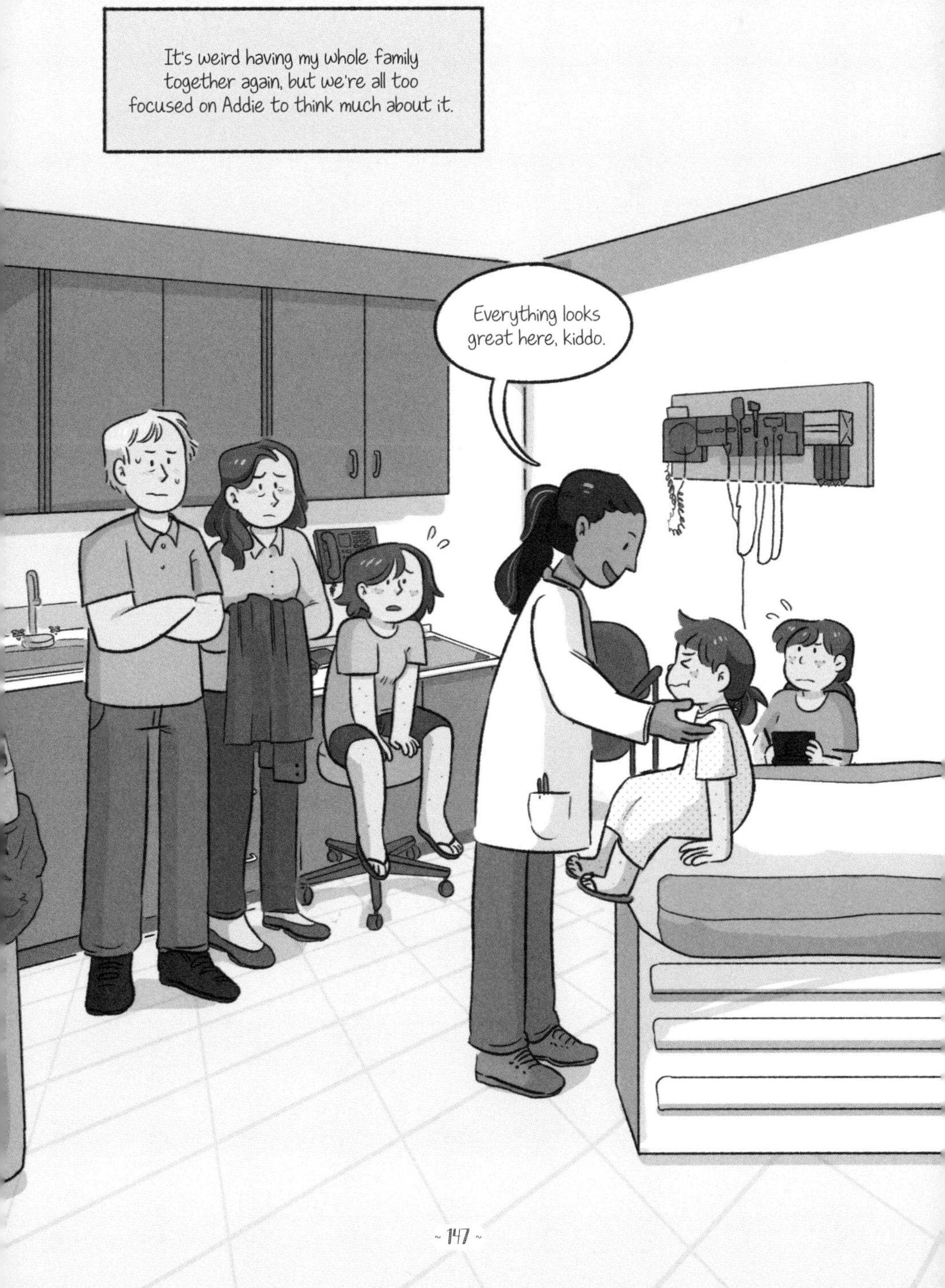
It's weird having my whole family together again, but we're all too focused on Addie to think much about it.
Everything looks great here, kiddo.

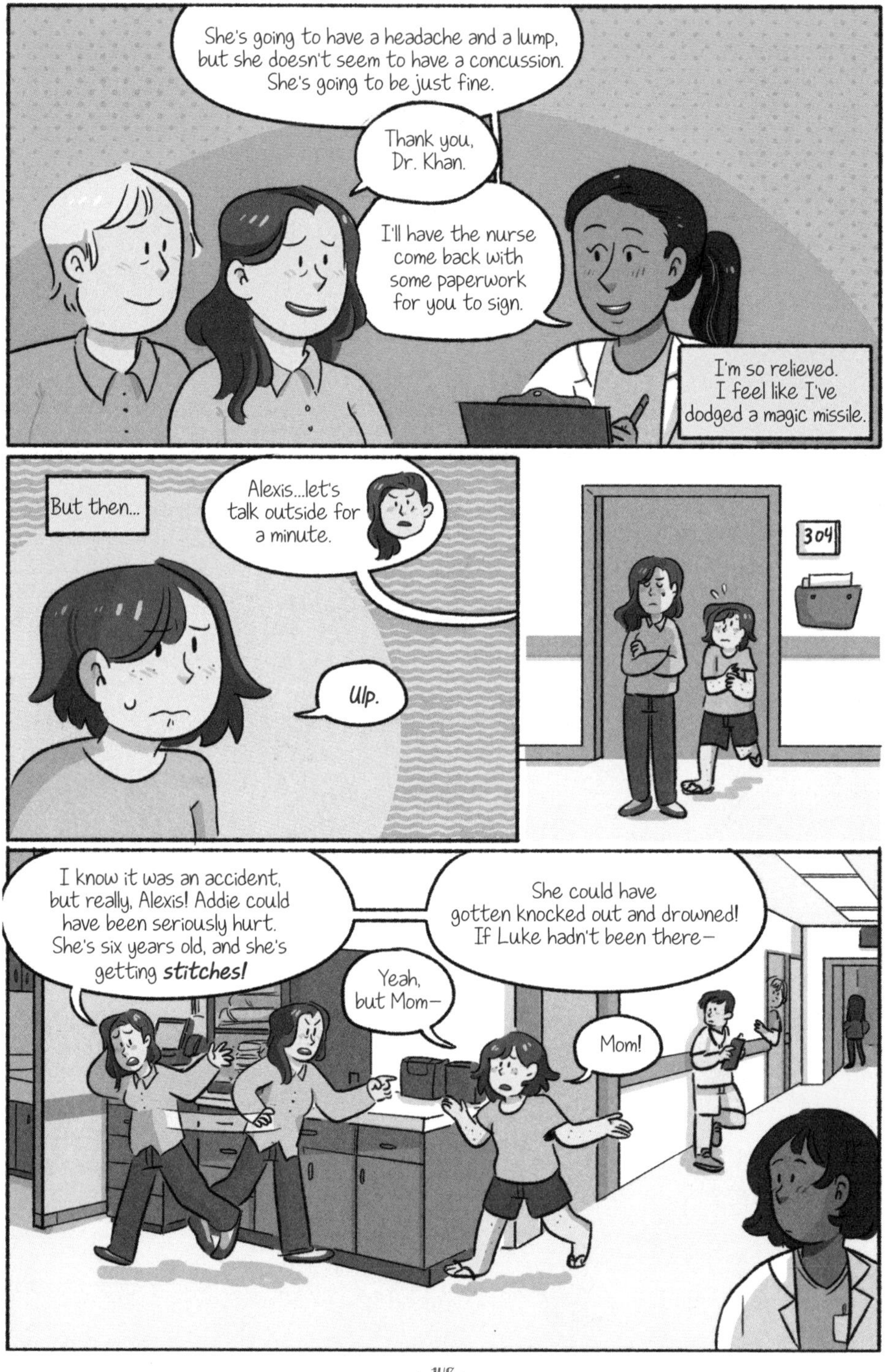
She's going to have a headache and a lump, but she doesn't seem to have a concussion. She's going to be just fine.
Thank you, Dr. Khan.
I'll have the nurse come back with some paperwork for you to sign.
I'm so relieved. I feel like I've dodged a magic missile.
But then...
Alexis...let's talk outside for a minute.
Ulp.
304
I know it was an accident, but really, Alexis! Addie could have been seriously hurt. She's six years old, and she's getting **stitches!**
She could have gotten knocked out and drowned! If Luke hadn't been there—
Yeah, but Mom—
Mom!

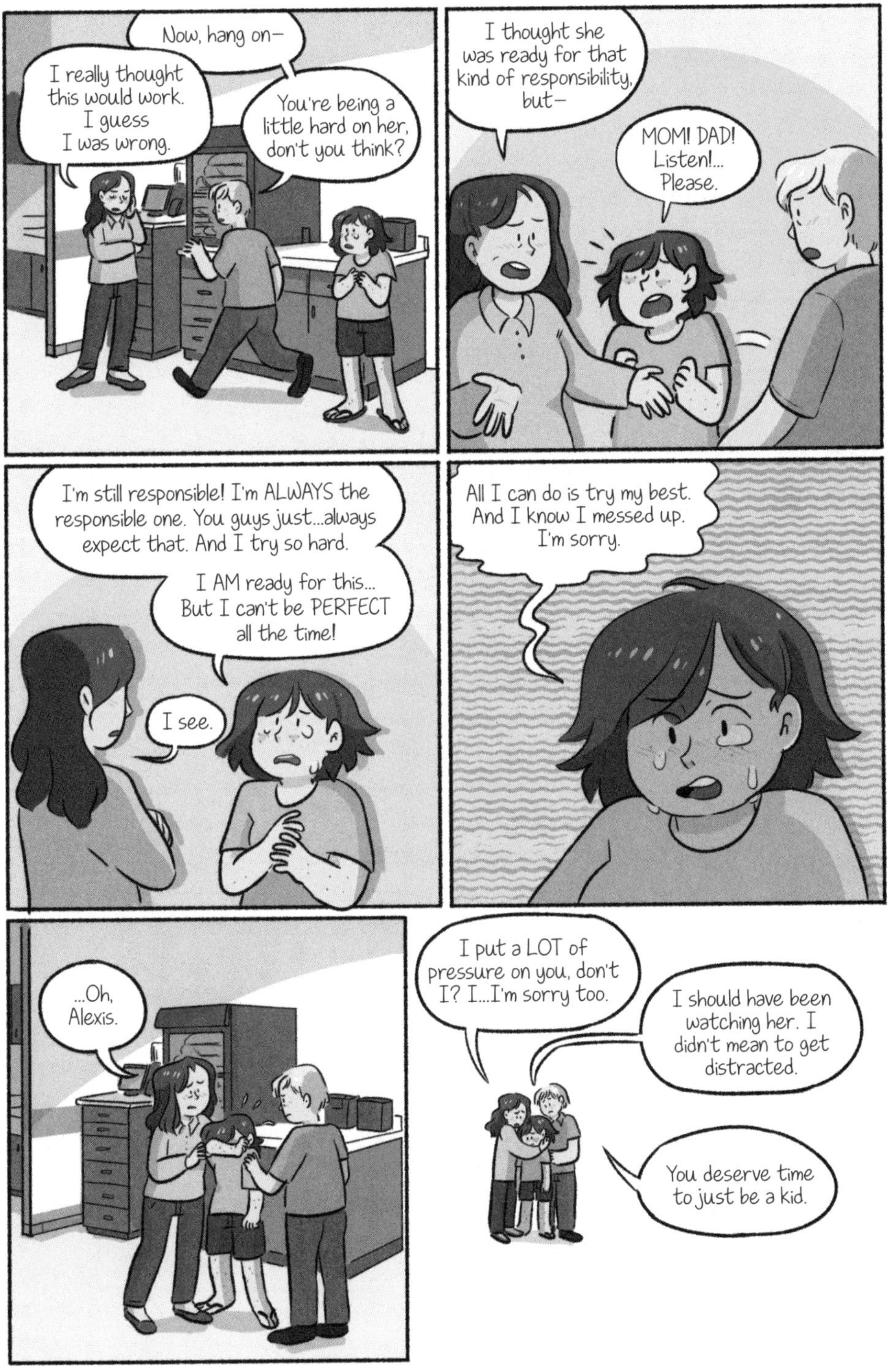
Now, hang on–
I really thought this would work. I guess I was wrong.
You're being a little hard on her, don't you think?
I thought she was ready for that kind of responsibility, but–
MOM! DAD! Listen!... Please.
I'm still responsible! I'm ALWAYS the responsible one. You guys just...always expect that. And I try so hard.
I AM ready for this... But I can't be PERFECT all the time!
I see.
All I can do is try my best. And I know I messed up. I'm sorry.
...Oh, Alexis.
I put a LOT of pressure on you, don't I? I...I'm sorry too.
I should have been watching her. I didn't mean to get distracted.
You deserve time to just be a kid.

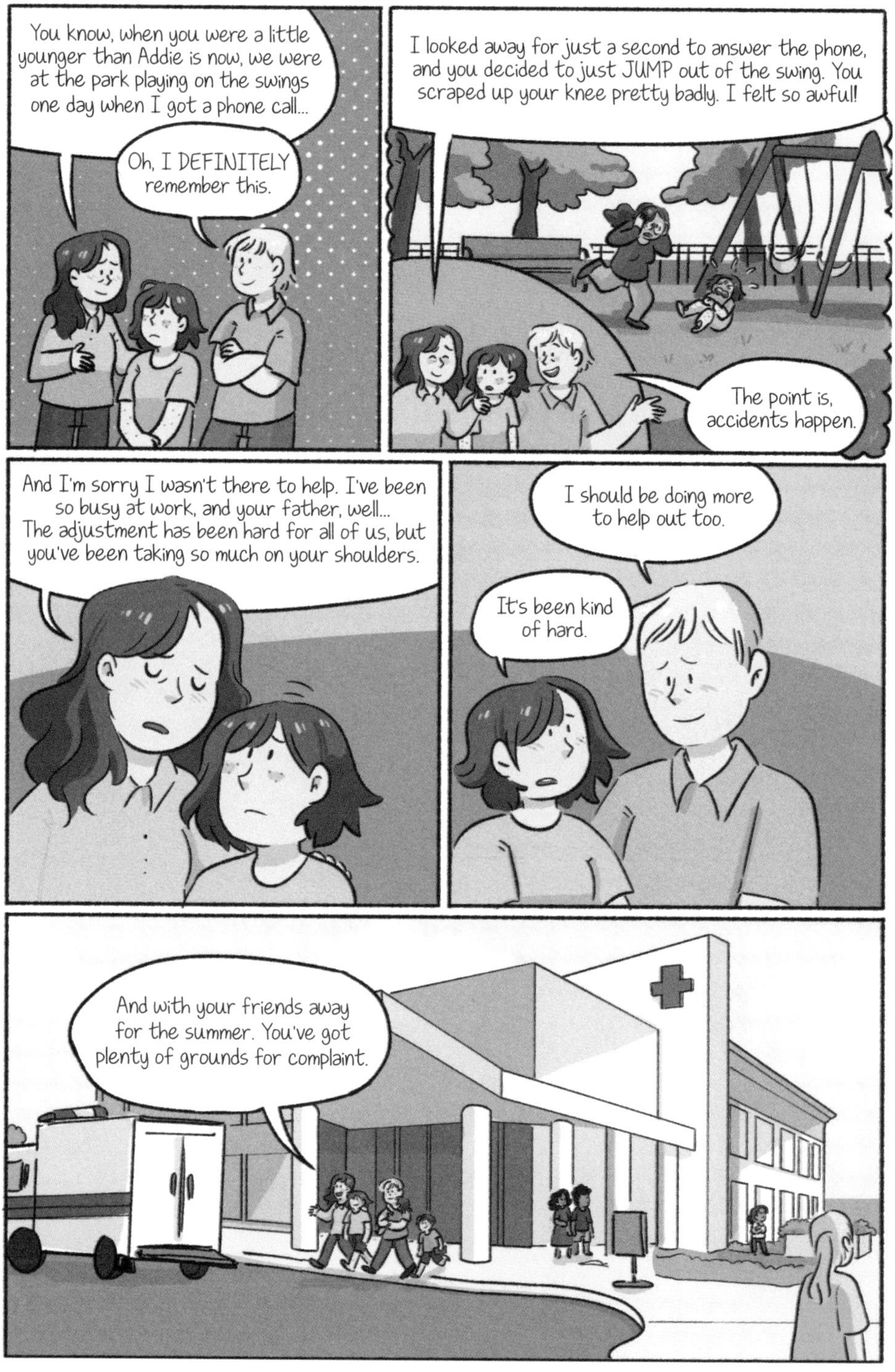
You know, when you were a little younger than Addie is now, we were at the park playing on the swings one day when I got a phone call...
Oh, I DEFINITELY remember this.
I looked away for just a second to answer the phone, and you decided to just JUMP out of the swing. You scraped up your knee pretty badly. I felt so awful!
The point is, accidents happen.
And I'm sorry I wasn't there to help. I've been so busy at work, and your father, well... The adjustment has been hard for all of us, but you've been taking so much on your shoulders.
I should be doing more to help out too.
It's been kind of hard.
And with your friends away for the summer. You've got plenty of grounds for complaint.

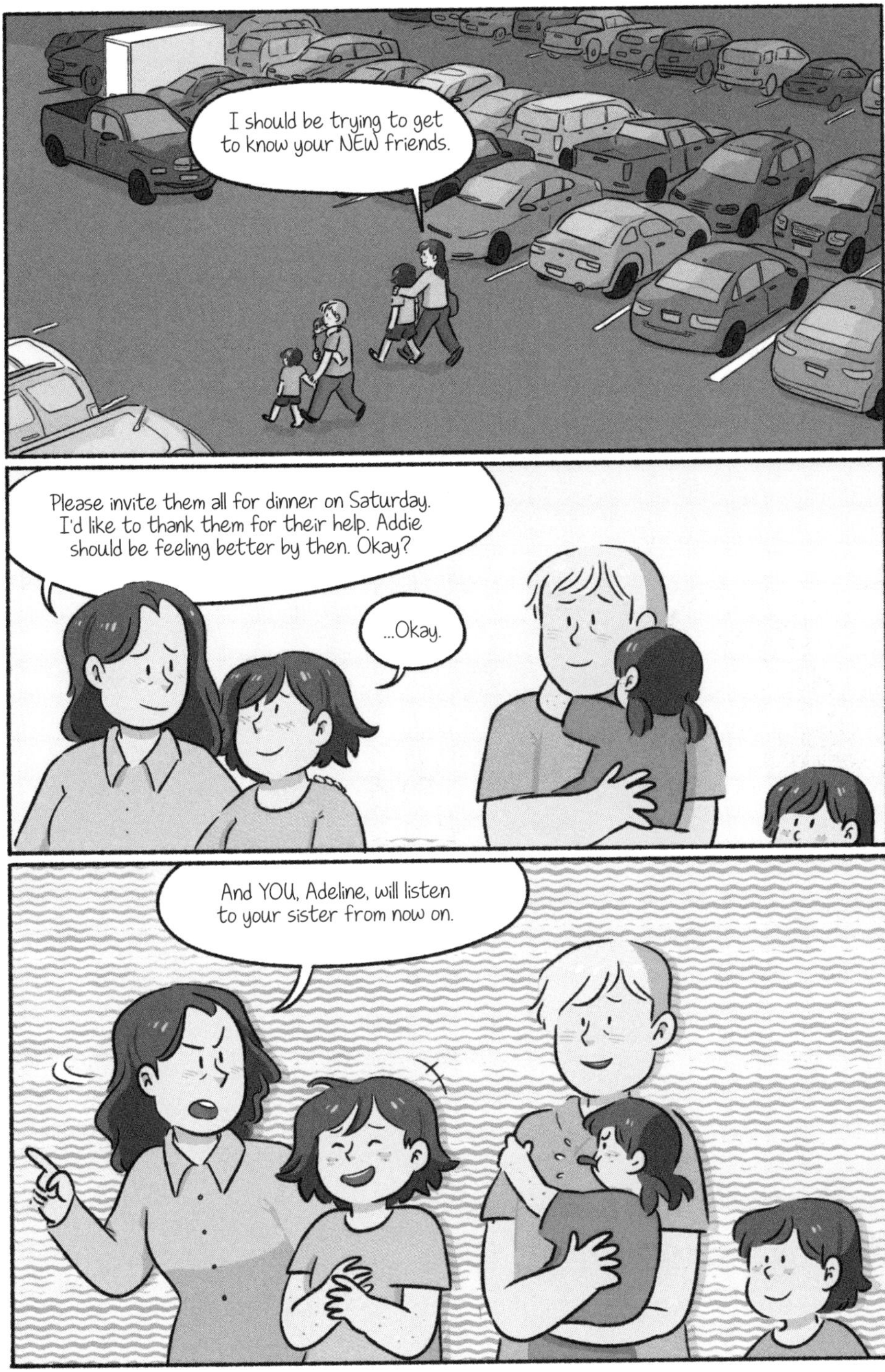
I should be trying to get to know your NEW friends.
Please invite them all for dinner on Saturday. I'd like to thank them for their help. Addie should be feeling better by then. Okay?
...Okay.
And YOU, Adeline, will listen to your sister from now on.

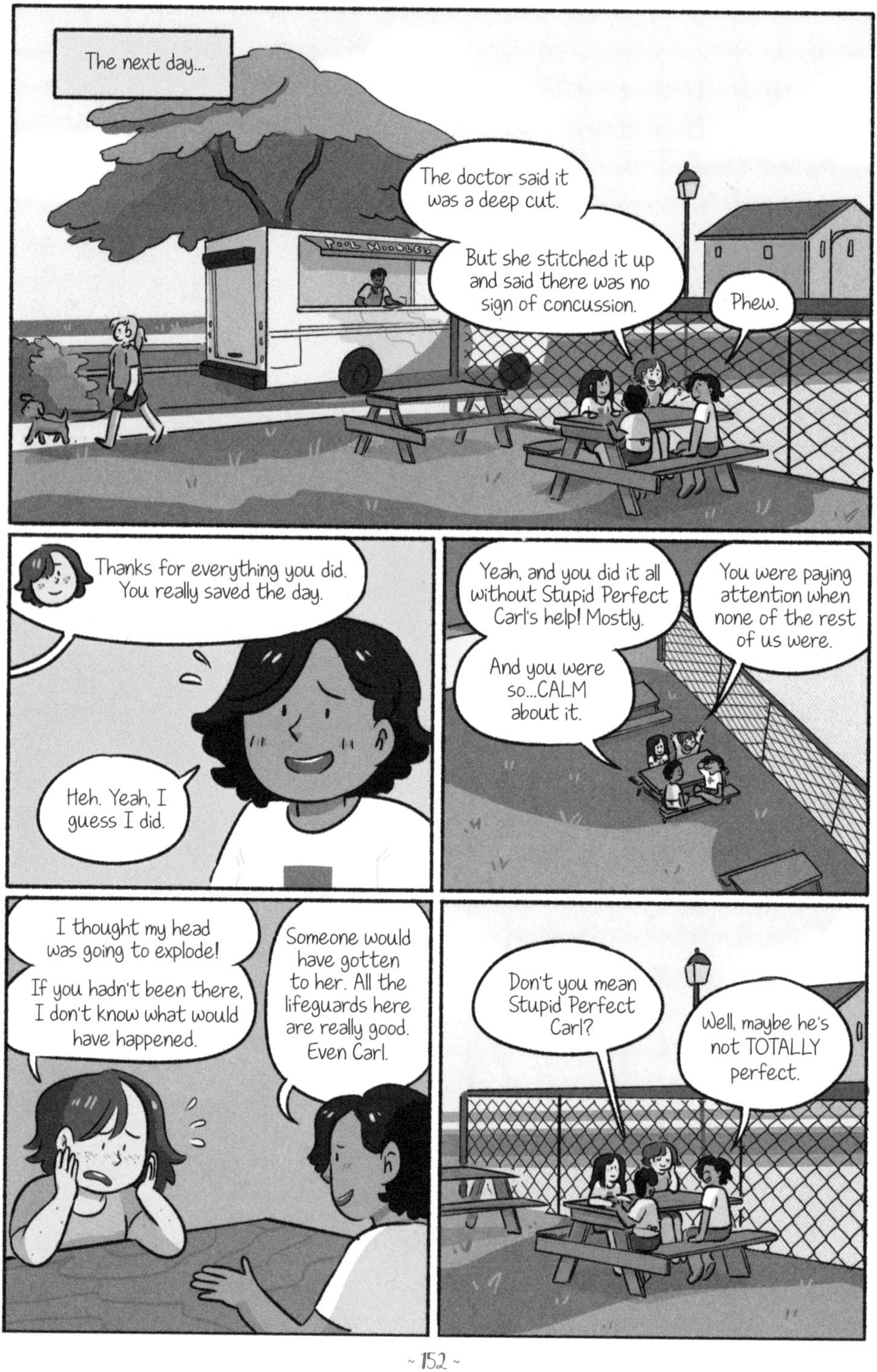
The next day...
The doctor said it was a deep cut.
But she stitched it up and said there was no sign of concussion.
Phew.
Thanks for everything you did. You really saved the day.
Heh. Yeah, I guess I did.
Yeah, and you did it all without Stupid Perfect Carl's help! Mostly.
And you were so...CALM about it.
You were paying attention when none of the rest of us were.
I thought my head was going to explode!
If you hadn't been there, I don't know what would have happened.
Someone would have gotten to her. All the lifeguards here are really good. Even Carl.
Don't you mean Stupid Perfect Carl?
Well, maybe he's not TOTALLY perfect.

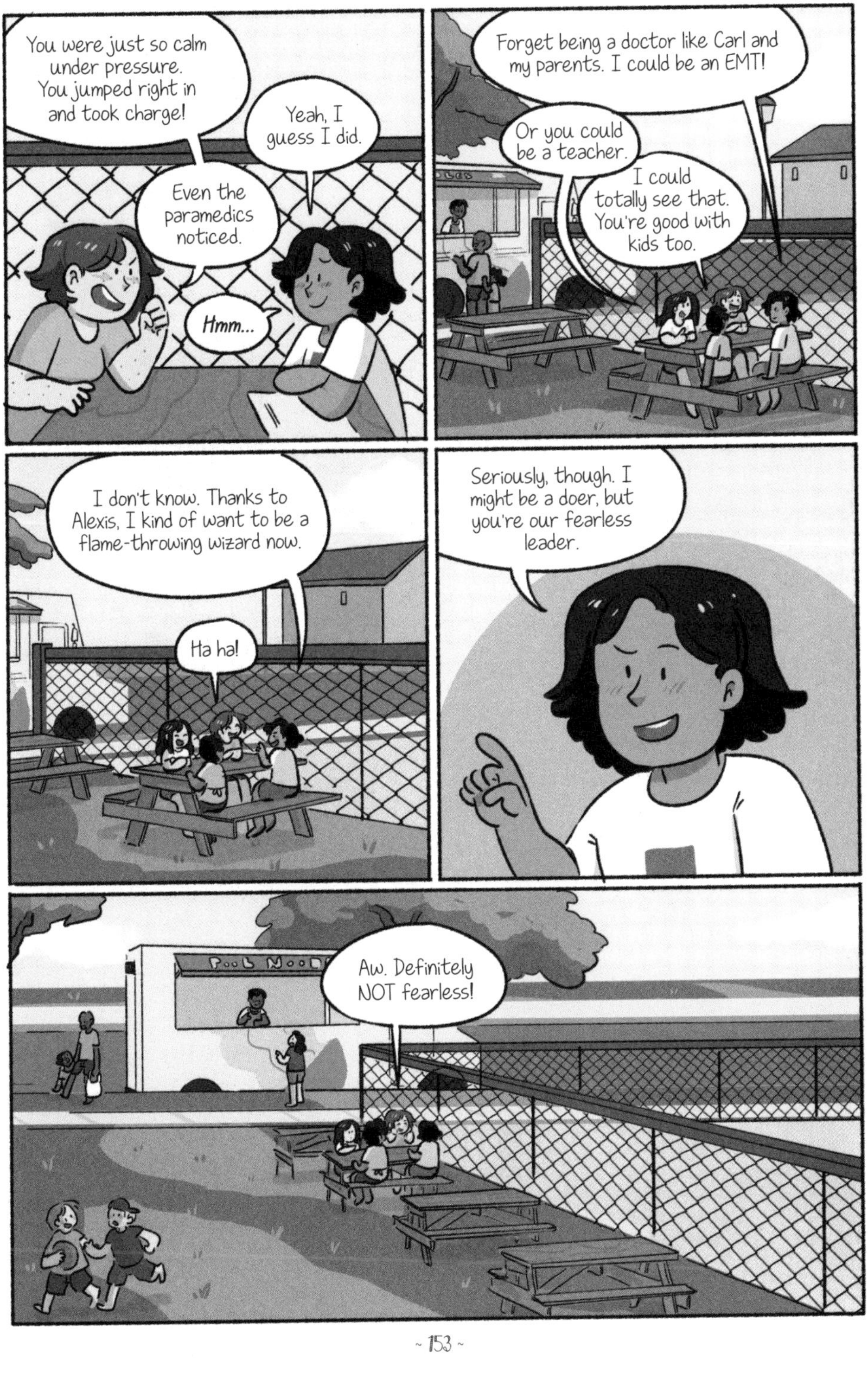
You were just so calm under pressure. You jumped right in and took charge!
Yeah, I guess I did.
Even the paramedics noticed.
Hmm...
Forget being a doctor like Carl and my parents. I could be an EMT!
Or you could be a teacher.
I could totally see that. You're good with kids too.
I don't know. Thanks to Alexis, I kind of want to be a flame-throwing wizard now.
Ha ha!
Seriously, though. I might be a doer, but you're our fearless leader.
Aw. Definitely NOT fearless!

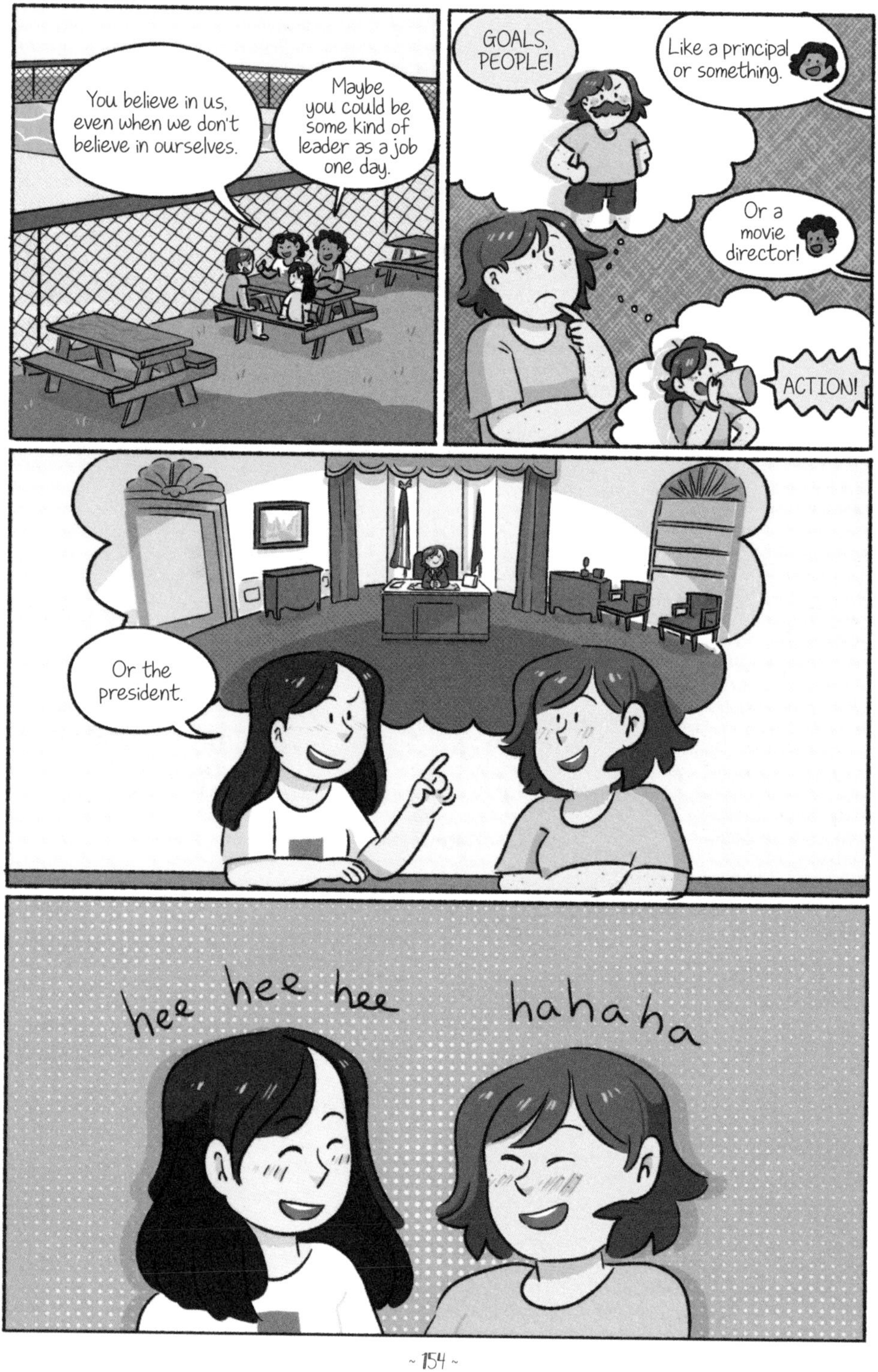
You believe in us, even when we don't believe in ourselves.
Maybe you could be some kind of leader as a job one day.
GOALS, PEOPLE!
Like a principal or something.
Or a movie director!
ACTION!
Or the president.
hee hee hee
hahaha

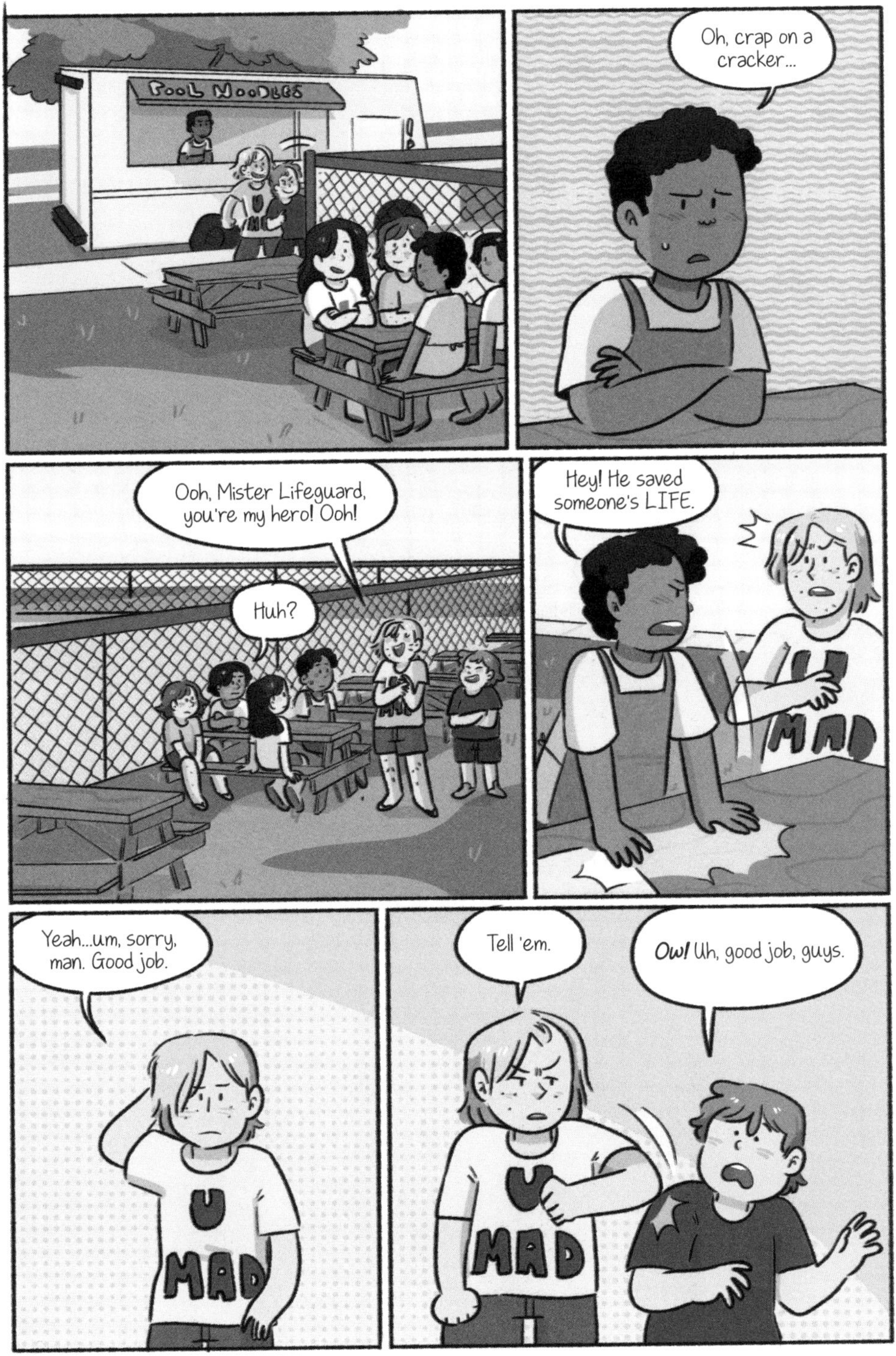

POOL NOODLES
Oh, crap on a cracker...
Ooh, Mister Lifeguard, you're my hero! Ooh!
Huh?
Hey! He saved someone's LIFE.
Yeah...um, sorry, man. Good job.
Tell 'em.
Ow! Uh, good job, guys.

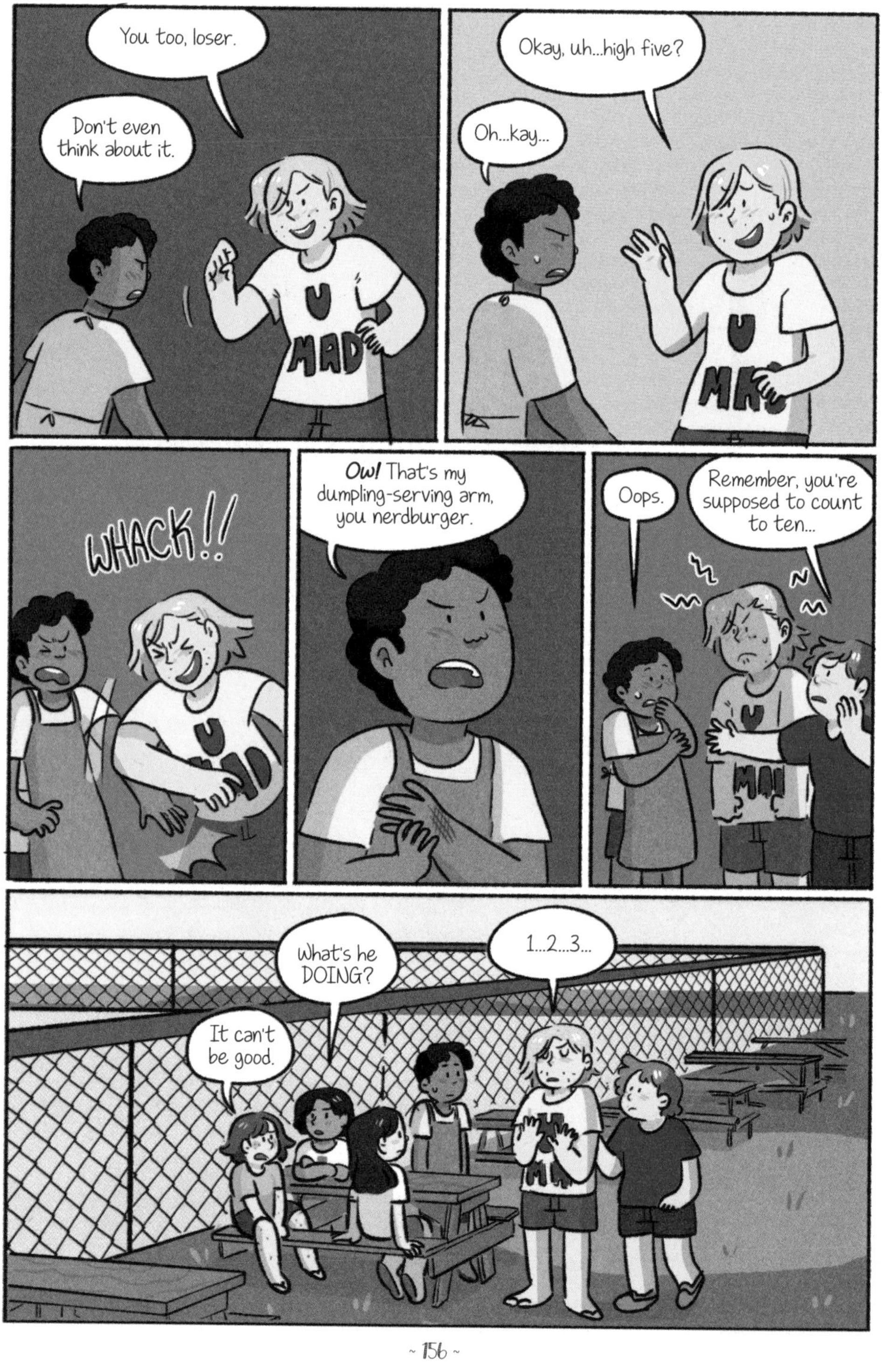
You too, loser.
Don't even think about it.
Okay, uh...high five?
Oh...kay...
WHACK!!
Ow! That's my dumpling-serving arm, you nerdburger.
Oops.
Remember, you're supposed to count to ten...
What's he DOING?
1...2...3...
It can't be good.

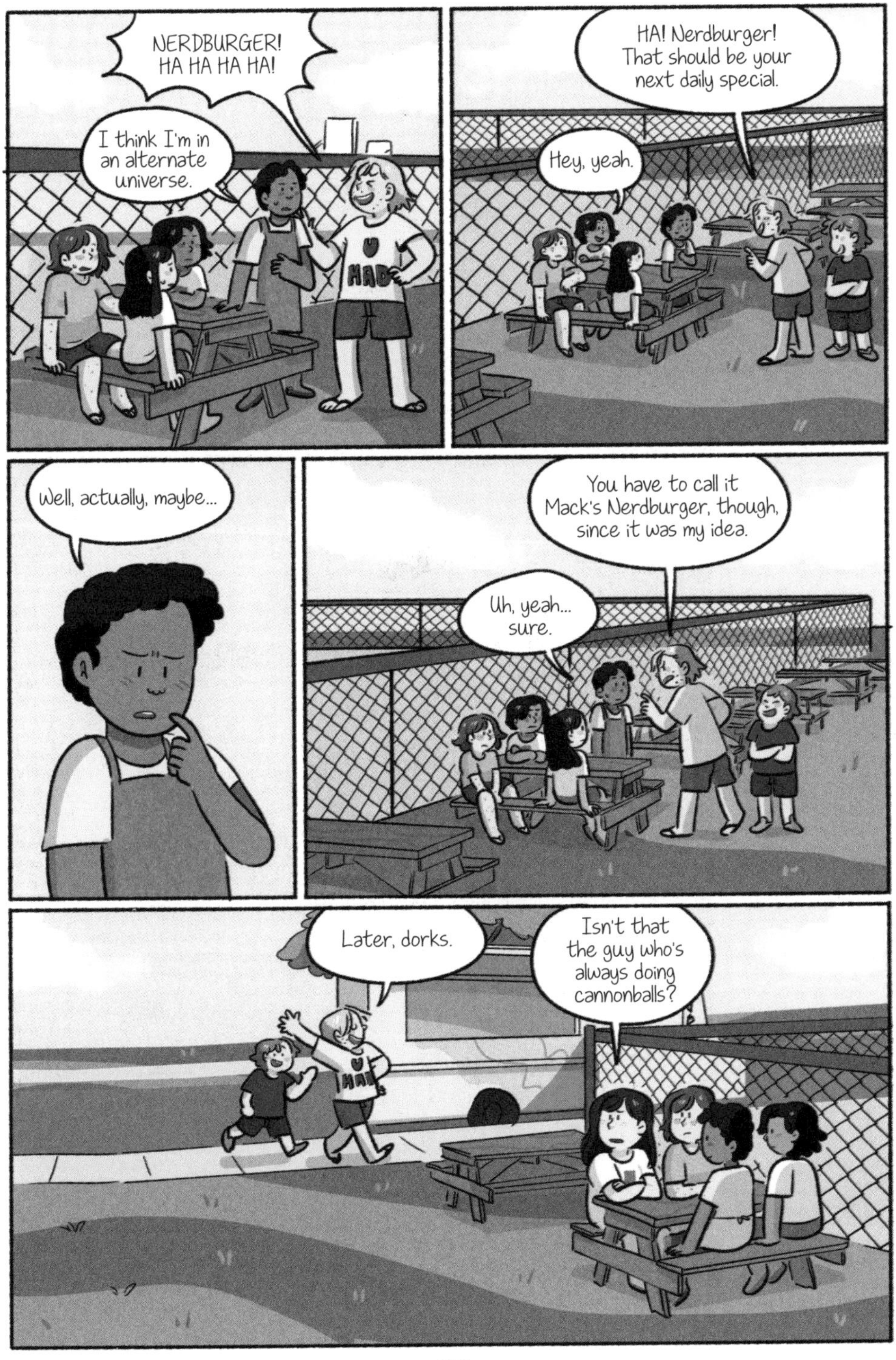
NERDBURGER! HA HA HA HA!
I think I'm in an alternate universe.
HA! Nerdburger! That should be your next daily special.
Hey, yeah.
Well, actually, maybe...
You have to call it Mack's Nerdburger, though, since it was my idea.
Uh, yeah... sure.
Later, dorks.
Isn't that the guy who's always doing cannonballs?

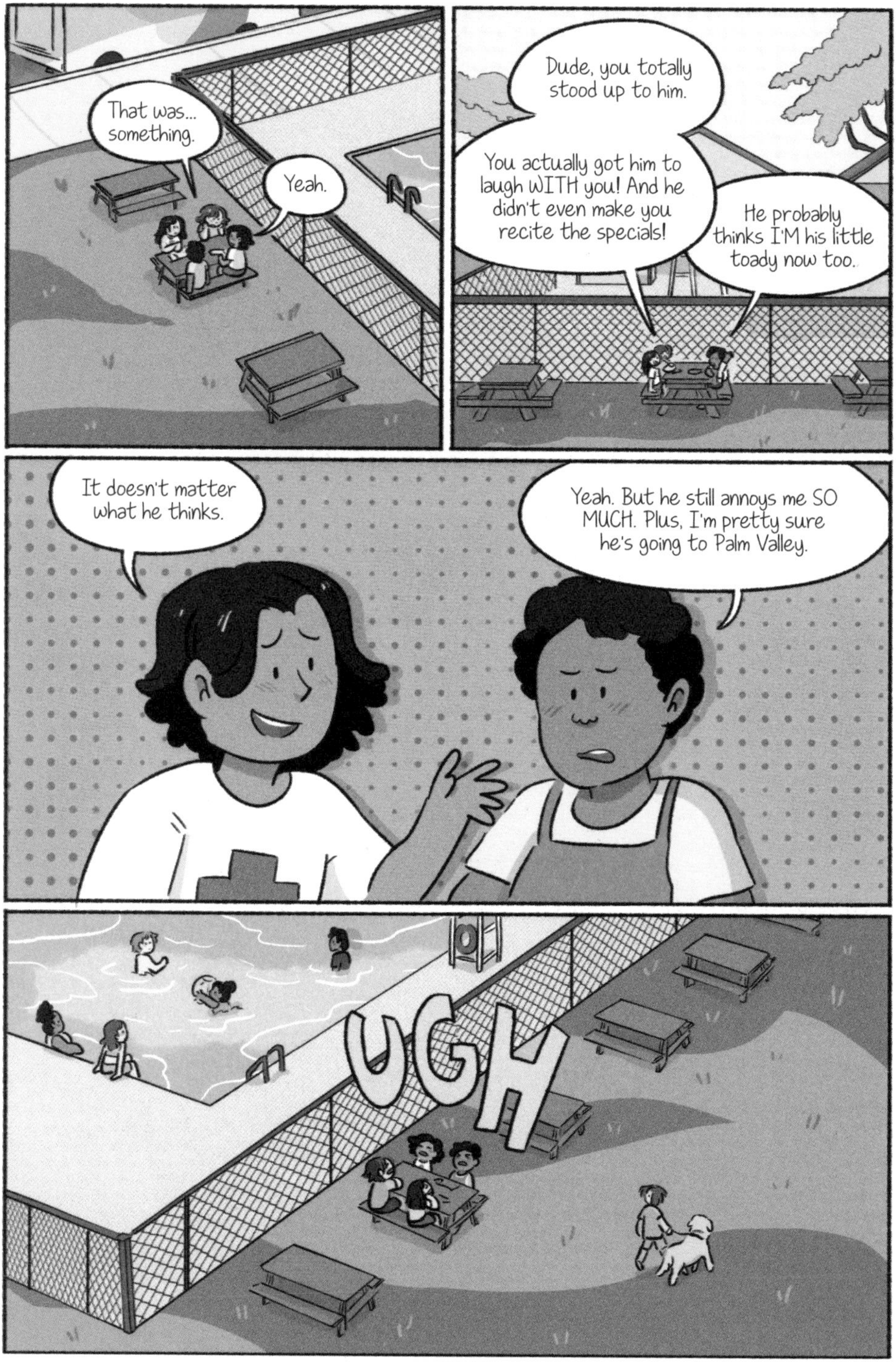
That was... something.
Yeah.
Dude, you totally stood up to him.
You actually got him to laugh WITH you! And he didn't even make you recite the specials!
He probably thinks I'M his little toady now too.
It doesn't matter what he thinks.
Yeah. But he still annoys me SO MUCH. Plus, I'm pretty sure he's going to Palm Valley.
UGH

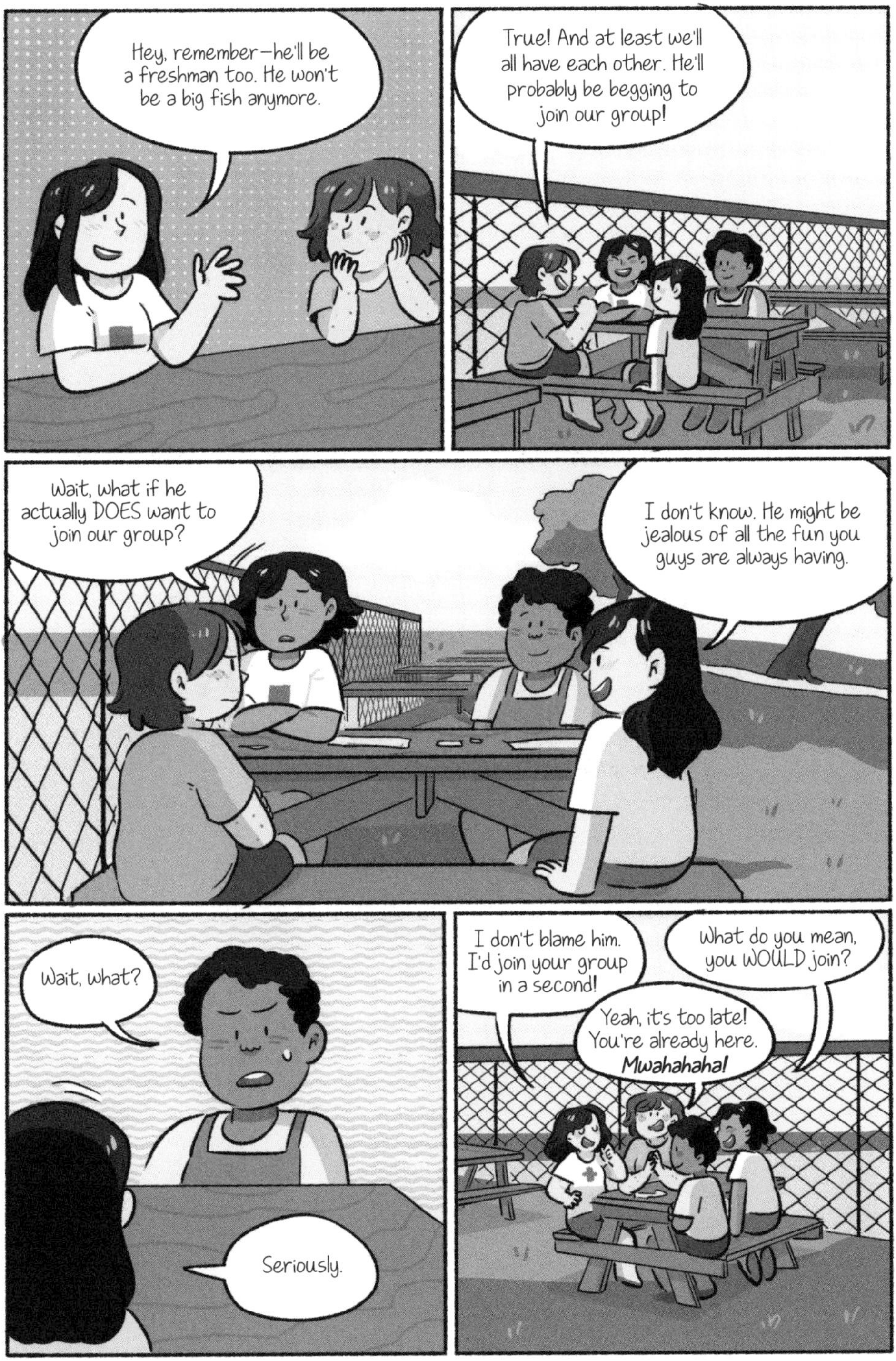
Hey, remember—he'll be a freshman too. He won't be a big fish anymore.
True! And at least we'll all have each other. He'll probably be begging to join our group!
Wait, what if he actually DOES want to join our group?
I don't know. He might be jealous of all the fun you guys are always having.
Wait, what?
Seriously.
I don't blame him. I'd join your group in a second!
What do you mean, you WOULD join?
Yeah, it's too late! You're already here. **Mwahahaha!**

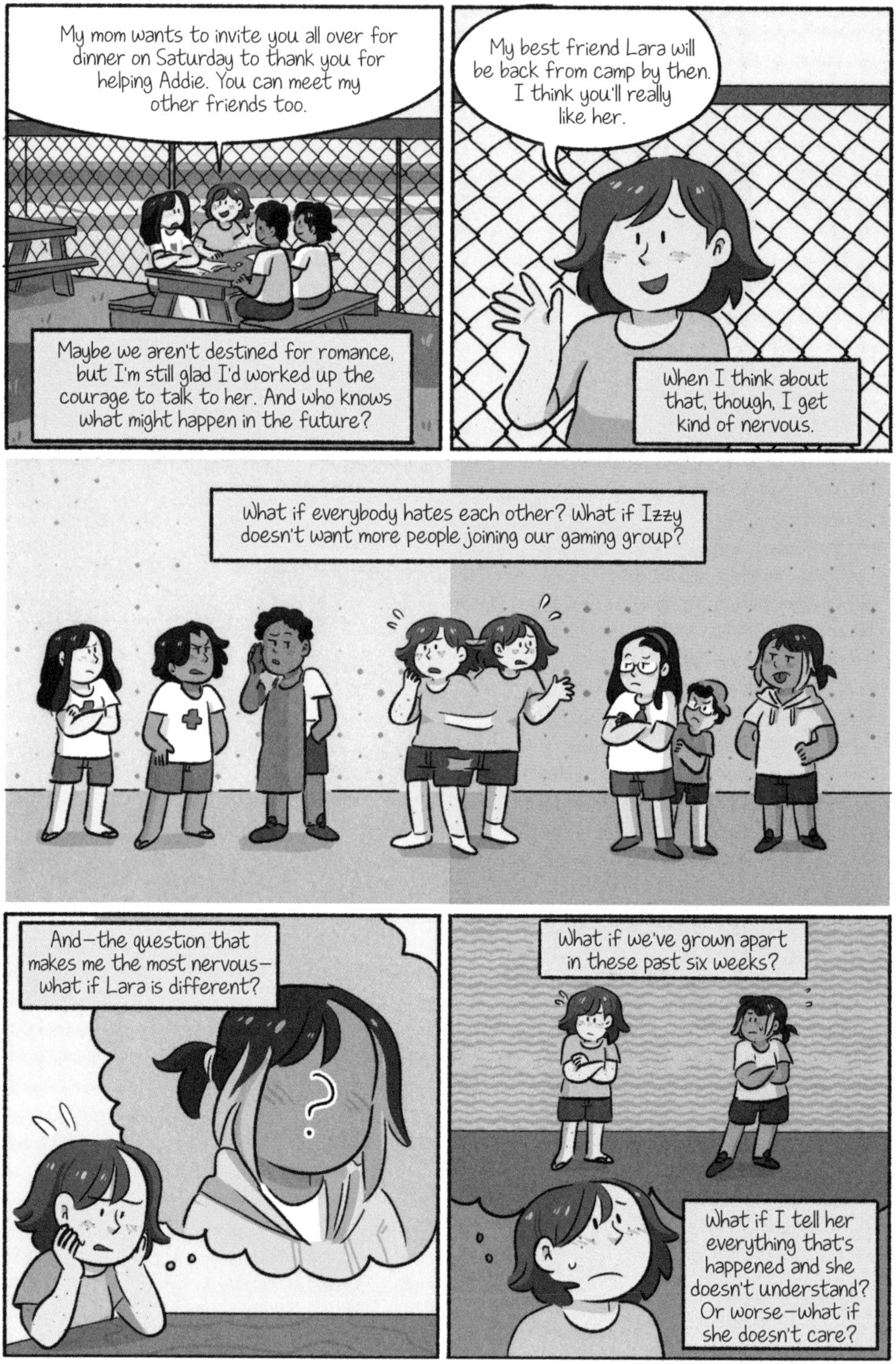

My mom wants to invite you all over for dinner on Saturday to thank you for helping Addie. You can meet my other friends too.
Maybe we aren't destined for romance, but I'm still glad I'd worked up the courage to talk to her. And who knows what might happen in the future?
My best friend Lara will be back from camp by then. I think you'll really like her.
When I think about that, though, I get kind of nervous.
What if everybody hates each other? What if Izzy doesn't want more people joining our gaming group?
And—the question that makes me the most nervous—what if Lara is different?
What if we've grown apart in these past six weeks?
What if I tell her everything that's happened and she doesn't understand? Or worse—what if she doesn't care?

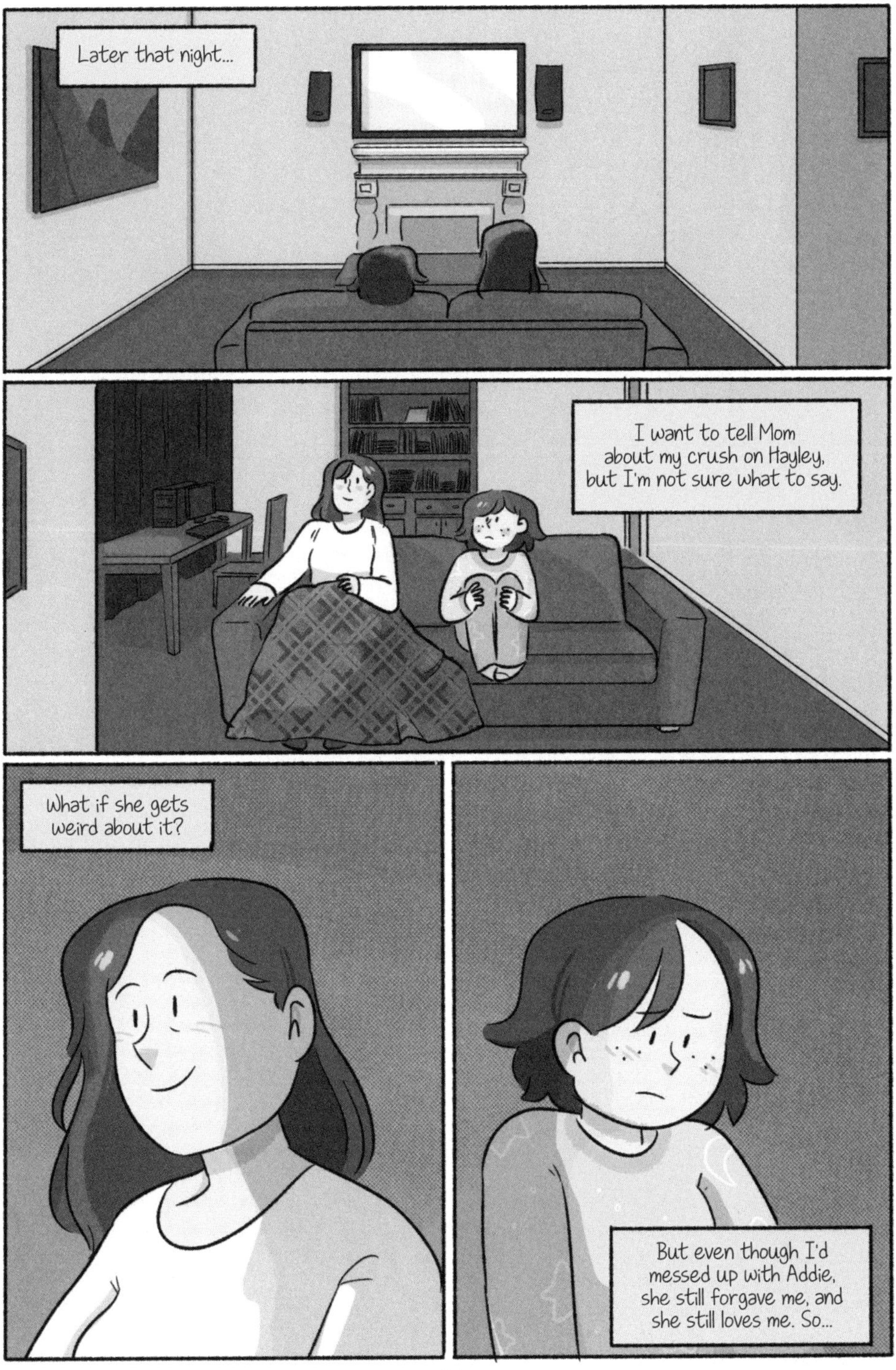
Later that night...
I want to tell Mom about my crush on Hayley, but I'm not sure what to say.
What if she gets weird about it?
But even though I'd messed up with Addie, she still forgave me, and she still loves me. So...

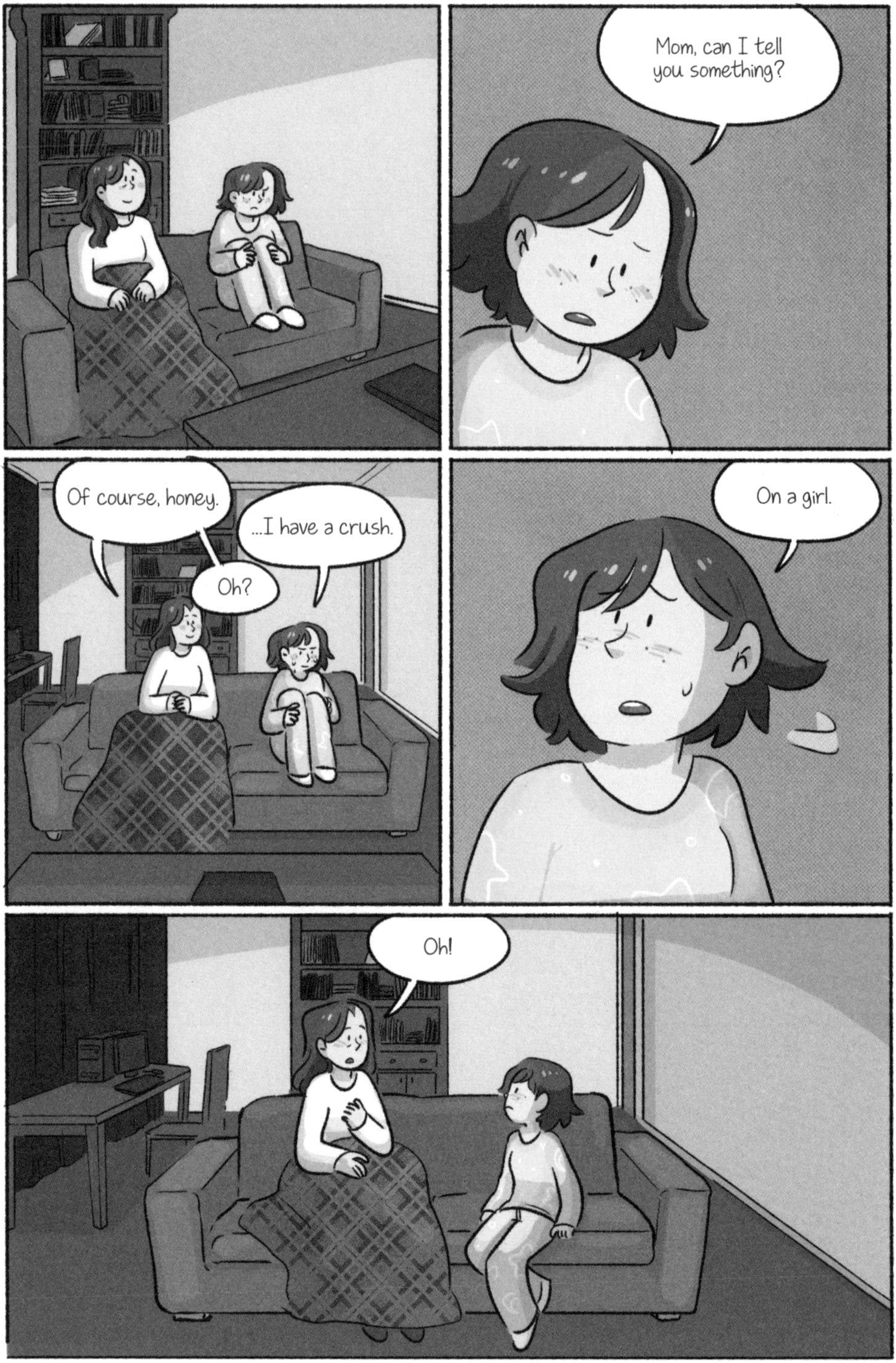
Mom, can I tell you something?
Of course, honey.
...I have a crush.
Oh?
On a girl.
Oh!

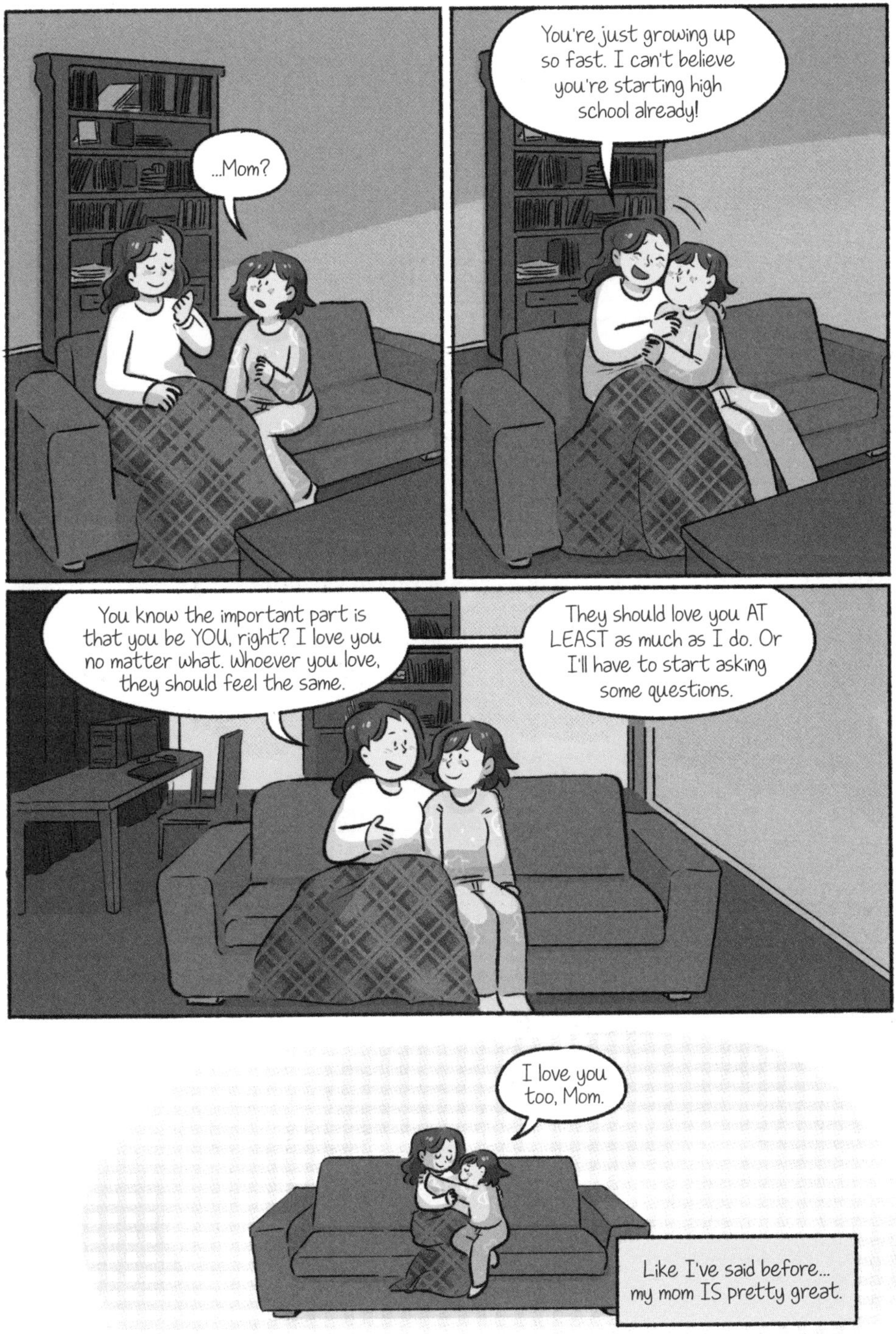
...Mom?
You're just growing up so fast. I can't believe you're starting high school already!
You know the important part is that you be YOU, right? I love you no matter what. Whoever you love, they should feel the same.
They should love you AT LEAST as much as I do. Or I'll have to start asking some questions.
I love you too, Mom.
Like I've said before... my mom IS pretty great.

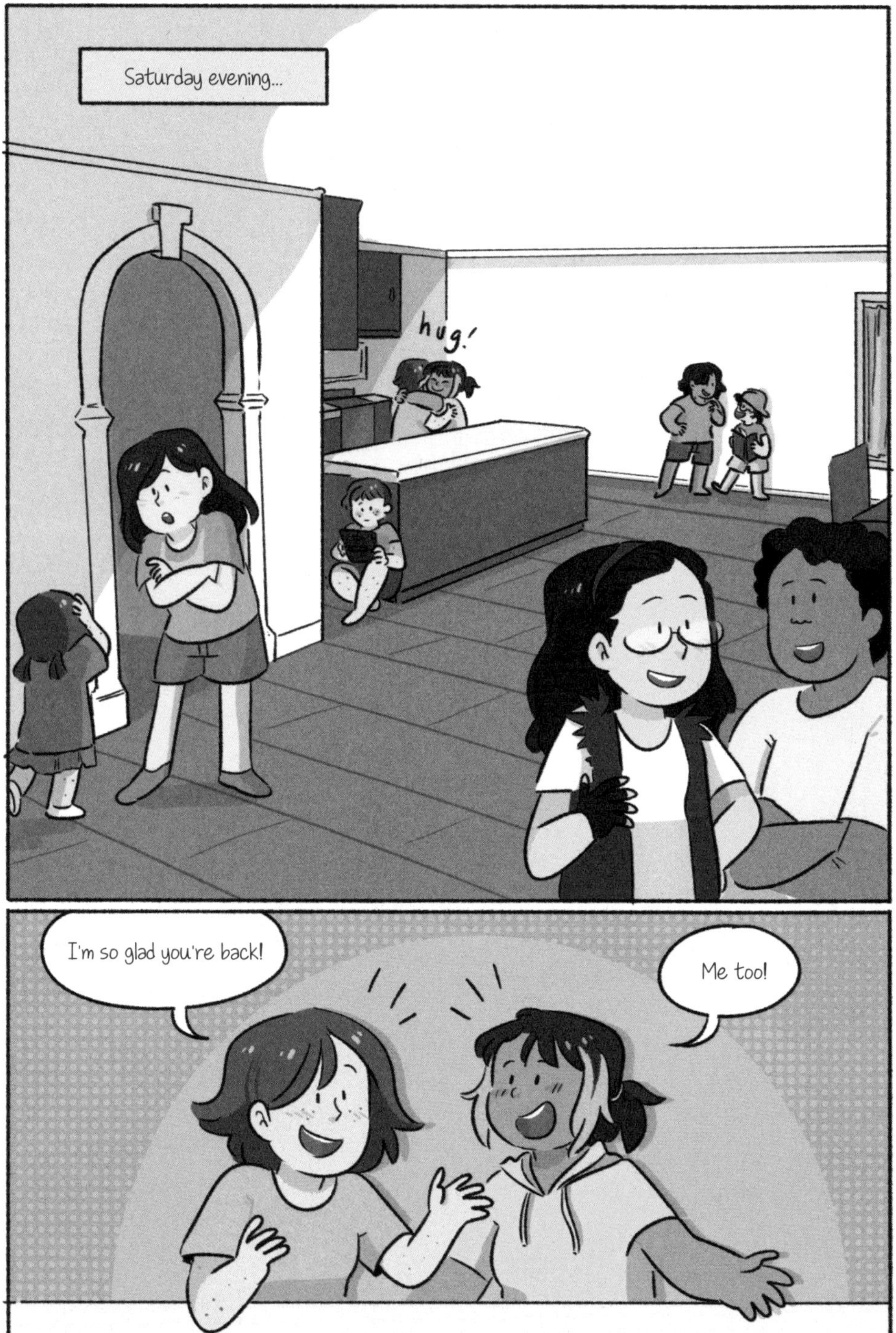
Saturday evening...
hug!
I'm so glad you're back!
Me too!

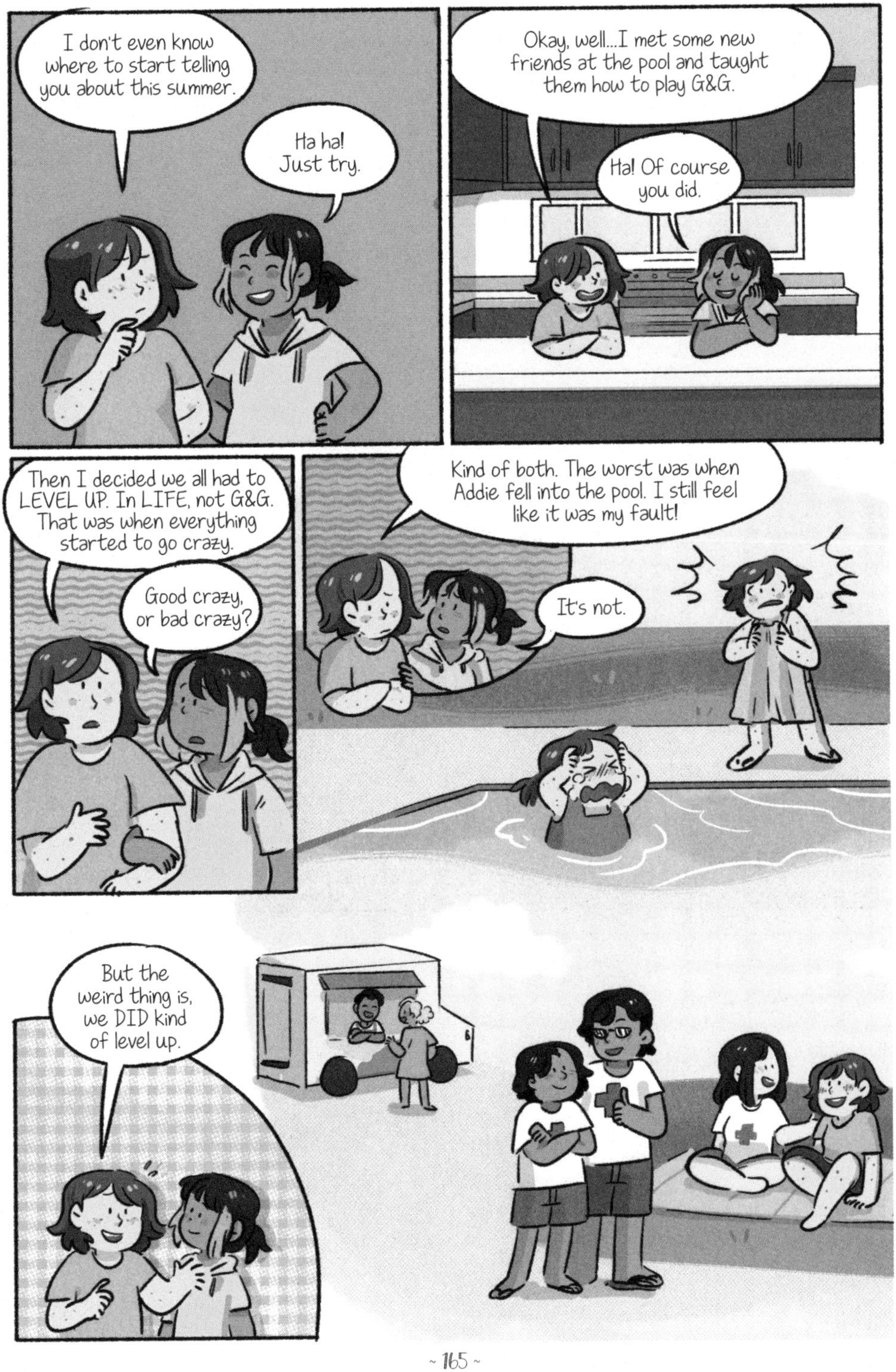
I don't even know where to start telling you about this summer.
Ha ha! Just try.
Okay, well...I met some new friends at the pool and taught them how to play G&G.
Ha! Of course you did.
Then I decided we all had to LEVEL UP. In LIFE, not G&G. That was when everything started to go crazy.
Good crazy, or bad crazy?
Kind of both. The worst was when Addie fell into the pool. I still feel like it was my fault!
It's not.
But the weird thing is, we DID kind of level up.

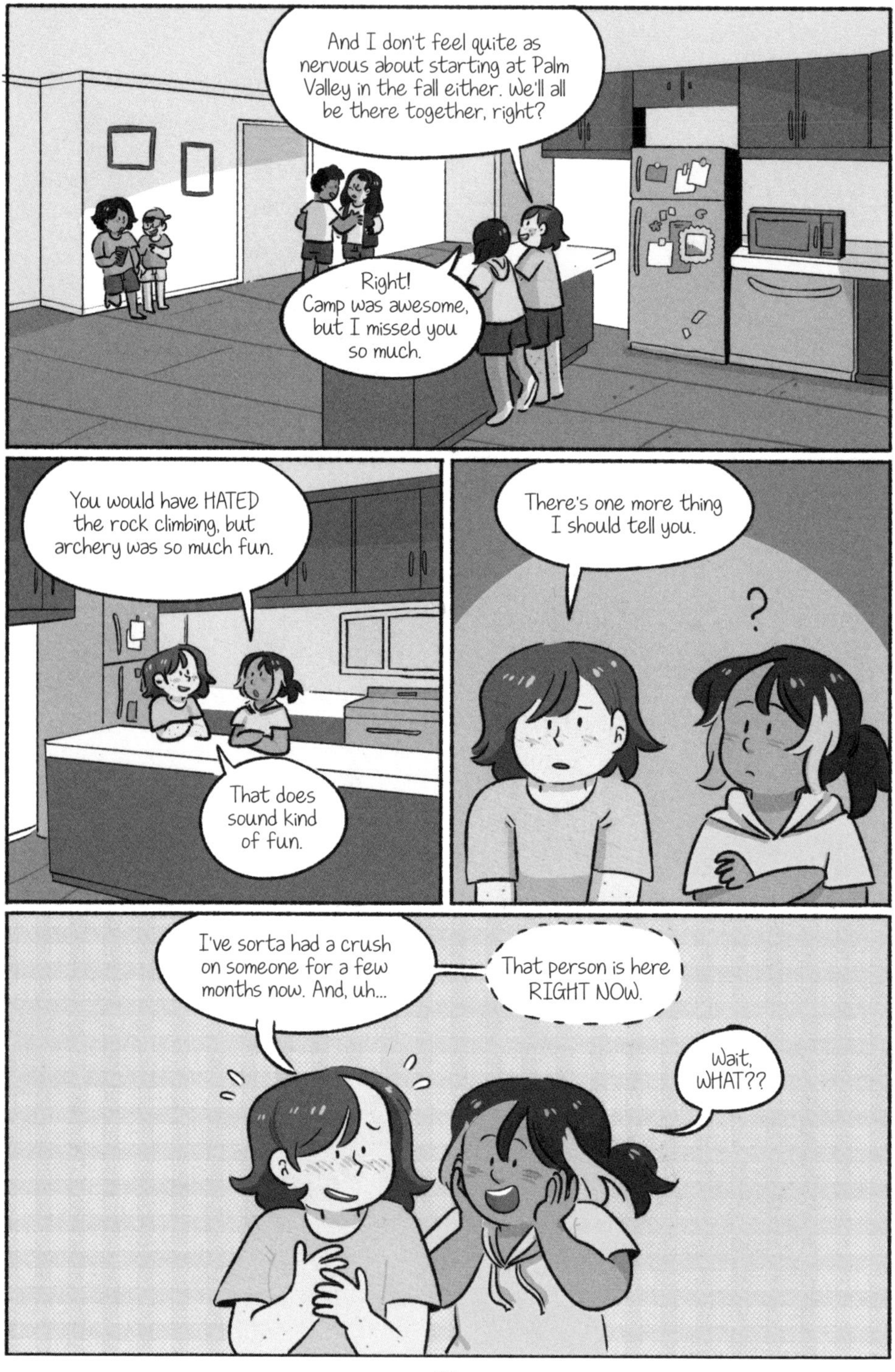
And I don't feel quite as nervous about starting at Palm Valley in the fall either. We'll all be there together, right?
Right! Camp was awesome, but I missed you so much.
You would have HATED the rock climbing, but archery was so much fun.
That does sound kind of fun.
There's one more thing I should tell you.
?
I've sorta had a crush on someone for a few months now. And, uh...
That person is here RIGHT NOW.
Wait, WHAT??

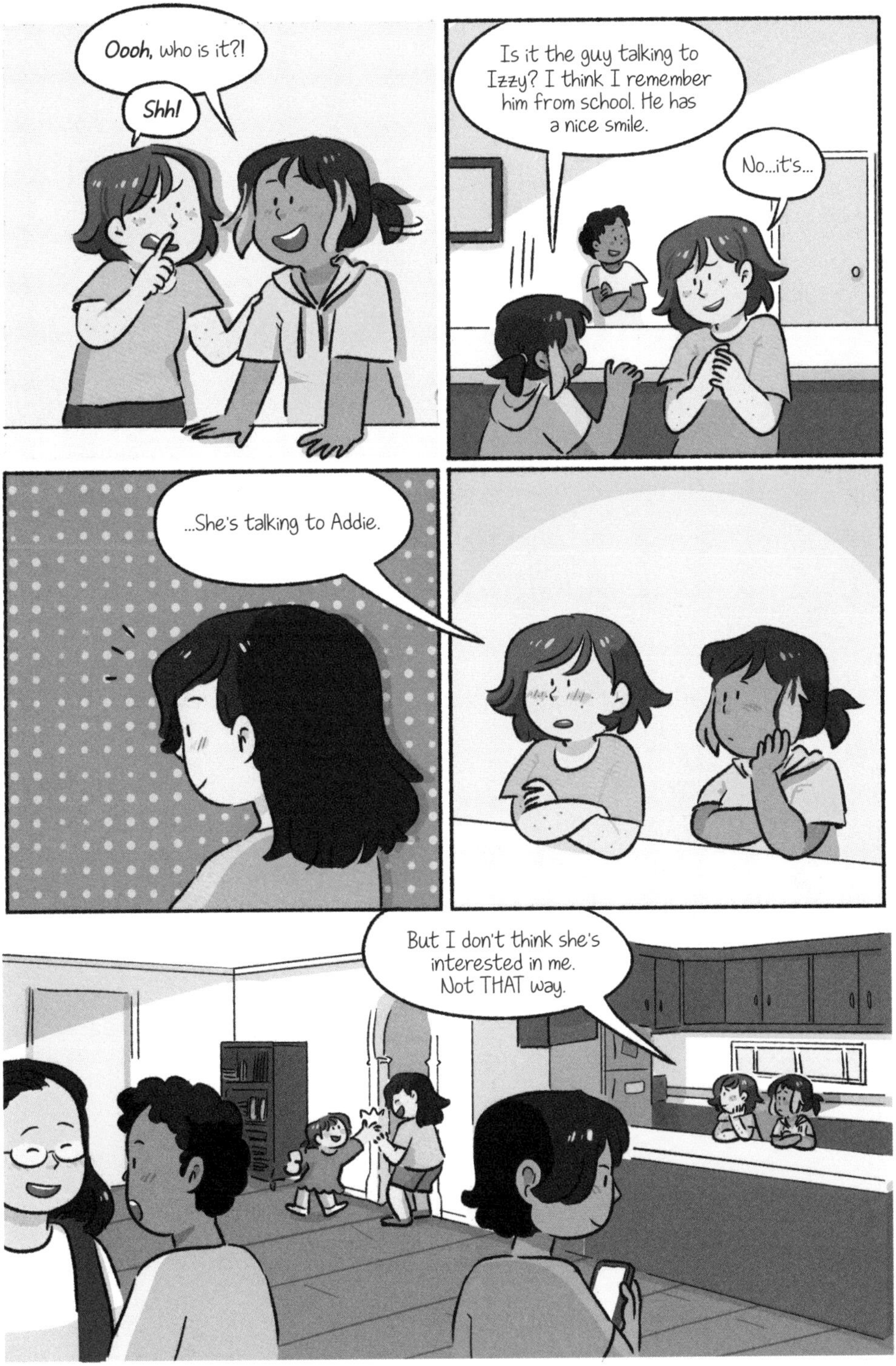
Oooh, who is it?!
Shh!
Is it the guy talking to Izzy? I think I remember him from school. He has a nice smile.
No...it's...
...She's talking to Addie.
But I don't think she's interested in me. Not THAT way.

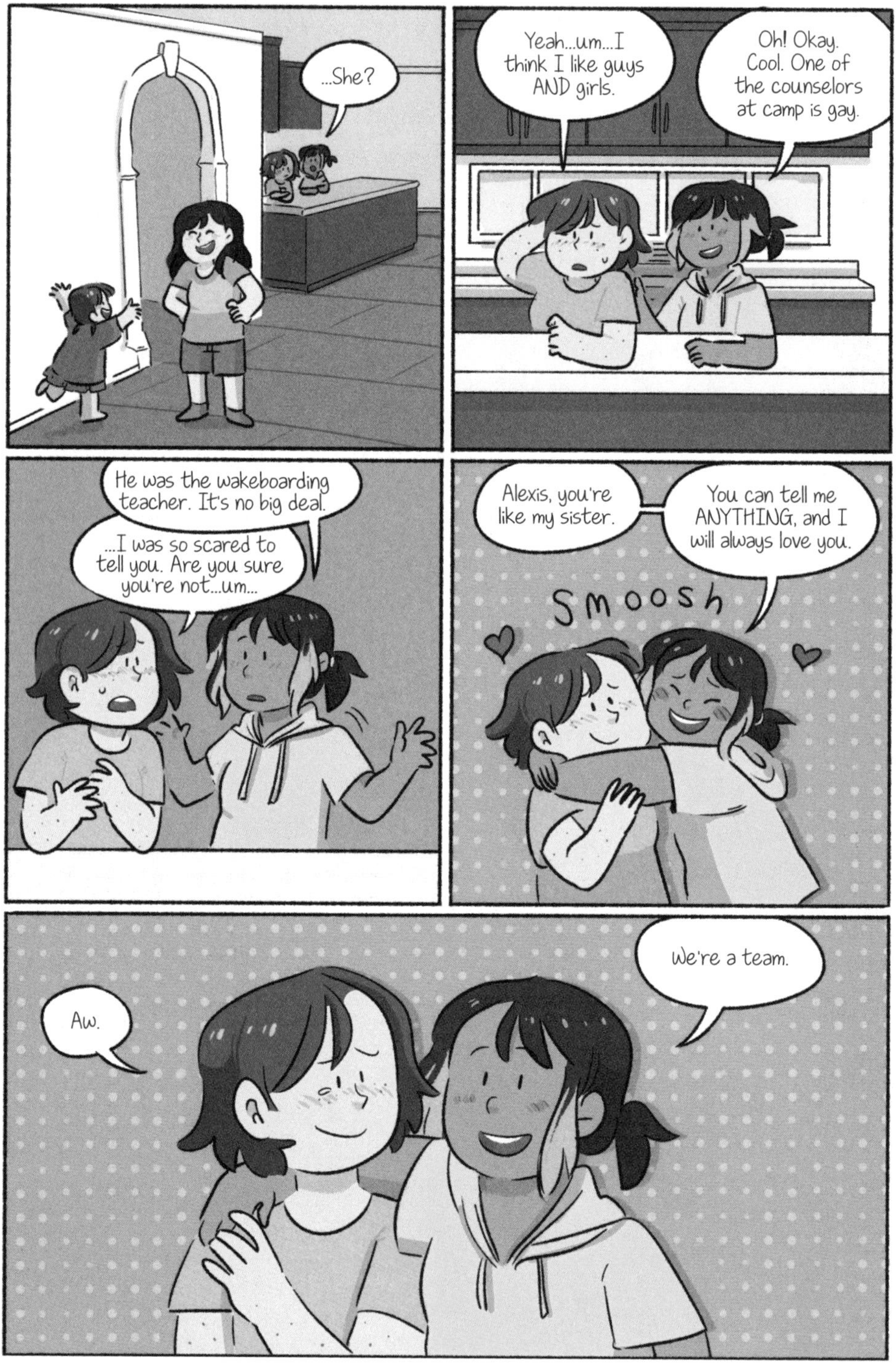

...She?
Yeah...um...I think I like guys AND girls.
Oh! Okay. Cool. One of the counselors at camp is gay.
He was the wakeboarding teacher. It's no big deal.
...I was so scared to tell you. Are you sure you're not...um...
Alexis, you're like my sister.
You can tell me ANYTHING, and I will always love you.
Smoosh
We're a team.
Aw.

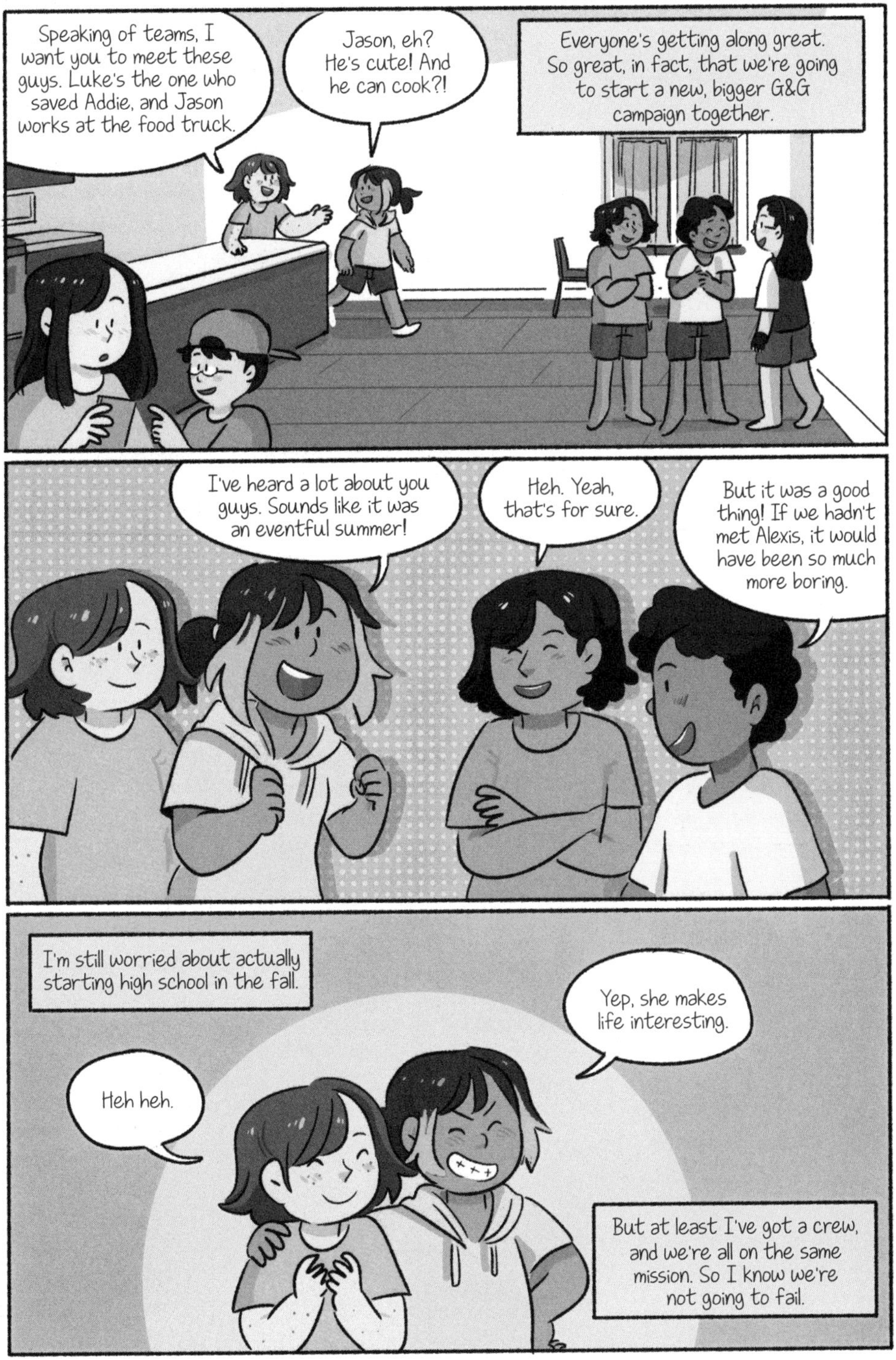
Speaking of teams, I want you to meet these guys. Luke's the one who saved Addie, and Jason works at the food truck.
Jason, eh? He's cute! And he can cook?!
Everyone's getting along great. So great, in fact, that we're going to start a new, bigger G&G campaign together.
I've heard a lot about you guys. Sounds like it was an eventful summer!
Heh. Yeah, that's for sure.
But it was a good thing! If we hadn't met Alexis, it would have been so much more boring.
I'm still worried about actually starting high school in the fall.
Yep, she makes life interesting.
Heh heh.
But at least I've got a crew, and we're all on the same mission. So I know we're not going to fail.

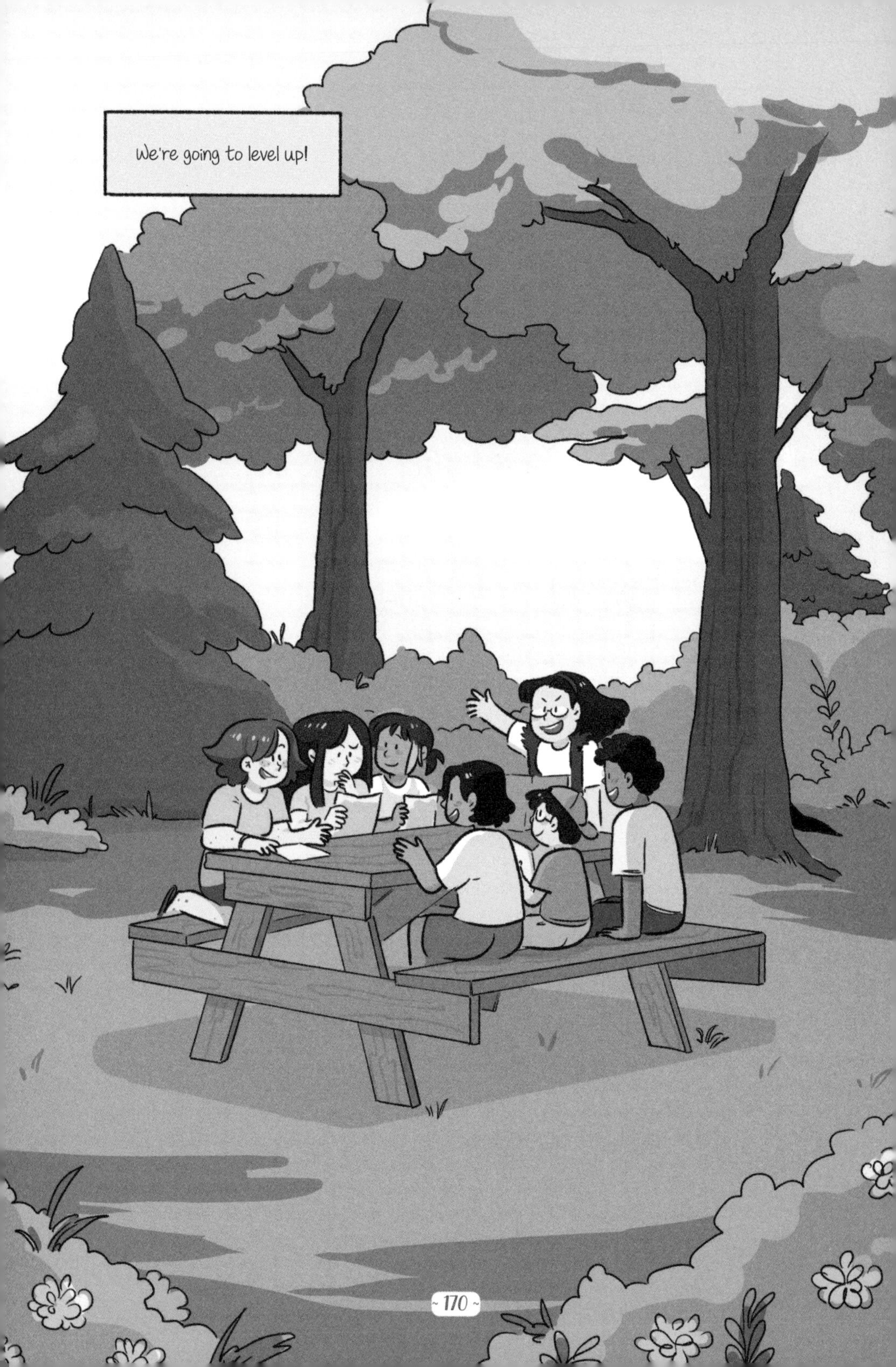
We're going to level up!

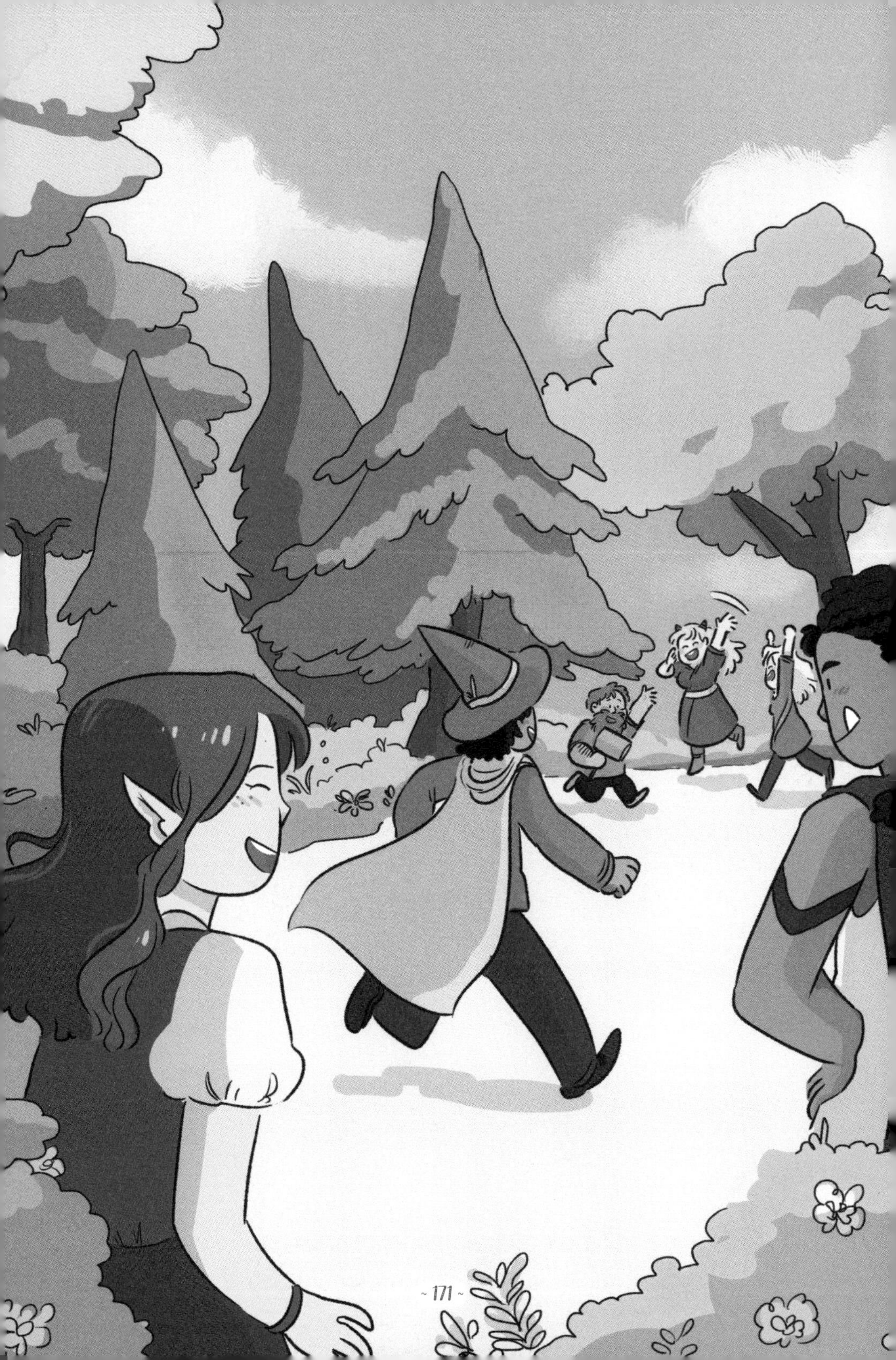

Looking for your next read?
Check out:

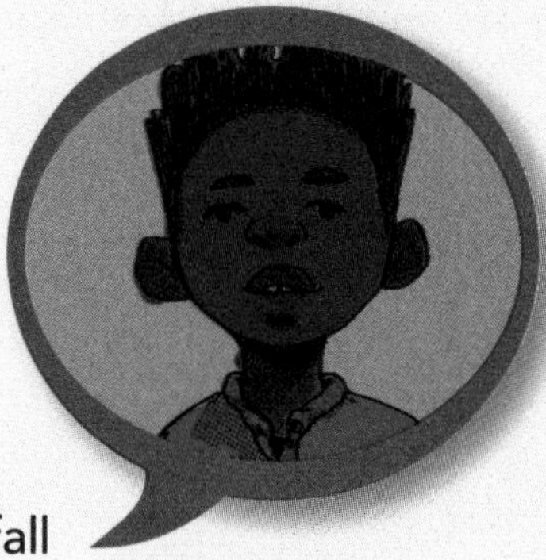

Duff Parker and the Downfall of the Dystopiad

J. Hill • Ian Moore

Thirteen-year-old Duff Parker has fallen in with a neighborhood gang. After he loses control and seriously hurts his adversary during a fight, Duff makes a break from the gang, losing all his friends in the process. As an escape, he turns to the graphic novel series he finds in his uncle's room and joins his middle school Sci-Fi Club. As he helps the club prepare for a costume contest at their local comic con, a whole new world opens up for him. But when the old gang comes back to settle a score, Duff must find a way to save the Sci-Fi Club before he loses more than just his reputation.

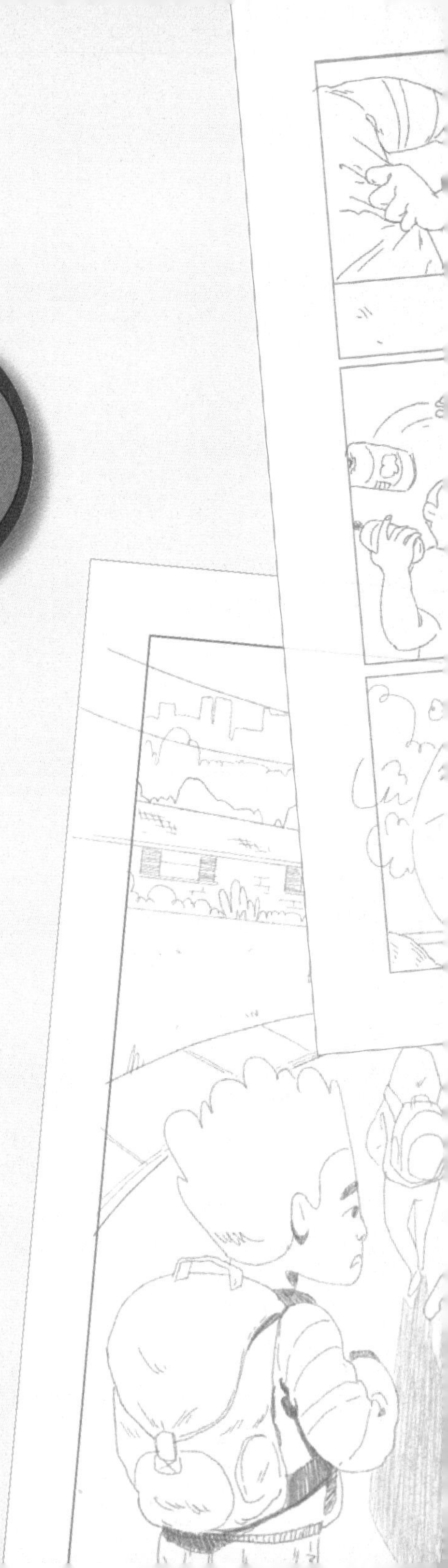

SLAM
HA HA
C'mon you guys!
Oof.
Wreck it!

Avenue A Books is a graphic novel imprint from Center for Responsive Schools that focuses on social and emotional learning for kids ages 5–14. This engaging and colorful collection is being created by a diverse group of talented children's book authors and illustrators. Kids will see themselves and their peers reflected in stories that depict real-world challenges that they experience both at school and at home. While these books offer subtle examples of how to navigate various situations with empathy and self-control, they are compelling, fun to read, and often laugh-out-loud funny. We offer a wide range of genres that will attract all kinds of readers, including action and adventure stories, mysteries, and coming-of-age dramas.

Learn more at

AVENUEABOOKS.ORG

Acknowledgements

I've wanted to write a graphic novel for a VERY long time, and so, first and foremost, thanks to everyone at Center for Responsive Schools and Avenue A Books for giving me the opportunity to plunge into this project. I especially want to thank Sera Rivers for being an amazing editor, organizer, and all-around awesome person and Heather Kamins (fellow Millsian) for bringing me on board AND for sherpa-ing this story into the world as its very first editor.

Very special thanks to Veronica Agarwal for bringing Alexis, Luke, and Jason to life and making me fall in love with the story all over again. It's a little scary to surrender one's writing to another person's artistic vision—being able to work with someone who really "got it" was a gift and a joy.

As with all of my writing projects that have managed to reach the eyes of readers, huge thanks are due to my writing group, WritingYA: Tanita Davis, David Elzey, Suzi Guina, Sara Lewis Holmes, and Kelly Herold.

Last but not least, thank you to my family: my mom, Bonnie Pavlis, who was my beta reader long before I ever became an "official" writer, and special thanks to my husband, Rob, for everything.

—Sarah "Why do my dice hate me?" Stevenson

Thanks to...

My parents and family, for their unending love and support of my artistic career.

Lee, for quelling my anxiety whenever I worried I wasn't good enough.

Susan Graham, for being the most wonderful agent I could have ever wished for—and an even better friend.

Alex and Wren, for being endless sources of advice, wisdom, and happiness.

All of Sunflower Station, for cheering me on and allowing me to do the same for them.

There's no greater honor than being able to make you all proud. Without all of you, I could never have accomplished illustrating this book.

Perhaps most importantly, I want to thank Avenue A and Center for Responsive Schools for giving me the opportunity to work on this book. This was my first solo project after college, and Sera and Heather put so much of their faith and enthusiasm behind me. I'm so incredibly grateful for that!

I also want to thank Sarah Stevenson for writing this story. When I first read the synopsis, I felt an immediate connection to Alexis, Jason, and Luke, and I felt so lucky to bring them to life. Thank you for trusting me with your characters and story!

Lastly, thanks to Polygon's video team, whose content kept me entertained while I worked on at least 70% of this book.

All my love,
Veronica

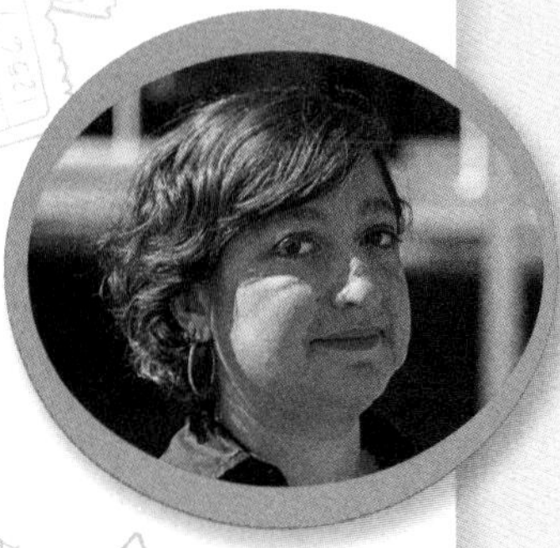

Sarah Jamila Stevenson is a middle grade and young adult author from Northern California. She received her MFA in creative writing from Mills College. She is the 2012 recipient of the bronze IPPY Award for children's multicultural fiction. Visit Sarah at sarahjamilastevenson.com.

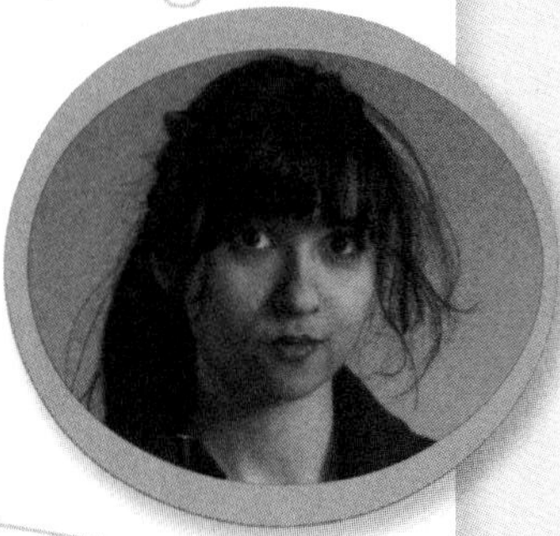

Veronica Agarwal is a cartoonist and illustrator from New York. She received her BFA in cartooning from the School of Visual Arts. Visit Veronica at wisbafolio.com.

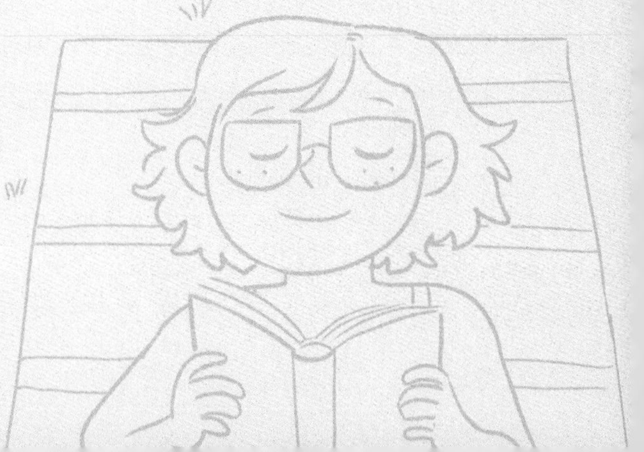